"I may not know the difference between a sigmoidoscope and a stethoscope but I do know the genuine article when I see one. And if there ever was a "genuine article" it has to be Dr. Tom Stern. Reading his thoroughly engaging book makes me yearn for the really "Good Ol' Days" of a family doctor in Sherwood, Oregon."

—**Victor Atiyeh,** former Governor of Oregon

"This fast-paced account by an obviously dedicated family physician and family man left me breathless. I knew pieces of the puzzle of his life before reading his story but found I wanted to know more. I couldn't put it down. What a fun read."

—**Sandra L. Panther,** Executive Vice President, American Academy of Family Physicians Foundation

"This is a superb autobiography of a family doctor who experienced the joy and satisfaction of practicing medicine at a kinder, gentler time when the blending of the 'art and science of medicine' was what family practice was all about. Clearly, it is the best book of its kind. Well-written, informative, and often humorous, it will appeal to a wide audience of readers."

—**Donald I. Rice,** C.M., M.D., L.L.D., F.C.F.P., International Center for Family Medicine founding member and past president

"House Calls is the autobiography of a self-made man who became a family physician in the mid-1900s after overcoming the adversities of the Depression, being orphaned on the streets of San Francisco, and serving in World War II as a Navy corpsman. His colorful and warm descriptions of medical practice in small-town and rural America in the 1950s are like episodes from Marcus Welby, M.D. In fact, he helped create the TV series in later years. But Dr. Stern's stories are better because they really happened to real people."

—**Richard V. Stenson**, M.H.A., M.B.A., F.A.C.H.E., F.A.C.M.P.E., author of *A Physician's Guide to Thriving in the New Managed Care Environment*

"This is not just a collection of physician stories, this is the life story of a boy who grew up to be a man at a very early age and overcame obstacles that would have buried most others. You will enjoy the stories, but more than that, you will see the development of a physician with great integrity and the ability to bond with his patients and the community he served in a very special way."

—**Joe Galassi,** Railroad Executive, Leawood, Kansas

"House Calls *captures the heart of family practice. Dr. Tom Stern was the quintessential family doctor—beginning in a small rural practice in Oregon, and then transferring his skills and insight to the metropolitan Los Angeles area.* House Calls *captures not only the development and maturation of Dr. Stern as a physician, but also the transition of the field of general practice into the modern specialty of family practice. The individuals and clinical situations described leave the ring of truth which could only come from a wonderfully empathic and sensitive family physician."*

—**Robert Graham,** M.D., Kansas City, Missouri

HOUSE CALLS

Recollections of a Family Physician

Thomas L. Stern, M.D.

 BookPartners
Wilsonville, Oregon

Library of Congress Cataloging-in-Publication Data

Stern, Thomas L., 1920–
    House Calls : recollections of a family physician / Thomas L. Stern.
      p.   cm.
    ISBN 1-58151-033-0 (trade pbk. : alk. paper)
    1. Stern, Thomas L., 1920– . 2. Physicians (General practice)—United
States Biography.   I. Title.
R154.S79A3   1999
610'.92—dc21   99-16534
[B]   CIP

Cover design by Richard Ferguson
Text design by Sheryl Mehary

BookPartners, Inc.
P. O. Box 922
Wilsonville, Oregon 97070

To Glad, my partner, my co-writer (her name should appear on the title page with mine but she refused), and the absolute love of my life. After you read this book you will probably love her a little, too.

To Don, Lee, and Pamela—I always wanted you to be proud of me, and now I am proud of you.

For Carly Elizabeth, Carrie Crawford, Alexis Hift, Elizabeth Ann, Alexander Thomas, Andrew Thomas, and Michael Frederick. I love all of you.

Contents

Foreword

I have been privileged in many ways throughout my life. One of these privileges has been the opportunity to travel extensively around the world in varying capacities. While thus engaged, I have come to believe that all of the nearly six billion people of this world are unique individuals and have their own unique stories to tell—some more interesting than others. Fortunately for the forests of our world, all but a few have chosen not to put their stories on paper.

Another privilege I have enjoyed over the past twenty-five or more years is my friendship with Dr. Tom Stern, who has a far more interesting story to tell than most others. Happily for his friends, acquaintances, and readers, he has recorded his memoirs.

His story is that of an individual who rose above early adversity to have a full and meaningful life of service to others. Many would say that he is lucky to have done what he has done, but luck is recognizing opportunities and taking advantage of them.

When he was fifteen years old, both of his parents died. Without notifying the school authorities, he worked to support himself and continued going to school. This solution is an early indication of how he approached life. His service in World War II as a U.S. Navy hospital corpsman afforded him the opportunity to enter college and medical school under the Navy's V-12 program. It was during this time that he made his best decision—the decision to marry Gladys, who brought her many excellent strengths to this union.

When the war ended and he finished his medical training, he started a long and very distinguished career in private medical practice, and later in medical education. His positive approach to life was reflected in his approach with patients, and later with the young physicians he helped train. Taking advantage of every opportunity to further the specialty of Family Practice, he rose to prominence at the statewide level in California and later at the national level. It was this prominence that positioned him to work as the technical advisor for the television series *Marcus Welby, M.D.* Medicine in the United States was becoming increasingly technical and far less personal. By working with Dr. Welby's character, he helped bring a believable idea to the public: that there were still physicians who were interested in them as individuals.

The people you will meet in this book are Tom Stern's patients. Some are unusual, such as Bill Riley, who is found sitting on a stump in his backyard with an ax and threatening to kill anyone who comes near him, or a beautiful but deaf woman who discourages her lovers when she throws up on them. But most of his patients are exactly what family physicians find in their practices—people with heart trouble; pregnant women; people with broken bones, boils, cancer, and the myriad problems that people have. There is also a cow with milk fever whose life a farmer asks Dr. Stern to save.

Dr. Stern's book ends at a certain chapter in his life, but his story continues. His contributions from that point on are no less important. He joined the staff of the American Academy of Family Physicians as the Vice President for Education and Scientific Affairs. In that role, he had a major influence on the training of all young physicians entering the specialty of Family Practice in the U.S. As the president of the International Center for Family Medicine for the Americas, Spain, and Portugal, he was able to influence the development of Family Medicine in many other countries. He founded the Residency Assistance Program, a quality assurance program that helps residencies in Family Practice improve and maintain the quality of their training. His friendship and influence with the early leaders in the new specialty helped mold it into one with a tradition of service to others. He is one of a very few true icons in Family Medicine in the world.

The book is funny and sad but, through it all, you have the opportunity to watch a real family doctor deal with human beings with humanity and look into his soul while he is doing it. The book is a celebration of the specialty of Family Practice, which Dr. Stern loves so much. Gladys is still a pillar of strength in their marriage, and provided great inspiration for this work.

His book is both entertaining and inspirational. It falls into that small category of life stories that needed to be written.

Robert W. Higgins, M.D.
Rear Admiral Medical Corps U.S.N. (Ret.)
President of the World Organizations of National Academies and Colleges for Family and General Practice (WONCA)
Past president of the American Academy of Family Physicians

Preface

I am blessed with seven grandchildren, but therein lies a problem. Whereas I live in the geographical middle of the country, I don't live anywhere near them. Three live in New York City, three in Southern California, and one in Oregon. When they were little (some still are) I worried that they might never get to know Grandpa. Both my grandfathers died before I was born and somehow, I knew that I had missed something in life. Many years ago I began to write stories of my life. I did this so that the grandkids might not remember me just as an old guy with white hair, who lived in Kansas City, but as a person who was young once, and really had some great adventures. And I hoped they would feel that I had contributed a little to the betterment of humanity.

The grandchildren began to grow. The four oldest, girls, became teenagers. They knew Grandpa and Grandma pretty well. Their need to know more about me became less. Good or bad, they had a grandfather they would remember. I thought that the boys, who were the youngest, might need a journal to get to know me better but they, too, were seeing me more often. Also, I had wonderful sons and a daughter who, along with their mates, reinforced the thoughts that Grandma and Grandpa were something special. Bless them for their love and wonderful understanding of what holds a family together.

Then I remembered my half-promise to Robert Young, made one day on the set of *Marcus Welby, M.D.* that I would write a book. So, in retirement, when events of the past seem to be crystal clear (in contrast to what happened last week) I adapted my life story for everyone. Thus began *House Calls*.

This work represents the best of my recollection of what happened over the years. I have changed some names and places in order to preserve patient confidentiality and privacy. There are people whom I have identified by their real names. I have done so because I would like the world to know how wonderful they are. Pinky, however, is the alter ego I never really had. He is the composite of three important people in my life. He is not actually real, but the things he says and does actually happened.

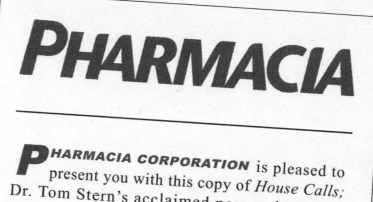

PHARMACIA

PHARMACIA CORPORATION is pleased to present you with this copy of *House Calls;* Dr. Tom Stern's acclaimed personal account from the front lines of medicine.

Stern's story reminds us all that in an age of unprecedented scientific advancement, it is you, the physician, to whom patients will always turn for help, for advice, for healing.

At Pharmacia, we aspire to support your work through our innovative medicines and through our people.

We hope you enjoy the book.

Sincerely,

Fred Hassan, CEO,
and the People of Pharmacia

Chronology

The twenties in San Francisco
    Childhood
    Grandmother dies
    The Great Depression begins

The thirties in San Francisco
    Mother and Father die
    Graduation from George Washington High School
    Works at U.S. Marine Hospital and as a salesman

The forties in the Pacific Theater and in Oregon
    World War II—joins U.S. Navy as a hospital corpsman
    Willamette University
    Tom and Glad marry
    University of Oregon Medical School (Oregon Health
        Sciences University)
    Donnel Bernard is born

The fifties in Oregon
    Graduates from medical school
    Completes training at St. Vincent's Hospital
    Lee Crawford is born
    Sherwood practice, family moves to Tualatin
    • St. Vincent's Hospital staff (Portland)
    • Tuality Hospital staff (Hillsboro)
    Pamela Ann is born
    Black Magic and Markie join the family
    The Stern family moves to Sherwood

The sixties and seventies in California
    The family moves to Palos Verdes Estates
    Manhattan Beach medical practice
    Family Practice becomes the twentieth medical specialty
    Establishes the Family Practice Residency at
        Santa Monica Hospital
    Technical advisor for the *Marcus Welby, M.D.* television series
    Glad and Tom move to Kansas City

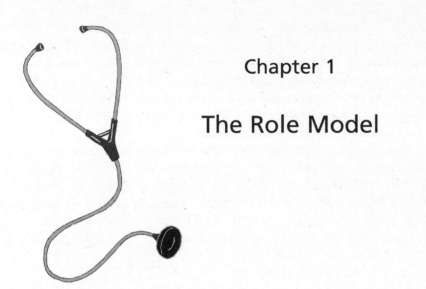

Chapter 1

The Role Model

Robert Young, star of the hit TV series *Marcus Welby, M.D.,* and I were playing backgammon in his dressing room. After we played a couple of games, Bob leaned back in his chair and said, "Let's talk." I guessed he was tired of playing backgammon with me as he usually won, and this day had been no exception. He went on, "You know, it's commonly thought that I'm an alcoholic. You knew that, didn't you?"

Inwardly, I jumped. Outwardly, I tried not to show any reaction. Why would he ask me a question like this? How should I answer? Robert Young was one of the biggest names in Hollywood: star of the *Welby* show, formerly the star of the very popular series *Father Knows Best,* winner of an Emmy; he had starred in over one hundred motion pictures. Now, here we are in his personal dressing room—and he wants to talk to me about his problems?

Bob stood up and walked over to the window, standing ramrod straight with his hands clasped behind his back in a typical Bob Young gesture. This was indeed just a gesture because, when looking out the window of his dressing room trailer, there was nothing to be seen—only the backside of the boards that shaped the set containing the *Welby* TV medical office.

When Robert Young moved, it was with force and dynamism. He was the consummate actor, mentally "on" all the time. He was tall, slender, in fine physical shape, and there were laugh crinkles at the sides of his eyes. The corners of his mouth usually showed his mood but the eyes described his feelings. They either sparkled with interest and excitement or they were unfocused and thoughtful—which often meant he felt depressed. As he turned and faced me, his eyes seemed to be peering into space and the corners of his mouth drooped. His mood was thoughtful, and I could tell he wanted a straightforward answer.

If we had been in my private office and this man standing in front of me had been a patient I might have said, "Let's talk about your depression." I might have scheduled him for a longer visit with the idea of getting to the root of the problem, written a prescription for an antidepressant medication, or suggested a referral to a psychiatrist or a psychologist. But Bob Young wasn't my patient; instead, he was a friend and also a colleague in a sort of cockeyed way, as I worked as the technical advisor to the show in which he was the star.

Because he was the star and had to be ready for most of the takes, retakes, side shots, over-the-shoulder shots, and closeups that are crucial to filmmaking, he tried to relax when it was not necessary for him to be on the set. Being the professional and veteran actor that he was, he had no difficulty in memorizing his lines or getting into the part emotionally. So, while the set was being changed or other actors were going through their scenes, Bob would stay in his dressing room reading, writing letters, or playing cards. When he was memorizing his lines he was always outside the trailer pacing up and down, script in one hand and gesturing with the other in a silent recitation of the lines for the next scene.

As technical advisor, I had attended a production conference in preparation for an upcoming episode of *Welby*. When the conference ended some of us went to the commissary for lunch. As we were leaving Bob had asked, "Can you come back to the set for a while? I have the backgammon board out and I've got time for a game." My first office patient was scheduled for midafternoon. Bob so rarely made demands on my time that I decided to take a chance on the formidable L.A. traffic and stay with him to play a game.

In answer to the dramatic remark about his alcoholism I said, "Well, Bob, I've heard rumors."

"I'm not a real drunk, you know. Oh, sometimes I have drunk too much and from time to time it's hurt me professionally, but it's not the alcohol I crave. No! You see, I get depressed and I don't handle it well. I have misused alcohol to help me get through my depression, but it's just that and it's not real alcoholism. I'm not the town drunk. Of course, it doesn't really help my depression either, but I haven't seemed to learn. I just wanted you to know about my foibles, as we're together a lot and I have great respect for you and your profession. If I should take a drink in your presence, don't get excited and wonder if I'm falling off the wagon. I'm just having a drink. That's all! You won't see me drink very often, and especially in public, as I know what people think and I certainly don't wish to sully my reputation any more than it already is."

His statement didn't require an answer. He wasn't asking for help. I recognized that he had opened his heart to me as a friend, therefore I wasn't terribly surprised when he said, "Now, I've bared my soul, tell me about you. What kind of a guy were you and what led to your becoming a physician?"

Well now, I thought, *should I tell this man my life's story?* Why? I knew of his tremendous interest in other people and the sensitivity he demonstrated toward others, but I also knew of his flair for the dramatic. Was this just a line from a part he had once played or did he really want to know? *Oh, well,* I thought, *it can't hurt to share with him a bit. I won't be verbose; and, if he becomes bored, I can quit and no harm done.*

I told Bob my story, but I made it short. He said, "You mean to tell me that from age fifteen you have been on your own? That's a pretty remarkable record. You could have gone bad anytime. How come you didn't?"

"Well, once I got over being mad at my parents for dying and leaving me in the lurch, and once I stopped being mad at God and the world, I guess I did what my mother and dad expected me to do, even if it meant becoming a doctor instead of a lawyer as my mother wanted."

That seemed to be enough. I didn't belabor him with my life history, but I guess in my own mind I really hadn't thought about why I was ambitious or why I had pursued a career as I had, when it might have been easier to just go with the flow. It just never occurred to me to do so. Sometime before they died and left me alone on the streets of San Francisco, my parents had apparently imbued me with the desire to try to keep myself afloat. I never remembered any specific teaching by my parents; but I had always known that a person must move forward and be productive.

Penniless at fifteen and alone, I knew that my driving ambition was to have a family. At seventeen, I told the insurance agent that I was eighteen, and bought a four-thousand-dollar life insurance policy so my future children wouldn't be completely penniless if I died young. Hell, at this point I didn't even have a girlfriend; at that age I couldn't afford one.

Bob said, "In the past you've told me all kinds of stories about your practice and the affection you had for your patients. Some of those stories have been the basis, if not the reality, for some of our shows. Now I find out that even though you were an orphan kid, you grabbed for the brass ring of life and here you are—a doctor. You've had so many interesting experiences. I think you need to document your life." He continued, "I want you to promise me that someday you'll write a book, at least for your children and perhaps for your grandchildren, so that all this lore won't be lost. Will you promise?"

I never answered the question, for at that moment there was a knock on the door and the assistant director said, "You're wanted on the set, Mr. Young."

Bob got up and left. I don't know what my answer would have been.

I do like to tell stories. I thought about it a lot. If I were to write a book telling the story of my life and times, as Robert Young had suggested, where would I start? There are stories about my adventures in Hollywood, with my patients, our family, and medicine as it was practiced in the days just after World War II. What should be first?

If the book was to be written for my grandchildren, I might start by saying, "My grandfather arrived at Battery Park in New York in a stream of immigrants in 1853."

If the target market was to be the general reader living anywhere, maybe I should start with a shocking patient anecdote. Perhaps a case history about Laura. I could say, "Laura was an exotic dancer who came to my office to have a wart removed. It grew halfway between the anus and the opening to the vagina and since she performed her act on a leopard skin hassock wearing only a G-string, she wanted to be sure there would not be a scar." (Incidentally, she was a single mother raising a delightful eight-year-old boy who wanted to be an airline pilot.)

However, regardless of who the reader is, neither my grandfather whom I never knew, nor my patient, Laura, is really germane to the story I would wish to tell. My story would be about my years as a general prac- titioner and the transition I had to make when, after eight years of a busy and fulfilling practice in Oregon, my partner and I had a falling out and, due to our contractual arrangement, I had moved. Now I was established in a beach town in sprawling Los Angeles County, still practicing the same way I had as a country doctor in Sherwood, Oregon; but I had acquired two additions to my life. I was the director of a training program for the new specialty of Family Practice, and I was the technical advisor of *Marcus Welby, M.D.*

It was a sweeter, gentler time, after the second World War, and just before a new age when medicine became divided into specialties and technology-oriented. But it was also a time of conflict. Bikini bathing attire became popular; at first I was shocked as I observed bikini suntan outlines on my young patients. Boys at the beach carried surfboards and dyed their hair. Smoking pot, free speech, and free love were popular. Peace medals sprouted on hairy male chests and between females' suddenly exposed, unencumbered breasts. The flag was being burned. Feminism had evolved, and brassieres were being burned too.

Even with all the scientific advances in the healing professions and the social changes, we can still look back at a time, all those years ago, when the doctor was not only a healer, but also a real friend of the family. Yes. I do want to tell my story, and I want to start where it began.

I began as a general practitioner, a country doctor. I never wanted to be anything else. I came into medicine as an heir to the medical advances which accrued to the world as a result of the war. Blood transfusions, new drugs (especially antibiotics), endotracheal intubation, antihistamines, new forms of digitalis, Rh blood typing, and new anesthetic agents were among the scientific discoveries doctors only dreamed about before the end of the war. And now we thought we had it all. At times we felt almost invincible.

Antihistamines were proclaimed to be the cure for the common cold. Well, that didn't work out, did it? We had solutions to other problems that didn't work out either, just as there are treatments today that will be passé in years to come.

I quickly learned that invincibility is not a human characteristic. One had only to look at history when Samson lost his hair or when David smote Goliath. The most important adage I learned in medicine was my first thought with every patient, the rule of Aesculapius: "Do no harm."

"Do no harm" is an idea that might be interpreted as "do nothing." But that is not what this book is all about. It's about house calls, delivering babies, my Oregon and California practice; about tragedy and humor. I'll tell you stories of the warmth of patients' feelings toward me as their doctor; but, especially, I'll tell you about how I loved each of them, the people who trusted me enough to refer to me as "my doctor."

Robert Young often referred to me as his role model for playing the Welby character. I told the stories of my life to producers and writers and they helped to shape Welby into the family doctor most people wished they could find. The television show was not the story of my life—but this book is.

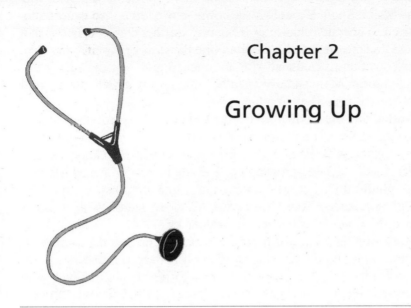

Chapter 2

Growing Up

Writing a book was not my earliest goal in life. My mother, who called me "Lambie Pie," wanted me to grow up and become a lawyer. Outlining a career for me was a more positive response than her reaction to my being born a boy when she had wanted a girl, to be named Katherine or Katie after her mother. For two days after I was born, she refused to see me; but after that she threw herself into mothering and reared me in an atmosphere of love and caring.

Mother had adored her own mother whom, I was told, I called "Baa." I guess my baby talk sounded like the bleating of a sheep. I don't remember Baa, who died of diabetes in 1922. My father was in China; the letters between my parents read like a medical history of the times. Mother and Dad exchanged daily letters which, because of the vagaries of mail service by ship between two continents, arrived in bunches. In a rapidly moving acute illness, the information—when it arrived—was always after the fact, I discovered many years later when I opened the neat little pile of letters I found in an old trunk. The trunk and its contents had been saved for me by my one caring relative during the pillaging of household effects by so-called friends, and by shirttail relatives when the social services agency broke up my parents' apartment and sent me to an orphanage.

The gist of the written conversation between Mother and Dad was that Baa was desperately ill with a bowel obstruction, but the doctors were afraid to operate because of the severity of her diabetes. The worse the bowel became, the more it affected her diabetes. Lying there for days with her bowel obstructed and with no relief from the excruciating pain, other than morphine, must have been horrible for my grandmother—and for Mother, who loved her so much.

During this time, when Mother stayed at Baa's side in the hospital day and night, I was cared for by Baa's sisters, my great aunts. Aunt Hattie and Aunt Sadie were a very important part of my childhood and very dear to me. As I was growing up, The Aunts usually invited Mother, Dad, and me for dinner at least once a week. In a way, they assumed the role of grandmothers. These were very Victorian ladies, with whom I associated the smell of lavender and burning string.

The lavender came from their eau de toilette and the sachets of lavender amid their clothes, but the string was burned in the bathroom as an air cleaner. The string was tied to a lighting fixture that had been fueled by gas but was no longer used due to electrification. After an odoriferous deposit in the toilet bowl, a match was taken from the handy box, and the string lighted. As a tot, I always wanted to use the bathroom when I visited The Aunts so I could set the piece of string on fire. After there was sufficient smoke to clear the air, my mother or one of The Aunts would lick two fingers and squeeze the burning string. I thought they were very brave and I was glad I didn't have to do that.

Baa's illness was a losing battle. Her doctor had heard of a new discovery made by two researchers (Drs. Best and Taylor of Toronto, Canada) that reduced the amount of sugar in the blood. If the blood sugar could be reduced, the doctors thought an operation that might save her life could be performed. They sent a telegram to Toronto requesting a supply of this new hormone. Best and Taylor hesitated for several days because the material was still considered experimental, but finally agreed to send a supply. All of this is documented in the letters of Mother to Dad—even to the point of daily reports of the progress of the train carrying the medicine west, and the hopes and anguish of Mother watching Baa slipping away from her.

The medicine arrived a day late. Baa had died without being able to use the new compound, which was named "insulin." Had the doctors in Toronto been quicker, my childhood might have been different. I grew up without any grandparents.

Mother was inconsolable. I was told that she wept for days, not only for Baa but for being alone, while her beloved Ben was far away in China. When he finally heard by cable that Baa was gone he booked passage for San Francisco, but it was about a month after the death when he arrived home. He decided during his ocean voyage that he would have to give up the best job of his life as the foreign representative of Associated Oil Company in the Far East. He didn't want to be away from his family anymore and would not consider taking us to China.

"China," he said, "is no place to raise a little American boy. The Caucasians treat the Chinese as if they are slaves. No American child should be raised in an atmosphere such as that. Why, just getting accustomed to having servants like there are in China would spoil him for life. And the dirt," he said, "is horrible. There are open sewers in the streets. I have to wear a fever vest in the summer to protect me from disease, and it's hot. A child couldn't stand it." Once he showed me one of his fever vests. They were simply tight muslin undershirts and what service they performed was never clear to me. Now, with my medical training, I know they had no value. I often wonder at the potions and folklore we humans subject ourselves to.

"I don't care how good the job is, I want to be home with my girl," he always referred to Mother as his girl, "and with T.L." That was me.

His "girl" was redheaded, with hazel eyes and alabaster skin. Once when I saw her wearing a long white formal evening gown—a string of perfectly matched green jade beads setting off her costume—and walking gracefully down the staircase that opened into our living room, I knew she had to be the most beautiful person in the whole world. I was six years old. I thought she looked like a queen and I fantasized for days that I was a prince.

Mother always said she was twenty-five years old when I was born. I didn't discover until many years after her death that she probably was closer to thirty-five. Dad was her first husband. But apparently, years earlier, she had a torrid romance with an itinerant preacher—which had produced a son. The child was raised by a family in San Jose whose income was supplemented by money contributed by Mother and Dad.

The Victorian era hadn't ended. Families had secrets they wouldn't share even with their own children. Perhaps they thought I was too young to know about such things. But there was frequent gossip at the dining room table, such as "Mabel and her affinity went to Marin County," (an affinity was a mistress or lover) or "Frank's son seems to be sowing his wild oats." I was left to wonder what an affinity was and why Frank's son was fooling around with oats, which so far as I knew was feed for the horses I saw pulling the streetcar on Pacific Avenue or the Railway Express wagons that delivered packages.

The fact that I may have a half-brother didn't surface until many years after Mother and Dad had died. I may have gone through life with a brother I never met. Alone in the world, I wished for a brother. What a shame that the mores of the times kept that secret from me.

I never thought of my mother as young or old—she was just Mother. Never Mom, never Ma, always Mother; she was too regal for anything less.

Dad went along with Mother's idea that I would become a lawyer. Dad was brilliant, albeit a contrarian. He ran away from home at the age of twelve because of a tyrannical father, and shipped out as a cabin boy on a sealing ship bound for Alaska. During his first voyage, the ship was trapped in Arctic ice. As cabin boy, he had to endure the anger and abuse of the ship's officers and crew when rations were short. His education came from books in the ship's cook's library. Dad remembered everything he ever read; he was a linguist fluent in several languages, but he lost jobs due to his lack of formal education and contrariness. Dad usually thought his boss was wrong and that he, himself, was smarter. Maybe he was, but informing his boss of that fact did not provide job security.

His greatest day, in my eyes, came when he and I were sitting beside a fountain in front of the San Francisco Civic Auditorium. A bunch of young white street toughs were harassing a Filipino man and his little boy, calling them "goo goos," and manhandling the father. My dad went over, put his arms around the Filipinos, and told the gang to beat it. They did. I was seven years old and very proud.

I grew up in San Francisco at a time when the streets were mostly safe and clean and a boy could move joyously about the city. The entire forty-two square miles of the city and county of San Francisco were my playground. My earliest memories are of the fog rolling inland from the west and the moisture sweetening the pungent aroma of the eucalyptus trees. I wore knickers—which I hated, but I hated even worse the hockey puck-shaped cake of camphor that my mother insisted I carry in the pocket of those knickers to ward off the fleas that inhabited the sandy soil of San Francisco.

When I turned six years old, I was allowed to play on the street alone and go to a nearby park. I had no watch, so Mother always said, "T.L., you come home when you see the lamplighter." The lamplighter came every night about five or six o'clock, carrying a long pole with a flint on the end. When he came to each of the gas streetlights he inserted his lighter through a small opening in the bottom of the light and "flicked his Bic." The lamp would hiss and sing for a moment and then glow, filling the bowl of the lamp with light and warmth, buttressing our street against the wet gloom of the fog.

The Great Depression caught up with our family while I was still wearing knickers. With my father's propensity for not getting along with his boss, he was soon out of a job. When it became evident that there wasn't enough money to buy groceries, I got an afternoon paper route delivering the *Daily News*. As a carrier, I was also obligated to sell papers on the street when breaking news caused the paper to print an extra edition. All the carriers were mobilized and we trotted down the streets shouting, "Extra! Extra! Read all about it, Lindbergh Baby Kidnapped!" Or, "Corrigan Flies the Atlantic Wrong Way!" or, "Negro Lynched in San Jose!" Sometimes the news wasn't as startling as it sounded but the paper wanted to increase circulation. People eager for news in the days before TV or regular radio news would come running out of their houses with a nickel. I liked that part of my job, as I kept four cents out of the nickel and often made as much as an extra dollar.

I was proud of my role as a family provider. Mother and Dad would praise me and I glowed all over. My biggest glow occurred when Mother didn't have the money to go grocery shopping for dinner until I came home from making my monthly collections on my route. Maybe it was at this time that my desire to succeed germinated and carried me through during the really hard times that I faced later in life. I thought about my dad and his lack of education and his frustration with not having all the tickets necessary to get along in life. I didn't realize how hard the goal of getting an education would be until my parents died a few years later.

It was during the Depression that Mother and her friend Bessie became traveling saleswomen. During the summer months, Mother and Bessie and I went on the road. They sold made-to-measure clothing for ladies in small-town America. I traveled with them throughout the western United States. Sometimes we had money to stay in nice places and sometimes we sneaked out of hotels in the middle of the night because we didn't have enough to pay the bill. And I saw America.

While the ladies were in a house measuring the occupant for a dress or suit, I often met bullies, and kids on the street who were suspicious of me because I was from out of town. But I learned to talk my way out of trouble and I met many kids who were friendly. It became a wrenching experience to be pulled away when we were playing and having fun; but it would be time to move to the next small town, and I knew I had to leave my new-found friends. After all, we had to eat. So Mother and Bessie had to find more paying customers.

I grew up in apartment houses on Pacific Heights and in a house in Cow Hollow near the Marina District. That was the best. The house was next door to a private tennis club where I was given playing privileges for tossing back the errant balls which flew over the fence into our backyard. I learned to play under the tutelage of Tomu, our Japanese houseman. Tomu was only a few years older than I and worked for us in order to become Americanized, hence he worked for room and board only. I was shocked when he received a letter from the emperor ordering him to go to Japan for military service. Tomu's father was from a military class when he emigrated from Japan, so despite being born in America, Tomu felt compelled to honor the letter calling him back to Japan, and he left.

This was during the time when Japan was first invading China. Dad was very disturbed over the invasion because he had many friends in China, especially in Shanghai. His number one boy or personal manservant, Chow Ping Sang, lived in the Chapei distinct of Shanghai, which was devastated by the Japanese. After Dad left China, Ping Sang had worked on President Line passenger liners. Whenever his ship docked in San Francisco, he would call to have Dad go to the docks and vouch for him so that the authorities would permit him to go ashore. His reason for wishing to come ashore was to see "the Missy and the Little Boy." He always brought me a gift—a pair of slippers, a child's laughing Buddha, or some lichee nuts; then he would cook dinner for us. After the invasion we never heard from Ping Sang again. During World War II when I was in the Pacific, I often wondered if Tomu was out there somewhere.

In the summer of 1934, the Depression was at its worst. Men were selling apples on street corners and well-dressed people sniped butts (picked up cigarette butts from the street). I once saw a man wearing a suit and tie notice a friend on the same streetcar. He sat down next to his friend and opened his silver cigarette case. He said—obviously being very generous—"Buddy, take a big one." The case was filled with sniped butts.

Dad occasionally found a day's work installing or repairing commercial refrigeration. He had designed and installed the refrigeration in the first truck to carry fresh produce to the East Coast. When he earned a day's pay, he came home with a sackful of groceries. After unloading a loaf of bread and a quart of milk, I could see that most of his money had gone for family treats such as smoked salmon, chocolates, or caviar with fancy crackers.

On an August day he had been job-hunting and had walked all the way downtown and back in order to save the dime carfare. I was out playing tennis. Instead of coming straight home as I had promised, I went to a friend's home to play Monopoly. When I opened our apartment door I heard sobbing from the bedroom. I had known that Mother was sick with lung fever. Now, I thought, *Mother is really sick; gosh, I wish I had come home earlier.* I rushed to the bedroom and saw my father slumped across the foot of the bed with my mother kneeling on the floor beside him. Mother was crying and Dad wasn't consoling her.

Mother looked up, and through tear-filled eyes sobbed, "Oh, T.L., you should have been here earlier. He's gone."

Gone? My DAD? Dead? How can this be? I love him. He will always be there. I need him. I got down on the floor with Mother and we wept together. I wept for my dead father and I wept for myself because I was already feeling lonely and because of the guilt I had for not being home in time to say goodbye.

Mother and Bessie went back into business and this time, instead of going on the road, they opened a dress shop. Every winter Mother had suffered from a lung infection. After four months of hard work and trying to maintain a home for me and Aunt Hattie (who had come to live with us), she became so ill that she had to go to a hospital. She died on Washington's Birthday, and I was alone.

We had not been a religious family and I certainly wasn't a religious kid. However, Mother had allowed me to go to Christian Science Sunday School with another boy who lived in the same apartment house. In light of my future career, I guess not much of the Christian Science teachings rubbed off; but I did say my prayers before I went to sleep at night. I started with the usual "Now I lay me down to sleep…" but when I got to the God-bless part I changed things after Dad and Mother died. I prayed, "God bless Daddy and Mother and make them happy and healthy and all better (I certainly didn't want them sick in heaven) and prosperous (this from a penniless kid in the Depression), and help them live together forever. And bless all the aunts I love." At this point I had only Aunt Hattie and Aunt Celia (Dad's sister) but Mother always had me call most of her friends "Aunt." I wasn't at all sure that I liked all of them and didn't necessarily want God to bless them; however, so as not to be pejorative and name names, I figured God would know which ones I liked and He would bless the right ones.

Becoming a lawyer no longer seemed important. I temporarily abandoned my goal of getting an education in favor of earning a living. I thought I wanted to be a radio announcer or a movie star. When I was without family, as a kid roaming the streets of San Francisco with no adult direction or love, a career that offered fame and fortune seemed most likely to compensate for what was lacking in my life. However, I had to work in order to live and so became an usher in a theater, a grocery stock boy, and a morning newspaper delivery boy and later, for a short period, I did get a job as a radio announcer.

I went to school when I could spare the time, and more than once I was picked up for truancy by a police officer. I was saved from the orphan asylum by David Opachatanu, a wonderful, loving man. David was assigned to my case as a parole officer of the juvenile court. I had run away from the orphanage because I wanted my independence and I wanted to finish high school. I wanted to be a good guy and do what my parents had planned for me, at least to be a success if not a lawyer.

The director of the institution had welcomed me to the place by showing me a heavy wooden paddle which, he explained, would be used for any infraction of the rules. Mother and Dad never believed in spanking. I had been assaulted with a paddle on my rear end by a neighborhood bully when I was a little boy and vowed that no one would ever do that again. On my first day at the orphanage, another boy was beaten by the director. No wonder I ran away the second night.

Several months later, after being caught and returned, the director told me that I would be paddled on my bare behind the next morning in front of all the other kids. I left that same night. I was classed as a chronic runaway. The probation officer, David, found me sitting outside the judge's chambers, awaiting my day in court. I guess I looked down in the mouth, for David's first words were, "Kid, do you feel all right? You're not sick or anything are you?"

I felt like saying, *Hell, yes, I'm sick. I'm sick of living, I'm sick of life, and I don't want to be here or in the damn orphanage where a kid loses his identity. Just leave me alone!* But I didn't say those things; I was in enough trouble. I said, "Naw, I'm okay."

David asked me questions and found out that instead of being a hardened criminal as my caseworker, Rose Minzey, had called me, I was just a kid anxious to make my own way in life, go to school, and earn a living. The day before, Rose Minzey had confronted me in her tiny cubicle in the Hall of Justice, and with the curly hairs on her chin waggling and sweat coating the black hairs on her upper lip, said, "You're no good. You're a chronic runaway, and one of these days you're going to San Quentin." I wondered at the time what twist of fate or act of God had taken my beautiful mother and left me to be hissed at by this harridan.

David told me to wait until he could see the judge and try to make some other arrangements for me. In about an hour he returned and asked me, "If I take you to my home for a little while and you live with my family—I've got two kids, they're younger than you but I'll bet you'll like them—if we do this, will you run away again?"

Would I run away? I so yearned to be part of a family that I would have done anything to please him. I answered, "Do you mean it? I'd get to live with you? Could I go to my regular high school? Oh, heck, that doesn't matter. Of course I won't run away. Thank you, thank you!"

I stayed with David and Sophie and the kids for several weeks, and then one day David said it was time for me to be on my own. He helped me get jobs—an early morning paper route and an ushering job in a theater at night. He helped me find a furnished room in a rooming house with partial board and saw that I enrolled in the high school in my new neighborhood.

Some nights turned out to be very short. If I had late duty at the theater and we closed at midnight, I still had to be on my paper route at 5 A.M. On those nights I consoled myself by thinking that I could try to sleep faster.

David, my benefactor, died an untimely death a few years later. I saw him frequently in the years while I was still a kid and living on my own, and I knew it was his intervention that gave me the opportunity to live alone, be on my own, and escape the Rose Minzeys of the world.

I concentrated on my new chosen career during my senior year in high school, studying journalism, public speaking, and drama. After graduation during the Great Depression, broke and alone, I wound up working in the laundry of a Public Health Service hospital. Later, I became a salesman of radios and appliances in stores in both San Francisco and San Jose. So much for law and the performing arts.

At the beginning of World War II, when I enlisted in the Navy, the recruiter asked what job experience I had. After hearing about my having worked in a hospital, and assuming that I'd had some training, or possibly because he had a recruitment quota to fill, he offered me a job as a Hospital Apprentice First Class, the equivalent of corporal. That I would be serving in the Hospital Corps seemed good to me for, obviously, that meant being shore-based with clean sheets at night. No seasickness for me, no wallowing around in the mud like an ordinary dogface. But what did I know? A hospital corpsman was the Navy's jack-of-all-trades in medicine.

My enlistment was the result of an overwhelming surge of patriotism and an acute case of big mouth. I was employed as a salesman of radios and appliances in a branch of a credit department store chain. One afternoon, about a week after the war started, I was schmoozing with a customer who was standing in line, waiting to make a weekly payment on his account. The guy was a shipyard worker and he was complaining about his wages.

"When the union calls for a strike vote, I'm gonna be first in line to vote for a strike. They want us to build ships, they're gonna have to pay us."

The newspapers had carried a story about the militancy of the shipyard workers and how a strike would impede the war effort. I questioned the big, burly guy with a smashed nose about his patriotism, when our soldiers and sailors needed ships and matériel so badly.

This hard case looked me right in the eye and said, "Kid, what the hell kind of a contribution are you making, selling stuff in this crummy store?"

I started to make a smart remark to the customer, when I noticed his balled fists hanging by his sides. He suddenly looked like Ike Clanton facing Wyatt Earp at the O.K. Corral. Well, I wasn't Wyatt Earp and I thought maybe I should shut up. Then I noticed that complete quiet had fallen over all the people standing around. Customers and employees, alike, were waiting for my answer. I glanced back and forth, looking for a sign or hint of what I should do. Even the store manager, attracted by the loud voices, was awaiting my answer.

I took a deep breath and, willing my voice not to crack, said in a loud, unquavering voice, "Tomorrow, I'm going downtown to enlist."

There was a collective sigh of relief from the group, followed by applause. I was the hero of the moment. The manager held up his hands for quiet, and spoke to me, so that everyone could hear, "You are not my son, but in your honor, I'm going to put a gold star in the store window." A great promotional idea.

"Not a gold star, Boss, that's for mothers whose sons have been killed in action."

The hard case muttered, "Kid, you'd better not be here next week when I come in to make my payment." He relaxed his fists and stalked out of the store.

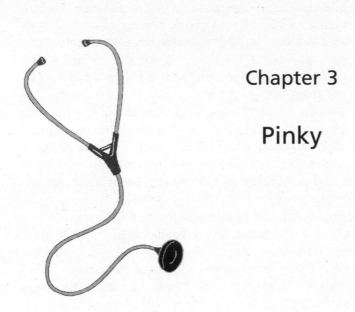

Chapter 3

Pinky

Pinky and I met the day I left San Francisco for Navy boot camp at the beginning of World War II. That momentous day eventually changed the entire course of my life. Auntie Clara, an old friend of the family (one of the aunts I wanted God to include in my prayers), had her chauffeur pick me up and deliver me to the train station for my trip to San Diego despite my protest that I couldn't arrive in a chauffeur-driven limousine to take a troop train. I convinced Claude to let me out a couple of blocks from the station so I could walk the rest of the way.

Our group of boots was met by a first class petty officer who organized us into platoons and into assigned rail coaches. I found myself sitting next to a freckled-faced, red-headed guy who looked at me strangely. It made me a little jumpy. Well, I was jumpy anyway. I was going to war, and I might get killed.

I was leaving everything I knew for a career in something I knew nothing about, amid strangers; and I had given up my privacy—my single bedroom and private bath. I had given up my personal freedom and I was under the absolute control of others. I had run away from the orphanage for some of those very reasons.

Out of the corner of my eye I could see this guy looking surreptitiously at me. Why? I didn't want to turn and look at him, but I couldn't figure out what could be wrong. I began to feel more and more uncomfortable. Finally, I couldn't stand it any longer. I turned toward the guy, told him my name, and stuck out my hand. He took it and said, "I'm Pinky."

I thought, *I'm not the one with a problem; my name isn't Pinky.* I said, "Where are you from?"

"Reno," he answered, "And I know where you're from. How come you're going to boot camp? With your money you could be an officer."

Money? What's he talking about? I did what they told us at the recruiting office, "Wear old clothes and carry only a little shaving kit and a change of socks and underwear." Oh my God! I thought, *he saw me arrive in the limo with Claude.*

"Why? Did you see the car I came to the station in?"

"Yeah. If I had a car like that I'd be in college with a draft deferment, not going off to boot camp."

"It's not my car, Pinky. It belongs to a friend of the family."

"Some friends your family has. With friends like that your family must be doing pretty well."

"Oh come on, Pinky, get off my case. What's it to you, anyway? If you want the truth I don't have any family. They're dead. My wealth consists of a 1937 Hudson Terraplane sedan, a trunkful of clothes I left at my cousin's house, forty-nine dollars in the bank, and a girlfriend I can't afford who's going to drive the Hudson while I'm gone and will probably wreck it. I enlisted because I'm damn mad at the Japs and the Germans and I want to get this thing over with. Now what about you? How come you're on the way to boot camp to get your ass shot off in this war?"

He didn't say much. We traveled quietly for a couple of hours and just before noon he reached into his ditty bag and, carefully, so as not to be seen, took out a brown bottle and took a drink. He started to put the bottle back and then thought better of it and passed it to me. Drinking before lunch was a new experience for me and the thought wasn't appetizing. Also, I didn't want the first class petty officer in charge of our platoon to catch me. I didn't know what the Navy's rules were for such things. I figured just being in the Navy was going to be bad enough without getting into trouble the first day. Pinky said, "You'd better have some; you won't get any in Dego. We're going to be locked up for six weeks. No booze, no girls, no fun." And he pushed the bottle at me again.

No booze for six weeks wasn't going to be a problem and I had promised myself to be true to my girl, but what the heck. I might as well go along with it and I grabbed the bottle. When I swallowed I almost choked to death. It was straight Scotch. I looked around to see if my choking and spluttering had aroused any interest from the petty officer. It seemed as if everyone but us was asleep. Pinky took the bottle back and took another swig. When he passed it back to me, I was much more cautious and took just a sip. It wasn't long before the atmosphere in our train seat became considerably more relaxed. Pinky started to talk.

His mother had run off with another man when Pinky was ten. His father was an alcoholic who was usually gone from their apartment. Pinky hung out on the streets of Reno on his own, sometimes not seeing his dad for several days. Because of his fair complexion, his face turned red when he was out in the sun for any length of time. He never tanned. This led to his nickname, Pinky. The neighborhood where he lived was in the toughest section of town and, with a moniker like Pinky, he constantly had to defend himself. He became pretty good with his fists—so good that a high school teacher, recognizing his talent, got him started in Golden Gloves. According to Pinky, this man probably saved him from going down the mean streets.

I told him that there had been a person like that in my life—David, the probation officer who had taken me in. I didn't know then that Auntie Clara had accepted the responsibility for my behavior until I was 18. The only monitoring I had was when I went to her house for dinner on Friday nights. This wasn't a hardship, as it was the best meal I had every week and, since Claude always picked me up and took me home, I was able to fantasize about life as a little rich boy. But it was only fantasy; Auntie Clara never helped me with money.

Pinky stopped boxing as soon as he got a job dealing blackjack in a Reno casino. He said he hoped the Navy would let him go into the hospital corps because he wanted to become a doctor.

The parallel in our lives was astounding. I really never had contemplated becoming a physician, but I was already in the hospital corps. Working in the United States Marine Hospital in San Francisco hardly seemed to be the beginning of a career in medicine. I had started the job by working in the laundry and graduated to running the front office and switchboard on the twelve-hour night shift for six nights a week. My only contact with patients came when I had to help an orderly wrestle with merchant seamen suffering with delirium tremens in the psychopathic ward. However, the recruiter said that having worked in a hospital qualified me to be a Hospital Apprentice First Class. The next step in advancement would be to the petty officer level, Pharmacist Mate Third Class. That was okay with me. The pay would be thirty-five dollars a month instead of the base pay for a boot of twenty-one bucks. The Navy hadn't told me there were hospital corpsmen on almost all ships, or that corpsmen provided medical care for the Marines, the Seabees, and isolated radio and ship observation stations. I didn't find this out until later.

The petty officer on the train saw to it that box lunches were handed out. The combination of food and Scotch led to an afternoon of sleep. I had dreams about my girl in San Francisco and my homecoming as a national hero with a parade down Market Street. When I awoke I felt good about the future. Talking to Pinky had relaxed me so that when we disembarked the train in San Diego after about twelve hours, with our only sustenance having been a box lunch, I wasn't prepared for Chief Petty Officer Waldorff, who was to be our training officer while in boot camp. This nice-looking man asked us to line up in a single row. When we didn't line up straight enough or fast enough he started yelling, thrusting his face into each of ours as we stood in line so that spittle sprayed into our eyes and mouth, while he referred to us as dog meat, queers, people of obscure parentage, and probably of Japanese ancestry (which at the time was the worst insult of all). The three weeks of hell had started.

Hell, that first night, was trying to sleep in a tent, fully dressed, on a camp cot, with no blankets and no food. I had been in San Diego once before when I had sold enough subscriptions to the *San Francisco Chronicle* to win a trip to the World's Fair and a newsboy's convention. It was a warm, lovely place; but my housing was different then and the time of year was different. I hadn't been lying on a cot in a tent on the parade ground of the Navy boot camp in January, with a north wind howling across my tired body. I went to sleep deciding that perhaps the Navy hadn't been prepared for our arrival. The torture of the night was quickly interrupted by our tormentor, the chief, indicating in stentorian tones that it was 4:30 A.M. and time to get a little exercise. He accentuated his remarks with pokes from a swagger stick he always carried. He said, "You've got ten minutes to get to the head and fall in. Anyone late will do fifty push-ups."

Pinky grabbed my arm and said, "The head is this way. Run!"

While running, jolting my bladder with every step, I managed to gasp, "What's a head?" Thinking, *Here I am running like a damn fool in this strange place to the head of something—don't even know what it is—and I have to go to the bathroom so darn bad I can taste it.*

Pinky said, "The head's the john, hurry up." The head was a four-holer for fifty men. Fortunately, due to Pinky's worldly knowledge we were there first and made it back to the formation with time to spare. The late arrivals did fifty push-ups each after we had all run ten laps around the grinder.

Breakfast was coffee, milk, an orange, and toast covered with a granular gravy substance. When I asked the mess cook what it was, this old salt (who had been a sailor six weeks longer than I) said, "Shit-on-a-Shingle, Mac. Keep moving."

I wondered why he thought he knew me and called me "Mac." I found out later that we were all Mac. Or worse. To the regular Navy, the reserves were "feather merchants" who were in for the duration and six months.

My next experience with the petty tyrants who were supposed to serve their fellow sailors was with the quartermasters who were in charge of issuing uniforms. Pinky and I stood in line for over an hour waiting to get into the building where uniforms were handed out. The chief had told all of us, in his charming way, to be in full dress blues. He sneered, "Wear your medals." Waldorff was an old China hand. He had a load of ribbons on his chest from service in China and stripes on his arm that signaled years of service. He added, "Be in front of your tents at 1100 hours."

It seemed like the most reasonable thing he had said to us so far—three hours to get uniforms and put them on. We should have known better. Once the two of us got in the door we saw a long line of tables piled high with clothes. The first table was underwear. "What size skivvies, Mac?" The word Mac was snorted like an expletive. I made a snap decision, deciding that skivvies must be undershorts and I answered, "Thirty-two."

The skivvy king threw a bundle of six undershorts at me. As I started down the line I looked at my bundle and saw that they were size thirty. I stopped and backed up, "Hey, these are thirty waist."

The guy glared at me and said, "Look Mac, you want to complain? Get a chit to see the chaplain. Next!"

Then I got skivvy shirts that were too big, dungarees that were too long, chambray shirts that fit—the shirt king wasn't paying attention or he would never have made a mistake like that—and dress blues that didn't come close to being my size. At the last station, where the demeanor of the minor tyrant was particularly obnoxious, I began to react. Pinky grabbed my arm and gave it a twist strong enough to change my direction and probably saved me from a lot of trouble.

I wondered what motivated the people I had encountered that morning. However, boot camp wasn't the last I saw of such people. Some were to be found in the mess halls, in the offices, behind the counters in the ship's service, in the shore patrol on the streets—and they were among my colleagues in the hospital corps.

The short-arm examination was performed by hospital corpsmen on all enlisted personnel whenever a sailor was transferred or whenever the powers that be decided that the risk of syphilis or gonorrhea was evident, such as a week after a ship left port. This was the most humiliation experienced by enlisted men. Officers didn't have to go through this, as it was assumed they were gentlemen. I wondered if that meant they were celibate. Some corpsmen seemed to delight in ordering enlisted men to "line up and drop your pants." Then they walked down the line telling each person to "skin 'er back and milk 'er down." By skinning back the foreskin, the observer could see if the chancre of syphilis was present and milking down could reveal the green discharge of gonorrhea. In all the years I participated in this dumb performance, either as a victim or an inquisitor, I never saw any positive results from it.

The worst example of this kind of tyranny occurred when one hundred fifty men awaiting transfer were lined up on a parade ground at Pearl Harbor, facing the main highway to Honolulu, and submitted to a mass short-arm exercise. Fortunately I was only a spectator, but so were dozens of motorists and pedestrians traveling down the highway. The crowd of mixed sexes hooted and laughed in hysterical fits while the sailors sweated and groaned in frustration and humiliation. We were taught the mechanics of the short arm later that first day but, blessedly, in seclusion. I learned then why hospital corpsmen were derisively called "chancre mechanics" or "penis machinists."

I always wondered what motivated persons in minor positions of authority to behave with rudeness and anger. I supposed it was their own inadequacy and the feeling of power over their fellow man. Given the ability to exercise that power, they sought payback for all that had been done to them.

The three hours given us by the chief to find and put on our uniforms were not nearly enough. No one had a uniform that fit. The area in front of our tents looked like Third Avenue in New York City as we exchanged clothes, trying to find something that fit. In addition, I had to take the sewing kit the Navy provided and attempt to sew on the red cross patch that I was admonished to wear on my left sleeve, "three inches down from the tip of the shoulder, Mac. Get it wrong and you're out of uniform. Oh yeah, you need three white stripes on each of the cuffs of your dress blues jumper instead of the single stripe of an apprentice seaman."

Sew? I didn't know how to sew. Well, maybe in the past, living alone, I had sewed on a button or two. But to do fine work on that red cross and those tiny white stripes, no way. I thought of the alternatives and the dressing down by Chief Waldorff and the spit in my eyes—and I sewed. The red cross was a little crooked and the white stripes didn't go straight around the cuffs, they sort of wavered here and there, but the chief didn't seem to notice. He was preoccupied with others whose uniforms fit so badly that, while spewing spittle in their faces, he threatened to have them court-martialed. Pinky and I had been fortunate in that we were both easy to fit and through trading were able to look halfway decent.

People had begun to buddy up. We were now a company divided into two platoons. By sticking together, Pinky and I were put in the same platoon and marched to barracks in Camp Paul Jones where we got bunks side by side. It was here that I made my first mistake. We were lined up in front of the barracks after noon chow, and the chief asked if any of us had prior military service. No hands were raised. Then he asked if any of us had college ROTC. One hand went up. He had this guy step forward. Next he asked for anyone who had high school ROTC. I raised my hand. Dumb! I was volunteering and didn't know it. Anyone knows that you never volunteer for anything in the military. Why hadn't I thought of that?

I had enjoyed ROTC in high school; in fact, it was the only course that I didn't fail the year my parents died. I liked the marching and the Sousa music. I had risen to the rank of captain and wore an officer's uniform with Sam Browne belt and saber. In high school it was fun—I had liked the drilling and marching, and the other kids marched with good humor. Now I was in the real world and the chief called me out and laughingly appointed a chancre mechanic, me, as platoon leader. I hadn't realized that in boot camp the sick and emotionally tortured sailors hated anyone in a position of authority.

We were all sick within three days. Not only were we given the various immunizations that gave us sore arms and low-grade fevers but we all had what the Navy called catarrhal or "cat" fever. The symptoms were flu-like, with chills, fever and runny nose. The cause was the exchanging of viruses from the upper respiratory systems of a group of young men from different parts of the country who, because they were thrown together in close contact with these bugs for which they had no immunity, got sick. The Navy looked upon this as a toughening process and allowed no time off. A visit to sick call resulted in a hand full of APC pills (aspirin, phenacetin, and caffeine) and a stern order, "Get your ass back to duty, Mac."

Every group of forty men has at least one who can't tell his left hand from his right. My trial and tribulation was Angelo LoBelli. LoBelli couldn't keep in step when marching straight ahead and almost always turned right instead of left, causing the marching sailors to stumble over each other. The chief's wrath didn't fall on LoBelli's head, but instead on mine.

"What's the matter, can't the chancre mechanic cure these daisies of yours from stumbling around?"

I was the only non-apprentice seaman in the platoon, so his constant reference to my exalted state inflamed the platoon's antipathy toward me. Pinky constantly cautioned me against responding to the taunts of my shipmates when the chief wasn't around, as he said they might turn on me violently. On about the tenth day of our miseries, LoBelli was out of step as usual. I finally couldn't stand it any longer and yelled at him, "Lowbelly, for god's sake get in step!"

Angelo had had it, too. He yelled back, "Goddamn you, my name is Lo-BELL-ee. You come on with 'Lowbelly' one more time and I'll kick your ass from here to Sunday."

I yelled back, "Lowbelly, get in step!" This was a dumb thing to do. I had a headache, my feet hurt, both arms hurt where I'd had the shots, and I was sick of this damn job as platoon leader and sick of being in the Navy.

Chief Waldorff heard the commotion. That sonofabitch had ears and eyes that heard and saw everything. He stopped the platoon, walked over, and asked, "Can't you girls get along?" Without waiting for an answer he said, "I think we'd better settle this the Navy way, with your fists. Be at the gym at 1700 hours and we'll see who's right, the penis machinist or the fighting wop. You're all dismissed. Now get out of here until after noon chow." And he stalked off.

Pinky walked over to me while the rest of the platoon gathered around Angelo LoBelli. It was easy to see who the guys would be rooting for. I said, "Pinky, that bastard Waldorff has just undermined any control I might have had over this outfit. LoBelli looks like a pretty tough Italian kid. He's going to beat the hell out of me. What a mess I'm in!"

Pinky asked, "Have you ever done any boxing?"

"Hell, no. My dad gave me a pair of boxing gloves when I was five and then refereed a fight with a kid from across the street named Theophilus Stevens who gave me a bloody nose. I traded the boxing gloves for a single roller skate which was no good to me but at least the skate didn't get my nose smashed. In the seventh grade I got into a fight in the schoolyard with a kid named Marshall who beat the hell out of me. I decided right then that I would always talk my way out of trouble; but it looks like talking isn't going to help, now. Shit!"

"Have you never had the satisfaction of really hitting someone you didn't like?"

"Yeah, I guess once I did. I was fifteen. I was delivering morning papers and a guy came along who was attempting to sexually molest me. I was scared to death and I knocked him down. The guy was getting up muttering curses about killing me, but I was saved by the milkman who was delivering in the area. He came along at the right time and chased the guy away. That's my only successful fight and it was only one punch."

"Are you scared now?"

"Sure I am."

"Okay then, you can fight and I'm going to teach you how. You've got to lick this thing. Waldorff is a dictator and he's no better than a dictator anywhere. He controls our lives. He tells us when to walk and where. He tells us when to run, when to sleep, eat, bathe, how to dress, and now how to settle an argument. It's not fair, but it's his method and the method of all bullies and dictators. He's intentionally building anger against you in the platoon. That way he unites the group, and united they will perform better and make him look good to his superiors, and the hell with how you feel. Now, here's what I want you to do. This is a three-round bout. LoBelli will come out swinging and I want you to cover up, like this." And he demonstrated some of the techniques he had learned in Golden Gloves. "Keep backing up. The crowd will boo. Screw them; it's your fight. Before the end of each round LoBelli will get arm-weary and drop his hands a little. Don't try to hit him until the third round, when he'll be pooped, and then, when his hands come down, hit him like you did that guy you knocked down when you were fifteen years old—and the fight's over."

"What about all the times he hits me on the arms? Isn't that going to be painful and weaken me, too?"

"Naw. You'll be wearing sixteen-ounce gloves, like pillows. Unless he hits you on the chin or nose, it won't bother you."

My poor nose. Not again, I thought. *I damn well will cover up.*

At 1700 hours I showed up at the gym in dungarees and Navy-issue high-top black tennis shoes. LoBelli was already there. Waldorff got us into the ring and told each of us to pick a second. Our seconds laced up our gloves. Pinky had trouble with mine as my hands where shaking. There was no bell to start the fight—instead Waldorff just grunted, "Okay, start fighting."

LoBelli did what Pinky had predicted. He swung at me from every conceivable angle, but I just covered up and backed away. He got tired. Round Two went the same way, only now Waldorff was growling, "Fight him, damn you." And the crowd was with him, booing and calling out for me to fight. In the middle of the third round I began to get desperate. I was getting tired of the pounding. Although he had not landed a telling blow it seemed as if he still had plenty of stamina. I thought I'd better ignore Pinky's instructions—it would be better just to survive and not risk my nose in trying to win.

But Pinky was yelling for me to go ahead and, sure enough, LoBelli's arms were practically at his sides. I threw a left and missed, but as he ducked it was obvious that the opening was there and I stepped forward, swinging my right toward his head. Alas, my foot had caught in a tear in the canvas cover in the ring. The momentum of my arm driving forward and my stumbling propelled me into LoBelli, my glove hitting his forehead; but my body crashed into his and we both went down in a tangle of arms and legs—with me on top. I looked into his eyes and started to laugh at the ridiculous situation we were in. For an instant he tried to get up but, suddenly, he too was overcome with laughter. The two erstwhile gladiators were no longer trying to commit mayhem on each other but were howling with laughter. The moment was won by the good guys. The rest of the platoon joined in the laughter and Waldorff was defeated. We were laughing with each other and at the tyrant.

Instead of the six weeks of hell that Pinky had thought we would have boot camp turned out to be only three weeks long. At that stage of the war there was too great a need for bodies to allow boots the luxury of lingering at Camp Paul Jones. As soon as we had completed our shots we were reassigned. Pinky was assigned to Hospital Corps School at the San Diego Naval Hospital for at least three months of training. Because I was already a Hospital Apprentice First Class and presumably knew how to be a corpsman, I was assigned to the Naval Hospital at Pearl Harbor, to be sent by the fastest available transportation. Three weeks and three days after I had left San Francisco, I was back, in transit at the receiving ship on Goat Island. I made one liberty to San Francisco and then boarded a transport for Hawaii.

Within three more weeks I was reassigned to the USN Mobile Hospital Number 2. Three months after that, when we heard that a new load of corpsmen was arriving from the States, most of us went to the master-at-arms' shack to meet the truck bringing the new fish we would have to work with. Pinky got off that truck! What a reunion. I made room in the barracks where my bunk was and eventually helped him to be assigned to the same duties I had. We were a team, again.

A year later when I was assigned to sea duty, Pinky decided he would take his sun-sensitive face under water and volunteered for submarine duty. We met in Pearl a couple of times after that. Then I received the news that his sub had not returned from war patrol and was presumed lost. It was as if I had lost a brother.

One day a bulletin from the Bureau of Personnel notified Navy enlisted men that there was an opportunity for a limited number of men to go to college and qualify for commissions. Some would, after a short course in college, go to ninety-day-wonder school and become line officers, while others could become pre-medical students and later become doctors. I applied for the pre-med program. To my absolute delight, I was accepted and sent back to the States for assignment.

The shooting war was over for me.

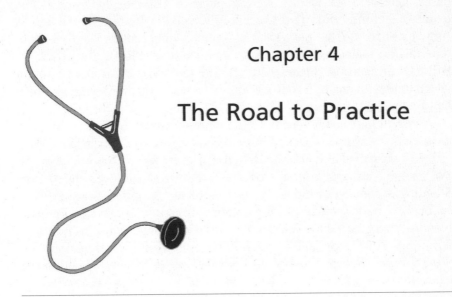

Chapter 4

The Road to Practice

When I got back to the States, I found that I was assigned to pre-med at Willamette University in Salem, Oregon.

Where?

I had applied to U.C. Berkeley, Stanford, and U.S.C. But the Navy, in its wisdom, was sending me to Salem, Oregon. I was from San Francisco, for God's sake! Salem had only about thirty thousand people. What was a big city kid going to do in Salem, Oregon?

My self-worth had been depleted not only because, as a member of the Navy's V-12 program, I had been demoted to Apprentice Seaman, but also because I had been the recipient of a face-to-face "Dear John" when I arrived in San Francisco after twenty-two months overseas. My girl had dumped me for an older guy with money and heart trouble that kept him out of the war. She had offered to get a blind date for me so the four of us could go out together. This, after I had faithfully written to her from my abstemious life in the Pacific where a shooting war was going on. Blind date? My foot! I left town after collecting the money from the sale of my Hudson (which she no longer needed after acquiring a rich boyfriend) to finish the remainder of my leave under the bright lights of Los Angeles and Hollywood before starting college.

Los Angeles was a great liberty town. There were no major military bases there, and servicemen were popular. A sailor couldn't spend his own money for a drink. There was always a civilian to pick up the tab. A former girlfriend lived there. She had been a singer in the Chi-Chi Club on Catalina Island before the war and was now "Rosie the Riveter," building airplanes at Hughes Aircraft. She took time off from her job to spend time with me, as a contribution to the war effort more relevant than building planes.

When I arrived in Salem I felt the need to show the kids there what a real sailor was like. I needed to polish my image—or I thought I did.

Upon arrival at Lausanne Hall, the quarters for the Navy students at Willamette University, I paid off the cabbie and surveyed the scene. Standing at the top of the stairs in front of the dormitory was a young sailor wearing leggings, with a garrison belt around his middle. He was obviously on guard duty. What in the world was he guarding in front of a dormitory in a sleepy college town in Oregon? Not much, I guessed; he wasn't armed. Where I had come from there were Marines armed to the teeth and looking angry. Come to think of it, Marines always looked angry; they must have been taught that in boot camp.

⚬⚭⚬

I had done a stint with the Marines and had the utmost respect for them. In the late spring of 1942, the master-at-arms where I was stationed called together all the corpsmen working in the two operating rooms and asked for six volunteers for a mission. He told us he didn't know the nature of the mission but he did know that we would be flying somewhere, as he had been informed that we could take only fourteen pounds of clothes with us and that we would be coming back; or being as how there was a war going on he thought we would be coming back. There were no sailors there as dumb I had been in boot camp so, of course, no one volunteered. The master-at-arms said he was shocked at the total lack of honor among us. His face became red as he said, "If I were qualified by being an O.R. tech, I would be the first to go. Now who's ready? Step forward!"

The guy standing next to me said, "Bullshit, chief. Having been in the Navy as long as you have, you would know better than to volunteer for a snafu mission like the one you're telling us about."

The chief growled but he understood, so he had us line up and count off by fours. When we finished he said, "Okay, odd men volunteer, even go back to work." And he laughed like the jackass he was and guffawed, "Odd men out. That's a great idea!"

I was number three.

He told us, "You've got two hours to get ready. Pack tropical gear, take only fourteen pounds..." I was glad to hear "tropical" because there had been fighting in the Aleutians, "...write a letter home but don't mention this mission...." *Write a letter home? That is ominous.* "...and be at the master-at-arms' shack at 1030 hours."

I wrote to my girl in San Francisco and tried to convey the idea that I was going to be in danger and might not come back. I wanted her to worry and love me more. Some months later I got a letter from her in which she mentioned that the letter I had written on May 30 was so badly cut up by the military censors that there wasn't much left but my name. "Loose Lips Sink Ships" was everyone's byword of the day.

We boarded a PbY2 flying boat and were airborne by midafternoon. The inside of the plane was filled with supplies and we had to find a place somewhere in the bare ribbed fuselage to sit. Within an hour we were putting on the extra clothes we had brought. I had flown in a seaplane from San Pedro to Catalina Island several times when I was romancing the gal from the Chi-Chi Club, but the plane had plush seats and never went over a thousand feet up in the air. I had no idea how high we were because there were no windows, but it was colder than a well-digger's ass.

After a couple of hours one of the pilots came back from the cockpit. This guy wasn't any older than I and he was flying an airplane. I hoped he was a better trained pilot that I was a trained nurse. He had a thermos of hot coffee, and when it was circulated he asked if we were okay.

"Yes sir," we answered.

I got my nerve together and asked, "Where are we going?"

The pilot began to laugh and said, "Where are we going?" More laughter. "You mean you guys have been sitting back here all this time and you don't know where we're going? That's amazing." And the laughter continued. I thought, *If this idiot doesn't stop braying like a donkey and tell us, I'm going to kill him.* The pilot must have read my mind.

"Men, you're on your way to Midway Island, the garden spot of the Pacific, where there's nothing but planes, Marines and gooney birds—and you're going to be Marines!" He was still laughing as he made his way back into the cockpit.

Everyone on Midway earned my respect over the next week, including the gooey birds. I thought that after the blitz was over they would be so emotionally disturbed that they wouldn't be able to fly. But they continued unperturbed, with graceful flights and their usual comical landings, crashing and rolling over and over as if they hadn't been able to lower their gear.

The sick bay with the huge Red Cross emblem on the roof had been demolished when the Japs dropped their first load of bombs. Luckily, the building had been evacuated earlier. We had to work out of kits and what remained of undamaged supplies. I dislocated my shoulder by diving into a bunker when I realized that the bullets and bombs were real. When I yelled loud enough, a doctor came by and, noticing my predicament, put his foot in my armpit, grabbed my wrist and yanked. The shoulder went back into place and I went to work as an aid man taking care of others. A month later, when I was back from detached duty with the Marines, I went to my commanding officer and asked if I could get a Purple Heart. He asked, "Where's your wound?"

When I told him that I had dislocated my shoulder, he said "No blood, no medal. Dismissed!"

❦

The guard at Willamette University looked about seventeen years old. Actually he was nineteen, had gone right out of high school into the Navy college program, and was a sophomore.

Never mind that I was to be a freshman, I wore ribbons and chevrons on the sleeve of my dress blues. I was a pharmacist mate second class in appearance, but really just an apprentice seaman—as he was. I had to agree to become an apprentice seaman when entering the Navy's V-12 program. Now I was eligible to wear only one white stripe on the cuff of my Navy blues for the first time since I had enlisted as a hospital apprentice first class at the beginning of the war. Even though at San Diego we had all been required to clean up our uniforms, denuding them of chevrons and white stripes, I had saved out a tailor-made jumper to travel in. I didn't want to look like a boot and be challenged for wearing ribbons because I was only an apprentice seaman.

The kid with the garrison belt came down the stairs and, seeing my chevrons, said, "Sir, may I help you?"

Well, "sir" wasn't something I was used to being called. Assuming my saltiest of salty-dog attitudes I said, "Kid, I have been assigned here— bring in my sea bag." To my utter amazement, he did it.

The V-12 students numbered two hundred seventy apprentice seamen, of whom twelve, including me, had been in the "real" Navy. The twelve of us were something of an oddity.

Quarters were dormitory rooms with two double bunks and four desks. Lausanne Hall had been a girls' dorm before the Navy took over. (Any lingering scent of perfume had been wiped out before I arrived.)

The Navy guys were practically the only men on campus. A few 4Fs and kids waiting to be drafted made up the rest of the civilian cadre of males; but, oh my, there were lots of girls!

Life in V-12 was a pain in the neck, despite the presence of so many beautiful coeds. What fun was it to be around girls if all you could do was look and you didn't have time to frolic? We had to take twenty-one academic hours each semester in this accelerated program, in order to be ready for medical school in under twenty-four months. Three semesters a year belied the definition of semester. One was allowed off campus Friday night until 10 P.M. and Saturday after inspection and parade (about 1 P.M.) until Sunday, at 10 P.M.

Academically, I was not doing well. I had been out of high school for six and a half years and even then hadn't prepared for any of the courses I had to take in pre-med.

With a great deal of mind-searching and sadness, I went to Lt. George Bliss, the commanding officer (a grade school principal before the war), and asked to leave the program. Maybe, if I went back to the "real" Navy, I would be lucky and be shore based.

I didn't want to suffer the defeat of academic failure. I had always suffered secret problems of self-esteem, feeling insecure in the company of others, especially those with advanced academic degrees. I carried these feelings deep within me, exuding a false bravado in my public persona. The damage that I would suffer through failure could be great. Quitting gave me an out. In the back of my mind there was conflict: I probably could not be better than my father, but on the other hand, I didn't want to go through life unable to succeed because of the lack of academic tickets.

Did I really want to quit?

Lt. Bliss did not want to accept my resignation, but I insisted. He informed me that such a request, because I was an officer candidate, would have to go through the Navy Bureau of Personnel. He said he would send it, but he also said, "During the time you are here, behave well and give it your all, or I will have you up for punishment."

I agreed and thought my college days would be over in about six weeks, so I relaxed a bit and began looking over the coeds. The coeds turned out to be what was known in those days as "San Quentin quail." All were too young for me. The U.S.O. (an organization for servicemen, where young women volunteered to dance and socialize with homesick young guys) seemed to be my only recourse.

On a Saturday night in November, after I had been at school for two and a half months, a friend and I decided to go to the U.S.O. First, we would stop at the Alpha Chi Omega House, where the sorority girls were having a get-acquainted mixer for the sailors. The mixer was held in a basement recreation room, with stairs leading down from the main floor, sort of like a chute. After a little bland punch and a few conversations with "San Quentin quail" who had been warned about men from the fleet, my buddy and I decided to escape to the U.S.O.

Then it happened! A girl came down the chute gracefully, with an erect carriage, snapping blue eyes, a lovely figure, not too tall, not too short, and with a smile that went from ear to ear when she said, "Hello, I'm Gladys." And she was over twenty-one.

I was immediately smitten and I still am. The idea of going to the U.S.O. to meet girls went out of my mind. We danced. We went downtown for a hamburger. We were late returning to meet the 1 A.M. sorority curfew, something Glad had never done before. The light was dancing in her eyes and our souls were singing.

We were engaged three weeks later, but not before Glad had to reckon with her sorority sisters' dire predictions of what would happen if she took up with a real sailor who probably had a girl in every port. Come to think of it, I guess I did have a girl in every port, but I was ready to meet the challenge of spending the rest of my life with a single mate.

As a pre-med student, I competed against men five years my junior who were right out of high school and had prepared for pre-med by taking physics, chemistry, math, and biology. My preparation in the fields of journalism, public speaking, and drama left me a bit confused and a lot behind.

Glad offered to help me study, but even that did not seem promising, as she was a music major and didn't know an atom from an equation. However, she knew one thing—she knew how to study. I knew two things—I wanted to stay where she was and I wanted to be a doctor. With Glad's help I made the honor role. I had to, for only those of us on the honor roll could leave Lausanne Hall for a Coke break during the evening study hours. We met at the Bearcat Cavern in the basement of the oldest building (Waller Hall) on this historic old campus. We held hands and drank our Cokes and looked into each other's eyes; and we both knew it was right.

When I went to see Lt. Bliss to ask him to withdraw my application for transfer, he grinned and said, "I never sent it. I thought you were just having trouble settling down from your freedom in the 'real' Navy and getting used to the commitment necessary for you to become a student."

What a wise man!

❦

We had met in December. By June, not being married was too much for both of us. We eloped. Well, we eloped if you consider it eloping to take Glad's father along to give the bride away, her mother to be the matron of honor, and Grammy, her grandmother, to be the best man. We were eloping from the U.S. Navy, which, with its typical intuition, had adjudged that the way to keep a man from being distracted from studies was to keep him single. Whoever concocted that decision didn't understand the mindset and the hormones of youth.

My grades improved dramatically despite my lack of sleep. I sneaked out almost every night after lights out, to be with Glad in our one-room apartment in the basement of a house down near the millstream. Sneaking out was a challenge. My room was on the third floor of Lausanne Hall (we called it Lousy Annie) and the way to escape was by way of a two-story, smooth, steel slide. This slide had been installed by the Navy in order to comply with some of its fire escape rules. They never imagined sailors escaping for reasons other than fire.

Taps was at 2200 hours and reveille at 0600. All of us had to be out of our rooms and on the athletic field by 0630 for calisthenics, where role was taken. Woe be unto anyone who was late or didn't show up at all. Glad and I invested in two alarm clocks. Getting back on time wasn't a problem during that fall. I always made it back up the slide before 0600. My room opened onto the balcony where the beginning or the end of the slide—depending on whether you were coming or going—was located. My roommates kept the window open for me.

On the morning of the first hard frost of winter, I arrived at the foot of the slide at 0555, ready to climb up to my room. The first few feet were easy, but suddenly my tennis shoe slipped. I fell flat on my face and skidded all the way down to the bottom. I reasoned that I'd better hang onto the sides of the fire escape with a tighter grip. I started up again. My ascent was Sisyphean—three feet ahead, two feet back. Progress was discouragingly slow. I cursed my slovenly habit of awakening at the last possible moment and wished I had more time.

Soon it was 0600. Lights were coming on inside Lousy Annie and outside, with the floods lighting the athletic field. The watch officer was making his rounds in the halls, pounding on doors, making sure that no one was still asleep. In seconds, I would be outlined by all this light. What to do? I flattened my body against the cold metal and cast desperately about in my mind for an idea.

One good thing—I was dressed properly for calisthenics. When I slipped out at night I always wore the clothes I would wear in the morning. I could stay where I was and then, when all the other guys were going down the stairs for exercises, I could slide down and join them. But would I be seen? Probably. Using the slide was forbidden. Not a good solution! I'd better get the hell out of here. I rolled over onto my back and slid down the half of the slide that I had successfully negotiated. When I hit the bottom I quickly dropped to my knees and crawled under the lee of the building.

I was safe for a few minutes. Should I creep into the kitchen where Pop Crary, the cook, was preparing breakfast, and seek safe haven? No, that would put Pop on the spot. What a stupid situation. Why hadn't I thought of this before? My roommates couldn't help either. I couldn't get in touch with them, and if I could what would I ask them to do—scatter a bucket of sand on the slippery slope?

Crouched on the ground on my muddy knees, I began to wonder if I had wrecked my career in a way that even Lt. Bliss couldn't fix. I looked around for a solution. There was a row of bushes along the far side of the driveway that led from the street to the athletic field past the south end of "Lousy Annie." The sailors emerging from the south end of the building in ten or fifteen minutes would pass close to those bushes and, if I could remain undiscovered until then, I could merge with the group and my future might remain secure.

The first problem was to get to the bushes. At any moment, one of the CPOs who were our bosses might drive into the parking area behind the building. I decided the sooner the better. As I gathered myself and stood up for the thirty-yard dash from my hiding place to cross the driveway and lose myself in the bushes, a pair of headlights rounded the corner from the street. I flattened myself as I recognized Chief McGuire's car. Had he seen me? I lay prone, cold and worried, as the car passed by. The chief parked his car and, without a glance around, entered the building. I picked myself up and immediately dashed for a hiding place in the bushes.

Another car came as soon as I was in place. The gods were smiling on me. But I was a mess, with mud up and down my front. If somebody saw my dungarees and Navy-issue black sweater covered with dirt and asked me how come I was so dirty just coming out of Lousy Annie, I was sunk.

We formed two ranks for calisthenics. I made sure to get behind a sailor who was six foot four and I felt might hide me. Some of the guys looked at me oddly because of the state of my uniform; however, no one said a word.

Suddenly my brain went into high gear. My salvation was at hand. During the jumping jacks exercise I fell down, bumped into sailors jumping on both sides of me, sprawled on my stomach, and collapsed my section of the ranks. I was on the bottom of a pile of irritated shipmates, but now I had a reason to be dirty. Chief McGuire ran over and, once he got us untangled, he pointed at me and shouted, "You clumsy sonofabitch. Is this how you real Navy men are trying to win the war? Look at your clothes. You're a disgrace!" I was happy to be a disgrace because of the dirt on my uniform and not disgraced by being drummed out of the corps.

Glad and I made it through college together.

After the war, off we went to Portland, Oregon; I to medical school and Glad to teach music in the public schools.

❧

Medical school started with a bang. There were seventy-five of us, eight of whom were women—a remarkably high ratio for the times. It was the avowed purpose of the faculty to flunk out anyone who couldn't stand the pressure. My worst bang was in the Department of Human Anatomy; we didn't get along. The chairman of the department was a sadist who delighted in torturing the students he felt were inferior—not real scholars as he was. He would tell us, shaking his pasty jowls, which were pickled by formaldehyde fumes, "You should be anatomists. This is an exact science. You identify an organ, it is there; others can see it. But you, what will you do? Practice medicine and always guess. Here you will not guess; you will learn anatomy." He taught anatomy for anatomy's sake, without reference to any practical use in our future careers.

One student was kicked out of school during the first month.

We all had been issued a wooden box filled with human bones to take home to study. The anatomist told us, while holding two carpal bones in his hand as if they were worry beads, "You will know all of these bones so that you can identify them with a blindfold over your eyes."

The purpose of that exercise always escaped me. As a doctor, when would I be required to feel bones in the dark? Nevertheless, we studied the bones with our eyes closed.

The student who was terminated had been involved in an auto accident and the trunk of his car came open. Police arrived at the scene and promptly arrested him for having human remains in his possession as well as a set of surgical instruments in his car. The morning papers carried the story, also stating that the arrested person claimed to be a medical student and if that were true, what in the world was he doing—hunting more bones? Was he body-snatching? We thought the school would bail him out, until a follow-up story documented that he also had lewd pictures in his car. The reasons for those never came to light. The guy was gone.

It was rumored that you could also be dismissed for not wearing a tie.

There were faculty in the school who became our heroes. The head of the Department of Biochemistry took extra time to tutor students, and the head of pharmacology was a practical joker who taught with humor and wisdom. The greatest of all was Dr. Howard P. Lewis, the Chief of Medicine, a tall, spare, quiet man whose knowledge, teaching ability and kindness made him my personal hero. Perhaps the greatest day of my life was many years later when Doctor Lewis and I sat on the same platform to teach other doctors.

I was scared to death and proud at the same time. I was afraid that I would say something wrong. But he was congratulatory and told me he was proud that I had been his student. Although we worked together many times after that, I never got over the feeling of pride of being with him and being known as his colleague. I just happened to be in the area when he had his terminal illness. The day before he died, I visited him in the hospital and held his poor, pale, shrunken hand. I said thank you, and I cried.

One evening, early in the junior year of medical school, I asked, "Glad, how would you like to make a baby?" She said, "Sir honey, that's a very seductive idea." Glad and I debated this wonderful idea. Maybe we should start a family.

We pondered, discussing the whys and wherefores. We had been married four years. We were aging rapidly, it seemed. I would be twenty-nine the next year when the baby might be born. That was almost thirty; indeed, a pivotal point in one's life. We speculated that if we waited, we might be doddering when our grandchildren were born. Glad said spring was the only time to give birth, because diapers are easier to dry in an Oregon summer than in the winter.

School would be out at the end of May. "Let's try for June," she said. But what if it did not happen right away? Should we put it off a year? After we debated for about ten minutes, we decided to try.

We wondered if enthusiasm benefited fertility, since the effort was successful.

As the date of delivery of our first baby came closer, we became more and more excited. The baby was due on May 20 and my junior general oral examination was scheduled for May 26. These two upcoming events occupied my mind during most of my waking hours.

Glad was insistent that I be present when our child was born, not an unreasonable request. The Chief of Medicine was even more insistent that I be present for my appointment for junior generals. The only excuse one could have for missing the oral exams was to be dead. You didn't show up, you didn't pass—you didn't go on to the final year of medical school.

The exam itself was not as great a worry as the anatomy orals had been at the end of the first year. In contrast to the irascible anatomist, we now were dealing with clinicians; and because the third year had been all clinical, we felt reasonably prepared. True, the clinicians were perfectionists, but they were also used to dealing with human beings rather than with corpses. The only impracticality was the absolute provision that one had to be there.

The May 20 due date came and went.

Worry!

A call to the obstetrician was not reassuring. "When the apple is ripe it will fall."

We tried an impractical solution: a car ride over bumpy roads. We traveled west of the city, out in the country over the worst roads we could find, not realizing that three years later I would be traveling these same roads making house calls.

No labor, yet.

More worry! My appointment for the junior generals was at 1 P.M. in Dr. Lewis' office on May 26. May 24 and 25 came and went. On May 26 Glad and I went to see the obstetrician in his office early in the morning.

"It's time," he said, and into the hospital we went for induction of labor.

Glad did not take long. I waited in the doctors' lounge because of my status as a medical student, without the companionship of other expectant fathers. So I paced alone. I was not allowed into the delivery room to watch. In those days fathers were excluded, not only as unnecessary but also as a potential hazard to the doctor. Apparently, sometime in the dim past a distraught husband who felt that the doctor wasn't doing enough for his wife attacked a doctor and wreaked havoc.

Donnel Bernard, an eight-pound-nine-ounce baby boy named after his two grandfathers, was born at 1:29 P.M. on May 26. In my excitement, the appointment for junior generals did not even surface in my mind until that night, and then only while I was having a celebratory beer and a cigar with some of my classmates.

Holy smoke! I had missed the single, absolute appointment that was necessary for my promotion. My friends looked at me with heartfelt pity. To have come so far and then to have lost my chance to graduate! They consoled me by suggesting that perhaps I could start over in another medical school—or become a dentist.

The next morning, clad in an immaculately clean white coat, white shirt and tie, I went to see Dr. Lewis. He kept me waiting. I fidgeted. I waited. Finally, the door opened and I was ushered into his office. The great man was seated at his desk, hands folded with the fingers peaked in front of him like a series of gallows.

Dr. Lewis, with eyebrows raised, said, "You missed your appointment." His face was very solemn.

I quaked and quivered. "Sir," I said, "I had a baby."

"How very remarkable," was the retort.

"I mean, sir, my wife had a baby."

"Oh?"

"Sir, could I make up the exam?"

"Mister." This was the term used by the faculty to make sure that—just because students had white clinic coats, carried a stethoscope and tried to look very professional—we made no assumptions about being doctors before our time. The title would come on graduation day and not before. Dr. Lewis repeated, "Mister, what time was the birth?"

I told him.

He contemplated his fingers, took the gallows apart, waited a minute and said, slowly, "It would have been difficult for you to have left at that hour, would it not? I shall let you know when to reschedule and I hope the mother and baby are well."

Lord, what a relief! I left, dancing about three feet in the air. The rescheduling never took place. I passed, anyway. I was the only student ever—up to that time—not to have taken the exam. The junior generals were canceled the next year in favor of national board exams.

❧❧❧

We decided that Glad was not going to return to teaching.

I needed a job. The medical school said that during the school year, I could work every day for one to two hours, pasting X-ray reports into patients' charts for forty-five cents an hour. Good grief, I was paid that when I worked in a theater as an usher and doorman ten years earlier. Actually, when I worked as doorman, I got a nickel an hour more. It was cold standing outside the door taking tickets. I had not risen much in the world.

Then I got another offer. I could do urinalysis for an insurance company two nights a week for one dollar per urine exam, and they would guarantee five exams for each trip downtown. I hated urine, but five bucks was five bucks and I did it. Now things were looking up. That was at least ten dollars a week added to my ninety cents per day for five days. I was, with four years of college and three years of medical school, able to earn fourteen dollars and fifty cents a week!

A big break came that summer. St. Vincent's Hospital (the teaching hospital where I later interned) had hired only two interns when they needed eighteen, so the hospital needed help. The administration decided that medical school seniors (externs) could replace the missing interns. They would do intake histories and physicals, make rounds, scrub in surgery, and work in the emergency room—all under strict supervision.

I took the job for every other night and every other weekend. It paid seventy-five dollars a month and meals when on duty. It was a great learning experience and went on for the entire year. I still pasted X-ray reports and muddled around in other people's bodily fluids for the insurance company during off-hours.

❧❧❧

Having a baby in those days was considerably different than it is today. Well, that is not exactly true, but mothers were more pampered. Glad stayed in the hospital nine days, at no charge, because I was to be an extern at the hospital.

The arrival of the baby was the fulfillment of a cherished dream. When Don was just over one year old, we fulfilled our second dream: I graduated from medical school!

On graduation day the faculty held a reception for the graduates. Dr. Lewis came over to where Glad and I were standing with little Don and said, "Congratulations, DOCTOR. I presume this is the young man who had you so worried last year. Madam, you should be proud of your doctor and your son."

Now, I was ready to face the world. I would try very hard to be a good doctor and a good husband and father. With my career in front of me, I envisioned a life with community respect and a good income to support my family, whose ranks we had every intention of increasing.

❧

My monthly salary as an intern was now fifty dollars a month. This princely sum was down from the seventy-five dollars I had earned as an extern. Market forces were at work; there were plenty of interns this year. I now had a bachelor's degree in biology plus a doctor of medicine degree, but I still could not earn a living wage. Further, I no longer had time to paste X-ray reports or do urinalysis for the insurance company. As a fourth-year medical student I had been able to earn one hundred and thirteen dollars a month. Now, after achieving my goal of adding two letters, M and D, after my name, I was way below the poverty level once more. One advantage was that all meals, uniforms, and laundry were free to interns; and their families could come to the hospital for Sunday dinner.

I chose a rotating internship over a specialty internship, with the expectation that I would become a general practitioner. I had never figured out which branch of medicine I liked better than any other; except that I knew that whatever I did, it had to be with people.

Interns spent every other night and every other weekend on call. My being away so much caused Glad to spend a lot of her time telling number one son that, indeed, he did have a father. She spent many hours rocking little Don and telling him that he had a "Daddy Boy." The trouble was, when "Daddy Boy" came home every other day, it was mostly for sleep and the baby had to be quiet. Don and I really did not get to know each other well until a year later, when I became a resident.

St. Vincent's was an old-fashioned hospital, run by Catholic sisters who were angels, but disciplinarians. When a doctor, even an intern, entered a chart room, all the nurses and student nurses were required to stand up. When boarding an elevator, the nurses stood back and let the doctors go ahead. This subservience got under my skin.

One day when I entered a busy chart room, work stopped and everybody stood up. I finally had had enough of this. I said, "Please sit down. For God's sake don't get up when I come in." I sat down and started to write on a chart.

The nun who was supervisor for that floor was in the room, working behind a filing cabinet. She emerged after my declaration and with a very solemn expression, took me by the arm. I knew I was in trouble when she walked me into the corridor. I thought I knew the reason for my imminent chewing out. I had used the Lord's name in vain. I prepared myself to beg forgiveness and swear off swearing forever, a truly formidable task, having spent four years in the U.S. Navy.

Sister's eyes bored into mine and she said, "For GOD'S sake Doctor, why don't you concentrate on learning to be a good doctor and leave the training of the nurses to me? Oh yes, and when you invoke God's name, let it be for a good reason."

The charity ward, 2 North, was my intern responsibility when I was on the internal medicine service. The head nurse was not only intelligent and extremely confident, but absolutely beautiful. She had long black hair, high cheekbones, pouty lips, and a figure that made me want to walk behind her instead of in front.

When I arrived on Ward 2 North on my first morning the head nurse led me into a room to examine a patient, admitted the night before with shortness of breath. The nurse told me that the gentleman in question was a devotee of the god Bacchus, an inhabitant of a section of the city known as Skid Row, and a frequent visitor to Ward 2 North.

The nurse said, "Good morning, Jack."

The patient grinned at her. Then he turned to me with a scowl, "I see you've got another kid for me to train."

I smiled in my best bedside manner, put out my hand, and said, "Good morning, Jack. I'm glad to meet you. What seems to be bothering you?"

The patient was lying, propped in bed, smoking a cigarette. He had dirty, unkempt hair and three day's growth of beard. The nuns would later have the hospital barber give him a shave, shampoo, and a haircut. Jack's mouth was permanently downturned at the corners, reflective of his attitude toward life.

Jack did not answer or shake my hand. He just scowled. I asked again, and the short-of-breath old buzzard wheezed his reply, "Kid, you're the doctor, you find out." He scowled again, took a drag on his cigarette, and blew the smoke my way.

This was his game, and I had walked right into his trap like any rookie. They had not taught me what to do in this situation in medical school. I retreated to the hall with the nurse and, holding out my arms with palms up, said, "Help."

The savvy head nurse told me that Jack came in several times each year and always tried his trick on new house staff. She suggested that the only solution was to get tough with him, show him who was the boss, and not take any nonsense. She advised me to go back alone, so that I could do whatever I pleased, short of mayhem, and without witnesses.

This was quite an open invitation, but how does one get tough with a patient? Even worse, how does one get tough with a patient as sick as this old buzzard? The kind of shortness of breath that I saw in the old man probably resulted from severe emphysema. This could be fatal if not promptly treated. And he was still smoking. Not a good sign and certainly a window on his own self-esteem.

I went back into the room. Now I wasn't there to save my face, but to see that this guy submitted to treatment for his own welfare. To reason with him was to continue to play his game of being the stubborn, crotchety old man embarrassing the kid doctor. I resolved not to play the game, but to take the nurse's advice and be tough.

"Jack," I said, "you were admitted from the emergency room last night with shortness of breath. The acronym for that is S.O.B., and believe me, pal, that is exactly what you are—an S.O.B. You help me straighten out your health problem or you're back on the street in one hour. Stay here and cooperate and I'll see that you get an ounce of booze four times a day, and you won't have snakes crawling up the wall or see purple elephants in the corner of the ward.

This time Jack grinned at me and obligingly said, "Okay, Doc, she told you about me, didn't she? But that's okay. If I get a little to drink, I'll behave."

We became friendly, if not friends. Jack left in a week or so, improved but hardly well. He would be back. If I was still on Ward 2 North, he wouldn't be a problem.

⌘

The ringing of the phone to a young doctor was like the klaxon horn on a battleship, calling everyone to general quarters. The ringing was like the sound of a voice in a dark alley saying, "Hands up, I want your wallet and your watch!" The ringing of the phone meant fear. It was the sound that stirred one's blood, caught one's breath, chilled one's limbs, made one's heart beat faster.

I had been an intern for about three months and had received many phone calls while on night call in the house staff's quarters across the street from the hospital. Some were like my first call, when a poor old lady had died and I worried about her not really being dead and popping up in the morgue. Other calls were for horrible accidents, slashings on Saturday nights, heart attacks, and respiratory failure.

Once again I was awakened by the phone. I jumped to answer it. A nurse on 3 South merely wanted a sleep order for a patient. When I hung up, I realized something was wrong. My heart was pounding and I was short of breath. My heart was pounding so hard my chest hurt.

"Oh God, I'm having a heart attack. I'm going to die." I staggered out of bed and into the room where the medical resident, Dr. Jim Blickle, was asleep.

"Jim, Jim," I cried. "Jim, wake up, I'm having a heart attack. Help me!"

Jim Blickle was a laid-back, cool, calm guy, just the kind that makes a great internist. He was also very Irish and adored a good joke. He opened one eye, cocked it toward me and asked, "You're having a what?"

I told him, "Heart attack, damn it. Do something!"

He looked again and without getting up reached for my wrist, feeling for my pulse. After a few seconds with my wrist in his hands, my heart in my throat, and my brain addled from fear, he made his pronouncement. "You have the three-month gallop. You'll be okay."

Now what does this mean? Will my heart gallop like this for three months? This must be a disease that wasn't taught in medical school, or I had been asleep that day. I wished I was asleep at that moment. Maybe I was and this was all a bad dream.

Jim said, "Sit down on the edge of the bed." He took hold of my neck and began to rub the large artery on the left side.

Carotid massage! Good grief, he was trying to convert a bout of paroxysmal auricular tachycardia (P.A.T.) to a normal rhythm by massaging my carotid sinus. I could have done that myself. My pulse slowed, my shoulders relaxed, and I suddenly felt stupid. "What in the hell is the three-month gallop?"

Grinning, Jim answered, "That's what happens to interns after they have been on the job about three months. The phone rings and a startle reaction occurs. Adrenaline pours into the blood from the adrenal gland, your heart speeds up, this scares you even more, and the first thing you know you have a P.A.T. It happens every year. This year, you're the first."

The phone became my demon. Many times during my practice years I dreamed that the phone had rung and I jumped up to answer it, only to hear a dial tone. Once I even went to the hospital to deliver a baby and there was no one in labor. I had been dreaming. Years later when I left active practice and there was no reason for the phone to ring at night, I continued to be terrorized by the telephone. Waking after a dream that the phone had rung, Glad and I decided to have the phone company put a telephone jack on her side of the bed. It worked. I was suddenly free of the responsibility and the dreams stopped.

❧

On July 1, I stopped being a rookie doctor and began a surgical residency. Now I was a real doctor and eligible for licensure. The secretary of the State Board of Medical Examiners was on our medical faculty and a good friend. During the first week of my residency he came to the hospital in great pain, suffering from a kidney stone. I jokingly told him that I wouldn't give him an injection of morphine unless he promised that I would pass the exam. His roars woke seventeen patients on the same floor who thought that either the hospital was on fire or a wild bull had made its way into the hospital. In order to get the people back to sleep we had to give them sleeping pills. Dr. Foster never let me forget my practical joke—telling it and retelling it in the surgeons' lounge—how this damn kid had pulled his leg. And I passed the exam without any help.

Working in a Catholic hospital, but not being a Catholic, gave me a certain awe of the Catholic clergy. The nuns wore habits and wimples and tight shoes, and had callused knees (they said). The priests were all Jesuits and, remembering from my classes in medieval history that the order was a devious lot, I was somewhat apprehensive of associating with them.

Not having matriculated at a Catholic school, I had never had my hands slapped by a teaching nun wielding a ruler, or been poked sharply in the back with a pointed finger when caught daydreaming in class, or even considered donating money for a pagan baby. I learned about these practices from the Jesuit priests at our hospital. They were trainees in their last stages of training. This experience was their instruction as hospital chaplains.

These young men, hardly devious, became pals. We hoisted a few together and they taught me what to do and say for last rites. Despite our friendship I still stood in awe when, on Sunday morning before mass, a priest paraded through the halls, swinging his censer, with incense smoke trailing along behind him. I always thought of Diogenes, looking for the honest man. I noticed that the Catholic nurses and other workers ducked into a doorway when the parade appeared. Not wanting to buck the trend, I just ducked out of the way, too. The significance of the ritual was unclear to me.

Later in life, a Catholic friend, when queried about why they did this, said that she really did not know. She laughingly suggested that in the early days of the church, perhaps the congregation, who probably didn't bathe often, smelled so bad that incense was used to clear the air as the priest moved down the aisle in preparation for holding mass. Piqued by this question and by my friend's response, I called the local archdiocese. They suggested that "the custom is a holdover from the Old Testament. It was a custom of the Israelites." My informant suggested I call the local synagogue and ask the rabbi for my answer. I shall do that, someday.

The other clergy were the nursing nuns. Some were pretty tough on us young guys, and the old guys too. We paid deference to the nuns who were really in charge of the hospital. We could hardly call them pals, as we did the young priests.

Sister Catherine, the chief of the operating room, and the one who scheduled all the surgical cases, invariably snarled at any doctor who scheduled a dilatation and curettage (D and C) of the uterus, saying, "Doctor, if you start it in your office, finish it there." The implication being that a D and C was often done on an incomplete abortion. Elective therapeutic abortions were verboten. The only cases admitted to the hospital were spontaneous abortions. But Sister never let the doctors forget that she was watching and nobody, but nobody, was going to abort a patient in her surgery.

Mother Pascal was Mother Superior. She ruled by love and kindness. She was a round and short lady who constantly roamed the corridors, talking with everyone she saw. She knew every employee and maybe every patient by name.

After I became a resident, I frequently scrubbed in surgery with the surgical chief, Dr. Dean Seabrook. I learned at the feet of a master. He was a master of not only surgical diagnosis and technique, but he had a masterful wit. The butt of his jokes was always himself.

A great honor came toward the end of my residency year, when Dean Seabrook offered to supplement my income for two more years of surgical training and invited me to enter practice with him, as his partner, at the end of that time. I demurred and have not regretted it, but the flush of pride remains.

Mother Pascal became ill. The hospital became silent. Dr. Seabrook was called in. I went with him to her room. After we examined her, Dr. Seabrook declared that Mother Pascal had a "surgical abdomen" and would require emergency surgery. Diagnostic procedures and examinations indicated a bowel obstruction in the descending colon. When this area is obstructed, it is usually from either a ruptured diverticulum with abscess, or from cancer.

Everyone waited, hoping for good news. The case was scheduled for 7 P.M., allowing time to get blood transfusions ready.

Dr. Seabrook said, "I want you to scrub with me." I was thrilled to be so honored, but concerned about the outcome.

We had dinner together in the cafeteria. Dr. Seabrook's usual jocular mood was subdued. We discussed the surgical approach we would use. At 6:30 P.M. we took the elevator to the fifth floor, where we would go to the surgical lounge and change into scrub clothes and then enter the operating room.

When we emerged from the elevator and turned to the right, we had to walk down a long corridor to the operating suites. Stretched out along both sides of this corridor, were all the black-robed nuns and priests, each holding a lighted candle and praying. The sight was awesome. We didn't know how to act, other than to walk straight forward with heads erect and try to behave confidently. As we passed each nun and priest, they crossed themselves, touched one of us, and murmured something like, "God be with you."

The strain was overwhelming.

We did operate on Mother Pascal. She had a cancer and we could not get it all; she died soon after. My memory of her is of a kind-hearted, loving person. That night, walking the gauntlet of clergy, still enters my dreams occasionally.

ജ൜ഠ

Glad and I assessed our financial state which was nil, we assessed my desire not to be limited to any special area of medicine, and we assessed the environment in which we wished to raise our family. The final decision was to look for a place where I could practice near a good hospital and one which would be best for the children.

Despite my upbringing in a big city, I was willing to try country life. The place we selected was rural but only twenty-five miles from Portland. We were bound for Sherwood, Oregon.

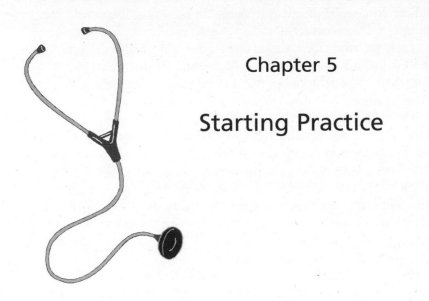

Chapter 5

Starting Practice

After sixteen years of classroom education, one year of internship, and one year as a resident physician—and because we were as poor as church mice—I was eagerly looking forward to entering practice, and doing what I had been working toward for so long: being a real doctor.

I was going to be a general practitioner. In medical school I had not found a specialty that I liked better than all the others; though I knew what I did had to be with people. A laboratory specialty was not my cup of tea, nor were the limited specialties in which I would have to concentrate on one organ system.

After I entered practice I was really glad—because of my adventure with Eddie Lucetti III (whom you will meet later)—that I hadn't selected urology. Excreted bodily fluids had never been high on my list of favorite things, so standing around in a urology surgery, ankle deep in someone's urine, was not appealing. Heck, I didn't even like to change a baby's diaper. Once I read in a book that the ancient Chinese brushed their teeth with baby urine. Such things didn't console me. I finally got accustomed to urine after a number of little boy patients sprayed me and we had a second baby boy ourselves.

One experience as a resident cemented my thinking that forever bound me to general practice, to being a real doctor who could handle anything—well, almost anything.

I was on call at the hospital one night when a respected internist on the staff called the switchboard in a high state of agitation and said, "I've got her here. She's bleeding like hell! I need help right now! Send somebody, quick!"

Dr. Pagar was one of the most erudite of all the physicians on our staff. He was the one with the right answers at the diagnostic conferences and he wrote the best papers for the scientific journals. The switchboard operator and I both recognized his distinctive voice despite his obvious agitation, but his garbled message was impossible to deal with. He didn't give his name, he didn't say where he was, and he obviously had forgotten that Portland hospitals did not maintain ambulance services. It would be necessary to call the ambulance directly. We couldn't even do that for him, as we didn't know where he was.

The switchboard operator was a toughened veteran of her job and accustomed to the vagaries of the medical staff, some of whom were not above a practical joke now and then. For example, Dr. Harry Blair, a well-respected orthopedic surgeon, arrived every morning to make rounds and always stopped in at the admitting office where it was understood by the admitting staff that they were to take care of his imaginary dog while he made rounds. Occasionally he would call the switchboard operator and indicate that his dog was lost and would she keep an eye out for it.

But she knew this call wasn't a practical joke. The distraught doctor on the telephone never saw anything funny in life. We called his home to see if his family knew where he had gone. They did not. We called his answering service to see if they had taken the call. They had not. Apparently the patient had called the doctor's home directly. There was nothing we could do but wait.

After fifteen minutes he called again, shouting into the telephone, saying essentially the same thing and once more he hung up quickly. Minutes later, when the third call came, I took the call rather than the operator and, without listening to his tirade, I began to shout his name and the words, "Listen to me," over and over until I finally got through to him. He stopped yelling and said, "This is terrible! I don't know what to do! This lady is pregnant and bleeding. I don't know anything about pregnant women. I'm just an internist. I need help."

After calming him down, I was able to walk him through a couple of emergency procedures while the operator dispatched an ambulance through another phone line.

When the patient arrived, I examined her and found that she was undergoing a spontaneous miscarriage in her first trimester and, tragic as all these cases are, her life wasn't in danger. In fact, she easily could have been driven to the hospital by a family member. I resolved right then and there that I wanted to be the kind of doctor who could handle any emergency—and certainly not one spooked by the sight of blood. I would even be patient when little boys sprayed me.

Before the war, when I had been a salesman, I guess I had developed a salesman's personality. I liked being around people. I also had an overwhelming desire to be liked. I thought I could be liked as a doctor, but I knew I would have to make unpleasant decisions. It would be my job to make those decisions as palatable for my patients as I could. I would want to explain and sell rather than dictate to my patients. I wanted to be in a practice situation where I would be able to take the time to talk to people. I was going to be that kind of doctor. Sound idealistic? It was! I still feel that way and have always tried to do it. Marcus Welby did it, and I wish more of today's doctors had the same attitude.

Physicians were in short supply in 1952 and practice opportunities were plentiful. I had many offers. As a young doctor entering practice I would be assured of a fine career, the opportunity to earn respect from the community and patients alike, and a decent income. Selecting the right place to practice was a challenge. What location would be the best? As I wanted to find a place where Glad and I could spend the rest of our lives, the decision was critical.

Sherwood, Oregon—a town of six hundred souls, just twenty-five miles from Portland—seemed to be ideal. In addition to the six hundred people in Sherwood, there were twenty-five hundred rural mail boxes, making a total population in the catchment area of about ten thousand. The town had one very old doctor who had already retired. The other doctor, who had practiced there four years, offered to hire me. The doctor who made me the offer was the same age as I, had three children, and owned a successful practice.

If a good book had been available on how to go into practice when I was starting out, its first page would have advised the young doctor on how to buy a new car before moving to his new home. Conventional wisdom dictated buying an expensive car, since upgrading a cheap one could be interpreted as flaunting behavior. "Your patients will think you're making too much money," said one older colleague.

Glad and I accepted this wisdom, perhaps too willingly. We yearned for a nice car. Our 1946 Chevrolet was okay, but our expanding family, increased by a second son, Lee, would not be accommodated comfortably in a Chevrolet roadster. Not yet in practice and earning only seventy-five dollars a month as a resident, how could we buy anything? Well, the second page of that mythical book would have said, "Your M.D. degree and state license to practice medicine can open bank vaults." They did. The heady essence of our newly acquired buying power got us in pretty deep, and later, when we tried to economize that, too, presented problems.

Car dealers drooled when I introduced myself as "Doctor." I suppose our naiveté showed. No two more wide-eyed car shoppers ever kicked a tire. Loans were available, probably because of the "Doctor" title; and the price was probably higher, too. But what the heck, we were going to make a real salary and the future was not only rosy, it was damned exciting. Finally, after eight years of marriage, we would be poor no longer.

We settled on a DeSoto. The DeSoto was a midrange Chrysler product, above a Dodge and below a New Yorker. The model we picked was a blue hardtop convertible with white leather upholstery. A hardtop convertible was really a two-door sedan with no post between the front and back seat. It was a truly handsome vehicle. We bought the car on Saturday and I drove it to St. Vincent's on Monday. After rounds in the morning, I invited all the house staff to the parking lot to view my acquisition. They stood around and murmured niceties while I expounded on the quality and luxuries of my new car. As the residents and interns began to drift away, I asked, "How many want a ride?"

Three people accepted, two for the back and Barbara, a pal from both medical student and resident days, was to ride in front with me. Barbara knew me as well as anyone since she and I had been among the four students sharing the same cadaver in anatomy lab. Having suffered anatomy together, ours would be a lifelong friendship. Mutual suffering binds people. With a flourish, I grasped the door handle on the passenger side to admit the lady to the car and, to my utter shock and embarrassment, the entire handle and its assembly came off in my hand. The roars of laughter cheered everyone else for the entire day, but not me. I drooped, but Barbara tried to make me feel better by saying, "Don't make such a fuss—it could have been a wheel!"

❧❧❧

I proudly drove the DeSoto to Sherwood, Oregon two months later on the day I started practice and saw my first private patient.

My boss, Sam, and I were the same age, but we had graduated from medical school four years apart. He had spent the war years in college and in medical school, while I had been in the Navy. About the time I finished my undergraduate work, he was completing medical school.

Sam was a bright guy who had been elected to the honor society, Alpha Omega Alpha. He was well thought of by his colleagues in the county medical society.

Our families matched each other. He had three beautiful blonde kids, and Glad and I had two boys and a third child planned. The boss's wife was a nurse who had worked in his office, but who was willing to quit when I arrived, as we all felt this might be a source of conflict. We agreed that the "marriage" of two doctors would be hard enough without any other distractions.

Glad and I instantly liked both of them. After looking over the practice, its books, the potential for growth, and what seemed to be the compatibility between families, we accepted the offer of six hundred dollars a month as salary (about average for a rookie doctor in 1952) for a six-month trial period. After that, if we both agreed, I would have the opportunity to gradually buy half of the practice.

Our medical practice covered an area of about two hundred fifty square miles. Making a house call was often time consuming, not only because of distance, but because of gravel or dirt roads and very few signs or markers to point the way.

The countryside around Sherwood was in part flat, in part rolling, and in part mountainous. We covered a territory from Bull Mountain (in a part of Tigard), west through Six Corners to Chehalem Mountain, south over Parret Mountain to the Willamette River and along its course north and east past Wilsonville and Frog Pond to the edge of Lake Grove, and past Wankers Corners up to Highway 99W to the edge of Tigard.

Within these zigzag borders were the Tualatin River and the sparse communities of Prosperity Park (no doubt named during the Depression, from which it never recovered), Tonquin and Malloy, and the Onion Swamp. The more populated areas were Norwood, Durham, Wilsonville, and Tualatin—where we bought our first home when we moved to the area.

I enjoyed driving the country roads—especially at night—because of the rich smells of the countryside. The earthy smell of freshly plowed

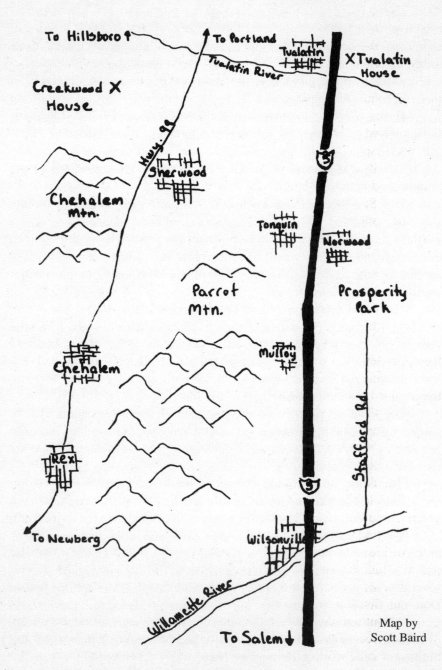

Map of the Sherwood-Tualatin area.

Map by
Scott Baird

fields after a rain, the perfume of new-mown hay in the spring, sometimes mixed with the pungent smell of a frightened skunk, merged into an aroma of the country. These were smells I would never forget. Even today, after the neighborhood lawns have been mowed, I hearken back to a hectic life of driving like mad along country roads to deliver a baby or respond to an emergency call.

Being a country doctor, I made many trips through the night to Portland and to Hillsboro, the county seat of Washington County, where Tuality Hospital was located.

Tuality was a seventy-five-bed rural community hospital where my partner had practiced before my arrival. We continued to practice there and added St. Vincent's Hospital in Portland, where I had done my internship and residency. "St. V" had about four hundred beds. The trip to the Portland hospital was twenty-four miles, to Hillsboro twenty-three miles; and the great circle for hospital rounds was sixty-seven miles, a difficult chore in the morning if only one of us was to see our hospital patients. Actually, unless we had surgery or other special problems with patients, one of us went to Portland and the other to Hillsboro.

The trip to Portland was scenic. My route took me across the west hills of the city, up to Council Crest, and then down past the Portland Rose Gardens to the hospital near 23rd Avenue and West Burnside.

During the four years of his full and demanding practice, my new friend and boss, soon-to-be partner had been waiting to take a vacation. Ten days after my arrival in Sherwood, he informed me that he and his family were going on a three-week camping vacation.

"We've been waiting a long time for this and, besides, it's a good way for you to get your feet wet," he said. We didn't know then that I would break one of those feet while I was getting them wet.

Sam left on the first of July with his wife and three kids in his ugly green Chevrolet station wagon. I had the duty.

We had just moved into the house in Tualatin, about six miles east of the office and twenty-four miles from Portland. The road was a familiar one to Glad and me; we had traveled it when I was in medical school, several years earlier, in a futile attempt at initiating her labor just before Don, our first son, was born.

About ten days before the announcement that I was to be on my own for three weeks, I had moved into the new house by myself for my nights on call, while Glad and the boys waited for the closing of the sale on our Portland house to be completed. The Portland house had been purchased with a GI loan, nothing down and interest of four and one-half percent. We had bought it brand new for eight thousand dollars.

My only furnishings in the new Tualatin house were a bed and telephone. On the first night I discovered the sad news. Munniksma's Dairy, across Sagert Road from our house, had a very large, very loud Holstein bull. The smell, when the wind was just right, was pretty over-whelming in its own right, but at least it was intermittent. For city dwellers, an amorous tomcat on the fence can disturb the serenity of sleep. Imagine an amorous two-thousand-pound bull stuck in his own corral, calling out to his ladies who were in the fields all around him. For all the years that we lived in that house, the bull bellowed most nights. The noise was outrageous. The only respite came during the times when the cows needed freshening and the bull and the ladies were locked together in a pasture on the other side of the barn. Fortunately, we were not able to hear the conjugal grunts and the mooing.

We didn't know all this when the real estate agent showed the place to us. Who would go to see the house of their choice during the night, before signing the contract? As a young doctor, I wasn't much of a busi-nessman.

On July first, Glad, Don and our second son, Lee Crawford (born just three months before moving day), arrived with the furniture. That same day, my boss had made his announcement about going on vacation. He probably imagined that, once we had sold our other house and physi-cally moved into the new one, we were hooked; and the news that I would be alone for three weeks would not scare me off.

Scare me off? Nothing was going to drive me away. I was as excited as a jumper checking out the length of his bungee cord, about the whole idea of fulfilling my dream and going into practice at last! I couldn't wait for him to leave so that I could jump feet first into medical practice. Of course, I was scared as well. My medical career up to that point had been one where I was always supervised, and I had thought that when I entered practice, Sam would be there. I would have someone to talk to, share problems with, and ask questions of—I guess I sort of imagined contin-uing as a trainee, under supervision. I never knew if Sam was very wise in throwing me into the water to sink or swim or if, as stated, he just wanted a vacation. Whatever his reason, the prescription was correct. I grew up in a hurry.

There were thirty-five to forty-five patients in the office each day, hospital rounds, and house calls. House calls in 1952 were common and usual. When we closed the office at 5:30 P.M., there were usually between one and eight house calls still to be made. These calls included emergencies that had come up during the day when the patients were not able to get in to the office, or routine follow-up calls on shut-ins. At that time, older people and the chronically ill usually lived at home, cared for by their families rather than being institutionalized.

The fourth of July fell on a Friday, so, in order to have the long holiday weekend free, I had to catch up on all my week's house calls on Thursday night. There were five calls to be made and I was late leaving the office. Since I had not had time to become familiar with all the patients and where they lived, I was pretty slow.

There were no street signs, only spoken directions: "Take Tonquin Road down to the second fork and turn south *Which way is south? It's dark, now,* go about a mile and you will come to the old Tomanjian place," *Tom who?,* "and pass that, then turn right at Petry's big white barn," *How will I know that it's Petry's white barn? The countryside is full of white barns,* "cross the creek on the old wooden bridge and, oh yes, be careful. Joe Loomis drove off that bridge last year and drowned, but he had a snootful. Well, anyway, you just keep on a-comin' and we'll have the light on for ya."

My first visit was a simple blood pressure and function check on a stroke victim who was recovering at home. The next patient was down in Tonquin-Malloy. Tonquin-Malloy should not have been linked together. Tonquin was mostly a rock farm, while Malloy was the area of the rich and fertile onion swamp. My house call was in Tonquin to see a kid with a sore throat and an earache.

The house was a ramshackle bungalow out in the middle of a weed patch. The porch had no railing, the stairs were rickety, and I was in a hurry to leave. I had done the usual: checked the kid's ear, given him a shot of penicillin, put drops in his ear, left a prescription for oral penicillin, and hurried off.

Medical bag in hand, I leaped off the side of the porch nearest my car, rather than taking the time to go down the steps since I was late already. I landed with one foot on a rock submerged in the weeds. The area was a rock farm and I had found a rock. My ankle went one way; my foot went the other. There was a loud snap, a shooting pain, and an embarrassing fall into the weeds while the nearby chickens and the cows in the pasture looked on. I got up, gritted my teeth, and hopped to the car on one foot.

During the next two house calls I was in real pain, hopping and hobbling along and reassuring the patients that I was okay, despite a dusty suit coat and grass stains on my pants. I did not want to seem lacking in the eyes of patients, no matter what. Both the quality of my medical care and my personal pride were extremely important to me in my first weeks in practice. (Such false pride has a way of diminishing with age.)

The last call of the night (at 7:45 P.M.) was from the village matriarch of the city of Tualatin, population two hundred fifty. Tualatin is now a bustling, industrial suburb of Portland.

The matriarch's old house, a glorious, three-story gingerbread relic of the past, still stands just across the railroad tracks from the town's main thoroughfare. The old lady's son was a retired Navy physician. The two of them and a housekeeper lived in the old house.

As I hobbled from my car to the door, I could see gray hair and a white face peeping from behind partially closed curtains in an upstairs window. I assumed she was my patient, as all my patients were new faces to me. I was meeting them for the first time.

The wind had started to blow, moving the curtain in the upstairs window, giving both of us a better look at each other. The dust from the driveway whipped around my head which was now soaked from the perspiration of pain. I wiped my brow and rang the doorbell. (This was one of the few houses I ever entered by the front door while practicing in Oregon farm country; barnyard back doors were customary.) Wiping my brow had produced dirt smudges on my face, further besmirching my appearance.

A servant opened the door and pointed me to a long, gracefully curving staircase. My patient and her doctor son were in the upstairs sitting room. I considered asking the lady to come down but, remembering that her age was ninety-two, I decided that I could manage. When I entered the upstairs sitting room the doctor was having an evening cocktail and the patient was sitting on a chaise lounge near the window with the blowing curtain. She was, indeed, the peeper I had seen in the window.

The lady, for it was obvious that she was a lady, had silvery white hair, a thin angular jaw, and piercing dark eyes, and wore a lace negligee.

I introduced myself, apologized for the lateness of the hour and my appearance, and hobbled across the room to examine my patient. The old lady looked at me with an appraising eye and immediately asked me about my welfare. I explained that I had suffered a slight fall. She made me sit down and told her son, a boozy-looking, white-haired man of military bearing, to examine my foot. He did. It hurt. It was swollen so much, it even scared me. It certainly scared the matriarch, who teetered across the room to have her own look. She immediately took charge.

"Young man," she said, "sit down and do not take another step." She ordered the doctor to fix me a Scotch. I would have preferred bourbon, but at that moment even Scotch was welcome. "Now," she ordered, "you'll go home. Can you drive?"

I replied in the affirmative and started to rise, getting out my stethoscope to perform my medical functions. My patient again took charge and refused my attentions, stating that I was to get right home and please take her cane, that I needed it more than she!

When I got home, I went right to bed with a throbbing ankle. Glad called Harley Hiestand, an orthopedic surgeon and old friend from my residency days, who lived about fifteen miles away at Lake Oswego. He came over and assisted me in getting to my office. I hadn't yet learned the intricacies of our office X-ray machine, but between us we managed to take a picture. The ankle was broken, not severely, but in need of immobilization via a plaster of Paris cast which he applied. In twenty-four hours, when the cast hardened, he would return and apply a walking heel, and a day after that I would become mobile without crutches. Meanwhile, he prescribed bed rest with my foot elevated on two pillows. Quite a way to start my first week alone in practice!

I felt that I had blown my start in a new practice. I had about forty-eight hours before I could even lower my foot off the pillows, let alone walk without crutches, and what if I had to make a house call? What if there was an emergency, an auto accident, a farm accident, a baby to deliver? My new boss was camping and totally unavailable. I had failed in the trust he had placed in me.

Glad and I pondered and tried to remember classmates in Portland who were still in specialty training. Perhaps one of them would be available for a brief locum tenens. Sure enough, Harry Proud, a general surgery resident at the university, and his wife, came out for the weekend, and he covered for me until I was once again mobile. I held forth on the chaise lounge on our patio, responding to his phone calls from the houses of patients.

In one case, he could not figure out the diagnosis of a kid with a rash and fever, and I suggested measles. Harry said, "Oh, my gosh, I've never seen a case of measles. As a surgery resident at the medical school I'll probably never see another, but I'll never forget this one."

This was certainly a commentary on medical training. Because the nation's medical schools were research centers, the unusual was the usual and students never saw patients who exhibited the types of cases that were the essence of everyday practice. At St. Vincent's Hospital, when I was an intern, the house staff asked the nuns to let us develop an outpatient clinic for the indigent. So, fortunately, we had an opportunity to see a sample of a normal patient load, as would be experienced in practice. I was better prepared to enter general practice as a result.

We made it through the weekend and no lives were lost.

The sequel to this story came a week later when Glad drove me to the hospital and watched as I, with my leg draped with rubber sheets, delivered a baby. On the way home Glad marveled at the poignant moment, observing the wonderment of birth. She also explained how being there had brought home to her the important role that I played in the lives of my patients.

If I had been elevated in her eyes, I was grateful. One of the most important reasons I have lived my life as I have is to earn the respect of my wife and my children.

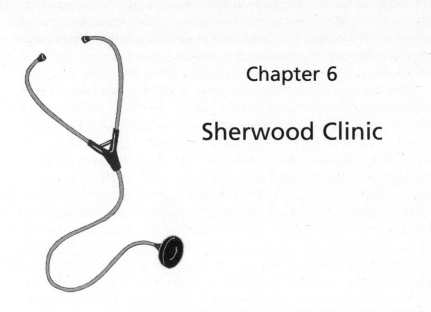

Chapter 6

Sherwood Clinic

My boss, without much forethought, had built a one-doctor office. After I arrived he didn't change it. We both worked in a one-man office.

There was a large reception room with a tiny reception cubicle, behind which was a desk for a secretary or insurance person. Down the left corridor there were two large examining rooms, each with a small desk containing prescription pads and forms requesting lab and X-ray procedures. Doing it this way saved taking a patient into a consultation room just to take a medical history.

"Using a consultation room won't work," my new employer said, "We have to see more patients. No time!"

Maybe he was ahead of his time and was behaving as his descendants in medicine would in years to come, as a seller of medical services instead of being a giver of health care. My idealism about taking the time necessary to talk to my patients was shaken. But he was the boss and had been doing it this way for four years and it had worked, so I listened and learned—not realizing that the very words I heard those first few days together were the issues that would cause the collapse of the partnership eight years later.

Rewards in medicine were substantial. There was money to be made sufficient to provide the good life for all practitioners; however, to me, the relationship with my patients and the trust they placed in me was the greatest reward I would ever have. In later years, whenever I picked up a patient's record and noted that the family had trusted me to be their doctor for a number of years, I felt a surge of pride and love for those people.

During my years as a medical student, intern, and resident I had fantasized myself as the kindly doctor sitting at my desk in the consulting room, discussing weighty problems with patients and family. This was a Hollywood portrayal, not a real-life one, according to Sam. Neither of us dreamed that that very role would be portrayed by Robert Young seventeen years later and that I would be the role model for his portrayal of Marcus Welby.

There was a place called "the doctors' office." Here there was one desk (I could have two drawers), a desk chair, a side chair, and a couch. We would share the office, use it to read and have conferences together. Yes, I could bring a patient in there once in a while if it was absolutely necessary, but Sam liked to rest in there or catch up on his paperwork when he was not seeing patients. Also, this was where we filled out insurance forms, received visits from pharmaceutical company representatives, stockbrokers, traveling insurance agents, traveling shoe salesmen, and other vendors who called on small-town doctors unable to get away to shop.

❧

My naivete knew no bounds. Bob Goodwin, an old friend, showed up after I had been in the practice about a year. I had known him when I sold radios and appliances at Sherman-Clay. Before the war he was a drummer with the big bands; his last gig was with Jack Teagarden. Bob introduced himself as a stockbroker and said, "I've got a wonderful deal for you. The Upjohn Pharmaceutical Company is a family-owned business, but it has decided to go public with some stock. I have a limited number of shares I can let you have."

Boy, I thought, *if it's hard to get it must be a good buy and if I owned Upjohn stock I would prescribe their products as would a lot of other doctors and the stock will go up* (a very unethical idea). I had never before considered purchasing stock, but I was flushed with the idea of having so much money in my hands. The boss had given me a raise and I was making seven hundred and fifty dollars a month. I asked, "How much?"

My friend answered, "Only twelve-fifty, and," he said, "there's no commission to be paid because the stock is just coming on the market."

Whatta deal. I did a lot of rapid calculations in my head, thought about the little savings we had squirreled away in the months I had been in practice. We were saving for the baby due in June but…. What the heck, a chance like this to make some real dough doesn't come along very often. "Can I get a hundred?"

My friend said, "You haven't established a margin account with us. Do you want to do that?"

"What's a margin account?"

"That's an account where you only pay for part of the stock now and you finish paying for it when you sell the stock if you sell it at a profit."

"What happens if it goes down?"

"Then you have to finish paying for it right away."

"Do you think it will go down?" I was frightened to lose the money. I didn't want to buy something like that on credit, either.

Bob answered, "Go down? Not a chance."

"Okay, I'll pay cash. When do you need it?"

My very happy and grinning friend said, "Well, in a deal this big I'd better have it tomorrow because we'll have to clear the check and that could take a few days."

"A few days? You can go down to the bank right now and get the cash—the banker is a patient of mine."

The broker studied me quizzically and said, "I wouldn't want to carry a hundred and twenty-five thousand dollars on me."

A what? He said twelve-fifty. He must have meant twelve hundred and fifty. My God, I haven't made that much money by adding up every dollar I've earned in my whole life. Hell, I may never make that much money if I live to be a hundred.

"Say, Bob, I think we made a mistake here." With my face the color of the setting sun, I stammered, "I haven't got that much money. We better forget it."

Bob left, still grinning. I think he knew all along I couldn't hack that kind of a bill. He was just letting me hang myself. Well, I would learn.

⚬⚬⚬

The pill pushers of the world, at the time I went into practice, the pharmaceutical company representatives, were called "detail men." One of the uses of our private office was as a place to see these people. The job of these professional representatives was to inform doctors about the glories of using their particular prescription drug to cure everything from athlete's foot to heart disease. In order to interest us, samples were given. Promotional gimmicks also played a significant role. The most common gimmick was a sales premium or gift. The gifts ranged from very useful anatomical models to copies of squat Indian figures of pre-Columbian art. Authentic artifacts have pristine beauty as historical relics; but a copy on a doctor's desk, with its fat belly emblazoned with the company's trademark, had no redeeming features. Nevertheless, these sales people were nice guys.

No women had cracked their ranks at this early date. Industry leaders had not yet figured out that women could do this job. They said, "Doctors won't accept advice or technical information from a woman." Maybe they were right, because medical schools had not figured that out, either—that women as doctors are as competent as men. Eight women made up ten percent of my class in medical school. This was an aberration for the times. All eight graduated, whereas twenty percent of the males didn't make it.

The detail men served a function in making physicians aware of new products. They were personally pleasant. We saw most of them because, as the only doctors in town, we knew that they had made a special trip to see us; and we felt obligated to listen for at least a few minutes. These guys lived or died by quotas. If they met their sales quotas they could get a year-end bonus; if they failed, they'd get a chewing out at least, and dismissal at worst. They also had contact quotas, so they were required to see a certain number of doctors every day. If they spent too much time waiting in our office, it might cause them to fall behind; therefore, we always made a quick decision about seeing reps.

Seeing these people was easier on some days than on others, but we didn't know which days would be better, because we did not make patient appointments.

What kind of a doctor's office was this? No appointments for patients? When I first arrived I questioned this method. But the boss said that he had been doing this for four years and it worked fine.

Before going into practice I had a mental image of spending time with each patient, first in a consultation room taking a history and later going to an examining room to complete the visit. This was the way the family doctor of my childhood, Doctor Joe Kavanaugh (replete with goatee and Viennese manner), had done it. Dr. Joe was a childhood hero. With only one office, and this one somewhat restricted territory, my dream could not be realized; but, at least, I thought we could make appointments.

"No," he said, "we have to see all the patients that show up. It doesn't matter whether they come in for a school physical or an acute illness. They'll wait their turn and then we'll see them."

"But," I countered, "Wouldn't it make more sense to schedule routine visits and fill in around them with emergencies?" We always dealt with severe emergencies at any time.

"The more the merrier," he said. "We don't want people to go someplace else because they are not able to get an appointment here when they want it."

This technique resulted in our seeing a record one hundred forty patients on one day during a flu epidemic. This is no way to practice medicine! Over the years I tried, repeatedly, to change the system, to no avail. Eventually this was another one of the important rifts between my partner and me that resulted in the dissolution of the partnership.

My feeling about the need for appointments was reinforced around the end of my first year in practice, when a tragedy involved a patient who didn't want to wait in our crowded waiting room to see the doctor.

Francis Skillicorn was an old-timer around town and had been a patient of "Ole Doc" before he retired. Ole Doc lived on a tree-shaded street three blocks from our office. He still maintained a little outbuilding adjacent to his home where he had carried on his medical practice. Francis had a cold. He wanted a penicillin shot. When he arrived at our office he noticed a whole lot of cars parked in front and when he poked his nose in the door his suspicions were confirmed. The place was jam-packed, full.

It was like going into a busy restaurant and asking the maitre d' hôtel how long the wait would be for a table. In this case the maitre d' was Cora, and the request was to see a doctor, not have dinner. She told him it would be between one and two hours. Francis decided his summer cold wasn't bad enough to sit around and wait. His original decision to see a doctor for a common cold was fuzzy thinking to begin with. To ask for a penicillin shot was a lousy choice. If I had seen him with a viral cold I would not have given him a shot. The choice was moot; we didn't have the chance to treat him.

When he left the office, he turned right and passed by Ole Doc's place. The retired doctor was in the front yard pruning and digging around in his rose garden. Francis pulled up in his pickup, got out, and greeted his old friend. The two of them schmoozed for a while and Francis told the story of not being able to be seen promptly at the other doctors' office, when all he wanted was a penicillin shot. Ole Doc said, "Hey, come on in. I've got some penicillin. I'll give you a shot for old time's sake." And he did.

The two old guys went outside again and chatted some more until Francis said, "Doc, I feel funny. I can't breathe so good and my skin is crawling. Look, here, Doc, I'm getting red bumps on my arm." And he rolled up his sleeve to prove it.

The doctor rightly diagnosed an acute penicillin reaction and had Francis come back into his office, where he prepared and administered adrenaline. Within minutes Francis was having excruciating pain in his chest. Ole Doc took Francis's pulse. He found it extremely rapid and forceful. When he took the man's blood pressure, it was so high that the old doctor ran to the telephone, called our office, and asked that one of us come right over.

I took the call. I found Francis unconscious, with pulse and blood pressure as the other doctor described, but now his breathing had become shallow and slow. I administered oxygen, sent for the ambulance, did what I could to lower his blood pressure; but to no avail.

Francis died within five minutes of my arrival.

Ole Doc was beside himself with grief and fear that some mistake he had made was the cause of this. He showed me the syringe which he had used to give Francis the adrenaline. It was a 5 cubic centimeter glass syringe. Ole Doc said, "I filled it only half full and I gave it slowly into his vein."

"You gave him 2.5 cc's of adrenaline?"

"Yes."

"My God, the dose is two- to three-tenths of 1 cc. You gave him ten times the recommended dose." I thought—but didn't say—*you killed him!*

Everyone was distraught: the widow, Ole Doc, and me. For months, I wondered if there had been anything else I could have done. I finally came to the conclusion that, although it wasn't our fault, if the office had been better organized and we had made it so that Francis could have been allotted his time and been seen properly, maybe this tragedy would not have occurred.

I also pondered, in awe, the tremendous responsibility given to ordinary human beings licensed to practice medicine. I was used to death. I had seen death in its many forms while in medical school and during my years of training and practice, but I had never seen so flagrant an accident caused by a physician. This was an accident that never should have happened. We, all doctors, have lethal drugs in our hands every day. We can control life or death in many instances. I resolved during this period of reflection on the death of Francis that I would redouble my efforts to be careful. I never wanted to be haunted by the ghost of an occurrence like the one Ole Doc had to live with.

ొ෪෪ు

One Wednesday afternoon—it was Sam's day off and I was swamped with a waiting room full of patients—our receptionist, Cora, told me a detail man was waiting for me in the back office.

"Gee, Cora, today? I'm so busy, can't he come back when I have a little spare time?"

"Doctor," said prim-faced Cora, who would not have minded a bit if I had run screaming from the building because of the pressure of so many patients waiting. She was my partner's receptionist when I arrived: she never did like the new doctor, and she was happy when I left, eight years later, still "the new doctor" in her eyes. "Doctor, he says he is an old friend. He has come clear out here in the country to see you. I think you should see him."

She thinks I ought to see him?

Hesitating for a moment, I thought, *If I make an issue of this, she'll be a sourpuss for the rest of the day.* "Okay, but tell him five minutes."

I went to the back office and, opening the door, faced a ghost whose name was Pinky, my pal from Navy boot camp and from our overseas station at Mobile Hospital Number 2. I was sure he had been lost at sea when his submarine failed to return from war patrol.

After hilarious backslapping and handshaking (he was real!) and exchanging information such as, "You haven't changed a bit," we settled down to talk. We didn't talk about the pharmaceuticals he was supposed to detail me on, but about old times.

I said, "Jeez, Pinky, you don't look dead." Pinky explained his miraculous reappearance. He had become ill just before his sub sailed on its fatal voyage, and he was evacuated to the mainland. Meanwhile, I left my ship and went to college. When Pinky recovered he had gone to advanced submarine school in New London, Connecticut, and then on submarine patrol in the North Atlantic.

After the war, when he landed the job with the pharmaceutical company and was sent to Oregon, he scanned the list of Oregon physicians and happened upon my name. Although that was before the age of computers (or even before the Age of Aquarius), these companies kept profiles on each doctor. When Pinky saw my name, he first thought it must be another person with the same name; but the profile fit me—born in San Francisco, corpsman in the Navy. He prevailed upon his boss to let him call on me, although I was not in his territory. We were so glad to see each other it was like brothers getting together. Ten years apart hadn't changed our affection for one another.

And so Pinky and I caught up. He came by every couple of weeks in his roll as pill pusher and, with his family, often came to our house as friends. I had no idea, at that time, of the many adventures we would share over the next few years.

❧

When I joined the practice Sam said, "Now that there are two of us, how about if we call this a clinic? Would the Sherwood Clinic be okay with you?"

My mind raced ahead:

A clinic! More doctors. As Sherwood grows, the current population might swell to six thousand or sixty thousand and we might be operators of a multidisciplinary clinic with all kinds of specialists working for us, and I would take only selected old patients. We would have a hospital. We would build it. The hospital, because of its research facilities and good care, would make us world-famous. We would be asked to speak in New York and London and Bali—I've wanted to go to Bali ever since I saw South Pacific. *This would be a place where poor people could have care without being made to feel that it was charity; and we would be so rich we really wouldn't want to charge. Our sons and daughters would study medicine and become partners, living happy and wonderful lives, with our family marrying into their family and vice versa. What joy, what a future this holds!*

"Sure," I said, "call it the Sherwood Clinic."

❧

Practicing, especially for a generalist, has to offer the same expectancy, the same thrill as fishing does for a fisherman. When I cast my line into the water, my arm would be taut, my eyes glued, as I waited for the next strike of a trout. The GP who has to treat the common problems that bother his patients could be lulled into boredom, were it not for the thrills of expectancy. Beyond the next door to the examining room might be the big one. No, not a trout, but an interesting case.

An interesting case isn't necessarily interesting to the patient; in fact, it can be a real pain. It can also be fatal. So when I open an examining room door, I feel that if it has to happen, let me see it, let me diagnose it, and pray to God—let me cure it.

During my first week in the office, I walked into an examining room to see Albert Scordelis. Albert was not sitting on the examining table as a patient would ordinarily do, but was pacing back and forth between the door and the desk at the side of the room. He didn't stop when I came in.

I said, "Good morning, I'm Doctor..."

Mr. Scordelis interrupted, "Jesus, Doc, I've got an awful pain in my butt. I can't sit down. I've waited all night and I can't stand it much longer." All this while still walking painfully back and forth.

I looked at the chart and saw that my patient was twenty-four years old. As a surgery resident I had learned that a male in his late teens or twenties who had a severe pain in his rear end and absolutely could not sit down, most likely had an acutely inflamed pilonidal cyst. I hoped this was the case. If it was a pilonidal I would be successful in immediately relieving his pain and later, after the infection cleared, I would be able to do definitive surgery and cure this patient.

I said, "Mr. Scordelis, lower your pants and lie face-down on the table." When I looked at the red bulging mass at the base of his spine at a point where the crease in the buttocks begins, I knew I was correct in my early presumption about the diagnosis. Within minutes I had injected a little Novocain into the skin and lanced the inflamed cyst.

Albert's relief was instantaneous. He said, "I heard that you're the new doctor in town; you are wonderful!"

⚜

When I opened the examining room door a week after helping Albert, I saw Emil Wishong sitting on the edge of the examination table, holding his lower abdomen with both hands. I felt a thrill of anticipation at the possibility of my first major surgical case as a private practitioner. I must have exuded electricity as I stepped forward to see this patient and grasped his hand, saying, "Mr. Wishong, I am the doctor. How may I help you?"

Emil Wishong wore bib overalls. He looked about fifty to fifty-five years old. His forehead was white above the line where his International Harvesters billed cap kept the sun away. The skin at the back of his neck, burned a deep brown by years of sun, was weathered with deep creases and resembled nothing so much as the well-worn back of an old leather chair. As we shook hands, my soft palms were hardly a match for his horny, callused mitts. He shook hands firmly; he was a farmer—the salt of the earth.

He said, "Where's the other doctor?"

"He isn't here, today. He's on vacation for another week."

"Oh." He was plainly disappointed,

He described griping abdominal pain gradually increasing in frequency and intensity, and a change in his bowel habits. Mentally, I made a diagnosis of incomplete bowel obstruction. When I examined his belly, I detected a small, fixed mass in the left lower quadrant of the abdomen, about where one would expect to find the junction of the descending colon with the sigmoid colon. The diagnosis, in my mind, was cancer of the lower intestine, probably treatable. This was a most interesting case and I was excited about it. This was what I lived for. I could help this man.

"Mr. Wishong, I think I know what your problem is and we don't have much time to lose. If my suspicions are correct, you'll need surgery. I'll need to call a surgeon."

I reached in a drawer of the examining table and withdrew a twenty-six-centimeter rigid sigmoidoscope. It looked like a foot-long silvery three-quarter-inch pipe. "Mr. Wishong, I'll need to examine you with this instrument." His eyes became round and large. "Then tomorrow we will send you to Portland to have an X-ray. You will be given a barium enema. They put an opaque substance in your bowel…" I burbled on, overwhelmed by my own diagnostic acumen and the absolute knowledge that what I was saying was correct.

I finished by saying, "I want you to go home and take an enema. That way you will be all cleaned out so that I can see what is going on in there. Come back right away and I'll scope you this afternoon."

"Where ya gonna put that thing, Doc?" he asked, pointing to the long shiny silver metal tube.

"Why, Mr. Wishong, right here." I pointed to his bottom.

"Oh." His eyes got bigger and rounder.

"Do you have any questions? I want to be sure that you understand. Time is of the essence. You are in danger of having your bowel totally obstructed and that will make surgery more difficult."

He looked me over, sizing up the new doctor in town. I wondered if he thought I was really smart. I guess he wondered if I knew what I was talking about.

The afternoon dragged after Mr. Wishong left. I wanted to get on with this life-threatening case. I called the radiology department at St. Vincent's Hospital and scheduled his barium enema for the next day. I called a surgical consultant and told him what was going on and he offered to see Mr. Wishong as soon as he was ready. Everything was all set.

Mr. Wishong did not return! At 5 o'clock I called his home and a woman answered. I introduced myself and asked for Emil.

The woman said, "I'm Mrs. Wishong. Emil is milking the cows, right now, and can't come to the phone."

"Milking the cows? Good Lord, Mrs. Wishong, he's a sick man. I need to see him right away."

"That was good treatment you give him, Doc. He done what you said and his bellyache went away."

I tried to explain that the problem was still there, that the enema had only temporarily relieved the partial obstruction and the pain. Only now could we see what really was going on inside his tummy.

I never spoke to Emil Wishong again. I phoned, I wrote letters; nothing worked. I had scared him, literally, to death.

A squib in the local weekly newspaper two weeks later stated: "Emil Wishong is seeing a chiropractor over at the coast. Mr. and Mrs. Wishong report that the chiropractor, who specializes in colonic flushes, will help after local doctors have failed."

The colonic flushes offered the same help that the single enema had and worked for a while. But they were deadly. Because as a result of the temporary relief they afforded, he never sought any other help.

His obituary appeared nine months later.

The surgeon whose assistance I had sought in this case counseled me, "When you have an interesting case, don't play all your cards at once. Sometimes it is more than a patient can stand."

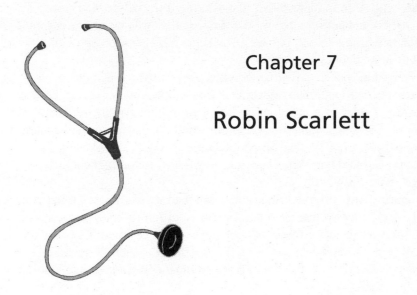

Chapter 7

Robin Scarlett

When I was seventeen I grew a mustache in order to look older. I still had it when I entered practice and I wondered what else I could do to keep from looking like the new young doctor in town. I thought about this a lot, particularly when a patient like Emil Wishong showed his distress at having to accept the services of the new doctor. His feelings were justified through my overzealous approach. I wasn't kidding myself—the problem was my enthusiasm—but also it was his distrust of the new young doctor.

My pride suffered every time I looked at the number of charts waiting for my partner, and then at the small number waiting for me. The receptionist, Cora, was my partner's ally, loyal to him to a fault. I overheard her tell a patient of mine, "If you wait a few minutes you won't have to see the new doctor."

Actually, the members of the staff were usually a tremendous asset to the practice. Each had her own attributes.

Cora, despite her subtle antagonism to me, had a smile for all the patients. She had lived in town all her life and knew all the townsfolk by their first names.

Blanche was our bookkeeper. Lloyd, her husband, was a long-time mail carrier on one of the rural routes. Together, they were active in local affairs, so they, too, knew everybody. Blanche wasn't above hitting on patients with a delinquent bill if she saw them in the grocery store. We never used a collection agency. We thought that was an unprofessional way for physicians to act, but with hawkeyes like Blanche and Cora, we didn't need an agency anyway.

Virginia was a part-time bookkeeper, part-time insurance clerk, part-time receptionist, and full-time charmer. She was married to Don, a banker and leader of a jazz band. They were related to three-quarters of the town's Catholics, a major asset in our small town. Virginia had a talent limited to only a few wonderful people in this world…she liked everyone and everyone liked her. When she dunned patients for delinquent bills, not one was ever offended.

During my time in Sherwood, we had two nurses, Helen and Marcia. Helen was a real gem because, in addition to being a registered nurse, she was also a certified lab technician and a certified X-ray technician. We were sorry when she left to be married, but then Marcia arrived. Marcia was small, dark and down-home; a most competent nurse, adored by the patients.

As a new and young doctor, I was sensitive about my practice ability. How many times have we heard people say, "At least I want a doctor that looks older than my kid," or "That doctor is still wet behind the ears." Medically, I was wet behind the ears; but I didn't want anyone to know it, and I was deathly afraid someone would find out. In a small town such as this, I felt I had only a few chances to make it or lose it with the community.

The tiny town of Sherwood was the marketing center for the area. The community leaders were the merchants and the town gossips. The farmers who came to town to shop got their news from them. These people included the mayor, Neville Van Dolah, who was the owner of the butcher shop in the Rainbow Market, and Woodie, proprietor of Woodie's Bakery, whose name on his chart at the office stated simply, "Woodie." Herb Dahlke ran the feed store and had a cat named Brinker. It was not until Brinker was over twenty years old that Herb started to feed Brinker once a day. Until then he had lived on a diet of mice. The old cat lived until he was twenty-nine, showing what a life of hard work and a good diet can do.

There were two hardware stores. The owner of one of those stores set up an unused attached garage as a TV theater. With the advent of broadcast TV, customers could sit in this little auditorium and watch TV; and some did, all day. I saw my first World Series game at the hardware store.

Tom Pfund ran the grain elevator; Lorn Drummond, the cleaners; Mr. Scarlett, the bank; and Avery Grundhagen, the cannery.

The Grange Hall and the American Legion Hall were where people congregated to have meetings, flower shows, and bake sales; and where the county agent spoke to the farmers when he came to town to discuss federal farm subsidies. There was a Junior Chamber of Commerce and a Kiwanis Club to which anyone who was anybody belonged. The American Legion Hall was not only for veterans but the square dance club also met there.

These people and these organizations were both the supporters and the conscience of the community. Businesses survived or failed based on the reaction of the leaders of the community.

I felt that these influential people were important factors for my acceptance. The other important factor for acceptance was to avoid scandal. During my first year in Sherwood I had three cases in which a bad mistake had the potential to damage my reputation and, perhaps, drive us out of town for a new start elsewhere. What an ignominious beginning that would be, and what a destroyer of my already fragile ego!

❧

Mr. Scarlett was the president of the local bank. The Scarlett farm, on the outskirts of Sherwood, included a stately two-story farmhouse, the Tara of Sherwood. The house, surrounded by orchards, beamed down on the community, constantly reassuring the locals that everything was all right. The Scarletts matched their home—they were stately people. Mr. Scarlett wore a high, starched collar and, although kind to a degree, carried the firmness of a banker's personality. Mrs. Scarlett was a grande dame in the strict sense of the word. The Scarletts had one child, a son named Robin. Of course, his name would be Robin in a town named Sherwood. Robin Scarlett rightly belonged to the orchards and the forests of the landed gentry.

Robin was in his early twenties, still lived at home, and he was expected to follow in his father's footsteps at the bank. Robin was fair of skin, with blond, wavy hair and a gentleness of nature that made him admired by every young maiden he came in contact with. Robin was a charming young man, with his future assured. But Robin became ill.

One night at about my bedtime, Mr. Scarlett called the common number that Sam and I shared and, because it was my night on duty, I took the call. He asked me to come over to see Robin, who was suffering excruciating abdominal pain.

Ruminating about my brief knowledge of the family while I drove the seven or eight miles from our Tualatin house to the Scarlett place, I wondered what it might have been like for me if my parents had lived and I had been reared in a genteel home such as this. But, even if they had lived, my life would never have been like the Scarletts' existence. My father, being a restless man and a wanderer, teamed with my mother's high spirits, could never have provided the quiet gentility I knew to be the Scarletts' life style. I envied them to a degree. But Glad and I and the three kids had a busy existence. I wouldn't have wanted to change it.

When I arrived at the Scarletts' house it was close to midnight. Mr. Scarlett was dressed with starched collar, although he had earlier retired. Mrs. Scarlett was dressed in a lovely, full peignoir, made of lace and other pretty stuff, the sort of garment one would assume a lady of the manor would wear at bedtime. Robin was in bed, writhing and moaning in pain.

The cramping pain had started two or three hours earlier, in the right upper quadrant of the abdomen, and was accompanied by nausea. His abdomen was tender where his gallbladder should be; he was extraordinarily pale, and had a slight fever. An injection of pain medication relieved him. We planned X-rays in the morning, suspecting gallbladder disease, even though the consensus of my teachers had been that the typical gallbladder patient usually exhibited the four Fs—fat, female, forty and farting.

The next day, Helen our office nurse, took a plain X-ray film of the abdomen; however, it didn't show gallstones and didn't help me make the diagnosis. I scheduled gallbladder X-rays at the hospital. Robin's excruciating pain had subsided, but the area was still very tender and he still felt sick to his stomach all the time.

Before his gallbladder X-rays could be taken, yellow jaundice appeared in the whites of Robin's eyes and in the palms of his hands. His stools had a whitish cast (clay-colored)—a result of obstruction of the common bile duct. Multiple small gallstones were the usual cause of such symptoms, so I reasoned that Robin had gallstones. Hepatitis could also cause jaundice, but the pain was so typical of gallstones, I could not ignore it. However, stones alone would not cause yellow jaundice, so I assumed that one of them had passed out of the gallbladder and had become wedged in his common bile duct, preventing the flow of bile into the bowel. I assumed that the pain was a result of the muscular walls of the common bile duct squeezing and relaxing in an attempt to expel the stones.

The pain returned periodically, but never with the severity of the first episode. However, I had to make several house calls to give him injections for recurrent pain. Gradually, Robin got better, although he had no sudden relief, as would be expected if he had passed a stone. His jaundice gradually cleared, a most unusual occurrence if he hadn't passed a stone. When we finally got the X-rays done, the radiologist at the hospital reported that gallbladder X-rays with orally ingested dye did not outline the gallbladder as they would have had it been normal. Therefore, his diagnosis was, "Non-filling gallbladder, diseased and nonfunctioning. It probably will require surgical removal."

After a sufficient interval to allow the inflamed tissues to return to normal, we scheduled a cholecystectomy (removal of the gallbladder) and exploration of the common duct.

I did the surgery, assisted by an older surgeon who had been one of my mentors during my residency. We found a normal gallbladder with no stones. I placed a needle in the common bile duct and injected dye, then took X-rays of the duct while the patient was still on the operating table. No stones were seen, but I did find blood in the common duct, a most uncommon finding. We did not explore the duct, but we did manually check surrounding tissue, lymph nodes, liver, duodenum, and stomach and found no abnormalities. Robin's immediate recovery from his surgery was good.

The hospital surgical board read my note of having found blood in the common duct and suggested that I had not placed the needle in the common duct, but had placed it in the hepatic (liver) vein, which lay just alongside. Remember, I was not a board-certified surgeon, and as a new member of the staff I was still on probation in the surgical department. The board directed that I would have to be watched more carefully. I was devastated and scared that I might have made a mistake, although the other surgeon assured me that we had done no wrong.

Three months passed. Robin became ill again, with pain, vomiting, and bloody bowel movements. This time he needed hospitalization because of the loss of blood. His condition became critical. Once again we opened his abdomen and found nothing but a large pool of blood in the abdominal cavity, and blood, again, in the common duct. Despite everything we could do for him, Robin suffered terribly for days and finally died.

The surgical board suspended my operating privileges, pending an investigation. Now I was really distraught because of the death of my patient, because my reputation in the community was in danger of being sullied, and because this one case could put a blemish on my professional status that I would carry with me wherever I went to practice medicine. I went to bed many nights only to lie awake visualizing Robin's handsome features ravaged by pain, his weight loss, and his inevitable slipping away from us. I mentally went over the operative site, searching for something I could have done differently, some thing I had missed. I became a two A.M. house walker, wandering around in my robe and slippers. I paid for my insomnia the next day by being chronically sleepy.

Fortunately, Mr. and Mrs. Scarlett were amenable to having an autopsy because we really did not know the cause of death. The surgical board suspected me of a grievous error in somehow missing the diagnosis or causing the hemorrhage. I wished to take the chance that an autopsy would either clear me or add to my knowledge. Contrary to the movies and TV, autopsies of non-homicide cases are not reported quickly. The removed organs sit in jars of formaldehyde, sometimes for weeks or months before examination, depending upon the pathology department's workload. In this case, it was weeks. I haunted the pathologist's office, seeking information and constantly being put off because of their heavy workload.

Finally, the day came when Robin's organs would be examined. I waited by the phone. Lunch time came and went. I couldn't eat. I couldn't see patients. My mind was in the lab with Robin and the pathologists. At last, about three in the afternoon, the phone rang. It was the hospital.

The pathologist, Dr. Joe Baumgarden, said, "I know how concerned you have been about this case and I finally have something to report. Your patient had a primary hepatoma (primary liver cancer), deep within the liver itself and not visible from the surface. He bled to death from the cancer. There wasn't a thing you could have done. It's a rare tumor and one you should report in the medical literature. The pain was from the obstruction of the common bile duct by blood clots and simulated the pain one would suffer from gallstones. The pain-free interval experienced by your patient was due to a temporary respite from the bleeding."

I said "Thank you," and hung up. Vindication was a hollow victory, but a victory nonetheless. I knew the Scarletts would be grateful that everything had been done for Robin that could have been done. I went over to the Scarletts' after office hours and explained the results of the autopsy report to them, and we cried together. We cried for Robin; and I guess I cried from relief, too, as my possible guilt in the eyes of these lovely people had been washed away.

After the autopsy, the surgical board rescinded its previous ruling, but did not apologize; nor should they have. They had done their job. Several months later, at the suggestion of a member of the surgical board, I was asked by the Portland Surgical Society to present my case at one of their quarterly meetings, an honor never before accorded to a general practitioner. It was their way of saying "Sorry."

⳩⳩⳩

Having escaped a storm of local public opinion on the Scarlett case, I felt I was pretty much okay with the community, until the wife of the owner of the cannery brought one of their children to see me. She had recurrent tonsillitis. Her mother had been a sort of sponsor of mine around the community, as she and Glad were sorority sisters in Alpha Chi Omega. The little girl met the criteria for a tonsillectomy and adenoidectomy, so we scheduled surgery.

The surgery went off without a hitch. I had warned the parents in my preoperative meeting that the little girl would talk through her nose for a couple of weeks after surgery because there would be a lot more space in the posterior pharyngeal and adenoid areas for air to accumulate. Also, children tend to use the line of least resistance, so if laryngeal talking hurts their throats, they tend to speak nasally until the soreness disappears and for a little while afterwards.

At the time of her two-week postoperative checkup, healing was progressing well; but it was obvious that the child had a nasal voice. *Oh boy,* I thought to myself, *here is an over-protective mother.* I said, "No problem, she will be okay in a week or two. Remember, I told you she would talk through her nose." And I patted the little girl on the head and asked her if she had enjoyed all the ice cream she had eaten when her throat was sore. I felt that I had done a good job and I was sure that everything was going to be all right.

Mother was appeased and the family left. Two weeks later the phone rang. It was Mother, complaining that their little angel was still sounding as if she had the granddaddy of all head colds. Couldn't I do something? I reassured Mom. I agreed a month was quite a while for a nasal voice to continue; but surely, in another week or two, her voice would return to normal. I was no longer quite so satisfied with myself. A month was a long time. I had never seen a patient speak nasally for so long. What could I have done wrong? The old nemesis of insecurity and lack of experience reared its head again.

The little girl's voice did not return. Not in a week or two weeks, not in another month. Kids in the neighborhood, and in the school, were making fun of the little girl. School officials were concerned. Daddy was concerned. And Daddy owned the cannery.

The cannery was our little town's major industry and Daddy had, prior to my arrival and when Sam had practiced alone, threatened several times to hire another doctor to care for the cannery workers. Daddy complained that one doctor was not up to caring for everybody in the community, and instead of paying for insurance, he thought he would bring in a salaried doctor to take care of what amounted to a substantial amount of the practice. My arrival had pacified him and we had not heard noises like that since I had come to Sherwood. I wanted that little girl to sound like a regular little girl again and not like a parody of an out-of-tune hillbilly singer.

I called an ear, nose and throat specialist in Portland. He reassured me that the problem would go away in a week. I explained that I had been telling the family that for three months. "Three months!" he exclaimed, "I didn't realize it had been going on for three months. Indeed, that's a problem of major magnitude."

Well, it was reassuring to me that he understood the extent of the problem, but when I asked him what I should or could do about it, he had no answer. "Never heard of anyone going on that long," he responded. "Lemme know if it continues."

That's a lot of help, I thought. *Keep him apprised of the situation even though he doesn't know what to do. That will help in court when the family sues me for malpractice and brings another doctor to town, and I have to slink away to take up practice elsewhere.* I was depressed.

After my consultation with the ENT specialist, I sought another consultant—this time a speech therapist. I described the case to her. She felt that she could help the child, so I arranged an appointment. I called Mom to explain what I had done.

"Oh dear!" Mother exclaimed. "I should have called you. Just yesterday, when my little darling got up and came to breakfast, she started speaking normally, just as you said she would, and the problem is over."

My spirits soared. I felt released and free; and I thought my troubles were over.

❦

The "Case of the Arthritic Ankle" was the final one in my triad of potential professional disasters that year.

Scandal!

It started on a spring day when a man was carried into the office by family members. This guy had rented a truck from the local trucking company to move his furniture into a newly rented house on the outskirts of town. He was from the city—not really a member of the community—so we had never seen him in our office before. He had accidentally fallen from the tailgate of the truck and had injured his ankle.

Upon examination, the ankle was magnificently swollen, tender, and turning black and blue. We X-rayed it and discovered that it was the site of an old injury. Over the years he had developed a significant amount of osteoarthritis in response to this old injury. There was a small avulsion (chip-fracture) of the tip of the bone on the outside of the ankle, which I treated with "soft casting" until the swelling went down. That was the usual and customary treatment. The case seemed routine at this point.

The fibula is not a weight-bearing bone, and this type of accident does not require a plaster cast. Mobilization of this ankle was the most important thing I could do so that the ankle would not stiffen due to the previous injury and ensuing arthritis. The patient returned twice. I started him walking as soon as possible, so that the joint would not stiffen. He missed returning for another follow-up.

I noticed some time later, when reading the local weekly newspaper, that my patient unsuccessfully sued the trucking company for his accident. The judge had thrown the case out of court. I thought no more about it.

Then it was fall. The patient with the arthritic ankle returned and asked to see me. I was greeted by a smiling man who said, "Doc, I hope you won't be mad at me, but I'm gonna sue you for malpractice. I have pain in my ankle sometimes and it's stiff when I get up in the morning. You may have heard that I sued the trucking company and lost, but you can bet somebody is going to pay for my accident. No hard feelings, huh, Doc? I know you have insurance. I thought you might want to see if they want to make me an offer. It'll save you a lot of trouble, Doc."

I gasped. A knife had just been plunged between my ribs. I couldn't breathe. For a minute I couldn't talk, then I got mad. "Get out of here, you miserable bastard!" I pushed him through the door and went with him to the front office where I told Cora to never let him into the office again.

No hard feelings? Why should this happen to me? I am trying to do a good job and here comes a klutz out of nowhere who falls down and now wants to ruin my reputation to line his pockets. Thoughts raged through my mind, day and night. I couldn't sleep. It didn't seem fair—I hadn't done anything wrong. I was so furious at the patient.

Cora went to Sam with a story of my anger and temporary loss of control. He admonished me to keep my temper in check, and didn't say a word about having faith in my competence or that my care for this patient had been good. Being out of his good graces further deepened my depression.

At that time, Oregon had an unusual system for handling malpractice claims. All doctors bought their malpractice insurance from the state medical society's approved insurance company, which had set up a Board of Peers to review malpractice claims. This board was the only trial which could truly exonerate or place blame on a doctor. The Board of Peers sat in judgment, honestly attempting to judge each case on its merits and render a fair opinion for either the doctor or the patient. The opinion of this group was passed on to the insurance company only as a recommendation to settle or to defend the suit. These doctors were not judging their colleagues to absolve them, but judging in the interest of the public and the medical profession, to see that fairness was accorded both sides.

The recommendation of settlement and a payoff meant that the Board of Peers felt the doctor was in some way at fault, while a recommendation to defend meant that the doctor's peers had judged him innocent. The insurance company inevitably acted on the board's advice. The legal profession understood the system and was usually reluctant to try cases that the board had reviewed and judged worthy of defending. In those times, perhaps lawyers weren't as greedy and juries weren't as willing to pay unreasonable damages.

Nevertheless, it was with a great deal of anxiety that I presented my case to the board. Prior to my personal appearance I had provided the board with all my office records and X-rays. My testimony would be the final evidence that the board would receive before rendering a decision. I presented my case with a trembling voice as I looked at ten stern faces sitting around the table. I was questioned. I had no inkling of their thoughts. After about forty-five minutes I was dismissed.

I went home to await the letter which would reveal the board's decision. I would have preferred placing burning hot splinters under the fingernails of the guy with the arthritic ankle. I thought about the case all day, every day.

At last, one morning, the letter from the insurance company arrived. I debated whether to open it or wait until the day was over, when I could sit down quietly and calmly read the letter and assess its contents. I knew that if the letter was for settling the suit, thereby implying that I was guilty, I would have to fight a monumental depression that could affect my family and my ability to care for patients.

I couldn't wait.

The letter said, "We have decided to appoint defense counsel to defend the suit brought against you by (the name of the patient was inserted). Please meet with counsel at your convenience."

I was exonerated and the lawyer for the plaintiff dropped the case. The nightmare was over.

Problems come in threes, and my three were over. I settled into community life with gusto!

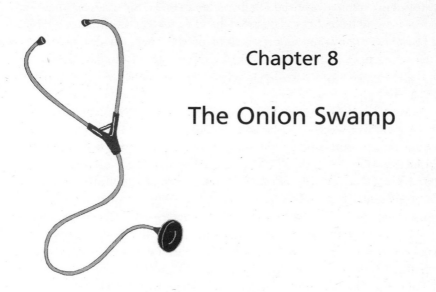

Chapter 8

The Onion Swamp

For two people who had struggled with dimes for the first eight years of marriage, having achieved solvency at six hundred dollars a month when I left residency, with periodic raises during my first six months in practice and the thrill of being accepted as a one-third partner afterwards was cause for celebration. When I first entered practice, we decided upon a third child. Glad always wanted spring babies. We opted for spring of the following year. This time spring ran into June, but there was still plenty of sunny weather for drying diapers. We were rewarded with a little girl baby, Pamela Ann. Our family was complete—and our pocketbook was empty.

Although my income had increased, so had our expenses. I was worried about our ability to make our newfound money stretch. That wonderful, imaginary book about how to go into practice that I wished I'd had when I first finished my residency would have said, "Don't let the thrill of having a few dollars in your jeans let you get carried away with your new prosperity. There's lots of time, Doctor; take it easy, and don't spend all your money in one place."

We thought an economy move was indicated. We decided to get rid of the old Chevy, which was no longer dependable, and downsize to a compact car with better gas mileage. This was a mistake we have never repeated.

Pinky Mayfield, my wartime buddy who seemed to be an authority on almost everything, advised Glad and me to buy a Simca, a car made in France. He said he had heard that they handled well and were dependable. All I have ever known about cars is that you start them by turning the key in the ignition. If that doesn't work, I'm stuck. In all things mechanical I'm liable to take any advice I get. When such advice is free, I usually get what I pay for.

Now, I know it snows in France and I know the French drive fast, having spent five weeks during one vacation dodging French drivers who had apparently consumed their daily liter of wine just before getting behind the wheel. I guess I was not used to the short wheel base, the lightness of the vehicle, or—being a Californian by birth—maybe I wasn't genetically competent to drive in the snow, or maybe I was just unlucky that snowy day on the flatland between Sherwood and Hillsboro.

I had driven the Simca several months before that fateful snowy day. I was on my way to do a delivery at Tuality Hospital when I skidded into a ditch three separate times. Maybe my adrenaline was flowing with the excitement of the impending delivery and maybe I was driving too fast for the road conditions; but I was a sucker for the unbanked curves of this dead-flat road. Fortunately, each time I hit the ditch there was a farm nearby for me to hike to in my wet galoshes and soaked lower legs, and a cooperative farmer with a tractor to pull me out. I explained to each farmer that I was a doctor on my way to deliver a baby and endured their looks of incredulity at my choice of vehicles. The mind-set of a farmer is a pickup or tractor, so they understood a doctor in a big car but not one driving a little Simca. The last good Samaritan who extracted me from a snowy, slushy, muddy ditch asked, "This the only car you got, Doc?" and when I responded negatively, he said, "How come you didn't drive the other one today?"

How do you answer such a wise man?

Of course, all of this going in and out of ditches caused me to miss the delivery. I could have gone home after the first ditch, as the mother popped the baby out about two hours prior to my arrival at the hospital. Fortunately she was okay, having been cared for by a colleague who happened to be in the hospital at the right time.

I started back to Sherwood, grumbling to myself, *Why did I buy this fool car in the first place? This darn-fool car will kill me someday! What kind of economy is this if I can't get to the hospital and my patients all go somewhere else?* And then I skidded into the ditch one more time. By this time I had patients awaiting my arrival in the office and I had run out of patience with the car.

My frustration with the Simca grew as I carefully drove home and deposited the car in the garage.

I burst into the house, yelling, "Glad, get that damn little car out of here by the time I get home tonight!"

I took the DeSoto and left for the office.

Glad nursed the Simca to town and came back with a Pontiac. The red Pontiac became a fixture around the countryside.

The next time I saw Pinky he remarked that he hadn't seen the Simca in the carport. "What happened to your new Simca?"

I explained my experience to him, including expletives, and asked him, if he thought a Simca was so great, why didn't he drive one? "Why," he said, "the company insists that I drive a Chevy. They claim it's safer and is better for the company's image."

"What about my image and safety, old friend?"

"Your image is made; you're a doctor! You don't need anything else."

It would be several years before I understood that remark.

❧

Both Tualatin and Sherwood had small industrial plants but the main industry in our area was farming. There were two kinds of farmers—those who farmed for a living and did well financially and socially in the community, and those who farmed as a sideline and had some other kind of job and never made it either way. Cora's country idiom for these people was peckerwoods.

Tualatin had a single industry: a horse-killing plant that turned old horses into canned dog food. This was an unwholesome place, but reasonably quiet, with minimal odors.

Sherwood was a different story. There were three industries and they all stank. The worst was the tannery. This malodorous establishment converted deer hides into leather for sport hunters. Florida paper mills were perfume factories, by comparison. All of the tannery's effluvium was dumped into the creek that ran through the town, much to the disgust of people living along its banks.

The next industry to disturb the community was the Nickel Cadmium Battery factory which contaminated air, water, and the general environment with lead.

The largest industry in Sherwood was the cannery. The cannery gave off various odors during the year, when it canned prunes, pickles, peaches and, late in the year, onions. At the same time the cannery was cooking onions, discarded onions were rotting in the Onion Swamp. If you are imagining the tantalizing aroma of onion soup, you may forget it. The smell around Sherwood did not even remotely resemble onion soup cheerily bubbling on the stove—it was more like the aroma of ripe garbage in a back alley. The entire area smelled. Sherwood's three industrial plants had few redeeming features.

The Onion Swamp, where the onions were grown, was about a half-mile wide and six miles long, running from Highway 99W through Tonquin and Malloy. It was probably a defunct river. Its soil was rich and black. Annual flooding of the north part of the swamp brought new deposits of plant food and sent the rotting onions downstream. People driving along Highway 99W in early spring thought it was a lake.

❦

The main farmers in the swamp were the Madigans. The family's widowed matriarch lived near the head of the swamp in a solitary, rustic cabin. The cabin was so rustic that it had no electricity or running water. She used a hand pump to get water from her well. The nearest road was a quarter of a mile away, accessed by a trail through the woods. The farm produce was hauled out the other end of the swamp by tractor, so the old lady claimed she had no need for a road and certainly wasn't going to spend the money for electrification. She had lived her whole life in that cabin the way it was and, "by jiminy," she was going to continue to do so. She stamped her high-topped men's shoes, and the floppy, broad-brimmed hat she always wore shook in emphasis as she said it.

One winter night, during the snowstorm that resulted in my driving my little French compact car into the ditch, I had a phone call from the lady who lived near the entrance of the trail leading to Mrs. Madigan's cabin. She had walked in to see the old lady a couple of days earlier to find out if she needed any supplies before the predicted bad weather settled in, and found her friend gimping around the cabin with an old, homemade crutch that had belonged to her late husband. She said she had fallen and her hip was sore. The neighbor wanted her to come out to see a doctor, but she refused. Now the neighbor was worried. Not having seen Mrs. Madigan for several days, she allowed as I had better go in and check her out.

"Why me?"

"You're her doctor!"

"I am? I've never seen her as a patient. I only met her once at the Grange Hall."

The neighbor replied, "She says you're gonna be her doctor if she ever needs one bad enough. She liked your looks." *Is this a good reason for a professional selection?*

"And it looks like she needs you, now."

I demurred. "Why don't you go on in and see if she wants me to visit her?" I had a real fear of intruding on a person's privacy and I especially feared being rebuffed by someone who didn't want me at all; I did not want to be thought of as pushy. I had seen the lady stamp her feet at the Grange Hall the night she brought in onions for the Grange ladies to serve at the Kiwanis dinner, and I knew she had a pretty caustic tongue.

"That's a waste," was the reply. "If she needs you, I'll have wasted my time and you'll have to go, anyway."

"Yeah, but…."

"No yeah-buts, you're her doctor and it's your responsibility."

With this kind of logic it seemed that I couldn't argue further. *Do I go on this wild goose chase and perhaps get chewed out by an irascible old lady, or do I sit home and worry about what I should have done?* I'm a worrier. I decided to go.

I put on galoshes and a heavy coat, ran a belt through the handle of my medical bag to be able to hang it over my shoulder, and drove the DeSoto to the head of the Madigan trail. (I hadn't had the Pontiac long enough to trust it on snowy, icy roads.) I started walking, with my bag banging against my back.

※

This old medical bag was sentimentally valuable. It had belonged to the surgeon who was my principal mentor when I was in my residency. He was by now in that great operating room in the sky.

The bag had a history of loss and recovery. When the bag had belonged to Dr. Seabrook, it had been stolen and found. By the time he got it back, he had acquired a new one. He was able to buy back his old bag from the insurance company for five dollars. After he bought it, he gave the old bag to me. Even surgeons carried a bag in those days.

Many years later I parked my station wagon in the parking lot at May Company in Los Angeles on the Miracle Mile on Wilshire Boulevard. I was there to watch some location shots for the Welby show and to talk to Connie Izay, the nurse who was always on the set checking the medical accuracy of the equipment, about some specialized equipment we would need for the episode to be shot the next week. When I returned to the car, the window was broken and my bag was gone. I reported this to the police and my insurance company. The police informed me that, undoubtedly, it had been stolen by an addict and was lost forever. My insurance company said there would be a thirty-day delay to pay off, on the chance that the bag would be recovered; but that I should go ahead and get a new bag right away, as medical bags were never returned.

They were both wrong. The bag was recovered. It was recovered within ten minutes after it had been stolen. The cops said I should come down to the station to identify it. When I went to the police to claim the bag, they refused to give it to me, saying that it was evidence and that I would be subpoenaed to identify it in court when the perpetrators were placed on trial.

My new bag never did feel quite right. The new one was smaller, lighter, and shiny. I liked the looks of the old one. I felt comfortable with it. Besides, it had wonderful little compartments where I could squirrel things away and find them again. The new bag was just a big, open space where everything got dumped and I never could find what I wanted—a fine mess during an emergency.

I took the day off when the thief was being tried for stealing my bag and I was to testify. My testimony took ten minutes but I hung around as a matter of interest. I was glad I had because the unique saga of my bag unfolded in the courtroom.

The man on trial (we'll call him Edgar) was a known petty thief whose modus operandi was stealing business machines, especially by breaking and entering gas stations at night. On this particular day he was in a poker game at the apartment of his fence for stolen goods, and the pot exceeded his ready cash. Edgar was dismayed. He begged for time to get a stash. The card players gave him thirty minutes and the fence agreed to put up the money if he returned with the proper collateral. Edgar set out to find collateral. All gas stations were open that time of day and, whereas breaking and entering was okay at night when no one was around, armed robbery was not in his M.O.

He knew he had to do something quickly, so he hurried over to the parking lot of May Company where affluent shoppers parked their cars. Luck was with Edgar. He spied my medical bag and soon was hurrying down Wilshire Boulevard carrying his collateral for the poker pot.

At this point luck deserted him, for who should drive by but the two detectives who had busted him the last time. Without Edgar's knowledge, the two detectives followed him to the apartment, because they found it highly unlikely that a man of his record and on parole could have suddenly, legitimately, acquired a physician's bag.

When Edgar entered the apartment, the two cops waited a few minutes, rang the bell, and politely asked for Edgar. When they walked in, Edgar was in the process of putting my bag into the poker pot, in hopes of winning. The only thing he won was another jail term.

Almost a year after the theft, I got my bag back. I never learned if Edgar had the winning poker hand; and I still have the bag.

CXXO

At the end of the trail, Mrs. Madigan's house was dark. I knocked on the door.

A voice yelled, "Git on in here!"

I went in and, with the help of my flashlight, saw Mrs. Madigan lying on the bed. I told her who I was and she said, "Well, it's about time somebody came and got me out of the mess I'm in."

"What's the matter?"

"Can't walk, doggone it. Light that kerosene lamp and fix me up."

I lit the lamp and looked around. The cabin had two rooms. A wood stove was the centerpiece of the main room, but it was dark and cold. The woman on the bed was hardly visible under piles of blankets. She looked drawn and unhappy, and she didn't smell very good.

"I messed m'self, doggone it. Git a fire goin' and git me some hot water and a towel and I'll clean m'self up."

I did as directed and then looked at the lady's leg. She had the telltale signs of a broken hip, probably about a week old. This kind of impacted fracture, where the bone ends are compressed into each other, will allow painful weight bearing for a brief period. When the spicules of bone, which have been driven together, then slowly dissolve as a result of being broken, the patient can no longer walk. A heck of a situation—a quarter mile from the nearest road in the middle of a snowy night.

I helped her clean up and wondered what my classmates in medical school, who had gone into specialty practice, would think of me, out here in a cabin, helping this gutsy lady.

And what about this lady? Despite her infirmity, she was lucid, trying to take care of herself, clenching her jaws with pain. I thought this must have been the way it was in the wagon trains during the settlement of the west. I was getting a look at the kind of courage people must have had in pioneer days.

I made her comfortable, got her a little water and bread, and headed out for help. I reached the road, wet and cold, and pounded on the neighbor's door. She let me in to phone the volunteer fire department in Tualatin.

The firemen also ran the local ambulance service. When they arrived the two firemen and I hiked back to the cabin. After I splinted her leg we managed to get our patient onto a canvas pole stretcher and started hiking out. Old Mrs. Madigan was not little, so the three of us took turns carrying her. I know that bumpy trip out to the road must have hurt like the very devil, but we never heard a squeak out of her.

After the ambulance left I went home, changed into dry clothes, called an orthopedic surgeon, and went to the hospital. We successfully pinned Mrs. Madigan's hip.

When she had fully recovered, she bought a small house in Sherwood and started wearing regular ladies' shoes instead of her old high-tops. She discarded her floppy hat in favor of a straw bonnet in the summertime and a ball cap, advertising fertilizer, in the winter. She became a confirmed town dweller, reveling in her hot running water and electricity.

"Goodness," she told me, "somebody even comes every week and takes away my garbage."

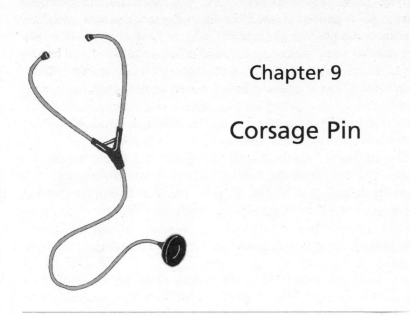

Chapter 9

Corsage Pin

My first visit to the Lucetti farm was soon after I began to practice in Sherwood. The patient that Sunday afternoon was one of the family's daughters, Maria. The poor kid couldn't keep anything on her stomach and her dad, Eddy Lucetti, Jr., was afraid that she was becoming dehydrated. I gave her an injection and had a cup of coffee with the family while I waited around to see if she would stop vomiting and fall asleep. When I called the next morning, she was taking a little fluid and keeping it down. She would be okay.

I was glad to have families like the Lucetti family in my practice. Eddy Lucetti, Jr. ran the family farm that had been started by his father, Eddy Sr., an early Italian immigrant in Oregon. The entire family worked in a truck gardening operation in the lowlands near the Tualatin River. The Lucetti compound consisted of the main house where Eddy Jr. and his family lived, including his oldest son, Eddy III, and several other buildings housing Eddy Jr.'s brothers and their families. There was a separate little house for Grandma.

Grandma was the family matriarch. Grandma smelled. She was clean enough, but she ate garlic. She did not take garlic pills but, instead, she ate the stuff straight. "Good for the heart," she said. Garlic is all the rage in the health food market today. So maybe Grandma knew something. I never understood whether the little house that was solely for Grandma's use was because of her position in the family or because of the pervasive aura of garlic that made her hard to live with.

The Lucetti men were all strongly built, but lean. They had dark curly hair, Roman noses, sensuous mouths, and laughing eyes. They were archetypal Italians and proud of it. When these men labored in the fields with their shirts off, girls in passing cars would slow up to admire the beefcake exhibited in the bean fields and lettuce patches.

Eddy III, as the eldest son of the eldest son, would eventually inherit the farm and head the family. He was fourteen years old and resembled his mother. Eddy III was a rotund, rather solemn boy, whose eyes did not have the same sparkle nor hair the same ringlets as the other male members of the family. Eddy III was bookish and shy. He did not exude the bravissimo of his father and uncles, nor of his younger brothers and cousins.

The family reminded me of the people from the San Francisco neighborhood where I lived as a child. Leo Iacaponi was one of my best friends. I visited at his home frequently. When I arrived at the time of the Sunday noon meal—which I did as often as I could—I was always treated to bread and wine, plus one or several of the main dishes such as chicken cacciatore, roast pork, and the ever-present pasta. The Lucettis had that indefinable something that set apart a happy Italian family and I remembered that from my childhood with the Iacaponis. Maybe it was the smell of oregano and garlic or the red wine on the table served in stubby old-fashioned glasses rather than tall graceful stemware, or the oilcloth cover on the kitchen table and the slices of hard salami on plates beside crusty bread.

I went to Galileo High which was affectionately called Galli-dago in San Francisco's North Beach, where I had other Italian schoolmates, including the Di Maggio boys, Joe and Dominick. I felt right at home at the Lucettis'.

The telephone rang about ten o'clock on a Sunday night. The caller was Eddy Jr. "Doctor," I thought I heard a sigh and then a slight quaver in his voice as he proceeded, "I'm having a problem with my son, Eddy, my oldest boy. I need your help."

"What's the matter, Eddy?" I asked.

"Doc, I'd just rather meet you at the office and have you see about it."

"Tell me what it is, Eddy."

I was tired. I didn't relish the thought of going to the office, if the problem could possibly be solved over the telephone. I insisted Eddy tell me what the problem was.

"Doc, Little Eddy has a pin stuck in him." The diminutive was a word caress, an indication of Dad's concern.

"Well, gee Eddy, can't you just pull it out?"

I imagined a straight pin, impaled through a finger and, although it might hurt to take it out, it wasn't as if it were barbed wire, or barbed like a fish hook. Sometimes, with fish hooks, we would have to take cutters, remove the shank of the hook, and pull it clear through. We didn't want to drag the barb through the finger or the patient's rear end, or any other place fishermen had a tendency to impale themselves. A pin might be a little painful but it should not be a major problem.

"I can't get hold of it, Doc. I really wish you'd meet me at the office." Eddy's voice had just raised about an octave in tone and several decibels in volume.

"Eddy, where in the world is it that you can't get hold of it?"

"Down near the groin, Doc. It's pretty painful."

"Near the groin" could mean anything. For once I had no visual image, no real point of reference that I could use to reassure my patient's father that everything would be okay. "Near the groin" was a pretty vague anatomical site. "Okay, Eddy, twenty minutes, at the office."

I hung up the telephone, put on my clothes, and went to the car. Eddy Jr. and Eddy III were waiting in the parking lot when I got there. We went into the office, turned on the lights, and I beckoned the two Lucettis into an examining room. Little Eddy walked strangely. *Well, if he had a pin stuck in his leg near the groin it might impair his gait.*

"Now, where is the pin?" I asked.

Eddy Jr. pointed at his son and said, "Go on and tell the doctor."

Little Eddy kept his eyes downcast and muttered, "In my pecker."

"Where?"

"In my pecker, Doctor."

I had a mental vision of a pin sticking in the side of his penis. Again, I thought, *removal must be just a question of pulling it out.* I said, "Lower your pants, Eddy, and lie on the table." It was cold in the office and Little Eddy shivered as he carefully climbed onto the table. His father stood by with jaws rigidly set, eyes fixed on the boy.

Little Eddy lay quietly. I looked at his penis. I couldn't see a pin. *What kind of a cock and bull story is this?* "Where is it, Eddy?"

"Inside," was the weak reply. Little Eddy's voice had almost disappeared.

I reached over to feel his penis and the kid grabbed at my hand, "It's pretty sore, Doctor."

I stopped. My mind boiled over with questions. *What shall I do next?* I asked, "What kind of a pin is it?"

He answered sheepishly, "A flower pin, Doctor. You know, a long one with a smooth round end like my sister got from her boyfriend when they went to the formal dance."

Now it was beginning to make sense. The boy had been diddling around with the smooth tip of a corsage pin. Although I could not imagine what fun that would be, I knew that a doctor should not try to relate a patient's action to his own experience. While fooling around he must have had an erection and the pin slipped all the way in. When the erection suddenly faded—from fear or pain—the pin became impaled inside the urethra. Boy, what a situation.

"Eddy, how did it get there?" I hoped to prove my theory.

"I don't know, Doctor. It must have been on my bedspread when I rolled over."

Okay, this is not true confession time. How it landed where it was, was immaterial; what to do about it was critical. If this pin perforated the urethra and came out the wall of the penis, a false passage might be created. If not successfully treated, this could cause Eddy to pee sideways, up or down, for the rest of his life.

This is not a job for me. I need a urologist. First, I would X-ray the boy to visualize the metal pin. That would quickly demonstrate the pin's presence and its direction.

I carefully helped Little Eddy onto the X-ray table and took a picture. Sure enough, there was the pin, as described. The head of the pin was deeper than the sharp point. The pin lay obliquely in the urethral canal, with the point sticking slightly into the wall of the penis.

After explaining the situation carefully to Eddy III and his father, Eddy Jr., I called a urologist friend in Portland. When he answered I explained, "John, I've got a problem here. It seems that a fourteen-year-old boy has a corsage pin stuck in his penis...."

The telephone exploded in my ear. "If you think this kind of goddamn joke is funny at this hour of the night you're a bigger horse's ass than I think you are. I never thought you were the kind of a misbegotten bastard who would pull a stupid stunt like this...."

"Hold it!" I yelled into the telephone. "Just shut up and listen to me. I've got a problem here and I need help."

"You've got a problem, all right, you sonofabitch. What you may think is funny is not funny to me."

At this point I slowed and deepened my voice, so the effect of my anger would not be lost, and said the key words, "John, I send most of my urology consultations to you because I believe you are a good urologist and because I like you. Right now I am beginning not to like you, and I am about to tell you that I will never refer another patient to you. Understand?"

John asked, "Are you serious about the boy?"

"Of course I'm serious."

"Oh, for God's sake, I thought you had been to the hospital and heard about my case and were calling up to kid me. I just came home after spending two hours getting a corsage pin out of a fourteen-year-old boy's penis and I'm pooped. I've never seen or heard of a case like this before. And you mean to tell me that this is the second case in one night?"

"That's what I'm telling you."

"Oh gosh, I am sorry. Send him right in. I'll meet him at the hospital."

I said I would send the X-rays with him. Then I jury-rigged a soft splint for Eddy III and he and his dad went off to the hospital.

John later told me that the only way the removal could be done was to insert a cystoscope into the penis and take the pin all the way back into the urinary bladder. Then he had to turn the pin around and remove it, headfirst. The job was successful and Eddy III was none the worse for wear the next day. To say that he was embarrassed was an understatement. Undoubtedly there was a major father-son confrontation following this experience. It is possible that Little Eddy thereafter marked his life as B.P. and A.P.—before the pin and after the pin.

Days after the case had ended, John and I spent some time going to the medical school library, checking the literature for other cases of this kind. We found none. John reported it to the local urological society and it became a part of medical history. John never again questioned or doubted me when I called him for a referral.

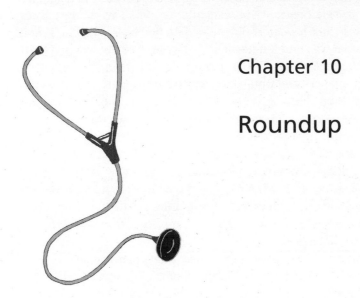

Chapter 10

Roundup

Because I was a city fella, now living in the country, I wanted to be a country fella, and part of being a country fella was to own a horse. It seemed wise that before owning a horse one should learn to ride. My partner Sam and his wife didn't know how to ride either, so the four of us decided to get riding instruction.

I had dreamed of riding horseback since I was a little boy. What kid growing up when I did hadn't imagined himself as one of the heroes of the silver screen. Tom Mix, Ken Maynard, Roy Steele, Buck Jones, and the incomparable William S. Hart of the silent screen were among my heroes. I was an avid reader of the great Western writer Zane Grey; and as a kid I hadn't cussed much because Gary Cooper in *The Virginian* had responded to having his mother referred to as a canine, by saying, "When you call me that, smile."

One of the problems in today's entertainment industry is the absence of the old-fashioned Western movie. What's the matter with the good guy getting the girl and justice being triumphant? I'm still a John Wayne fan and watch his Western reruns whenever I can. So when we moved to the country I was ready to learn to ride and maybe have my own horse.

About ten miles west of Tualatin was the Lake Oswego Hunt Club. This club was a boarding stable for pleasure and show horses and, we later found out, polo ponies, but no cowboy horses. What the heck, we reasoned, learn to ride one and you can ride 'em all. The riding master agreed to give us riding lessons—but we had no horses. He had no rental horses either, but he was much interested in the fees two doctors and their wives would pay for lessons. Being a resourceful person, he contacted some of the polo players and obtained permission for us to ride the polo ponies as part of their daily workout. While they were working out, we could learn to ride. A neat deal for everyone involved, we thought!

Polo ponies are full-sized horses, not little ponies. Polo ponies are trained to start and stop quickly and to turn on a dime. They respond instantly to the rider's commands. Woe unto the rider who doesn't know the commands. Inadvertently signaling the horse to execute a move that you are not expecting spells disaster. After getting up off the ground and dusting off your clothes, it's best to review your prior actions and promise yourself not to do that again.

I don't know what we expected that first day, perhaps just to walk our horses around the enclosed riding ring of the Hunt Club. But the riding master and the ponies had other ideas. First, he taught us to mount. Second, he taught us to hold the reins properly, how to squeeze with our knees and gently kick with our heels to cue the horse forward or to turn. So far we hadn't moved. "Now," said the master, "take your feet out of the stirrups. If you're going to learn to ride, you're going to sit your seat, and you'll never learn to do it with your feet in the stirrups. Only when you can really ride will I let you use the stirrups."

Whoa, no stirrups? I had a momentary vision of myself, landing face down in the tanbark and horse droppings. *The next thing this guy might take away from us is the saddle, and then we'll be bareback riders. Well, not me!*

"I want to use my stirrups, okay?"

"Nope."

"I'll fall."

"Not if you sit your seat."

I sat. I bounced. I slid. And I fell off (thankfully, I missed the droppings, that day) but eventually I did learn to ride. I learned in a very few lessons. Had I not learned quickly, I'm afraid I would have needed skin grafts between my buttocks and on my thighs, but soothing ointments and proficiency overcame the weaknesses of the flesh.

Glad and I were ready to get a horse.

✺

That fall we spent a weekend at the Oregon beach. We rented horses from a stable at the little vacation village of Neskowin, where we galloped on the sand and through the surf. The freedom of being aboard these eager horses with their manes flying, and with the spray in our faces, encouraged us to take our next step. There was a sign on the front of the stable that asked, "Do you wish to board a horse for the winter?"

Sure, we wanted to take a horse home for the winter. What fun! In fact, we wanted two horses; but where would we put them and how would we get them home? Minor problems, indeed. We went back to Tualatin and consulted our neighbors, the Van Hynings, who lived across the road east of Munniksma's dairy, home of the noisy bull. They had a barn, a twenty-acre filbert orchard, and a three-acre pasture—but no livestock.

Yes, we could stable our horses there for a small fee and if we would buy the hay and grain, they would do the night and morning feeding. Cleaning out the stalls was our responsibility. Thus we learned our first real lesson in country living: What goes in, must come out. And someone has to haul it away.

Wes Bright, a neighbor with a horse trailer, volunteered to transport the two horses, so back to Neskowin we went to pick out the two best horses to keep from October to May.

Alas, all the horses had already been taken away by surrogate owners like ourselves, except for Comanche and Princess. We were assured that these were the two best horses, reserved especially for us. Uh-huh! If we had believed that, we might as well have been offered a famous bridge. However, we decided to make the best of it and took our prizes home without incident.

Comanche was a sorrel with a light mane and quarter horse configuration. His mane was cropped but, at its base near his withers, the hair had been left quite long for about a six-inch strip. The significance of this temporarily escaped us.

Princess was black and nondescript, probably more thoroughbred than anything else, and she seemed quite docile. The stable owner mentioned that she had raced occasionally at county fairs and had done quite well. It appeared that her racing days were over.

At home the horses' personalities emerged. Princess always wanted to be in front. Every excursion was a race. It didn't matter if it was just to the other end of the pasture, or out on the trail, this horse wanted to be in the lead. She had been trained well for racing, but not for trail riding. If we went on a group trail ride, the trail master would become miffed by my constantly riding in front, especially since I didn't know the way.

She was a joy to ride when Glad and I took the horses out on the graded road surface that was to become Interstate 5 from San Diego to Seattle. The stretch of this road near our house had been graded and packed in 1941, prior to World War II, in anticipation of the highway. The war scrapped those plans for over ten years, so we had a nine-mile racetrack, running from the Willamette River at Wilsonville to the Tualatin River at Tualatin. The thrill of riding these horses on the open dirt road, without the danger of gopher holes, brambles, or other obstacles was a never-to-be-forgotten excitement—and, oh, how Princess loved to run! Our riding ability and horsemanship improved immensely, or so we thought.

About this time a local farmer came to me with a proposition. He wanted to buy a herd of twenty-six Black Angus cattle—thirteen cows, twelve yearlings, and a purebred registered Angus bull named Jock. All the cows had been bred to Jock. The farmer had ten acres of pasture lying fallow, but no money. He thought I was becoming a cowboy (this, from seeing me ride by his house on Princess) and could put up the cash. He would do the work, supply the pasture, and we would split the profits. Because I was committed to becoming a country fella, we shook hands, sealed the deal, and became partners.

The herd arrived. They were beautiful. When I walked out in the pasture, the twenty-five critters, Jock excluded, would gather round in a semicircle if I stood still, and with great curiosity, watch me. One day I pretended they were a choir and I was their conductor. As I waved my arms sideways or up and down, twenty-five bovine heads followed every move. Finally, they walked up to me, with their big, soulful, brown eyes, and wet muzzles, touching my arm. I felt like a real rancher.

I went out and bought a Stetson hat.

One day the farmer came to the house and said, "The cows will be dropping calves soon."

"Wonderful," I replied, thinking of nice profits and a growing herd.

"Well," he went on, "My ten acres won't hold all them cattle. Whatta' we goin' to do?"

Gee whiz and aw shucks, I thought; but I said, "I thought you had plenty of pasture."

"Uh-uh. Not for another thirteen critters."

"Well, can you get more?"

"Uh-uh."

"Can we sell the yearlings?" I asked.

"Market's poor and they ain't big enough," he answered.

"Gee whiz."

I pondered this awhile and thought about Harvey Baker's place. Harvey was a surgeon friend we had lured out from the city to become country folks, like us. I called. He did have eight acres of grass and no critters, yet. He was planning on getting some yearling sheep, but not until the spring lambs were older; and it was just now spring. We agreed on a deal and made a date for the following Sunday to separate our yearlings from their mothers and take the twelve of them over to Baker's pasture for the rest of the spring and summer.

Harvey ventured that probably we would need a truck to haul the cattle the four miles or so to his place.

"Nope," I said. I had a Stetson hat and two horses, and we would have a roundup and cattle drive. *(Oh, what fools we mortals be.)* By now my partner, Sam, had bought a horse, an American Saddlebred sorrel mare, Western-trained, named Penicillin. He called her Penny. With our two horses, Penny, two family cars, wives and six kids, we would commit Sunday afternoon to the cattle drive.

I contacted neighbors about crossing their stubble fields and got their permission. The members of our community, where we were the only doctors and they were all our patients or would be, were only too happy to let us cross their land. We assured everyone that we would take great care moving the animals and would pay promptly for any damage done.

One-not-so-friendly soul ventured that his summer garden had just started coming up and he had no intention of letting any of those critters wander around in his vegetables. He said, "I'll be back from church by one o'clock. Don't you start this damn fool stunt till I'm there. I want to be ready to take care of my own."

❧❦❧

One of the perks of knowing everybody in the community was the freely given permission to cross their land on our Sunday cattle drive. There were also downsides to knowing everybody—we had almost no privacy. Patients came freely to the house in an emergency or with a sick child—so often that I enlarged the entry hall at the back door of our house to accommodate a small table and chair. This was a result of urging by Glad who, after hearing the doorbell ring late one night, got up to see what was keeping me, and found a child stretched out on the dining room table. I was examining his tummy for appendicitis. The child alarmed

Glad, not only because of his dirty clothes and shoes on the dining room table, but because he said, "I think I'm going to throw up."

On another occasion we were playing bridge at the home of the grade school principal and his wife, John and Jane Brown. Jane had been a college chum of ours at Willamette University. When the doorbell rang, Jane went to the door and admitted a mother carrying a sick child. With a perplexed look on her face, Jane turned and called me to the door.

Remember, this was a very small town. We didn't have an answering service and beepers were not yet available. At that time, the only people with electronic devices of that complexity were Flash Gordon and his pals. Sam and I alternated nights on call and were able to switch our phones back and forth to ring at one house or the other. This was his night on call, but he was out delivering a baby.

The mother of the sick child bundled up the patient and took off for my house. No one was home. Our kids were with us, asleep in John and Jane's bedroom.

"How in the world," I asked, "did you find me?"

"Oh," replied Mom, "we know who you run with, and drove around until we spotted your car. Can you help my little boy?"

I could, and did, and reflected on the rigors of country practice. But, I also reflected on the satisfaction of helping the child and being an integral part of the neighborhood. Fortunately, I had learned never to leave the house without my medical bag.

❦

The Sunday morning of the great cattle drive dawned a little cloudy. We didn't want to be hindered by rain, so we started early. Shucks, the neighbor with the vegetable garden wouldn't care, as we would be well out of the way by the time he arrived home from church. We were glad we had not spent the money to rent a truck. Others of our neighbors from whom we had sought the "rights of passage" also came out to see the fun. It was a jovial, happy time and we were pleased to be a part of the local scene. The disadvantages of never being totally free of the responsibilities of our practice did not disturb us on that spring morning.

We organized our cowpunchers. The wives were assigned to the automobiles and were in charge of the children, the oldest of whom were to be foot soldiers. The men would ride the horses, Sam on pretty little Penny and I on my nondescript charger, Princess. We would ride into the field, separate the yearlings from their mothers, and send them out the pasture gate to be surrounded by autos and kids. When all twelve yearlings were in place, we would start across the country with our herd.

We opened the gate and rode in. Penny took one look at the cows and their babies, turned tail and ran. Her attitude was that a pretty little American Saddlebred mare should not get down and dirty with a bunch of cows. She lifted her skirts, left, and would not return.

Princess and I rode in and went right up to the cows, clear through the herd to the other side, scaring the cows into running. This was right up my black mare's alley and she ran faster, all the way to the other side of the pasture, turned and looked back at the cows, as if to say, "I won, anyone else want to try?"

We tried once more and Princess outran the cows, again. Now, what good was that? Stumped, I looked for Glad. Wisely, she had left our kids in the hands of my partner's wife and headed home to get Comanche.

Comanche was a knothead. He had bad habits, one of which was pulling back and breaking his halter rope when tied up. The other was jumping straight up and sideways upon seeing a gum wrapper or foreign object along the trail. However, this knothead of a horse was no worse than a lot of other horses I have known. Horses are pretty animals with their long, graceful legs, arched necks, flowing tails, soft muzzles, and rounded haunches; but they are really big babies, living in a fantasy world. To extract the most out of an everyday, possibly dull existence, they play games.

The gum wrapper alongside the trail is a rattlesnake—jump sideways; the empty can is a hill of fire ants—jump straight up (ants can't jump); a dead leaf blowing in the breeze is one of the gremlins of the horse world—rear up on hind legs and whinny; and a white rock is a gremlin's house, to be avoided at any cost.

Comanche spent a lot of time playing his games. He was most unpredictable. Therefore, we had not assigned him an early role in the roundup, nor had we assigned Glad a riding role. After all, she was female and didn't even own a Stetson hat.

Glad came back on Comanche, who earlier had been saddled to be ready for the easy part of the drive across open fields. I hesitated before opening the gate and letting Glad and Comanche in. This was dangerous business. Comanche was sure to be spooked and Glad might fall and be trampled by the herd (the choir with the soulful brown eyes).

But Glad insisted. She and Comanche went into the field. He looked at the cows—the cows looked back. Some sort of hidden communication passed between them, perhaps of the type that passed between Babe, the shepherd pig of motion picture fame, and his flock.

She guided the horse straight into the herd. Suddenly, Comanche became serious. This was his business. He was a cutting horse. All by himself he worked the yearlings over to one corner of the pasture, bowing and jigging in the style of a horse trained for this kind of work.

By now, Glad was just sitting in the saddle, hanging on, radiant because her horse was getting the job done. We later found out that the long hank of mane, down by the withers, was a trademark of a cutting horse. Cowboys trimmed their horses' manes so that when they needed a horse from the remuda during roundup time, they could quickly pick out an appropriate mount for the job.

I wish I could say we got the job done without a hitch after that. We didn't. Once we opened the gate, even Comanche could not keep all the yearlings together. Some of the six-hundred-pound yearlings, hungry for green grass, spotted the neighbors' lawns and went directly to them. Others sighted the succulent young heads of lettuce, radishes and carrot tops in the neighbor's vegetable patch and headed there. Others thought the world to be better across the road and went there. Some went north, some south, and some went east and west. We wound up paying for destroyed vegetable gardens and azalea bushes, and we didn't get two of the critters back until the next day.

The neighbor with the vegetable garden probably never forgave us. We never saw him as a patient, but maybe he never got sick.

When we started out cross-country with ten yearlings, we had a borrowed Guernsey cow, named Daisy, who wore a bell. She was docile and dependable. Daisy was to be the bellwether; the yearlings were supposed to follow her to their new pasture.

It looked as if we might yet be successful until, three-quarters of the way across a neighbor's one-hundred-acre stubble field, Daisy thought better of the idea and wanted to go home. She turned and ran back toward where she belonged. No problem. I was on Princess. Princess could outrun anything, including Daisy. I started out and ran right past that cow. Princess won again.

Having bought a Stetson hat, I had also bought a lariat which was now tied to my saddle. I stopped Princess, loosened my rope and, as Daisy trotted by, I dropped the noose over her head. The other end was wrapped around my saddlehorn and tightened quickly. Daisy was running. Princess ran ahead of her. The rope was taut and I couldn't get either critter stopped—and so we went, all the way home, inseparably united by my symbol of cowboyhood, the lariat.

My Stetson flew off and I had to go back later to retrieve it. Glad put what was left of the herd in their new pasture and the roundup was over.

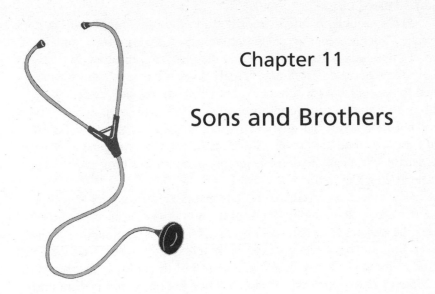

Chapter 11

Sons and Brothers

In Sherwood, Oregon, there was no emergency room where we could send patients, so we made house calls—lots of them! Doctors had not yet abdicated their position as part of the family's life in the home. We didn't know that the house call would become a lost art. For the sake of convenience, we sometimes met patients outside of office hours at our office, especially when we suspected that X-rays or lab work were needed. We usually visited the patients at home.

Often I was invited to sit down for pie and coffee, or even to stay for a full meal if mealtime was close. When invited, I would call Glad and tell her my estimated time of arrival at our house. If I had several more calls to make and was going to be late anyway, she would say, "You'd better eat now—I know you'll get hungry," or she might say, "You'd better get yourself home—I fixed a special dinner!" or, "The children need to see you before bedtime."

The breaking of bread with families deepened my relationship with them. My patients became my friends. People didn't invite their "Health Care Provider" to dinner, they invited the family's most respected counselor other than the minister: their family doctor. Their doctor was the person who helped them when there was illness, bereavement, trouble with the kids, or any time they needed a friendly shoulder to lean on. This was a role I gladly accepted, and I was proud to be a real part of the families I cared for.

The question of life's priorities for me was simple. First, the practice. Patients' needs were met at the expense of my own family. Of course, my family wasn't neglected in the physical sense but, at times, I believe they were neglected emotionally. I wasn't always there for them. I tried to be available for school events, celebrations, and family outings; but I wasn't home every night to tuck them into bed or sit at the dinner table and hear about the day's activities, or their successes or failures. And I missed some big events as well. How could I have done otherwise when there was a baby to deliver, surgery to be done, a broken arm to set, or a heart attack to treat?

Glad never wavered. As a general practitioner's wife, she knew what to expect. She continually reinforced my position in the family by telling the kids what a great dad they had, and never complaining. Would I do it differently if I were going into practice today? Yes. I would be a person of the times today, as I was a person of the times in Sherwood in the 1950s. Today's doctors combine practice and personal life differently. I'm sure their families are better off and maybe, if they read this, they will understand that they are.

My relationship with my patients grew through mutual under-standing and respect for one another. Seeing people in their natural surroundings gave me insight into their problems which could be gained in no other way. For instance, the orthopedic surgeon who pinned Mrs. Madigan's hip saw an elderly lady with a fracture of the neck of her femur, while I saw a pioneer lady who would need careful nurturing after she left the hospital—one to be enticed, not forced into a different life style. With her family, I was able to help her make the transition with the dignity befitting her personality and station in history. She was able to substitute a garden patch in her backyard for the onion swamp, and she even seemed to enjoy "dressing up" after she got used to it.

⸎

Drinking alcoholic beverages with patients was not my usual custom while making home visits, except when I went to see an elderly Russian lady and her two large and awesome sons.

The boys (in their late twenties or early thirties), were what I would draw in my sketchbook if I were to make drawings of Russian peasants. They were big, not gigantic, but big all over. They had big blonde square heads, big hands whose fingers looked like little loaves of bread baked brown on top, and heavy, thick square bodies. Their voices were deep, guttural, and heavily accented. Their eyes had the hint of an Asian look about them.

This family lived a quarter of a mile from our house in Tualatin. It was my practice to stop in to see the mother about once or twice a month. She was virtually bedridden from a collection of degenerative diseases. After the first visit or two, the boys invited me to have a drink of "wadka." I refused.

Their offers of a drink continued, until one night I was later than usual and the boys had been at the wadka before my arrival. After visiting Mother, I closed my bag and started out of the bedroom, only to be seized by either arm and physically removed to the kitchen, plopped down at the kitchen table and told, "Tonight you will have wadka." This was not a request, but a demand: "You *will* have wadka!"

Vodka was one kind of liquor I had never drunk, and I thought it looked like water. I watched the boys each take a swig of the clear liquid from the bottle before handing it to me. They did, carefully, wipe the bottle top with hands that looked as if they had just slopped the pigs.

This was not a habit I wanted to get started so, again, I thanked the boys and said, "No, I don't drink when I'm working."

The response was that I was on my way home and my day's work was done. Then they leveled the clincher at me. "Maybe you just too good for Russian peasants, huh, Doc? Maybe you don't like us. You just come to see Mama and take our money, but you don't like us." This speech was delivered by one of the boys in a flat but ominous tone.

Maybe I was reading animosity into what was probably just a little irritation and the Russian concept of hospitality augmented by having a little wadka. But I couldn't let that go. I wanted to be accepted by them as I was accepted by so many of the families I took care of (certainly, it wasn't for the seven dollars they paid me for a house call!). So I reached for the bottle.

"Take a big drink, Doc; it warms your toes."

I drank. It was liquid fire. My toes curled straight up and pointed toward the ceiling. I spluttered. The boys laughed.

"Have some more, Doc."

"Do you have any mixer?" I asked plaintively.

"Ho, ho, ho! Take another drink; you're a good man."

I drank. The heat in my throat was less, now; perhaps it was because I was sweating profusely. My vision was getting blurred, my lips were becoming numb, and the boys were looking better by the minute.

When I finally left, I drove home carefully. In the future, I planned to make calls at this lady's house in the morning or early in the evening, before the boys had uncapped the bottle. However, I am sorry to say that the flesh is weak, and several more times I arrived late and sat at the kitchen table to enjoy a sort of a rollicking camaraderie with my friends, the "Russian peasants."

❦

For a while it seemed as if large, overgrown sons played a significant role in my life. After the first adventure with the Russians, I was called one Saturday afternoon to see an elderly lady from the Tonquin area. "Mama's got pains in her chest, Doc; come quick!"

In the heart of a physician, the words "chest pain" or "heart attack" or "the baby is coming" strike a chord of anxiety. With those words comes the tightening of one's own chest muscles, as if you had just missed another car at an intersection or heard the siren and seen the red lights of a trailing police car while doing fifty in a thirty-five-mile-an-hour zone. In my practice, at that time and place, a doctor grabbed his medical bag and took off. In today's world the patient calls 911 or goes to the emergency room. The family's doctor might not hear about the crisis until the emergency room physicians have stabilized the patient and then found the time to notify the attending physician.

❦

It was in California that the citizenry learned to practice the fine art of "sue the doctor." This was exemplified later in the sixties when a California colleague of mine received a call from a woman who mentioned "chest pain" in the description of her husband's problems. The physician declared, "I'll be right there," just as I had replied that Saturday afternoon to the family of the lady (in Tonquin) who also had chest pain.

The California physician got in his car and took off. He arrived in twelve to fifteen minutes and examined a patient with crushing chest pain radiating to the jaw, rapid pulse, sweating, and low blood pressure. He made a quick diagnosis of posterior wall myocardial infarction (heart attack). The doctor called an ambulance from among several private ambulance services in the area, the only medical transportation available. He waited until the ambulance arrived, administering to his patient as needed. He then followed the ambulance to the hospital in his own car.

While being transferred from the ambulance to a hospital gurney, the patient suffered a cardiac arrest. Attendants rapidly moved him into the hospital where the E.R. staff applied a new cardiac treatment called "defibrillation," administered with a pair of electric paddles.

The patient died. The widow sued the doctor and won the malpractice suit, stating that the doctor should not have made a house call after hearing the history as described by the wife, but should have called an ambulance and sent the patient directly to the hospital. This action would have obviated the delay of the twelve to fifteen minutes it took the doctor to arrive at the patient's home, the two to five minutes it took him to evaluate the patient, and the additional ten to twelve minutes for the ambulance to be summoned and arrive. The widow contended that had the patient been in the hospital when the cardiac arrest took place, the patient's life might have been saved. She may or may not have been correct, but the jury thought she was right, and the rest of us recognized that a new era of practice had arrived.

ຕະແ9

That Saturday afternoon, when I received a call from the Tonquin area, I got in my car and drove as fast as I could to the patient's home— but time was not a factor. The patient was dead when I arrived.

Now, one has to understand that Tonquin looked like a part of Appalachia, transported to Oregon. It was a rock-pile aberration in the fertile valley between the Willamette and Tualatin Rivers. The houses were rundown and the people were worn out from trying to hold a job, run a small farm, feed a herd of moth-eaten-looking livestock, and not making a success of any of it. Our office receptionist, Cora, would have called all the people in Tonquin, peckerwoods.

The house where I arrived that day was standard Tonquin, with one exception: a trio of very large, very sturdily built, and very upset sons awaited me.

"Mama has fainted," they told me.

Despite their mother's lack of respirations, pulse, or movement for some time, the arrival of the doctor promised solution. I was grabbed out of my car and rushed into the house where the poor soul lay dead on the floor.

I was concerned. I knew this family only slightly, but I knew that the boys were a little below average on the intelligence scale, were hell-raisers, and were generally thought of as no good. Their father was already deceased; their mother was the glue that held the family together. With Mother gone, it seemed as if this group could be in a lot of trouble.

These thoughts were running through my head while I knelt on the floor, doing the usual doctor things, using a stethoscope to try to find her pulse—unconcerned about my own health. I should have been scared to death.

I looked up at the three boys with what I thought was a sympathetic face and murmured, "I'm sorry; it's too late."

The roof fell in!

One son started a high-pitched, keening wail, while the other two began to shout, "It's not so, Doc, it's not so. Do something!"

I replied that there was nothing to do—then things became ugly. One of the shouters lowered his voice and—right out of a grade B movie—said, "She's our mother. You save her or you're goin' with her."

Neither medical school or life had prepared me for this. I decided that maybe they meant it. They certainly didn't seem to be kidding. I bought time.

Closed-chest CPR hadn't been thought of at that time, so I reached into my medical bag and came up with a syringe, a three-inch needle, and a vial of adrenaline. I injected a bit of the medicine into a vein and when that did not elicit a response, as I knew it wouldn't, I plunged the needle into Mother's heart, injecting another small amount of the adrenaline. Then I fiddled with the blood pressure cuff and my stethoscope with trembling hands, as the noise level from the three sons had increased. As the decibels rose, so did my fear. What to do next?

Manfully, I stood up and said, "I cannot do any more."

The loudest brother took his two work hardened hands and grabbed me around the neck. He started to shake me back and forth, my feet just off the floor, teeth clacking as my lax jaws banged into each other. Breathing was difficult, but not yet impossible. He was shaking me and hadn't started the choking process yet.

Suddenly, there was relief! The second loudest brother grabbed my ankles and lifted me up off the floor, thus relieving some of the pressure on my neck and throat. However, his was not an act of kindness; but, rather, he wanted his piece of the action. Now I was being rattled and shaken from both ends. I began to think I might break. I heard my pockets empty of coins and car keys and reflected that, if I did break free and run for the car, I couldn't start it. When it seemed as if my neck was about to be snapped, I thought, *If only my friends the Russian peasants would suddenly arrive on the scene, I would be saved.* No such luck. It appeared I was doomed to fatal injury.

By no means was I cooperative in the boys' efforts to dislodge my brain from my skull. I was trying to kick and trying to free my arms, and I added my voice to the din whenever I got enough breath to make a noise.

Suddenly a new voice was added to the fracas, this one stentorian, as if from a pulpit, "WHAT IN HELL IS GOING ON IN HERE?"

The boys looked around and immediately dropped me about three feet straight to the floor, cracking my head on a table leg.

The voice *was* from the pulpit. It was Father O'Hara, from the Sherwood parish. He had been called at the same time as I had, but had taken longer to arrive.

Father O'Hara, himself a pretty big guy, roared at the boys. He informed them that they had disgraced the memory of their poor, departed mother, and if they didn't go stand in the corner and stop this nonsense, he wouldn't perform last rites.

While the priest did what was necessary, I departed from the house as quickly as possible. I had no dignity left to preserve.

That night as I lay in bed half-awake, half-asleep, counting the various places I ached, I pondered on what that day might have been like if I had felled one brother with a karate chop, tripped the second, and kicked the third, straight into his testicles. Would I have felt any better about myself? Probably not! And I fell asleep thinking, *What if... .*

⸙

During my childhood I thought *What if...I had an older brother?* Sometimes being an only child was a bit lonely. After my parents died, I would really have liked to have had a pal and protector.

When I was about five or six years old, a twelve-year-old boy in the neighborhood was the resident bully. The bully's name was Norton.

There was a park just a block from the apartment house where I lived with my father and mother. All the kids in the neighborhood played in the park. On a good day, Norton did not come to the park. But on a bad day, he was there, scheming and executing ways of making our lives miserable.

One of his favorite tricks was to beat us with a paddle he had fashioned in manual training class, in school. When we played ball, he demanded the best baseball glove from us. If we refused, we were forced to bend over and be whacked, hard, on our seat with his paddle. On several occasions, he forced two kids to pair off and fight with their fists. Refuse, and we were whacked with the paddle; and if the fighters weren't going at it hard enough, he used the paddle anyway.

Norton was able to maintain his supremacy over us by threatening to hurt us badly, or even kill us, if we told on him. We took him seriously and no one ever said a word.

One day his cruelty took a new turn. He made all of us go with him to an area behind a cluster of bushes where no one could witness what was going on. He made my best pal, Terrel, and me take down our pants and our underpants. We stood there, very embarrassed, wondering what would happen next.

"Now, you little shits put your little pricks touching end to end, and then piss on each other. All the rest of you watch because you're gonna do it next."

I said, "No."

Terrel said, "No."

"Bend over," said Norton and he whacked each of us, hard, on our bare buttocks.

We both cried with pain and shame. This was the first any of us had been forced to take our pants down or been hit so hard.

Norton, again, ordered us to carry out the obscenity that he had created for us. Again we refused, and again we were beaten.

Some of the other four or five kids were also crying. It looked as if everyone might bolt for home and Norton, apparently, thought that he had better get the situation under control.

He said, "If you don't do it this time, I'm gonna give each of you a real spanking. I'll spank you so hard, you may die."

The options had become intolerable. We did it.

Urine spattered and flew everywhere, down our legs, onto our downed trousers lying on the ground, up the front of our clothes and into our faces. Now, we were both sobbing and crying. The entire scene became too much for all the other kids who suddenly took off, running in all directions. Norton could not corral them, but when he left us to try to catch them, Terrel and I pulled up our pants and bolted for home.

But we couldn't go home in the shape we were in because our mothers would see that something was wrong. At this point we were still too frightened to tell anyone what had happened. We decided we would never go to the park again. We also decided that if we saw Norton on the street, we would run for home and not come out. We could probably outrun him. We had seen him play with the older boys and he certainly wasn't very good or very fast at sports. We agreed that we would not tell our parents.

After drying out as well as we could—miserable, sore, and over-whelmed with fear and disgust—we sneaked home.

That night, during my bath, I was careful not to let my mother see my sore, red bottom.

The next day in the apartment lobby I met a boy who often took me to Sunday school. I was always thrilled to be in the company of this mature, grown-up, fourteen-year-old. He treated me as an equal, rather than as some little kid. His name was Bill Fenstermaker and he was with his pal, Joe Kane.

Bill said, "C'mon, get your glove and I'll get a bat and ball and we'll go over to the park and hit a few."

"I don't go to the park anymore."

"C'mon, what's the matter? Is there a bogey man over there?" With that said, he reached down and gave me a comradely swat on my seat.

By now my bottom was swollen and even more painful than on the day before. I winced, noticeably, and a few tears trickled down my face.

Bill said, "What's the matter?"

"Nothing."

Joe came over and asked, "Your dad give you a licking?"

"No. My dad would never do that."

"Then what in the world is wrong with you? You won't go to the park, you don't want to play ball, and your rear end hurts. If your dad didn't spank you, who did? I think I'll go upstairs and talk to your mother."

At this point it all came out in a series of gasping statements, inter-mingled with sobs and tears. "I know Norton will kill me. I'm gonna die." I continued to sob.

The two boys took me by the shoulders and told me that I wasn't going to die. Instead, they were going to fix it so nothing like this would happen to me, ever again.

They found Norton and knocked him around a bit, convincing him that his behavior was unsatisfactory and that he should stay away from the little kids or they would work him over good. Then they told my parents what had happened.

My dad went to see Norton's dad. Within a short time Norton was sent to a military academy. During vacations, when he was home, he was never seen on the streets.

I came away from this experience thinking that fourteen was the best age that a boy could be. Had I been lucky enough to have had a brother, I wished he could have been just like Bill Fenstermaker or Joe Kane.

❧

Glad and I were thrilled when our second baby was a son. Lee would have an older brother for a role model and for a friend. Don would have the opportunity to be a pal, to include his little brother in his activities and be a protector, if necessary. The boys were three years apart. Pamela showed up fourteen months after Lee.

Our Tualatin house was built like an H. The cross bar on the H contained the living room, dining room, and kitchen. The west vertical arm was the two bedrooms, with one bathroom. The east vertical arm was the garage.

When there were just two boys, they shared the back bedroom. When Pamela arrived, it was obvious that we were a bit cramped for space. Our solution was to convert the oversized two-car garage into a combination playroom and sleeping room for the boys. We added a half-bath beside the furnace room.

As soon as Pamela was old enough to realize that she was isolated from her beloved boys, and as soon as she was coherently vocal, the first words we heard every morning were, "Where's dose boys?" This emanated from her crib until she was able to crawl out of it. Then we usually heard her as she was passing our door on her way to see "dose boys."

Don was a very serious kid, accepting responsibility with enthusiasm, as is the case with many firstborns. After all, Don had lived three years as an only child.

Lee was adventuresome, giving up nap time and his playpen very early. He was a mischief maker and a kid who thought he could do anything his older brother could do, which got him in hot water periodically.

Glad and I, being only children, watched the dynamics of our family with interest and with awe. We weren't sure what to do when conflict arose. One year when the internecine quarreling became too much for us, we warned the kids that Christmas would be less than they hoped for if they didn't start getting along better. I guess they didn't believe us because the spats continued. Christmas eve at our home was when the main presents were distributed and each one of us "ooed" and "ahed" over the wrapping and the contents of each package.

That year, Christmas Eve continued normally, with piles and piles of gifts under the tree for everyone, mostly given by Mom and Dad. After the children went to bed, Santa Claus would come and fill the huge knitted stockings hung from the mantle above the fireplace. We had told the kids that Santa knew who had been good and who had been naughty. Don was old enough that he wasn't entirely sure about the existence of the jolly fat man, but the other two believed devoutly.

On Christmas morning, when the excited kids ran into the living room to see what Santa had brought, all they found in their stockings were a stick (symbolizing a switch) and an orange, as their only gift. They still talk about that Christmas. After a while they figured out that we were the perpetrators. They have never forgiven us. Did it stop their familial bickering? NO! Did I ever advise a patient to use this as a ploy to deal with their problems? NO!

When counseling patients about behavioral problems, my own family was always a laboratory; but I never told the patients what my resources were.

At the customary age of six, Don was ready to start school. Lee thought he was ready, too. He was mad at everyone because we would not let him go off to school the same day as Don.

Right after lunch on Don's first day at school, Lee began watching from the front window for his brother to come walking down the road. Finally, when he spied Don, Lee rushed to the door. In his hand was a brand new book that no one had ever read to him. His first words to his brother, on this momentous day were, "Don, read my new book to me."

Don looked bewildered and said, "Lee, I don't know how to read yet."

Lee scowled at his brother with utter disgust and muttered, "Humph! If I'd been in school all day, I'll bet I'd know how to read."

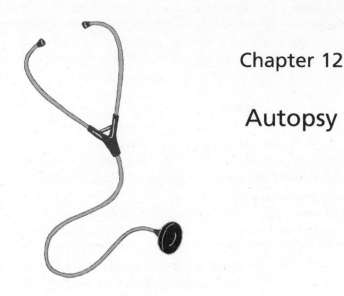

Chapter 12

Autopsy

Have you ever considered how difficult it would be to learn English if it were not your mother tongue?

Consider the word "post." The *Merriam-Webster's Dictionary* I'm using on my computer lists thirty-eight different uses for the noun "post," let alone the many adjectives, verbs, and adverbs. But when you ask a medical student or intern a question such as, "Did you get a post?" or "What did the post show?" there is no question in their minds about what that question is referring to.

The questioner is not asking about a fence post, the mail, the metal stem of a pierced earring, a goal at the end of a football field or what a rider does on a trotting horse when riding an English saddle. What the questioner wants to know is about the autopsy—an item I did not request from the bereaved boys in Tonquin that day when their mother died. I left that matter up to the coroner. I wanted no more to do with Father O'Hara's three burly parishioners.

An autopsy is a postmortem examination to determine the cause of death. When medicine emerged from its Dark Ages in about 1917, medical schools were required to increase their research activities. Medical licensing boards required that all doctors graduate from an accredited medical school. Accreditation required a certain amount of research. Schools found the easiest way to produce research publications was to determine the cause of death for all patients succumbing in their institutions. Thus the percentage of autopsies obtained through soliciting agreement from bereaved families, measured against the number of deaths, became the hallmark of institutional excellence for medical schools.

◈

When I was fourteen years old, my dad was a victim of a sudden, unexpected, fatal incident, probably a heart attack. Because he wasn't in a hospital, and because our family's physician was willing to sign the death certificate, there was no autopsy.

I have suffered severe guilt for not having gotten home in time to talk with my father, whom I respected and loved dearly. I was late because, after playing tennis following which I was supposed to come right home, I went to a friend's house to play Monopoly. My compulsivity for arriving early at every function I now attend perhaps stems from this teenage trauma. Glad sometimes plaintively wonders, as we drive to a dinner or bridge party, if we always have to be first.

Glad and the children have always been disappointed that I would never play board games with them, especially Monopoly. I am not aware that I have any covert dislike of the game, but rather I sense an antagonism to Park Place and Boardwalk that keeps me from enjoying the game or playing well.

Mother never completely recovered from the lung infection she had when Dad died. Three months later she entered a hospital from which she never emerged.

On George Washington's birthday, the call came from the hospital. I was at a friend's home, having a holiday breakfast, when Aunt Hattie (actually my mother's aunt, quite an elderly lady who was dying of breast cancer and who had come to live with us to help defray expenses after Dad had died) told me that the hospital had called and wanted me to come over. I said, "I'll go right away; but why does she want me to come now?" My routine was to go every night during visiting hours. I had seldom missed a night during the two months of her hospitalization.

Aunt Hattie replied, "I didn't ask; maybe she's going to come home soon."

So, with spirits buoyed, I left on the familiar trip. I took the cable car from the foot of the Fillmore Street hill, transferred to the No. 22 Line and got off at Post Street. While I walked the last three blocks, I envisioned how I would help Mother when she came home. I was so excited to think about her homecoming that I could hardly contain myself. My beautiful, lovely, adoring mother was going to come home. My great-aunt, although she was a sweet old lady, hadn't been much of a substitute mother.

When I reached the hospital I didn't wait for the elevator, but ran up the three flights of stairs. I burst into the six-bed ward, where Mother's cubicle was the first one on the right. She had been allowed to move over against the wall as one of the perquisites of longevity. A corner bed was sought after because at least one side afforded privacy.

Her bed wasn't occupied; in fact, it had been stripped and the mattress folded over. I thought, *She's getting dressed to go home.* The lady in the next bed saw my perplexity but simply said, "Your mother is next door in the treatment room."

I went to the treatment room. The door was closed. I opened it and peered in, expecting to see my mother dressed and waiting for me. Instead, she was lying on her back, very still and very pale. I moved across the room and spoke to her. She didn't answer. The door behind me opened and a hospital employee said, "What are you doing in here? You have no right to be here—now, get out!"

I backed away from this woman and said, "I want to talk to my mother."

She looked at me strangely and hurried out. I went over and picked up Mother's strangely cold hand. It began to sink in. *She is dead! God!*

The nurse arrived seconds later, took me by the arm and led me outside. She said, "Your mother has passed on. Is there anything I can do?"

Is there anything she can do? Is there anything I can do? Is there anything anyone can do? Dad died five months ago. Mother is dead? My God! I saw her just last night. Let's go back to last night and start over. She can't leave me; she loves me. I love her. What should I do?

The nurse took me to the solarium and a man wearing a white jacket came in. He said, "I'm the doctor."

"You're not my mother's doctor."

"No," he said. "I'm the intern; I've come to ask your help."

"What do you want me to do?" *I don't want to help anyone; I want someone to help me!*

The intern said, "It's very important that we know why people die. We want to do an autopsy on your mother to determine why she died."

I thought, *She was here two months and you don't know what was wrong with her?* but I said, "What's an autopsy?"

He replied, "It's really nothing—just a small operation to make sure we have all the answers about her. The autopsy may provide us with a new scientific discovery and help somebody else. Almost everyone has this done because it's so helpful to us to know how to treat the next person who has the same disease."

I didn't want to help anyone; I just wanted to get out of there. I said, "Okay."

I signed the necessary papers. I had just turned fifteen years old. I hadn't even cried yet!

When I left the hospital I really didn't know what to do. Go home? To what? A doddering old aunt who knew so little about what was going on that she thought Mother had been ready to come home? I walked the three blocks to where I could catch the street car for home and, without thinking, turned into the ice cream and candy store where I had often stopped at night after visiting Mother at the hospital. Even on those nights, going home to my aunt, who would already be in bed, hadn't been much of an option. I didn't have anyone to turn to; so I would buy a sundae and talk to the lady behind the counter.

The proprietress of the store spoke with an accent. I didn't know where she was from until one night she had told me she had been born in France, the daughter of a confectioner in Marseilles. Her name was Colette. After World War I, Colette and her father had come to San Francisco to work in a candy factory, but the candy maker had died and the factory went out of business. Her father had opened this little store. I asked her the name of the candy maker and, sure enough, he had been my uncle. We had a connection.

I must have looked strange that night when I shuffled into Colette's store. When she asked me what I wanted, I replied, "Nothing."

She asked, "Are you broke? I'll fix you something."

I said, "No, I'm not broke. I just don't want anything."

"Then," she said, "you must be sick." And she came around from behind the counter to feel my forehead to see if I had a fever. When she touched me, I could no longer hold back. She wasn't family. She wasn't even a real friend, just a person I had talked to on lonely nights when I had nowhere to go. I threw myself into her arms and began to sob. I needed a sympathetic breast to put my head on and sympathetic arms to hold me.

Colette understood and she held me tightly, rocking back and forth in rhythm with my sobs, saying, "Mon petit, mon petit, ta maman est mort, n'est-ce pas? Mon Dieu, mon Dieu!"

I never saw Colette after that night. The neighborhood was not one in which I usually traveled. Later I wished I had seen her to say "Thank you for understanding."

❧

My life went on. I went to war and saw dead, dying and maimed sailors and Marines. I went to medical school and, on the first day, a cadaver was assigned to me for dissection. These things had steeled me, I thought, for any eventuality. Wrong!

As a second-year medical student, while I was enrolled in a course in pathology, I was assigned as an observer at an autopsy. I didn't give this a lot of thought until I walked into the mortuary, carrying the pathologist's bag, and realized that this was the kind of place where I had been to my parents' funerals. The memories began flooding back. The sweet smell of dead flowers, the shielded area off the main chapel where the family sat during funerals and where I had sat with one of Mother's friends and felt as if I were in a new, miserable world. And the chapel where I was told to walk over to the open casket to say goodbye. I didn't want to see my mother lying there. I wanted her alive, but I did as I was told because it was the right thing to do. Ever after, I wished that I hadn't.

It had been twelve years since Mother's and Dad's deaths, but it seemed as if it were happening all over again. I began to get cold. Flashbacks shot through my mind. My hands shook. I told myself to stop this nonsense; I was going to be a doctor and I would have to be professional, no matter what. We went into the autopsy room and there was a body of a middle-aged female on the dissecting table.

The pathologist unpacked his tools, turned on a water spigot connected to a short length of garden hose and said, "The water is to keep the body clean while I work. Your job is to see that the embalming fluid and other stuff is washed away." With that, he took a scalpel and made an incision from the front of the base of the neck to the pelvic bone.

The woman could be my mother. They had done this to her; I had let them do this. My beautiful mother. I began to cry quietly. The pathologist was talking to me, explaining what he was doing. He asked a question, and I was too choked up to answer. He turned, looked at me and said, "Jesus Christ, a medical student pansy."

I stayed, spraying the water when necessary. I couldn't explain what my trouble was and I sensed he didn't care. It was my problem; solve it for myself or get out and fail the exercise. The next hour was as rough a time as I had ever experienced, but when it was over I knew I had survived one of the rites of passage in becoming a doctor.

During the years that I worked with the television show I tried to make Welby and Kiley appear to be *real* doctors. No matter how hard those of us on the production staff tried, we were faced with the problem that the words put in the actors' mouths came from writers whose life experiences were not medical. They hadn't had the emotional trauma of a medical student seeing his first autopsy, of having the first death of a patient, or the thrill of a successful conclusion of a desperately sick patient and the gratitude of a patient and the patient's family.

It was presumed that both Welby and Kiley went to medical school. In fact, during the series, references were made to classmates and alumni meetings; but they didn't go to a *real* medical school and they didn't have my anatomy professor. I had been well schooled in adversity during my freshman year by the professor who was the head of the anatomy department.

That professor was a sadist. At exam time, he created anatomy tag tests, in which obscure anatomical parts of corpses lined up on the dissecting tables in the anatomy lab, were tagged with a number. Students filing by were required to name each numbered tag on their score sheet. He never tagged anything common, such as a large muscle or bone—only obscure little bits of stuff, hidden under something else which one was forbidden to move in order to get a better look.

His other creation was a sausage slide. In this student horror he literally stuffed sausage skins with bits of tissue, mixing nerves, brain tissue, heart muscle, bowel wall muscle, mucus surfaces, and other tissues, then fixing the whole mess with formaldehyde and making microscopic slices, he gave these to students as unknowns on which to be tested. Looking at this conglomeration of disparate parts under a microscope and drawing them and naming them was the test. I was a lousy artist and found it very difficult to transpose what I saw under the microscope to a sheet of paper. I thought, *What's the use anyway? I've been a corpsmen in the Navy and I know enough about medicine to know that being able to identify bits of tissue isn't a part of patient care.*

There was so much to learn and so little time, and I fumed silently about wasting my time and risking my grades on exercises such as this.

In all my years of practice, very little that I was tested on by the anatomists made any difference in the way I treat patients. Of course, I learned human anatomy, but the tests lacked practical application and seemed to demonstrate the disregard that the anatomists have for physicians. Anatomy class in those days was for anatomists and the tests seemed to be an attempt to demonstrate their point that anatomy was a provable science, but the practice of medicine was simply a lot of intelligent supposition.

The anatomy lab was on the third floor of the medical school, down a dark corridor, at the end of the hall. Most of the corridors were dark in this less-than-prepossessing structure. The building lacked the character of age or the brilliance of youth. It was a government building built in the 1930s. The turnaround drive, fronting on Marquam Hill Road, boasted a flagpole as its sole attraction. The glory of the location was only visible from the back parking lot and from all the classrooms facing north or east; for there, for all of us to gaze upon, were the wondrous, snow-capped peaks of the Pacific Northwest. The north-facing windows of the anatomy lab, with its sordid display of human remnants, looked out on the pristine white slopes of Mt. Hood, Mt. Adams and Mt. St. Helens.

The lab's two rooms were separated by a washroom. Each barracks for the dead had ten tables, five to a side, each holding a cadaver wrapped in strips of muslin, looking for all the world like an ancient Egyptian mummy. Heads to the wall and feet to the center, each body had a name tag. We were cautioned to refer to our cadaver with respect, such as "Mr. Jones," or whatever appellation was proper. The cadavers were all men, as Oregon women had a benefactor whose money had kept them from paupers' graves and off our dissecting tables. The only women present were the eight female members of our class and one female cadaver, snatched from somewhere when no one was looking and dissected by anatomy assistants for demonstration purposes only.

On the days when written or tag test scores were to be distributed, the prof would tell the students to gather in the hall after class. After a delay sufficient to make all of us nervous wrecks, the prof would emerge, stand on a chair and ask, "How many of you think you passed?"

A few hands would go up.

"How many of you believe you failed?"

No hands went up because none of us wanted the monster to see our insecurity, but he knew the terror was there. We were a select group, the best of our classes in college; we were expected to succeed. Upperclassmen passed down the word that anatomy was the course that could easily fail a student. It seemed that the school's policy was to stress students to the point at which only the emotionally strong would survive.

Then he would say, "How many want your scores today?"

All hands would go up.

The prof would smirk, "Maybe I will just wait a day or two."

During this exercise I would take little short breaths to keep from yelling, "Give them to us, you bastard!"

This toying would go on for several minutes and then, mouth open in a soundless laugh, he would throw the papers on a table with such a flourish that many of the papers slid off onto the floor. The trembling, future doctors had to scramble on their knees to find their exam papers. We each hoped we would find our own quickly in order to cover our embarrassment, so the others would not see our failures. We were reduced to the lowest level of interpersonal relationships.

Perhaps this served a purpose in humanizing us for the future. It is hard to feel godlike, as a healer, after scrabbling around on the floor looking for your examination paper. Perhaps he felt that the terror and debasement had merit if its purpose was to weed out the weak and to humble the remainder; but some of us wondered if it should have been such an obvious source of pleasure to our tormentor.

At the end of the freshman year, before being promoted, each student had to sit for an oral anatomy examination conducted by the anatomy prof and others in the department. I was okay until the prof said, "What is the function of the thymus gland?"

I replied, "The thymus gland is a vestigial organ with no function ascribed to it." I was quite confident that I was correct.

Prof: "Is that your answer? A lot depends on this quiz. You had better take time to think this over."

At first blush, one would have to think that maybe it was the wrong answer and the professor was offering a kind opportunity for me to reconsider. I thought about that. I reasoned that a human being totally devoid of any of the milk of human kindness was not offering an olive branch, but, rather, was inviting me to pluck an apple from the Eden tree. Certainly the apple contained, if not a snake, a worm. I said, "No function."

Prof: "You are wrong."

Now I wasn't so sure. I was inwardly quaking, a condition the prof knew was going on and relished, but I decided to stand or fall by my answer.

Answer: "No, I am not wrong."

Prof: "That is all. You are dismissed."

Never a word that I had passed or failed—just "...dismissed."

In the hall were several of my colleagues awaiting their turn. We agreed that my answer was correct, but I never knew what my score was until a promotion list was published.

Although the answer was correct then, it would not be now. The thymus gland has been proved to serve a function in the immune system by producing the C-cells.

The anatomists' superior attitude toward physicians who simply practice medicine, as compared with anatomists whose calling is an exact science and always provable was dashed the day when C-cells were discovered. My regret was that the professor who quizzed me that day in my freshman year had died and escaped swallowing the bile of being wrong in what he had taught us.

A student who advanced to the second year of medical school had a far better chance of staying the distance. The lectures in pharmacology were lively and loud. Our pharmacology professor was a robust, laughing man who enjoyed his work and particularly enjoyed playing tricks on his students, but not the same types of tricks that the anatomy prof used. The pharmacologist was Norman David, and we nicknamed him "Stormin' Norman." Although seemingly cruel at the time, his tricks were designed to teach.

Stormin' Norman's first trick was a laboratory exercise to measure gastric acidity. How does one measure gastric acidity? With stomach fluids, of course. And whose stomach fluids did we use? Ours! And how did we obtain that fluid? Through a nasal gastric tube. Half the class passed a tube the first week and the second half passed a tube the next week.

Most of our class had never seen or contemplated a nasal gastric tube. Playing football at Stanford, flying a P-40 in the South Pacific, or matriculating as a chiropodist had not prepared anybody for this exercise. My partner in this exercise was lucky. Passing a gastric tube through the nose was a cinch for me. I had done this many times as a hospital corpsman in the Navy.

That first morning at 8 A.M., on an empty stomach, sixty-eight students (seven had already failed, been expelled, or dropped out) gathered in a laboratory. Thirty-four of us were passers and thirty-four of us passees. The apprehension of the passees was as great as the lack of skill among the passers. Within minutes the sounds of gagging filled the air. The sight of distraught medical students was fearful to behold. Stormin' Norman circulated throughout the room, encouraging and helping people, but we all felt as if this was his annual practical joke on the medical students. The exercise did have a use, though, for now we all knew what it was like to have a nasal gastric tube passed; and we would be absolutely sure it was a necessary procedure before ordering it for a patient!

Another application of the exercise (practical, if one subscribes to the theory that only the strong shall remain and the weak shall be vanquished) was that we lost a classmate. About midmorning, after gagging and vomiting around the tube for two hours, one irate student pulled out his tube, yelled epithets and obscenities at our prof—and left. We never saw him again. We now numbered sixty-seven.

Four weeks later, Stormin' Norman unveiled his second exercise in practical therapeutics. We all took an injection of morphine sulfate.

Morphine is a potent opiate. It is addictive, but it is a marvelous analgesic or pain reliever. It has side effects. It can slow respiration, contract the pupils of the eyes, slow bowel activity, and produce nausea and vomiting. Pain is the antidote for morphine, meaning that the more pain one has, the fewer side effects one suffers from the morphine one takes to relieve it.

⁂

Some years ago my coronary arteries clogged and I had to have open heart surgery. I had wonderful care. I was possibly never safer in my lifetime than I was in the hands of my doctors and the postoperative cardiac intensive care nurses. Six or eight hours post-op I remember awakening, and I still had my endotracheal tube in place. This is the tube the anesthesiologist places through your mouth into your windpipe. You are not supposed to wake up while it is there. I awakened. The tube hurt, but you can't talk with that thing prohibiting your vocal cords from closing. I grunted. The nurse came and said, "What can I do for you?"

I didn't answer. I couldn't. So I made a writing motion with my hand, like one makes to a waiter in a restaurant when calling for the check. She brought paper and pencil and I scribbled MS (for "morphine sulfate"). She understood immediately, put my injection into the I.V. tubing, and I went back to sleep. When I next awakened, the tube had been removed painlessly, but I was left with a sore throat and a sore chest. Morphine sulfate saw me through the next few days.

❦

That day in the pharmacology lab, none of the students was in pain and we did not tolerate morphine very well. We teamed up. Half of us took the injection while the partner monitored the nauseated, sedated colleague. The next week we reversed the process. Most of us vomited. We were all nauseated and vowed never to take that filthy stuff again unless we absolutely needed it, a valuable lesson in preventing addiction among a population with high tension and easy access to addictive drugs. Stormin' Norman had his tricks, but he taught us a lot.

When I wrote medical information for the Welby series I knew that, because the actors were good in their roles, to the public they would seem to be *real*; but to me they were only *reel*. None of them had ever been forced to watch an autopsy, the death of a real person, or a bungled operation. They could even laugh over the single word that is forbidden in the surgical theater: "OOPS!"

The series was not documentary; it was a dramatic show and a good one. Bob Young told me, "I don't think of myself as a doctor but as an actor playing an important role. It's your job to make me sound like a doctor."

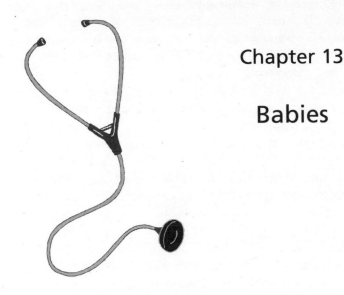

Chapter 13

Babies

"Doctor, come quick! I think the baby's comin'!"

It never matters when or where the call comes, everything stops for baby, because a baby stops for no one. It might be late at night, with a knock at the back door, or in the middle of a busy day at the office, or when Glad and I were having guests for dinner and she expected me to cook the hamburgers; the baby's needs took over. I might mutter to myself, *Why don't they ever come at my convenience,* and our children might complain about Daddy's going out again. Pamela, at age two, couldn't understand why her daddy was always running out to see some "Old Bees." But the issue about whether or not I would go was never in doubt. I went.

As a country doctor, delivering babies played a large part in my life. Maybe it was the most fun part of practice. By and large mothers were happy, fathers were happy, and by being the stork, the doctor who offici-ated at the baby's entrance into the world became the family's hero. With girl babies sometimes a personal relationship develops that lasts into their own motherhood. I still receive wedding announcements, birth announcements, and other celebratory messages from some of the babies that I delivered many years ago. The wonder of it all! I never tired of the thrill at being on the spot when new life enters the world.

The world looked pretty good. We had defeated Hitler and Tojo, the Korean war was winding down, and these babies seemed to be entering at a time of normalcy. The baby business was booming. Babies were popping out all over. Military veterans now back home and in secure jobs wanted to expand their families. We didn't know it then, but we were contributing to the Baby Boomer generation.

Life was simpler for doctors, as we did not have to worry about pro-life or pro-choice; it was all pro-life. The law prohibited abortion. The idea of performing an illegal abortion never surfaced in our everyday thinking. Life was simpler for doctors, but may have been harder for women.

A new family came to the office one day and asked me to take care of her expected confinement and to care for their new baby. I examined the woman and found her to be a healthy, robust twenty-year-old, married to a strapping, handsome young farmer. This was her first pregnancy. I gladly told them that I saw no problems. The couple explained that they lived up on the far reaches of Chehalem Mountain in a house they were building, and asked what I would do if there was an emergency that required a house call.

"I will come, of course," I responded, and the couple left, hand in hand.

Their next visit was uneventful; the pregnancy was progressing normally. Then, on a hot August afternoon, a Jeep screeched to a halt in front of the office. The young farmer came racing into the waiting room full of people, shouting my name and the fact that his wife was bleeding. The receptionist quickly recognized panic among the patients who were waiting and ushered the young man back to our office. I came quickly. The farmer told me that his wife had developed sudden cramping, abdominal pains, vaginal bleeding which was severe; and he had come to get me for the promised house call.

I asked, "Why didn't you phone?"

"No phone, Doc. I ain't finished the house yet," was the reply. "I stopped on my way out and got a neighbor lady to go over to my place. She'll take care of my wife till we get back. We gotta hurry."

I remembered the crowd in the waiting room and thought about all the people who would be disappointed because of my making a house call in midafternoon, but bleeding was bleeding, and a promise was a promise; so I grabbed my regular bag and an emergency bag full of stuff that I didn't usually keep in the car, and we ran out back toward my car.

"Come with me, Doc," the distraught husband said, as he grabbed my arm and attempted to hurry me around front to his Jeep.

"No, I'll take my car."

"Can't," replied the farmer. "At the end of the road we have to take the Jeep, anyway."

At the end of the road? Where in the world is this place? He said Chehalem Mountain. This must be way, way up the mountain if the only way to get to it is by Jeep.

I climbed into the Jeep and we spun our wheels in the gravel parking lot, throwing sand and gravel against the waiting room windows, calling attention to my sudden departure. I hoped it would assuage the injured feelings of the other patients, seeing their doctor hurrying off on an errand of mercy. All the while I thought, *I'll bet this thing is a false alarm and boy, am I going to be pissed!*

When we reached the end of the road, we took off on a track bordering a strawberry field, then through the woods and out into the sunlight. We hit a series of ruts and bounced so hard that I feared I would fly out of the vehicle. I hung on to the bar in front of the windshield and clenched my teeth to keep my jaws from rattling; after a quick jolt I felt a pain in my back, as though I had been stabbed.

I recognized this sensation, having suffered the same symptoms before, and knew that I would have to deal with this pain for days to come, just as I had after being roughed up by the boys in Tonquin whose mother had died so suddenly. Pinky, always the pragmatist, had asked, "What if you get a call some day to see one of them? Will you go?"

"No," I answered. "I would see them in the office if it was necessary. After all, we are the only doctors around here. But," I chuckled, "only one of them at a time."

Whoever said the practice of medicine was safe? Up to this time I had been beaten by irate family members, coerced into drinking straight vodka on an empty stomach by Russian peasants, falling and breaking my ankle during my first week in practice, and now I was in danger of suffering a back injury—all in the interest of saving humanity. Maybe I should have been a lawyer, as my mother had wanted.

Suddenly, we came upon a road. Around the bend was an A-frame house with smoke pouring out of the chimney and four cars parked in front. I reconstructed our route later and found that, by road, the trip was miles longer, but my driver's white lie about the absence of a regular road got us there faster. I weighed the evidence—my back versus my patient's blood loss—and the farmer with his Jeep won.

When I rushed into the house through a door that opened into one large room, there were three ladies in one corner, but no patient. The husband pointed to the rungs of a ladder (constructed by nailing boards against bare, vertical two-by-four studs) leading to a hole in the ceiling. He pushed me toward it, and said, "Up there."

The sleeping loft in this A-frame was above the main floor, under the eaves. I grabbed my regular medical bag and started toward the loft. I felt like a fly walking up a wall without any support. A fly with a sore back. As I poked my head through the ceiling opening, I saw my patient lying on a mattress in the middle of the loft. She called out, "Help me, Doctor!" A fourth neighbor woman, who had been sitting with my patient, climbed down through the hole in the floor.

The woman was having trouble. She was ashen and sweating, and had a rapid pulse. She was bleeding heavily; the bedclothes were soaked. I got down on my knees beside the mattress and began to massage her womb through pressure on the abdominal wall, in an effort to stop the bleeding. A tiny fetus and afterbirth had already been expelled, but the uterus would not contract down as it should to control bleeding. I supposed a segment of the placenta had broken off and was causing the problem.

It was hot in that loft. I took off my jacket and threw it over a stool in the corner. The farmer hovered, as husbands do, so I sent him for a hammer and nail and the other medical bag which I had left in the Jeep.

I became warmer; sweat was really rolling down my back and under my arms. I prepared a syringe of medication to force the uterus to contract and stop the bleeding, and injected it intravenously. Then I went back to my external massage of the uterus. The bleeding slowed. I became hotter, yet. I knew that two-story buildings always have hot attics and this one had no ceiling insulation, but this was ridiculous. I pulled off the tie and flung it over my jacket. A jacket and tie was not my usual attire on a hot summer's day; but I had been to Portland to a breakfast meeting earlier, and had played the game of conforming.

The farmer returned with a hammer and nail that I pounded into one of the four-by-six exposed beams. I took a liter bottle of 5 percent glucose and distilled water, hung it on the nail, and started an I.V. in the patient's arm.

She was hot, too. We were both so hot I didn't think it was good for either one of us; and I doubted that I would be much help if I were flattened by heat prostration. She had lost a lot of blood and didn't need the extra fluid loss resulting from sweating so vigorously. She needed to conserve fluids to reduce shock. Further, every time I stood up, I banged my head on the inside of the roof. We needed to get the patient downstairs, but she was too weak to climb down that ladder. I sent the farmer to ask one of the ladies to go to the nearest phone, call the volunteer fire department, and ask them to send the ambulance right away.

Next, my shirt came off; I was down to a T-shirt. I had never been so hot in my life. But, now I noticed a peculiar phenomenon. It was becoming foggy in the attic. Maybe I was blacking out from the heat. I went back to massaging the uterus. The bleeding had almost stopped. I told the farmer about the fog.

"Yup, Doc," he said, "the ladies are boiling a lot of water on the wood stove and the steam is comin' up through the spaces between the floorboards. I ain't had time to put the plywood down yet."

Well, I had seen as many old movies as the next guy; and I knew that when a birthing was about to happen, everyone boiled water. It was never clear what they had done with the hot water; possibly it was to be used for sterilizing instruments. My instruments and syringes, catheters and emergency umbilical tape were all sterilized and prepackaged in my bag. I didn't need the water. I peeked down through the hole. The three remaining ladies each manned a cauldron on a red-hot wood stove. I had suffered through Shakespeare in high school and I didn't remember much but I had a fleeting image from Macbeth, and started to giggle.

Double, double, toil and trouble;
Fire burn, and cauldron bubble.

I thought, *I'd better get out of this attic. If I'm giggling in this situation, the heat's gotten to me.* As I leaned over the hole, sweat dripping onto the floor below, I was tempted to shout, "Get that damn hot water out of here and put out the fire; you're killing us." Instead, in order not to hurt feelings, I said gently, "I guess we won't be needing the water, ladies; thank you."

The ambulance arrived. The firemen were surprised to see me shirtless. The patient was put in a steel-meshed Stokes litter, sometimes used to transfer patients off ships at sea. She was lowered through the hole in the ceiling and whisked off to the hospital. I went home and took a shower, went to the hospital, and got the situation under control. We both needed to have our fluid levels restored, she by intravenous routes and I by mouth. We both recovered.

⊂⟊⟊⟊⟆

There is no such thing as a run-of-the-mill delivery, not when the hospital is more than twenty miles away on a two-lane road. Having a baby is not a disease, but a normal physiological act, according to the books. Ask any rural physician and the answer may be different.

First, babies seem to come at night or other odd hours, such as during office hours. One old doctor once told me that, "A pregnancy lasts exactly nine months. They start 'em at night, they come at night." Then he laughed and said, "You'd better hope all your husbands go home for nooners and you won't have to get up at night at all." When did a doctor ever go home right after the office closed, have a leisurely dinner, proceed to the hospital to deliver a baby, and get home in time for a full night's sleep?

Second, there is always a rush of adrenaline sometime during the birthing process that speeds the physician's heart. It is the "what-if…" syndrome. What if the baby is stuck in an abnormal position? What if the baby's heart rate falters? What if mother has excessive bleeding or develops a cardiac arrhythmia; or, what if…what if…? There is no time to consult texts or other physicians. The doctor on the scene is it. Decisions are mandatory *right now* and must be correct or lives are lost.

Third, delivering a baby in a rural hospital is a lonely job. At St. Vincent's in Portland, residents, interns, and other staff were always around, including anesthetists, nurses, and other delivery room personnel. In Tuality Hospital in Hillsboro, we were usually alone with a single nurse for a helper. We gave anesthetics by pouring drop ether or by a saddle block. Lamaze had not been accepted yet, even though we recognized that less sophisticated peoples of the world were having spontaneous, nonmedicated deliveries all the time.

And finally, we worried about trying to deliver a baby that did not fit the pelvic opening, such that a cesarean section might be required.

A primiparous (first pregnancy) petite woman, who lived just down the road from our house in Tualatin, came to me for obstetrical care. She was a wee one, but of course, it's all relative between the size of the baby and the size of the pelvis. When I first checked her she seemed to have an underdeveloped pelvis and perhaps could not deliver vaginally. We put off the decision about a cesarean section until the last trimester. That was when the baby's actual size could be compared with the passageway that the baby would have to travel in leaving its mommy.

During the eighth month, I suspected she could have trouble with the fit so I asked a consulting obstetrician in Portland to see the patient and offer an opinion. He obtained X-ray pelvimetry, measurements of both the baby's head and the pelvis, and came back to me with a report that definitely indicated a cesarean section was necessary. We scheduled an elective section for about a week before her expected due date, but explained to the patient that she must inform us of any abdominal or labor pains before then.

One evening, right after dinner (which belies the tale that all deliveries are at odd hours, doesn't it?), the husband phoned. "Doc, the baby is comin'!"

Now, I grew up knowing that it took awhile to have a baby. My mother used to regale the family with tales of how, after she began having her first pains while I was trying to get born, she cleaned the apartment and cooked a large Sunday morning pancake breakfast for Dad and my godfather. At this point, Dad always finished the story by pointing out that he knew the exact time of my birth, because even from out in the hall he knew when Mother yelled the loudest. My sophistication about anesthesia and delivery came many years after they were gone; but I have subsequently wondered what was going on in that delivery room during the days when anesthesia was king, but my mother was still yelling.

"Nonsense!" I told the young woman's husband, now using my knowledge as a physician rather than my childhood memories. "Remember, she isn't due for two weeks. This is her first labor and she has a small pelvis. It is true that we will have to do an emergency cesarean section if she really is in labor; but it just won't happen quickly." With that gratuitous and pontifical explanation out of the way I then asked, "How often are the contractions?"

The father-to-be, somewhat abashed by having panicked, said, "Gee, Doc, I'm sorry, but she has had only one pain."

"See," I said.

"But Doc," offered the husband, "I'm worried."

"Sure you are, Joe. I'll be right there and check her over. Don't worry anymore."

I went right away and found my patient still having her first contraction—and *only* contraction. It hadn't stopped. Her uterus was in full-time activity. I checked her and found the cervix dilated about one-third of the way. I told Joe that it was necessary to take her right to the hospital. They had previously selected Tuality Hospital in Hillsboro rather than St. Vincent's in Portland. Her confinement bag was already packed, so they left right away.

I went home, called Sam, and told him we had a c-section to do. He said he would pick me up in five minutes. My house was on his route to the hospital.

When we arrived at the hospital and hurried into the doctors' entrance, we saw a crowd that had gathered around a hospital gurney in the entry hall where another doctor, who happened to be walking through the lobby, had been pressed into service. He was holding a seven-and-one-half-pound bouncing baby boy who was hollering his lungs out. My patient had not made it to the delivery room, and certainly hadn't needed a c-section. So much for pelvic measurements before the use of ultrasound!

During my tenure in Sherwood, she happily delivered two more, but I managed to be present for those.

∾∾∾

Pinky, my buddy from Navy days, and his wife, Carol, asked me to deliver their next child. Although Pinky had been a hospital corpsman in the Navy and had seen all kinds of medical procedures, being stationed at a mobile hospital or on a submarine had not afforded him any obstetrical experience. Pinky asked if he could watch. Carol thought it was sweet that he wanted to be there.

A request for the father to be in the delivery room when his wife was in the actual process of delivering the baby was still thought to be dangerous to the doctor, the mother and baby as well. Every hospital had its horror stories about distraught fathers going berserk and attacking the doctor, or trying to grab the baby themselves when they imagined the process of the delivery to be too slow or the mother or baby to be in danger. Dad was welcome in the labor room; but when the nurses wheeled the patient into the delivery room, he was banished to the hall, to pace with the other expectant fathers.

I asked for permission for Pinky to watch the delivery at Tuality Hospital, where Glad had watched me officiate at the birth of a baby during my first weeks in practice. I was turned down flat. It was okay for my wife to watch, but a father...never!

By now Pinky and Carol had become fixed on the idea of his participation (they were ahead of their time). They insisted that I request permission from St. Vincent's Hospital for Pinky to be in the delivery room. I knew better than to ask Sister. She would only say no with a snort and a stamp of her foot.

I had a better idea. The staff at St. Vincent's were accustomed to having trainees hanging around and would not be concerned if I introduced Pinky as a medical student who was doing a preceptorship with me.

I was sure the plan would work, but only if Pinky and Carol were able to act as if they had no relationship. This meant no hugging, no kissing, no "Does it hurt, darling?" or, "Tom, can't you do something to make it easier?" We had to act professional.

The idea of a father being in the delivery room made me nervous, but not as nervous as the first time it occurred. That time, it wasn't a father, it was a grandfather—and he was another doctor. Kile Hardesty was a very good friend and I was honored when his daughter asked me to deliver her first child. With Kile in the room during the delivery I wasn't afraid of being attacked, but I was concerned about this being a perfect delivery. Kile was a radiologist; but before the war he had been in general practice and in the baby delivery business himself. At the proper time, Kile donned a cap and mask and stood behind me while "Little Louise" was born. Although the delivery was normal, I sweat bullets.

I thought that it might be easier for me having Pinky in the room, as he wouldn't know if there was a crisis; but we were breaking the hospital's rules. I worried that Pinky or Carol would crack under the strain and Pinky would be exposed as the father-to-be.

The delivery progressed in the usual fashion. Labor lasted about six hours and I stood by Carol's and Pinky's sides every minute. When there was no nurse in the room I would occasionally remind them of our bargain. Pinky held up his end of the agreement well, giving Carol little hugs when they were alone but behaving in a very circumspect manner when anyone was around.

Finally it was time for all of us to go to the delivery room. I had to leave Pinky and Carol alone with the nurse during a very critical time while I went to scrub-up and put on my sterile gown and gloves. When I returned, Carol was grunting and Pinky looked a little pale. Sister Paul, the delivery room supervisor, had come into the room but because nothing was said, I assumed there had been no breakdown in Pinky's characterization as a medical student. I kept up a running patter of information as I would, had he been a regular student.

I gave Carol a saddle block. She was very comfortable and still able to push. As the baby's head began to emerge, I performed an episiotomy while encouraging her to push harder. Suddenly Pinky's voice was heard over my right shoulder, "Push, Carol, for God's sake, push! Oh my darling girl, push! Oh God, it's coming."

Oh, oh, I thought, *Pinky's blowing it.* I looked up. Sister's eyes were questioning behind her mask. I said, "Second year student, first delivery. He's very emotional."

Now Pinky was crying and laughing and muttering some unintelligible words. Suddenly the baby, whose head had completely emerged, let the world know that here was a new citizen by letting out a big howl. I heard a thump behind me and out of the corner of my eye I saw a nurse moving quickly around the table. Pinky had fainted dead away. Sister said, "They don't make 'em tough anymore." I didn't know if she was talking about fathers or medical students. Since I heard no more about the incident, I guessed correctly that Pinky had not blown his cover; or maybe I just didn't hear about it because of Sister Paul's personal predicament.

❧⚶❧

Sister Paul was a young, delightful, slim, pretty, fun-loving nun. She was adored by the nurses and patients and respected by the doctors. She ran a tight ship, but she was always ready to play.

One night there was a snowstorm. It rarely snowed in Portland; instead, winters were wet and chilly, and occasionally icy when a silver thaw whistled its cold winds down the Columbia River Gorge from eastern Oregon and turned rain into ice. Then the world became quiet, with great fir trees drooping from the weight of ice and a silver sheen covering all that was beautiful, as well as that which was tawdry, making the entire scene one of a shimmering silence. The tragedies of such storms were broken tree limbs and bushes and downed power lines with their inherent risks. This night it only snowed, but it snowed a lot.

The hospital was backed by a large hill covered with trees, but there was a clear strip in the lawn between the hospital and the nursing dormitory, a perfect place for sledding. An ideal braking area lay between the end of the slope and the street. Here, hospital maintenance men had cleared the sidewalks and heaped the snow along the curb, creating a snowy, moderately steep slope about two hundred feet long (two-thirds the length of a football field) that ended in a short braking area and a wall of snow.

Sister Paul was originally from the northern Midwest and longed to go sledding. Alas, there were no sleds. What could a nursing sister do in order to improvise? Why, of course, raid the hospital central supply and liberate enough stainless steel bedpans to accommodate a gaggle of student nurses and herself! Bedpans make great sleds, or more aptly, luges. Sister Paul and the nurses had a great time sliding down the hill. This was followed by rosy cheeks, hot chocolate, and a warm fire in the nurses' dorm common room.

The next day the sun came out briefly, causing a small amount of snow melt. Then it turned cold—really cold. That night, Sister Paul and her companions again brought out their shiny bedpans for an evening of sledding. Now the fun was greater because the slope had become an ice chute. Great speeds were obtained coming down the hill, but all control vanished. Braking was done by the sledder digging in her heels in the flat braking area.

Sister Paul came whizzing down the ice chute and stuck out her heels in order to brake—but her heels hit a sheet of ice and she was unable to slow up. She hit the snow pile at the bottom of the hill and, whereas her luge stopped, she became airborne.

She did a forward one-and-a-half, and landed headfirst in the snow. All that could be seen of Sister Paul were two black-stockinged legs sticking straight up in the air, and a round bottom covered by bloomers. Her white nursing habit collapsed around her to blend with the white snow while her disembodied legs waved like wands in the sky.

Flashbulbs began to pop. Student nurses' rosy cheeks paled as they witnessed Sister's predicament. Male onlookers hurried to Sister's legs and began to pull. More flashbulbs popped. Someone had told the newspapers that the hospital nurses had been having fun in the snow the night before, and a photographer and reporter showed up to document what seemed to be a good human interest story, only to find the story of the week—a nun, upside-down in the snowbank, with her bloomers showing. The story made the front page of the second section of the daily newspaper with the headline, "Nun Crashes Her Bedpan."

Sister Paul was none the worse for wear, but shortly thereafter, after the laughter and jokes died down, she disappeared, having been recalled to the mother house, never to be heard from again.

What do you suppose the punishment is for a naughty nun?

❧❀❧

I received a call from the office one morning while making rounds at the hospital in Portland, asking me to get in touch with a woman in the Frog Pond community. She was calling about one of my patients.

When I spoke to the caller, a neighbor of my patient, she explained that my patient had not felt well for a couple of days so she had gone over to see her. The patient said she felt pretty sick with a bellyache and that she was too sick to go to the office. Because she didn't have a phone, she asked her neighbor to ask me to make a house call. This sounded like Mrs.

Madigan in the Onion Swamp all over again. This was different, though, in that I had seen this lady in my office a number of times; hence I was not worried about not being wanted. Furthermore, she had asked me to come—whereas Mrs. Madigan's neighbor had made some assumption which, at the time, I hadn't felt was appropriate; but thank God I went to see her, anyway. Usually, when a person complained of abdominal pain, I would have asked her to come to the office because of the possible need for a blood count or X-ray or some other test. But here was a patient, home alone, and too sick to travel. I had been to her house before and knew she was not an alarmist, so I went.

When I reached the farm, I went to the back door and knocked. No answer. I knocked again—no answer. I hate it when people ring the door bell or knock again before I have a chance to answer the first summons, so I waited awhile before I called out—no answer. Alarmed, I then did a most uncharacteristic thing; I went to the front door to see if there was a doorbell. There wasn't but, peeking through the window, I could see that the front door, as usual, was a non-entrance. A sofa was backed up against the opening. In this part of the country using a front door meant that you were putting on airs. "Y'all come in now, hear?" meant you-all come in the back door into the kitchen. That was where the action was. No one used the parlor.

Returning to the back door, I knocked and called again without any luck, so I pushed open the screen door and walked into the kitchen. I immediately spotted a substantial puddle of fresh blood on the floor.

Recently I had been involved in a homicide, when a deputy sheriff and I had opened the door of another house and tracked a trail of blood to a bedroom, where a man lay dead of a shotgun blast by a person or persons unknown.

Is this another homicide?

Is the perpetrator still here?

Am I in danger? Probably! There was danger in the practice of medicine. I had already proved that in Tonquin.

I backed out and thought about it. *The next house with a phone is a half-mile away. I would need to drive over there, call the sheriff, and wait for him. How long would that take? Maybe fifteen to twenty minutes. What is going on? I'd better go back and find out if someone is bleeding to death.* That seemed to be the greater danger.

Back I went. The blood in the kitchen trailed into the dining room and stopped. There were two exits from the dining room—one to a parlor and one to the bedrooms via a hall. Betting that an injured person, perhaps shot, would head for bed, I proceeded down the hall. Bull's eye! More blood.

The first bedroom was empty. The door was open to the second bedroom and I peeked in, afraid of what I might see. My patient lay collapsed across the bed, soaked with blood and unconscious. Beside her was a blanket. Out from under the blanket peeped a telltale stump of umbilical cord.

Good grief, my patient had had a miscarriage! And she was still bleeding. I began to control the bleeding by uterine massage and medication. As I was working on the mother, I heard a faint sound from the other side of the bed, like a cat. Now wouldn't that be a mess, with a cat prowling through a dead fetus and afterbirth? I pulled back the blanket and, with the blast of cold air, the newborn let out a healthy yell, *wah-wah!*

Holy smoke, here I am with a mother bleeding, a premature newborn that probably doesn't weigh four pounds, and no phone or help. The loneliness of the situation hit me. She might need constant care, but her husband, who worked in town, wouldn't be home until five or six o'clock. I could be marooned until then. The office would have police out looking for me before that. *How much longer am I going to be stuck here?*

I just kept plugging along, and after another half hour the bleeding stopped. I wrapped up the baby in a clean towel. About that time the mother's eyes began to flicker and, with a dose of smelling salts, she woke up and said, "What happened?"

I answered with, "You've had a baby."

"Is that what was wrong?" she ventured.

"Didn't you know?"

"Well, I wasn't having any periods, but I'm over forty, and I thought I was going through the change."

Mother held her baby while I went to get help. I called the ambulance and both patients were transported to the hospital safely. Mother and baby were sent home about a week later, after I had tied her tubes so this wouldn't happen again.

My patient continued to be mystified about being pregnant and not recognizing her condition. I was mystified, too—having never completely understood the human predicament. She later told me that they had telephone service installed, so that in an emergency she would be able to call. I hoped it wouldn't be necessary, but I was sure that if she did call, it wouldn't be for the same thing.

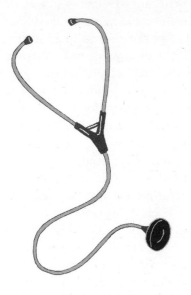

Chapter 14

Aunt Lucy

My grandfather, Joe Halberstadt, died when my mother was a little girl. My grandmother, Katie Lewis, had married Joe Halberstadt of Portland, Oregon, in 1882. She never remarried. She and my mother, Alice, were perhaps closer than most mothers and daughters. So my mother wanted to have a girl baby named Katie, when I came along. Horrors! She got me instead, a disappointment she managed to overcome.

The Lewis family had emigrated from Illinois to Oregon over the Oregon Trail and homesteaded a section of land along the Columbia River just east of Portland. We lost that land for taxes during the Great Depression. Portland International Airport rose from our tears. Katie's brother Leon was the treasurer of the city of Portland from 1871 to 1873. He died a wealthy man as a result of his success in the dry-goods business, but his fortune was dissipated by squabbling relatives. As far back as I can remember, my mother was waiting for her ship to come in from her Uncle Leon's estate. This anticipation was exacerbated during the Depression, but it wasn't until the homestead was lost to taxes that the fact really sank in. No money was left. She and Dad were on their own.

My grandmother died when I was two years old and my mother died when I was fifteen, so my knowledge of my maternal lineage is rather sketchy. My mother's maiden name was Alice Sarah Halberstadt. There is

a city in Bavaria named Halberstadt, and I believe that my maternal grandfather's family must have originated there. Because Halberstadt was in
what was then East Germany, I supposed that I would never get there. So
it was with interest, after I had been in practice for several years, that I
climbed out of bed one stormy night about 2 A.M. in response to a call from
a patient named Regnar Anderson. He was calling on behalf of his recently
widowed sister, just arrived to live with him, a Mrs. Lucy Halberstadt. Reg,
a bachelor, had told me that his sister was coming, for which he was very
glad as her company seemed a godsend to ease his loneliness in later life;
but he had only referred to her as Lucy. Mrs. Halberstadt, according to
Reg, had a high fever, severe cough, and was out of her head.

While on the road to the Anderson house in the Durham
community, about three miles across the river from our home in Tualatin,
I thought about the name, Halberstadt. I wondered if this could be a long-
lost relative. Even if she wasn't, maybe this woman could tell me about
the city of Halberstadt.

I also pondered the romanticized tales of my grandfather. Joe
Halberstadt was a well known man about town in Portland near the end
of the nineteenth century. Among my keepsakes is an old medal,
proclaiming Joe as the most popular man in the city for that year. Portland
wasn't a very big place around the turn of the century, but it was larger
than Sherwood, Oregon (where I won the Distinguished Service Award
from the Junior Chamber of Commerce about fifty-five years later).

Family lore related Joe's great love for his daughter and the unusual
gifts he brought home from his trips as a traveling salesman. Two such
gifts were a bat in a cage, and a baby alligator that took up residence in
the bathtub. The gator eventually went to the zoo. I never learned of the
disposition of the bat.

On my way to the Anderson place, I drove across the old Tualatin
River bridge. A glance out of the car window at the muddy waters below
led me to consider its stability. The ancient, cantilevered structure seemed
to groan with the weight of my red Pontiac. In the brief illumination of
my headlights, the river was high. Across the bridge, I turned right onto
the river road and went to Regnar Anderson's. This area had flooded in
the past and I wondered what the chances were of a flood occurring this
rainy season. Reg had lived alone as long as I had known him and, as a
bachelor, he kept himself pretty mobile. When the waters rose, he left.
Now there would be two of them. Would Reg and Mrs. Halberstadt, née
Anderson, if she were as sick as Regnar claimed, be able to evacuate the
area quickly should the need arise?

As I entered the Anderson driveway, it seemed the storm had increased its ferocity. The stately fir trees that surrounded the house bent in response to the sudden gusts of wind. Big Douglas fir trees are pretty tough old guys and seldom fall over in wind storms; but some of the large branches were known to snap off during storms and a big one could crush a house. The headlights of my car revealed the usually sluggish, muddy waters of the river, out of its banks and rising on the lawn. Another foot or two of floodwater would threaten the house.

Reg met me at the door with a worried look on his face. "She's bad," he said. "I can't control her. She's raving."

Reg preceded me into the bedroom where I beheld a most unlovely sight. Mrs. Halberstadt was a witch!

No doubt about it. She was a disheveled old witch.

She was ugly. Her wild hair streamed out of control in all directions, her eyes shone with a crazed light as they darted about the partially lighted room; and the laughing cackle that emanated from her snaggle-toothed mouth was constant and eerie. As I came closer, I noticed a large wart-like excrescence erupting from the tip of her nose, much like a miniature rhinoceros horn.

Gulping back my first reaction, I approached the bed. "How do you do, Mrs. Halberstadt. I am the doctor. What seems to be the trouble?"

Cackle, cackle, cackle!

"How long have you had the cough, Mrs. Halberstadt?"

Cackle, cackle!

"Would you please hold the thermometer in your mouth, under your tongue?"

It fell on the floor and broke.

Her arms flailed about, gesticulating wildly in what seemed to be magic incantations, especially at 2 A.M. on a wild and stormy night. The fury of the storm seemed to increase as the seemingly mad old lady shrieked her insane laughter. I wondered if Reg regarded the situation with the same sense of unreality that I experienced.

I took my stethoscope out of my bag and asked her to breathe through her mouth and please not talk.

Cackle, cackle.

She never stopped. I could hear nothing. But, as I placed my stethoscope on the front of her chest to try to hear her heart tones, it hit me.

The lady was drunk!

The smell was overpowering. I looked at her dilated pupils, her suffused skin, and her gesturing and cackling. I decided that I had better things to do than to try to treat a drunken old biddy, even if her name was Halberstadt. In reality, I couldn't treat her, as I didn't have any diagnosis except for what Reg had said; and with the vigor she was exhibiting, I presumed she would not die before morning.

I told Reg that when she had sobered up, he should take her into Portland to see a doctor. I cautioned him to keep watch on the river and not delay too long to evacuate, should that be his decision. I pointed out that extra time might be needed because of his sister's condition. I went home to bed. I had a dream that Disney could have made a movie about, full of witches and monsters who all seemed to be after me.

About twelve hours later, in the midst of my usual busy day at the office, Cora, the receptionist, called me to the phone, saying that it was a patient on whom I had made a house call the night before and how come I hadn't told her about the house call? Her inference was that I had pocketed the fee and not turned it in. *What fee?* Cora didn't like me when I arrived, didn't like me at the time, and furthermore, it was now apparent that she didn't trust me, either.

I wanted to refuse the phone call. I wasn't exactly in the best possible frame of mind, having had little sleep—most of which had been restless as a result of my encounter with the "witch"—and now Cora hadn't lightened my mood. But the name Halberstadt continued to tickle my sense of the bizarre. Imagine having a witch as a relative!

I went to the phone and said, "May I help you?"

The "witch" replied with well-modulated tones and without any semblance of a cackle, "Doctor, I want to apologize for my behavior last night. Reg explained what happened. I don't remember it, but he tells me that I was drunk. Doctor, I am so sick. Would you come to see me?"

I thought, *She's hung over, but what the heck.* I said I would come. As I drove back to the Anderson house on the river on my way home from the office late that afternoon, the storm had ended. When I entered the driveway, it was obvious that the storm had been particularly vicious, because of the number of large tree limbs scattered about the yard; fortunately none of them were house-crushers. The flood waters had receded. In fact, the sun was just beginning to pierce the clouds, sending down beams of God-light to the upper branches of the tall fir trees.

Her story unfolded this way. Lucy Halberstadt had always been a teetotaler. She had developed a heavy cough and a fever. A helpful neighbor brought her a bottle of bourbon and told her to sip a little bit to cut the phlegm. She was having a lot of phlegm. Being a nondrinker, she did not recognize what was happening.

Now, with her dental bridge in place, her hair combed, and the cackle eliminated, she was a very nice lady—not handsome, but nice. She still had a warty nose. Within weeks I removed the blemish on her nose with an electric needle. She definitely was not a witch. She became better-looking as she recovered from pneumonia.

I found out that she was my great-aunt by marriage. She had married one of Joe Halberstadt's two brothers. All three left the city of Halberstadt, Germany, when quite young, and settled in Canada. Joe was the prodigal—living in the States, siring my mother, and then falling off a train. His brothers hadn't known what had happened to him, and now both of them were gone.

I took care of Lucy for the rest of that fall. We planned to try to research my family tree. Unfortunately, we never finished it.

∽∾

It was later that year when a local support group for Native Americans asked physicians to volunteer to provide health care to students enrolled in the Indian school at Chemawa, located near Salem. I decided it was time for me to give something back to the community in return for the education I had received.

Actually, we gave something every day. Patients who couldn't pay were not charged, or if they were charged, they were not harassed if they got behind. When a mother came in with three sick kids and it seemed that they all had the same acute illness, they were only charged for one office visit. On house calls, when I saw more than one family member, I billed only one house call. We acted as team physicians for the high school as a community service and I taught residents and interns at St. Vincent's as part of my staff responsibility. In order to do more on a formal basis, I volunteered for one afternoon a week for one month each year at the Indian school.

My interest in Native Americans stemmed from an experience as a child when I witnessed an event of flagrant exploitation of Native Americans. I was about nine years old when I went on a trip with my mother and her business partner, Bessie McCoy. Driving the Redwood Highway north of San Francisco, we came upon a group of American Indian marathon runners. They were running from San Francisco to Eureka, California, for prizes and to demonstrate the plight of the Indian people. Actually, they were being exploited by the promoters who had organized the run. We hadn't heard about any of this until we came upon one of the runners, somewhere near Ukiah, California.

This man was the first runner we came to, and he was the last runner in the race. He wasn't going anywhere. He was fat, pooped, hot, discouraged, and sitting along the side of the road in his running suit with a number on his back. We passed him and stopped for gas near Ukiah. In the middle of summer this seemed the hottest spot on earth. The attendant told us about the race but thought all the runners had already gone by. We bought a Coke and sat in the shade to drink it, when along came "Tail End Charlie." We asked him if he would like a Coke. "Yup," he said, and so we shared.

Tail End Charlie told us how he happened to be there. Each runner paid his own way to the race, and if he finished he got fifty dollars. The promoter had scheduled "Indian Festivities" in towns along the way for which he charged admission, but did not share the proceeds with the runners. Any of the Indians who didn't finish—tough! They received no money and then had to get home on their own. Tail End Charlie didn't look as if he would finish. He didn't look as if he would get past Ukiah.

We asked him if he would like a ride. "Well," he said, "I guess if I could just catch up with the others, maybe I could get my fifty dollars."

So, what the hell, we took him in. We went a long distance with him crouching down on the floor in front of the back seat; in fact I had my feet on his back most of the time. He didn't seem to care. Apparently, none of his brethren, whom we passed, saw him. When we neared the middle of the pack of runners, we let our passenger out where he couldn't be seen, and we went on into Eureka.

My sense of justice was satisfied by helping a nice guy get what I thought he had suffered for. In these days of the Depression, the fact that we were helping this guy to cheat did not register with me and, if it had, it probably would not have mattered. I saw only a hot, tired guy who was trying to earn a buck.

The large, elegant Eureka Inn, where we stayed for several nights, was where the race ended. On the night when the awards ceremony was held, we saw Tail End Charlie get his fifty bucks. Once the awards had been distributed, the promoters continued the "Festivities" while the tired Indians were bused to smaller quarters in a lousy section of town, where there was no racial or color code. It seemed as if no one expected Indians, no matter how brave or athletic they might be, to stay at the fancy head-quarters hotel!

This was my first introduction to segregation by race and I didn't like what I saw.

❧❀❧

During my first session at the Chemawa Indian School as a volunteer physician, I realized that I was seeing a lot of kids with strange-looking eyes. Their upper lids were bulging slightly; some of them had inflamed conjunctiva (lining of the eyelids), and some showed a lot of scar tissue on the surface of the eyeball. The Native American nurse who was assisting me called my attention to the fact that this was trachoma, or Egyptian conjunctivitis.

I knew about the problem but had never seen a case. The disease is a highly contagious bacterial infection, endemic in some Mediterranean countries and among the American Indian people of the Southwest. Transmission is by hand-to-eye contact or by flies. It is also a by-product of crowded living conditions and dirt. Treatment was (and still is) through the application of a suitable antibacterial ointment for a period of four to eight weeks. The ointment was expensive, difficult to apply, and required long-term perseverance that seemed difficult for people not attuned to modern medical care.

The result of poor patient compliance, or of not being treated at all, was what I saw that first day in the clinic at Chemawa. Little kids had white scars that inhibited their vision over the surface of their eyes. Others had eyelids that turned outward so the eye wasn't protected, which caused ulceration of the cornea. Some of these kids were partially blind. I hoped that someday I could do more to help the Native American kids like those I met at Chemawa.

❧❀❧

That winter it rained. Of course, in Oregon it rains a good part of the time. But that particular winter, the everlasting drizzle and clouds turned into an everlasting downpour. Fields had standing water, the Onion Swamp resembled a lake, and the layers of mud on kitchen floors increased to new thicknesses from kids' muddy boots tracking it in from outside. House calls became rain calls and muddy lanes leading to farmhouses often were not traversable. My galoshes were covered with mud, the car was as dirty as a mud wrestler emerging from the ring, and I was discouraged. Furthermore, the river was rising again, having subsided from its high when I went to see Aunt Lucy. To top it off, my friend Pinky was making noises like he wanted to go back to Nevada where he had come from or maybe get his company to let him move to California.

The Tualatin River is usually benign—a slow, meandering, brownish stream. Trees overhang its banks. Numerous bends and back-waters are the hangouts of large-mouth bass. The river often seems discouraged and apathetic, like a human down on his luck, who just "don't want to make no trouble."

This year was different. It was trouble. It was raging, savage, undercutting its banks, overflowing fields and farmyards. Finally, it even spread into the town of Tualatin where we lived. This was too much. It was vacation time. Glad and I stashed the kids with Pinky and his family.

I wanted to see Aunt Lucy Halberstadt before we left on our vacation, so I braved the Tualatin River Bridge one more time. I told her that Glad and I were going on a trip and hoped that we could get together upon our return. We wanted to try to start recording my maternal family tree. Aunt Lucy was enthusiastic about the project and said, "I'll get on it as soon as I feel a little better." She had not had a recurrence of the pneumonia that had necessitated my first house call.

"What's wrong?" I asked.

"Nothing," was the reply. "Just a little flu bug. I'll be better in a day or two."

I checked her over. She seemed okay except for high blood pressure, for which I was already treating her.

Glad and I drove to Long Beach, California, to see her relatives. The visit was cut short when it began to rain, again. We headed east in the general direction of Phoenix.

Just before dawn, we turned into Joshua Tree National Monument, to experience our first sunrise in the desert. We parked the car at a little campground beside the beautiful, clear water of Cottonwood Springs and ate our breakfast, packed by Aunt Emma, one of the Long Beach relatives, who had intended it for our lunch. The blue-shaded hills in front of us, studded with small cacti, hid the rising sun, but allowed the light to begin to clothe the desert scene—changing colors and illuminating canyons and cliffs until, all at once—like a lightning bolt—the sun launched itself screaming over the mountain to bathe us and the whole world around us in its golden rays. We shed our jackets and basked in its warmth, as one would bathe in a heated pool, and luxuriated in our first experience in the desert.

When we arrived in Phoenix, we selected an inviting resort just off the highway. There was a pool, surrounded with rooms opening onto it and palm trees strung with colored lights. It seemed splendid and probably was not bad for Phoenix in the fifties. We didn't know about the luxurious Arizona Biltmore in the hills or Camelback Inn in Scottsdale. Phoenix had not yet attained worldwide resort status.

Next morning we breakfasted al fresco, poolside, and soaked up sunshine throughout the morning. It was a relief to wear swim trunks rather than rain gear.

About noon, just before it seemed time for a Tom Collins, a woman emerged from the men's lavatory just behind the pool, shrieking, "Help, help, I need a doctor!"

I rushed over and said, "I'm a doctor."

She pointed to the men's room, and at a still form lying on the floor. Her husband had complained of a pain, gone into the bathroom, and died. She had waited awhile and finally had gone looking for him. That's where I entered the picture. As on that day in Tonquin, here was a family member who could not accept sudden death. Who can? But this lady had long fingernails. When I could not bring her husband back, she turned on me. During her assault on me, she scratched my back until blood ran. After trying unsuccessfully to console her, Glad and I retired to our room. We washed my wounds and I again pondered the dangers inherent in the practice of medicine.

The place seemed a bit tarnished. And it had begun to rain, so we packed up and headed home.

Upon our return to Oregon, we found the floodwaters had receded. But one night during a blinding rain before the storm ended, a truck had careened into one end of the Tualatin River Bridge. Although the force of the impact was not great, it was enough to end the life of the old structure. It collapsed into the river.

Even with a new bridge I would never again cross the river to visit Aunt Lucy, for she had died during our absence. I had lost the opportunity to get to know her and to explore her knowledge of my heritage.

When we went to Pinky's house to claim our three children, he had a funny story to tell us. Our youngest, Pamela, was an intrepid little soul. While visiting Pinky and his family, she had wandered into the barn by herself. Interested in what the cows were doing, she crawled up on the edge of the manger and fell in. When Carol found her, she was laughing and giggling—delighted with a big old bossy cow whose large tongue was busily licking her face.

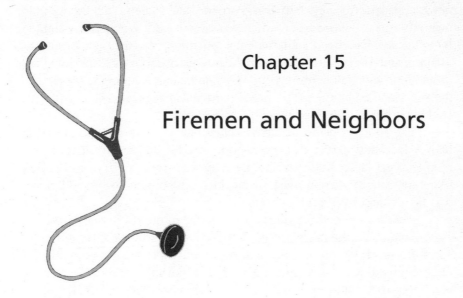

Chapter 15

Firemen and Neighbors

The Tualatin Volunteer Firemen not only put out fires, they also manned the local ambulance. Seven of the firemen were on the paid staff. These regulars, including the chief, worked in pairs and they were the ones who drove the ambulance as well as fighting fires. The volunteers, who were local businessmen and farmers, came in response to an alarm. The main fire station was in the city of Tualatin. There was a branch in Sherwood.

∞

The firemen posed some interesting problems for me from time to time. One night the doorbell rang and a father stood in the driveway with a baby in his arms. "Doctor," he cried, "my baby has turned blue."

"Quick, put him on the dining room table." Whoops, I did it again! Well, a cyanotic baby is a true emergency. I could see the reflection of the blinking red light of the ambulance as it waited in my driveway to see if they would have to speed this child to a hospital. Knowing the firemen were there was reassuring.

I checked the kid. Everything looked normal—heart, lungs, airway, reflexes—all okay and with normal color.

159

The story was that this out-of-town family was driving down the newly opened freeway between Portland and Salem, where we had formerly run our horses, but which was now paved. Wonderfully lighted interchanges had been built at each off-ramp. As the family neared Tualatin and the Tualatin off-ramp, the mother observed that the baby had turned blue and Dad, a resourceful man, immediately spun the car over to the right lane and exited. The fire department was in the center of town. Dad burst in, yelling, "My baby has turned blue!"

The firemen never hesitated. They put an oxygen mask over the baby's face and escorted the family to my house. It took less than a minute to get there. Upon arrival, the baby was crying lustily and fighting to get that smelly, rubber mask off his face. The only color I could detect was his redness from crying.

Another source of crying was when one of our own kids, awakened from sleep by all the noise and commotion, began to wail. Glad got up to comfort our child and I comforted the patient's parents by pronouncing the baby well. Reassured in the knowledge that their child was all right and their trip could continue without difficulty, the family left. The firemen went back to the station and I went back to bed. Glad was still up, trying to get our own little one back to sleep.

In thirty minutes the doorbell rang and there was the father with the baby, again.

"It happened again, Doc, as soon as I got back on the freeway. I had to go ten miles to get to the next exit before I could turn back."

I checked the baby. All okay! My head began to work. I asked, "This only happened when you neared the off-ramp?"

"Just then, Doc."

"And how was it when you went back onto the freeway?"

"Well, Doc, it seemed to happen again, just as we got back on the interstate here in Tualatin; but it was okay until we got near Wilsonville. Then it got worse."

I had just solved the diagnostic problem of the ages. "Your baby is okay," I told the parents. "Whenever you passed under the blue arc lights leading up to the off-ramps, your baby appeared to change color."

The parents left, chagrined. The firemen owed me one.

❧∞❧

Patients no longer come to the doctor's home, not even in Tualatin—which has grown to be a wealthy suburb, thanks to the paving of that dirt strip we used for a race track. Tualatin has its own hospital and I doubt that the volunteer fire department still exists. When we lived in California, events such as patients arriving at our front door or chasing me down at the home of friends didn't happen as often; but they did happen.

On a Saturday afternoon when Glad and I were starting our new hobby of gourmet cooking together, our next door neighbor had a gastric hemorrhage. I had rushed off with him to the hospital and was gone all afternoon and evening while our guests came and went.

Then there was the father who came to the door during the dinner hour, bearing a little glassine packet of grassy-looking material he had found in his car after his son had borrowed it. He suspected the teenager of smoking pot and wanted me to identify the stuff and then tell him what to do. Raw cannabis was not on the demonstration agenda of Stormin' Norman, the pharmacology professor, so I wasn't a lot of help. I told the father, "Go see Johnny and ask him quietly. If the answer is yes, don't lose your cool; and if it's no—believe him."

He did as I suggested, and the kid said, "Oh boy! There's the catnip Mom had me pick up at the store when I got her groceries." The father immediately called me with the good news, thus further disturbing the dinner he had interrupted the first time.

Perhaps the most dramatic visit of a sick neighbor occurred on a night when Robert and Betty Young came to dinner. Having the Youngs to dinner was heady stuff for an ex-country doctor, and we prepared for days in advance so that everything would go smoothly. I checked out to the other doctors in my call group so that the evening would be free for entertaining our guests.

The Youngs arrived in a limousine with chauffeur, a sight not common in our neighborhood, and apparently noticed by at least one of our neighbors, whose son, Jocko, had an earache. Jocko, actually Casimir Jackson Levine III, didn't like his real name. If someone unknowingly addressed him by his first name, as I did the first time we met, he drew himself up to his full height of thirty-nine inches and said, in his five-year-old soprano, "I'm not Casimir! I'm Jocko!" No one really knew where the name "Jocko" came from except that it was probably some kind of a contraction of Jackson, but it was his name and you had better not forget it.

Jocko and his family were all patients of mine. They were a little unusual in that Mrs. Levine, having heard of me through other neighbors, made an appointment to interview me as her prospective family doctor. Whereas in Sherwood, Sam and I were the only physicians unless people wanted to travel some distance, in Los Angeles County there were twelve thousand doctors, and in the South Bay area where we were located, there were at least a thousand to choose from. Interviewing your prospective doctor was, and still is, a good idea. When I passed muster, I became the Levine family doctor. They lived so close that a couple of times when Jocko or his brother was slightly ill, I had said, "Oh, just bring him over."

On the evening when the Youngs came to dinner, Mrs. Levine, who knew my home phone number and didn't have to go through the answering service, called and said, "I know you have company. I saw that big car in your driveway, but little Jocko has an earache and you told me always to call right away. I'll bet you've checked out to another doctor and if I call the answering service I'll have to explain everything; so, I thought if you could just call in a prescription for the same stuff you gave him before, you wouldn't have to see him, and I'll bring him to the office tomorrow or whenever you want." All this was said without taking a breath, as if she were afraid that, if she stopped, I might say no.

I covered the mouthpiece of the telephone and whispered to Bob Young, "You want to make a real house call?"

He bobbed his head affirmatively, so I said, "Mrs. Levine, I think someone should see him. My new assistant is here having dinner with us. I'll send him down to take a look at Jocko's ears."

Jocko's mother protested saying, "Please don't go to any trouble; I don't want to interrupt your dinner party; just call in a prescription." I told her that we hadn't started dinner and this was a good time for the family to meet my new assistant, anyway, so I would send him right down.

We took my car, a two-door Olds Cutlass, with Robert Young driving and with me crouched down in the back seat. I wasn't too sure about his driving, never having seen him drive a car because Universal Studio provided him with a car and driver. However, we made it safely down the street. When we arrived, Bob got out of the car and, with my medical bag in hand, went up the walk and rang the doorbell.

I knew it was time to raise my head when I heard Stephen, Jocko's older brother, yell "Mom, Dr. Welby is at the front door!" Mrs. Levine screamed when she saw my new assistant, Marcus Welby, M.D., standing there. We all had a great laugh. Dad got out his camera and memorialized the event and I treated Jocko by calling in the prescription that Mrs. Levine had asked for in the beginning.

To my knowledge, Robert Young made only one other house call that was not a part of the television show. That came when he was auctioned off for charity and had to go to Texas to make the call. The auction price was fifty thousand dollars.

He didn't charge the Levines.

❧

One misty, cold morning, at 5 A.M., the Tualatin fire department called to ask if I would come to an accident scene. A man was trapped under a car. A sedan had failed to negotiate the right angle turn at the corner of Nyberg and Meridian roads less than a mile from where I lived. The outside curve of the turn had a narrow shoulder and then a sharp dropoff of about eight feet, covered by blackberry brambles. Ironically, this is the site of the present Meridian Hospital.

When I arrived, I could see the bottom of a car with all four wheels pointed heavenward. Fire and police vehicles had arrived. A tow truck was standing by, waiting for me to determine the status of the human whose only visible part was a hand, protruding from beneath the roof of the car and almost hidden by the interlacing wild blackberry vines.

I climbed down the bank and immediately tore my pants. I hadn't taken time to choose old clothes, but grabbed the first pair of pants available. "Son," my father had told me when I was about ten years old, "never empty your pockets at night before you go to bed. Always hang your pants in the same place, so they're easy to find; if you do this, and there is a fire at night, you won't waste time looking for your trousers, and you won't find yourself out on the street at night with no pants, no keys, and the front door locked."

So I ripped a good pair of pants, but I didn't much care, because the person under the overturned car was a much greater concern. The tow truck operator and the firemen were awaiting my instructions as to whether or not to lift the car, fearing that if the person was alive, tilting the car back on him might cause more injuries.

I got down on my hands and knees (further wrecking my pants, and my hands as well) and tried to take his pulse. I couldn't feel one. The absence of a pulse did not help me to determine if the victim was dead or alive, because the edge of the car roof was pinching the outstretched arm just above the wrist and could easily be shutting off the blood supply, obliterating the pulse.

I tried to shove my fingers up to a point where I could feel more of the victim or see into the tangled vines. This didn't work. So, two firemen, a state trooper, the tow truck operator, and I lifted the car very carefully, so that I could squeeze a little way under. I felt the victim's arm. It was cold and clammy, but so was the weather and the man had lain there for an hour or more.

I needed to reach in farther. I asked the guys if they could hold the car higher, so that I could crawl in. They thought they could.

Thought they could? Gee, if they can't there will be two guys stuck here, and one of them will be me. This was a real danger, worse than being attacked by distraught relatives, worse than breaking my ankle in a farmyard, worse than constantly being exposed to infectious disease. *If that darn car falls on me, I could be killed.* There wasn't time to debate the pros and cons of what to do; I crawled in. I was shaking so that I was afraid I might dislodge the vehicle.

With my head under the car I heard a sound, more like a gurgle than anything else, but emanating from a trapped victim. Someone was alive. Was the sound from the owner of the hand or were there others in there? The men continued lifting the car, very slowly and evenly, by hand rather than with the tow truck winch.

They lifted.

I crawled in a little farther. I heard labored breathing. There was at least one live person in there. I crawled on. With the aid of a flashlight, I saw a face—and it was breathing. The victim had been thrown out of the car and then the car had rolled on top of him, but he was cushioned by the brambles. They may have scratched my hands and torn my pants but the brambles had probably saved this man's life.

The firemen passed me an oxygen mask with a long hose attached to the oxygen tank, located in the fire department ambulance. One fireman left the scene to get more oxygen, in order to be prepared for the long process of extricating the victim.

By now, the guys had propped up the edge of the car, with rocks and debris holding it in place—not a very reassuring foundation for safety. I backed out and the firemen took over the extrication process.

There was only one occupant, and he was alive. He had severe crushing injuries, but he survived. When I arrived home before going to the hospital with the patient, Glad remarked that I must have had to clean out a den of wildcats.

"No," I said. "Just blackberry bushes—and no berries ripe enough to eat. How about some breakfast?"

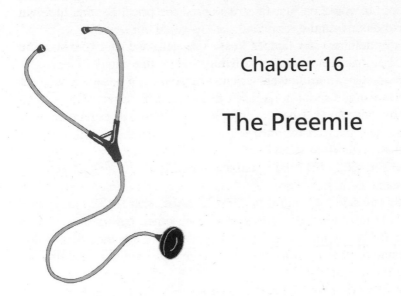

Chapter 16

The Preemie

Before I started medical school, just after the end of World War II, the school notified me of materials that I would need to purchase. One of these, and by far the most difficult to get, was a microscope with an oil immersion lens. I wasn't sure what a new one would cost, but whatever it was we couldn't afford it. We haunted surgical supply companies looking for a used scope, to no avail. Shortages resulting from the war had caused people with this kind of equipment to hang onto it. They certainly didn't have new ones for a lowly medical student; new models were going to their best customers, such as commercial laboratories, colleges, hospitals and the medical school itself.

Finally, as we were about to give up hope of ever finding one, we saw a newspaper ad that inspired us to respond immediately. We made an appointment and were at the advertiser's house within an hour. The young man who greeted us told us that there had been several calls after ours, but we were the first ones to arrive. He explained that his mother was doing the selling and she hoped we would be the buyer because, as I had told her on the phone, I was a medical student. Her recently deceased husband had been a physician and she hoped that a doctor, or a soon-to-be doctor, would be the buyer.

The physician's son took us into the house, where we examined the microscope. It would do just fine. We asked the price. By this time the widow had come into the room and she answered our question.

"Fifty dollars," she said. "I know you will take care of it like my husband did. It was the war that killed him. He retired in 1940, but went back into practice after the war started because there was such a need for doctors. He worked so hard." A tear slid down each cheek.

Glad looked sad. I had a difficult time talking, as it seemed as if something was stuck in my throat. I finally squeaked out, "You can be assured that I will do my best."

The son said, "I'll carry it out to your car."

"I can handle it."

"No," he said. "I'll put it in a box with the other stuff."

Other stuff? Glad and I looked at each other, but by now he had disappeared down a set of stairs into what I assumed was the cellar. When the son came back up he was carrying a large box. "You can take this out to the car while I get the rest."

For fifty dollars we had purchased not only the microscope, but all of the doctor's instruments. We had bone instruments for doing orthopedic surgery, Simpson forceps for doing deliveries, ear-nose-and-throat tools for doing office examinations, a complete set of instruments for drilling holes in the skull for brain surgery (complete with a Gigli saw for turning a cranial bone-flap), and another silver case containing a complete set of instruments to do a tracheostomy (cutting the windpipe to provide an airway). There was also a leather case containing vials of old-fashioned powders that the doctor had used as a portable pharmacy.

When we got home and checked the equipment I was flabbergasted. I knew what most of it was used for, from my experience as a surgical assistant in the Navy during the war. Would I ever use any of it? Probably not.

But Glad and I are sentimentalists. We quickly decided that, in order to honor the doctor who had previously owned this stuff and to carry out our promise to his widow to take good care of not only the microscope, but all of the medical and surgical paraphernalia we had acquired, we would make good use of the microscope and carefully store the rest.

I used the microscope throughout my medical training and during my years in practice. I still have it in my office where I can see it now, as I am writing. Its presence honors the life of J. T. LeFebre, M.D., of Portland, Oregon, a pioneer of medicine who died as a result of the war—

not on the battlefield—but as a war casualty, nonetheless. At the time I didn't realize that the most important set of instruments that I acquired that day was the tracheostomy set.

Delivering a premature baby is a dicey situation at best. Anything can go wrong during the delivery or in the neonatal period. Premature babies cannot be cared for in a general hospital but must be transferred to a neonatal intensive care unit. In the mid-1950s, there was no such thing. The best treatment available in our area was Doernbecher Children's Hospital, associated with the University of Oregon Medical School in Portland.

When I delivered Betty Schlemmer's baby at Tuality Hospital, he weighed only three and one-half pounds. After the delivery I called Children's Hospital and told them I had a seriously underweight newborn. The pediatrician on call advised me to watch the baby for a few hours and, if the vital signs were stable and I felt that it was safe for the little guy to travel, send him in by ambulance with a pediatric nurse in attendance for emergencies.

I had some very anxious hours waiting around the hospital in Hillsboro to see if the baby was stable enough to travel. I wanted that wee soul out of my hands and into the hands of experts with all the latest equipment as soon as possible. After three hours of checking vital signs, color, and general condition, I couldn't stand it any longer and called the fire department to send the ambulance to Hillsboro, pick up the baby and take him to Portland.

"Not us," said the chief. "We don't have equipment for that sort of thing."

"Nor does anyone else," I answered. "Furthermore, they suggested that we send a pediatric nurse with the baby. There isn't any such thing outside of the medical school hospital or Children's Hospital, so I'm going to ride along; and if I can go, you can go."

The baby arrived safely in Portland. My car languished in Hillsboro for a couple of days until my partner and I could arrange to ride together to make hospital rounds and I could pick it up. I received weekly reports on the preemie. Finally, the pediatricians let me know that, in about a week, the baby would reach five pounds. It was their policy to send the baby home at that weight. They would tell the mother to bring the infant to my office for a regular checkup in ten days.

The Schlemmers were peckerwoods. They lived quite a distance from the office, out in the country. In the past they hadn't demonstrated much in the way of thoughtful care of their kids. They weren't bad folks but, maybe, not too smart. I was worried about a fragile, five-pound baby at the Schlemmer house.

Mrs. Schlemmer notified the office on which day she would bring the little one in for a well-baby checkup. When she and the baby arrived at the office, there was quite a commotion in the front office. Marcia, our nurse, came running into the room in which I was seeing another patient and shouted, "Doctor, come quick!"

She scared the hell out of the patient I was seeing and scared me too. Marcia was not an alarmist. As we ran down the hall she blurted out, "It's the Schlemmer baby. He's blue!"

This wasn't some kid whose mother had mistaken the blue vapor lights on the interstate for cyanosis; this kid was not only blue, he was turning black!

I asked the mother how long his color had been bad. She answered, "Just started on the way over here, Doctor."

"Has he been sick?"

"Just for a couple of days, Doctor."

"Why didn't you call?"

"Well, we were coming in today, anyway, and I thought he would be all right."

During this time I had been checking him over. The baby had a high fever, congested lungs, and a stiff neck. He had acute spinal meningitis with pneumonia. His breathing was labored, and his color was worsening. He was going to die in a few minutes. His airway was obstructed and, because of the meningitis, he hadn't the strength to forcibly push the air down into his lungs. I needed a way to get oxygen directly to his lungs.

Because of all the commotion my partner wandered in. He took one look at the baby and said, "Jesus, we'd better get him off to Portland, fast!"

I said, "Marcia, go into the storeroom and get that old tracheostomy set, the one with the bright silver case. Hurry!"

My partner looked at me with awe. "You're crazy! You can't do a trach on a five-pound baby. You're going to kill him!"

"He's going to die, anyway. Will you help me?"

"Oh hell, come on, let's do it."

With an old tracheostomy set, a relic of World War I that the old doctor had in his office and had never used because it was not a usual office procedure—either in his time or ours—the two of us, with Marcia's help, pulled it off. As soon as we made our incision, controlled the bleeding, and inserted the infant cannula (breathing tube) into his trachea, the blue-black color faded to a dusky red. The baby was still a very sick kid, but looked as if he would survive long enough to get to Children's Hospital. I called there and told them what we had done and that I was sending him in. The firemen came again and took the baby and the mother to Portland. This time I didn't ride along. There was nothing else I could do.

Hours later the medical director from Children's called. He said the baby was still alive and, with the aid of intravenous antibiotics, looked as if he might make it. He said, "I don't know how you guys had the courage to do what you did."

In hindsight, I didn't either.

That baby was still alive because of the bargain Dr. LeFebre's widow had given to a poor medical student years before. I called to tell her about it, but the phone had been disconnected.

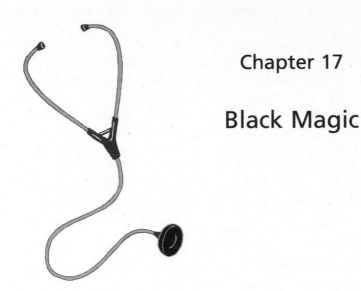

Chapter 17

Black Magic

It is certain that, had I practiced black magic in its usual sense, it would have been frowned upon by the American Medical Association and by the Oregon State Board of Medical Examiners. However, my Black Magic was a horse, properly named Bourbon's Black Magic, Kentucky bred, and about to become the focus of my love-hate relationship.

After Princess and Comanche returned to their home at the beach, I was left with a Stetson hat, half a herd of cattle, and no horse. Going about rectifying this situation prompted a deep discussion between Glad and me. Who would take care of a new horse? Where would it be housed? Would we both have horses, and where would we find enough pasture?

As I traveled about the countryside I admired the sleekest horses with big, round, powerful rumps and no ribs showing. If we acquired a horse, we would want it to have enough pasture with plentiful green grass. During the winter and spring, when we had Comanche and Princess, I almost drooled whenever I saw farms with grass going to waste.

Our little plantation was a single acre, occupied by our three-bedroom, one-and-a-half-bath house, a formal garden with beautifully scalloped flower beds, and about half an acre of grassland beyond the back fence. We decided we could manage to have a horse, but we needed more pasture. The neighbors across the road, with whom we had stabled the beach horses, came to our rescue again. They said we could use their barn and pasture, as before; so with all our ducks in a row, we set out to buy a horse.

The act of buying a horse seemed to be no great problem. We thought about one hundred twenty-five to one hundred fifty dollars would buy a fairly good riding horse of dubious lineage. We were not going in for a fancy horse, just some comfortable old horse. We hadn't counted on Slim.

We went to the local horse dealer. Slim was what one would expect in a cowboy—tall, lean, range-worn. He wore a Stetson, jeans, and a chambray cowboy shirt with a sack of roll-your-own Bull Durham hanging from its pocket. Slim had been a wrangler all his life. He bought and sold horses; he trained horses; he provided horses for parades, carriages, and breeding. Slim was an all-around horse trader.

❧

The term "horse trader" was one I learned early in life, from seeing a 1930s Will Rogers movie entitled *David Harum*.

Movies, when I was a kid, were the thing to do on a Saturday or Sunday afternoon. For a dime, a kid could go to a neighborhood theater and see a double feature, a cartoon and a newsreel, plus a serial like *Zorro* or *The Lone Ranger*. On Monday night, he could be eligible for a drawing for a basket of groceries; on Wednesday night, bank night, he could win as much as fifty dollars or get a set of dishes, one plate at a time, if he went every Friday night. Whatta deal! And sometimes, during Saturday matinee, there would be a little stage show with a contest—like who could spin the best yo-yo or do the best tap dance.

Nobody ever accused David Harum of being dishonest, just a good horse trader—and so was Slim.

"Doctor, you don't want just any old nag. You're a man of means, people look up to you in the community. You want a horse you can be proud of. You need a fine horse that, when you sit on that horse and ride down the road, people will look and say, 'See Doc on that fine horse? There's a man of substance!'"

Well, I was becoming a man of substance, all right, and I thought riding a horse and cleaning the stable would reduce the substance I was accumulating around my middle. But any old horse could do that.

"Now, Doc, I just happen to have a fine horse in my barn. I wasn't going to sell him at all, but just because it's you and because you really need a fine horse like this, I'm gonna let you have him. You remember seeing him in the parade over there in Sherwood last month? He was one of the team of black horses that pulled the carriage for the Queen of the Harvest Festival."

I remembered the Queen of the Harvest Festival. She was the daughter of a patient of mine. But the horses that pulled her carriage? I thought she rode in a Buick convertible. Well, maybe there was a carriage, but for goodness' sake, what did I want with a carriage horse?

"Remember that horse, Doc? I'm gonna saddle him up and put you up on him and you'll know you're on a fine horse. He's five-gaited." Slim left to get the horse.

I pondered what he had said. First, it is true, I secretly wanted a fine horse—at least one better than my partner's hoity-toity little mare who was too good for cow-work, the one that chickened out and ran away during the roundup. Second, I wondered about five gaits. My experience was walk, trot, and gallop. What else was there? Finally, I did not own a carriage, did not plan to own a carriage, and what good would a carriage horse be in another roundup? I should have realized that Glad would forbid another roundup if the subject ever came up, again.

Slim emerged from the barn atop the biggest, blackest, fire-eatingest horse I had ever seen. The horse's eyes rolled. A fleck of foam hung from his lip, his neck was arched like a show horse (which he had been), and his tail was held erect, curling over his sleek rump. The horse danced sideways as he approached. This was not the horse for me; this horse needed a real horseman, not a country doctor turning cowboy.

Slim dismounted and handed me the reins. "I want you to set up on this horse. I want you to feel the e-e-asy motion of his rack."

What is a rack? I didn't want to embarrass myself by asking, so I agreed. But then, I asked, "This horse won't want to run away with me, will he?"

"No, Doc, he's magnificently trained. He'll respond to your commands beautifully; but remember, he has a hard mouth. You gotta show him who's boss."

Slim helped me to mount. The black horse turned his head very slowly and looked me over. He evidently did not like what he saw, for he reached back, took the toe of my shoe in his mouth and bit.

"Ouch!" I said.

"Don't let him do that," commanded Slim.

Now, this horse weighed one thousand one hundred pounds, stood sixteen and one-half hands high, and had a mind of his own. I pulled his head around and kicked him in the flanks with both feet. Whoops! I shouldn't have done that. We took off at a gallop from a standing start, just like Roy Rogers and Trigger.

Slim was yelling, "Slow him down, so he'll rack."

Hell, I wanted to slow him down so I wouldn't fall off and break my neck, so I pulled on the reins. The horse did have a hard mouth, characteristic of this kind of show horse. However, pulling hard on the reins slowed him down. Suddenly, we settled into a new gait, one in which there was no bouncing and no jolting, just a little wiggle in my seat—like being in one of those beds in a cheap motel where, for a quarter, the bed vibrates and you get an electric massage. *So, this is the slow rack!* I later learned he also had a fast rack that was just as comfortable but a heck of a lot faster. The rack was also the gait for pulling a sulky in fine harness. In a horse show, sulky drivers careened around the ring at breakneck speed, racking their horses.

The horse and I returned to where Slim was standing with Glad. "Well, that was some ride," I offered.

Slim replied, "Black Magic will always give ya a good ride."

"So his name is Black Magic?" I asked.

"Yup, Bourbon's Black Magic, Kentucky-bred, shown in the ring—never defeated in fine harness," replied Slim.

"Why have you got him and why isn't he shown anymore?" I wanted to know.

Slim answered, "Had him gelded, lost his fire."

"Gee," I said, "it seemed to me he had a lot of fire."

Slim became really conspiratorial and lowered his voice. I guess he didn't want Glad or the horse to hear. "He's an original."

"What's that?"

"Why, Doc, when they castrate a horse, if they leave one of his testicles or a piece of the testicle, they call him an original; cause he still acts like a stallion. Maybe this horse just never forgot that for seven years he was a stallion and covered a lot of mares. He still likes the ladies. This is a showy horse, Doc. You put two people on a corral fence and he'll think he's in a horse show, and he'll fart and lather and foam at the mouth, just remembering the good old days. People will look at you on that horse, Doc, and they'll say, 'Why, that doctor is a fine rider, ain't he?' And all the time you'd jes' be sittin' there, and the horse is dancin' and foamin' and makin' you look good; but he's gentle as a kitten. You better buy him, Doc."

"How much?" I asked, hoping the price was right. Slim was correct; I sure wanted to have that horse. I thought he was the handsomest animal I had ever seen. I would be proud to be seen riding on Black Magic.

"Well, he's worth a lot more; but for you, Doc—because I know you'll tell people where you got this fine horse and they'll come here lookin' for a horse for themselves—just for you, Doc, a thousand dollars."

I was flabbergasted. A thousand dollars for a horse? Out of the question. That was a little less than my monthly income, and it had only been a short time ago when it was almost twice my monthly income. It was obvious that this horse was meant for me, however. I glanced at Glad, who smiled that enigmatic smile—sort of like the Mona Lisa with a toothache. With thoughts of all the other necessities of life that we would have to forego, she nodded her approval; so I made a counter-offer.

"Five hundred," I said.

Once Slim had me bidding, he had me hooked. I was committed. We dickered for a while and I paid more than I should have and he never went to his lowest price; so I bought my first horse. Not a cowboy horse, but a purebred American Saddlebred horse, an original, who had been retrained to western handling.

Slim cautioned me to let Magic know who was the boss—and when we got home, I tried. Oh boy, how I tried; but, after a few months, I had to admit the horse had me buffaloed. He would deliberately step on my foot or bite, whichever was easier. He would pull the lead rope out of my hand and run off thirty to fifty feet and watch me; and when I approached him, he would run another thirty to fifty feet until he became tired of the game.

When I tried to bridle him, he would toss his head so I couldn't reach it and hold his jaws closed so I couldn't put the bit in his mouth. He would not load into a trailer. This caused no end of problems. I wanted to go on trail rides with the other riders in the community. No sir! Not Black Magic. He did not want to go anywhere in a trailer. Getting an eleven-hundred-pound animal to go anywhere he doesn't want to go is a real problem. This was causing a severe strain on my image of myself as an emerging rancher.

Wes Bright, a neighbor and a true horseman, offered to take my horse in his trailer when there was a trail ride scheduled. Wes soon realized that the two of us could not coax, cajole, drag, beat, or push that damn stubborn horse into a trailer. It took four grown men to do the job, and that presupposed that I could catch the knotheaded horse in the first place. The four men deployed themselves: two on either side of the back end of the horse, dragging ropes forward against his hindquarters, one on a lead rope, and one with a stick, batting him on the rear end. The rear end fell to me as this was the place where flying hooves could do the most damage. Well, after all, he was my horse. Once on the trail Magic was okay and loading him to come home was only about one-third of the problem we had starting out. Who said horses were dumb?

His most objectionable habit was to slowly but steadily wheel away from me whenever I put my left foot into the stirrup preparing to mount. This caused me to hop after him, one foot in the stirrup and one on the ground, like some kind of insane acrobat.

Slim had told me that the only way to manage Magic was to demonstrate to him who was the boss. I tried this technique for the better part of a year and failed, miserably. I guess I wasn't a very good boss. How do you boss a horse, anyway? I reflected on the way I treated animals. I liked animals. Pets that we had seemed to like me and seemed willing to do my bidding. After all, I had obedience-trained our collie, Markie. Even Princess and I got along well, so long as I let her run. But Black Magic was nearly always in charge.

With all my frustrations about Black Magic, we still went ahead with the construction of a three-box-stall stable in the back half-acre. Even after we completed the stable, we would still be able to rent the pasture across the road. We wanted to have three horses—one each for Glad and me and one for the children.

We acquired a pregnant, black American Saddlebred mare named Conga Lady. Conga had been bred to a fine bay stallion and would foal in six to seven months. Glad was to ride Conga until she foaled and eventually we could train the foal for Glad to ride.

Conga also had a problem. She was gentle but, in contrast to Magic, she had very little personality. She was easy to saddle and mount, but once you pulled back on her reins, she would rear up on her hind legs and paw the air with her front feet, the way wild horses do in the movies. When you got on this horse you felt like Gene Autry, without a guitar. In real life this was scary. We worried that the darn fool horse would fall over backwards with her rider landing underneath, sporting a broken head.

We received a lot of advice on how to break Conga of rearing, but nothing worked. Finally, Wes told me of the ultimate treatment which he had learned from his granddaddy. When you mount the animal that rears up, carry a short length of a two-by-four board with you. When the horse goes into its act, bring the flat edge of the two-by-four down sharply on its head, right between the ears, and that horse will never do it, again. Or so he said.

When the day came for the ultimate treatment, nobody explained "sharply" to me. When Conga reared, I raised the two-by-four over my head and hit her "sharply" between the ears. Down we both went. Fortunately, I fell free; but Conga was cold-cocked and down for the count. She regained consciousness in a few seconds, but evidently didn't remember what had happened to her; she continued to rear. We never risked the ultimate treatment again.

Well, now we had a horse for me that I could scarcely ride because of his mastery over me; Conga, that Glad did not want to ride because of the fear of falling over backwards; and we still needed a mount for the children. We acquired a pinto Shetland pony mare. Having read a children's story in which the kids fed sugar to the horses and because our middle son Lee liked the name Sally, we called the pony Sugar Sally.

One day when I was out in the stable area cleaning out the stalls, I thought about the futility of spending my time cleaning up after the horses. Shoot, about the only real pleasure I got from having Magic was to look at him. He was a beauty, though merely looking at him was not reward enough. I thought, *Magic, you'll have to go.*

About this time he stuck his big ol' head out of the half-door on his box stall and I spoke to him. "Magic, you great, big, black devil, I love ya, but I can't put up with you much longer." I spoke in soothing tones and I put my hand up and scratched between his ears.

Maybe it was my tone of voice or maybe it was the first time that I had not taken Slim's advice about being the boss; he put his head down and nuzzled me. Now I wrapped my arm around his neck and scratched under his forelock. *What's this?* I thought. I tried again, and he nuzzled me, again. I said, "Hey Magic, let's you and I be friends." I cautiously slipped the head stall over one ear, put the bit in his mouth, threw the saddle on his back, and climbed aboard. I triumphantly rode up to the house so that Glad could see me on my big, black charger, and then we went thundering across the road and up over the hills. We had become a pair. We were a single unit, moving together in rhythm. Our relationship had changed completely. We were pals and enjoying each other's company!

Magic became easy to handle except for loading him into our truck. We were now the proud possessors of a three-quarter-ton Chevrolet pickup truck with a two-horse stall and hood built on the back. The long tailgate served as the loading ramp that Magic still would not climb.

Now, Magic had fallen in love with a girl half his size, our Shetland pony. Like any male in love, he became sort of dopey. For instance, after Sugar Sally had been around for a couple of days, he began to follow her wherever she went. He was moony-eyed.

Don, our older son, wanted to take Sugar Sally to town one day to ride with some friends; so I loaded the pony into the truck. Now, the big black horse was having a fit, stamping and kicking in his box stall. I saw what his problem was. I put a lead rope on his halter, opened his stall, and he ran into the truck. Forever more, loading Magic was a snap, so long as I put Sugar Sally in first. Even when I took her out of the truck after loading Magic, he didn't seem to care. Like all males, he liked a day out with the boys, as long as she stayed home; but she was his girl, and if she left home, he felt the need to chaperone her.

Even after the debacle with Conga Lady as a riding horse, we decided to keep her for breeding. She dropped foals, Mayday Mischief and Mayday Madcap, on two successive May firsts; both were beautiful bay horses. The two young colts would not be ready to ride for three years, so Glad still needed a horse. One of those fine, round-rumped, quarter-horse types that I had so admired became available and we bought him.

Little Joe was half Arabian and half quarter horse. He was full of spirit and, if not ridden hard and often, he became a handful. Because Glad was busy with the kids and their projects, much of the time it became my job to exercise Little Joe. One Saturday in the fall, I rode him up through the filbert orchard across the road, passing a stubble field, to a pasture where sheep were grazing. At the west end of the pasture, far away from the grazing sheep, someone had dug a pit large enough to trap an elephant. Emanating from the pit was a noxious odor that made my horse fidgety. Looking over his head into the pit, I could see sheep carcasses, rotting and covered with quick-lime. Apparently there had been some kind of catastrophe at this ranch, and the owner had disposed of the dead sheep.

Little Joe thought this was a bad place and tried to turn home. I thought it would be a good lesson for him to know who was in charge. He balked. I put the spurs to his flanks; he still resisted. I did it, again, and he began to buck. He wasn't doing little hippety-hops; he had decided to go home, with or without me. With each buck, he tried to wheel around for home, and with each buck I pulled him back. Soon we were bucking and wheeling and bucking and wheeling. This makes bucking in a circle—the worst kind—and I lost my seat. A large, wooden, Mexican stirrup guard caught me in the head as I departed from the horse and I was knocked out. I came to with no horse and a bump on my head, and had to walk to a nearby farmhouse to hitch a ride home. Little Joe was eating grass on the front lawn when I got back.

Subsequently, Magic and I cemented a relationship so friendly that, when I was out working in the yard, I would let him out and he followed me around, poking his big black nose into everything I was doing.

He dearly loved a parade. One year at the local festival, we hired a Portland disc jockey to be Grand Marshall. This guy affected a cowboy demeanor and wore Western clothes, so we supposed that, as Grand Marshall, he would ride a horse in the parade.

On parade day we had Magic all saddled and cleaned up for the drugstore cowboy to ride. The D.J. took one look at this big, black horse who, anticipating a parade, was already strutting around like a big fire-eater, and he said, "I'm not gettin' on that animal or any other animal. I want a convertible."

"We don't have a convertible, but this is a gentle horse. He won't give you any trouble."

"No. No. NO! If I don't get a convertible, I'm not going to be in this stupid parade."

"Look friend, we'd like to point out that you have a contract that doesn't mention how you lead this parade; it just says that you will lead it."

After giving the D.J. a minute to think this over, I said, "You won't have to do a thing. I'll just tie the reins around the saddle horn and you pretend to hold them. The horse will follow the marching band."

Magic knew that he was in a parade and put on one of his best acts. He walked when the band walked and stopped when the band stopped. Sometimes he walked sideways, as if controlling him took a major effort; and when the parade was over, his body was covered with lather. The D.J. never touched the reins. People commented on his fine horsemanship.

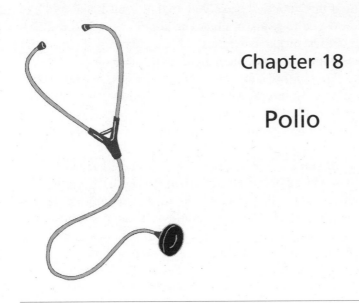

Chapter 18

Polio

Church bells rang throughout the city; the noise was deafening. Was the war over? Could this be a bomb alert? No, we had sirens for that. I was frightened that we were under attack. Bombers with red balls painted on their tails were flying overhead; the noise was too much. I was afraid, I was crying, and my patients would know I was scared. Glad shook me and said, "Answer the phone!"

I woke up, sweating. It was 1:30 A.M. on a Monday morning in the summer, two years before the momentous announcement by Dr. Jonas Salk that a vaccine for the prevention of poliomyelitis, the most dreaded of all childhood diseases, had been developed. Annette Fox, supermom, who spent all her free time on her children's activities, was on the phone. She had four kids. She was forever either carting them around, going to the PTA, having slumber parties, or feeding bunches of kids in her Bull Mountain aerie. There was always a crowd in their home.

This was an active family. If one child wasn't getting cut on a barbed wire fence or falling out of a tree and breaking a bone here and there, another had a runny nose or cough. Supermom took it all in stride, dealing with the minor traumas and vicissitudes of life with aplomb. She had told me, "I don't sweat the petty things and I do pet the sweaty things. I love 'em all."

This night was no exception. She opened the conversation with, "I'm sorry to call at this hour and wake you up, but I felt I had to talk to you. Though I know you're going to think I'm silly."

I wasn't glad to be awake but, at least, I was rid of my nightmare. I didn't know I was going to enter a new nightmare, a real one.

I never had thought this lady was silly. Gregarious, maybe. Active and happy, yes. But silly, no. She had her feet firmly planted on the ground. She knew who she was and where she was going.

I said, "Come on now, Annette, I never think you're silly. What's the problem?"

"Well, Doctor, you know I don't need much sleep. I read in bed a lot. Tonight I was reading *Ladies' Home Journal.* They have a story this month about polio. I know I shouldn't get alarmed over stuff like this in women's magazines, but Margie has been a little sick and has some of the same symptoms as the magazine says happens with polio, Doctor."

I had never seen a case of polio in private practice. I had suspected polio in a number of cases, had done the necessary diagnostic tests, and they had always been negative. I hoped this wouldn't be the first case of polio I had to treat. "Tell me about it, Annette."

Annette reported that Margie had been slightly ill for a couple of days with some vague flu-like symptoms and with a little fever. That night her symptoms had changed and she told her mom she had a headache. What alarmed Annette the most was that Margie had trouble raising her left arm. "Doctor, am I being silly, what with reading that darn magazine? Am I imagining stuff?"

I told her I had better come over. It was six to eight miles from our house in Tualatin, through Durham and Tigard, then up Bull Mountain.

On the way over I had time to reflect on polio, or infantile paralysis, as a lot of people called it. This was a rotten disease. It was endemic, with a few cases here and there every summer, but it sometimes occurred in outbreaks. There were mild cases that never showed any paralysis, and there were cases in which parts of the body became paralyzed through damage to the anterior horn cells of the spinal cord. These cells did not repair; and when the damage was extensive enough, children grew up having to use braces, crutches, and wheelchairs. This was not a happy outlook, but somewhat better than the kids or adults who had bulbar polio (a disease of the brain stem where certain functions like breathing are controlled). Some of these kids died suddenly. Others with respiratory failure were consigned to an iron lung (an automatic breathing machine), often for life.

⟨≈⟩

No doubt Margie had just hurt her arm playing and, like a puppy with a sore paw, would not use it. Years later, when I practiced in California, I heard a great "sore puppy paw" story about a patient of my good friend, pediatrician Paul Pabst.

A mother brought a little patient who was dragging his left leg, into Paul's office. Paul examined the five-year-old and took a history. There were no pertinent findings. The little guy had started to limp the day before he was scheduled to see Paul for a well-child checkup. Worried about a condition of the hip joint called Legg-Perthes disease (aseptic necrosis of the head of the thighbone), Paul sent his patient to an orthopedic surgeon, who took X-rays of the joint but saw no problems.

The orthopedic surgeon sat the little boy down and gently talked to him, then asked him, once again, to walk across the room to demonstrate the problem with his leg. The little guy limped forward with a sort of dragging motion to his left leg, saying, "I just love Dr. Pabst." The diagnosis was instantaneously revealed. The Dr. Pabst loved by the little boy had polio as a grown man and wore a brace on his left leg. The little boy was imitating his hero.

⟨≈⟩

Thinking about what could prompt a false alarm and hoping that this would be one, I still worried. Over the telephone, this sounded like the real thing. It became obvious when I examined Margie that she was not suffering from a sore puppy paw syndrome. She had weakness in her left arm. She had nuchal rigidity (a stiff neck); and worse, her breathing was labored. Even without a spinal tap, the key to confirm a diagnosis of bulbar polio, I felt sure she had the disease.

I sent for the ambulance and rushed her off to Doernbecher Children's Hospital in Portland, where she was immediately placed in an iron lung. She was now out of my care, but I received daily reports and spoke to Annette every day, both of us hoping for improvement.

Three days went by and another patient came to the office with a fever and stiff neck. We did a spinal tap on the spot and it was consistent with polio. This child also went to Children's Hospital, but without the complication of bulbar polio.

Everyone in the office was now sensitized to the idea that we might be facing a real polio outbreak. When we heard of an adult or a child with a fever, we insisted that they come to the office to see us immediately. We asked any patient with a fever to wait in the car until it was their turn to be seen, so as not to spread germs in the waiting room, then had them come in the back door through the carport. It was almost futile to try to see these patients at home because we usually had to do a spinal tap to confirm or rule out the diagnosis of polio; that wasn't a house call procedure even in those rough and ready days.

Then, as now, there was no definitive treatment for polio; but many alternative health care practitioners had novel ideas about how to defeat the dreaded disease. One of these practitioners was an Australian nurse named Sister Kenney who proclaimed that a series of hot packs and exercises was curative. There was probably some benefit through physio-therapy, in preventing stiffness and contractures of joints and retaining as much muscle tone as possible, but curative it was not.

The weirdest scheme of the day was the notion that if, during an attack of polio, one would refrain from using a particular muscle, then that muscle would not be weakened, or the weakness could be minimized. We hadn't yet realized that the cord itself was the problem and the muscle paralysis was only a symptom of what was wrong in the spinal cord.

On Thursday of the week that Annette's daughter went to the hospital, my partner's son developed a fever and stiff neck. His condition was followed at home by his dad and also by his mother, who was a nurse.

Friday saw our older son, Don, develop a low-grade fever, a runny nose, and aches. At any other time we would have called it flu; now, it was potential polio—and we were scared. Glad and I decided to subscribe to the theory that a muscle not used would be uninjured and, although the theory seemed weak, what the heck, it wouldn't hurt to render the kid immobile. Poor Don lay in bed, not allowed to raise his arms, walk to the bathroom, or feed himself. This was before we had a television set, so we took turns reading to him. We tried not to convey our worst fears to our son, so we laughed and told stories and tried to keep him entertained, with fear as our constant companion. We worried about my partner's son and all the other neighborhood kids, but it's hard to be thinking of others when your own is in danger.

I knew I would never treat a case of polio if one turned up; I would refer it. Polio was treated only in medical centers, not in small towns or general hospitals. Therefore polio had not been an important issue to me. I was insulated from it.

Oh yeah? Not anymore, not when I saw the first case in my own patient. This wasn't a situation in which a professor was using as an example a patient for whom I had no responsibility. Sure, when I had seen patients being demonstrated I had felt compassion for them, but when it happened to someone for whom I had the primary responsibility, my thought process changed. I was involved from the very first minute. It became a personal matter to me, not only because my own child was involved or the child of my partner, but because I felt personally involved with every case I saw. These were MY patients and what happened to them was my overriding concern.

Saturday came and went. The Children's Hospital reported Margie's condition as unchanged. I called the hospital several times a day and I made it a point to speak to Annette or her husband after every call. My partner called to say his son was stable and still at home. He had seen one more case of polio and referred the child to Children's Hospital.

❧

On Sunday morning at 5:30, the doorbell rang. A distraught father was at the door. He told me that his fourteen-year-old daughter was bleeding badly and he wished I would come over.

I said, "Where is she bleeding?" I thought that if it were bloody urine or a nose bleed, perhaps I could get by with some advice and go back to bed.

"You know, Doc," said the embarrassed father, with his hand sort of vaguely defining an area that lay somewhere in the neighborhood of the genitals.

The word "vagina" was apparently not in his vocabulary, or at least not where his fourteen-year-old daughter was concerned. I realized that further conversation was futile. I would like to have asked him if this was her first menstrual period, and with an affirmative answer, advise him to have the mother show the daughter how to use a sanitary napkin. But, I said, "Hold on a minute while I dress and I'll follow you home."

We went down Sagert Road, turned south on Meridian Road to Prosperity Park, then drove into the yard of a run-down peckerwood farm. It was dawn; the barnyard was awake. Chickens scattered and a cow bellowed. Rusty hulks of farm equipment and a couple of derelict autos attested to the condition of the family's exchequer, but provided roosts for the chickens, though eggs were probably hard to find.

We went into the house through the kitchen and into the living room where the daughter lay on the couch on a pile of newspapers, covered with blood. A six- or seven-week fetus lay among the clots. I was able to stop the bleeding and help Mom clean up the mess. Dad sat on the back step. I said to Mom, "What are we going to tell her father?" I recognized that this was going to be trouble. If the women of the family hadn't been able to talk about the event, it probably meant that Dad might have a very closed mind on this subject.

Mom cried a bit and asked another question instead of answering my question. She asked, "Will you see the boys in the back bedroom? They've had colds for several days."

I recognized diversion when I saw it. Mom did not want to talk about the miscarriage. Probably the boys were not even sick, but it would give her thinking time prior to dealing with her husband. Besides, once she got me in the house, she probably figured she might as well get everybody seen, since the house call fee was assumed to cover everyone under that roof. Looking at the surroundings, I guessed that I would never be paid, anyway. So, in for one or a bunch, it didn't matter.

We went into the little back bedroom where six- and eight-year-old brothers lay in twin beds. Both had fevers, stiff necks, and early paralysis. My God! We had two more cases of polio—and three sick siblings in one house!

Also, Mom had her diversion.

I went to a neighbor's to call the ambulance. Mom and Dad worried together about polio as the brothers went off to Children's Hospital. Whether or not they ever discussed the miscarriage, I don't know. I hope someone discussed the facts of life with the fourteen-year-old. The family moved away soon after the brothers came home, so I wasn't able to follow up. They did not seem to suffer any ill effects.

❧⚬⚬⚬❧

At the end of the first week, we had diagnosed six definite cases of polio and one suspected case. Our son proved to be okay and was liberated from his motionless existence. My partner's son recovered quickly, but during the next week we had eight more confirmed cases. Three cases were bulbar; one case was an adult. None died, but several had permanent paralysis and I worried about every one of them. The Children's Hospital staff was most gracious in responding to my calls and being supportive in helping us with the diagnosis. Without their help I don't know how I would have emotionally endured the stress of the mini-epidemic. The two-week period ended our local polio epidemic, but we had been sensitized; and until winter arrived and the polio season was over, we imagined polio in every patient. Margie got out of the iron lung, but she had a disabled arm.

Two years later, Dr. Jonas Salk announced to the world that a polio vaccine had been discovered and was ready for use. The world would never again need to fear the scourge of poliomyelitis.

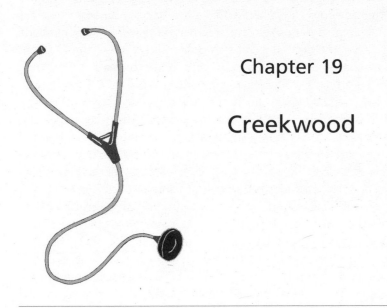

Chapter 19

Creekwood

Lines in front of our bathroom doors had grown as the children became older. Squabbles in the morning before school started the day on a discordant note.

We enjoyed living in our Tualatin house. It was the base from which I began to practice, the place where we brought newborn Pamela when she and Glad came home from the hospital, and it was where we had converted our garage to a most satisfactory bunkhouse and playroom for our sons, Lee and Don, but the house did not lend itself to further expansion. The formal garden, so lovingly conceived, planted and tended by Glad, and the memories of her parents' forty-fifth wedding anniversary reception held in the garden would be hard to walk away from. However, we still had the smelly old dairy across the road with its nocturnally bawling Holstein bull and the dog that had bitten nearly every kid in the neighborhood. And the darned bathrooms! So, we decided to search for a larger place.

We also wanted to be closer to the office. I had to drive six miles to get to work in the morning, even if I didn't make hospital rounds, or to see a patient at night in the office in lieu of making a house call. We were not yet ready for the expense of a new house, so we looked for an older place with the space we needed.

I had a yen to do a little ranching on the side. I guess I hadn't thought I would become a peckerwood farmer; I just wanted a place for the horses, which now numbered five, and maybe space for a couple head of beef cattle. Just the right place came on the market. Glad and I bought a ten-acre farm, three-quarters of a mile north of Six Corners and less than a mile from the office. I would be a gentleman farmer.

This old farm had a sign in front of the driveway proclaiming it to be Blueberry Dell. Because the blueberry bushes were long gone, and because of the deep woods at the back of the house and the creek that ran through the property, we promptly rechristened it Creekwood, but did not erect a sign to that effect. The name was our private way of thinking about our new home, not something for the public domain.

We were on a hill; the flat two acres on top fell off rather quickly to the lower pasture land down by the creek—the smelly stream that all the Sherwood industries dumped into. Smelly or not, it still held a limit of cutthroat trout on opening day of the fishing season each year. The fish seemed untainted by the odor of the creek. Glad's dad and I thought they had just come up from the river downstream from the contamination, and hadn't been in the creek long enough to become tainted. The hillside was covered with Douglas fir, maples, and several different types of ferns and wildflowers, including the beautiful Northwest trillium and Solomon's seal.

Glad envisioned herself sitting in the shade of the trees on a summer afternoon, reading a good book and reliving the peace and quiet she had experienced as a child growing up on a farm. What a dream! Three boisterous little kids and a husband—who, because of the exigencies of medical practice, couldn't be depended upon to be home sharing the responsibilities of child-rearing—soon relegated the peace and quiet to fantasy land. Glad, always the pragmatist, enjoyed her family and never looked back.

A weedy and overgrown family burial plot lay back under the trees between the house and the big old barn. The plot contained both fallen and erect headstones, mostly covered by wild grape vines. Names on the stones attested to the demise of one Eliza Coley, her husband, and other members of her family. Eliza was buried in 1898, according to the headstone; her first husband had died forty years earlier. As the local story went, Mr. Coley had been murdered by Eliza and the hired man, who ground up his remains in the mill they operated down near the creek. Eliza and her hired man lived out their lives together until he apparently couldn't stand her any longer or, fearing for his life from the old lady, knocked her in the head and ran off—or at least that was the story.

The remodeling of our ranch became a consuming project. The big white barn, which we subsequently painted red, would be large enough for our horses now and in the future. The existing house had been erected in the 1920s from the salvaged timbers of the original land grant dwelling built in the middle of the nineteenth century. It needed considerable updating.

Just after the remodeling began, our dear friends, Kile and Louise Hardesty, asked to park their Airstream trailer on our land while Kile did a locum tenens as a radiologist at the Portland Clinic. It was the Hardesty's granddaughter, Little Weezy (short for Louise), whom I had delivered with her grandfather standing behind me making me nervous. Their arrival was a break for us. We not only had friends nearby, but built-in caretakers.

Kile, who had been a general practitioner in Indiana before the war, had also worked at the Portland Clinic as one of their radiologists during my years as a resident at St. Vincent's. The Portland Clinic with its large number of physicians on staff had the greatest number of hospital admissions of any group; therefore, many of the patients I took care of were the private patients of the clinic. Kile and I had many stories to swap about some of the more puzzling or exciting cases we had shared in those days.

One of the cases we talked about was one of the worst accidents I cared for while on duty in the St. Vincent's Emergency Room as an intern.

As a result of a major accident, all four members of a family arrived at the hospital in two ambulances within minutes of each other. The mother was unconscious. She would have been horrified and shocked had she observed the carnage suffered by the other three members of her family.

The first thing I did was to stabilize Mom, a handsome blonde lady whose abundant hair had been in a chignon. Now her hair was matted with blood from a head wound that was still oozing. The combination of the coil of hair and the chignon styler called a "rat" probably buffered the blow and saved her life. Since her eye signs were okay and she responded to stimuli, we felt she would awaken with only supportive treatment.

I went on to examine Dad. Dad was lying stiffly on a stretcher on the floor in the hall outside the emergency room door, moaning occasionally. He was frighteningly pale. A rescue ambulance blanket covered his body. His eyes, head and neck seemed intact. I reasoned that the damage must be under the blanket. As I raised the blanket, the sight of coiled whitish-pink writhing snakes of exposed bowel, oozing out of the abdominal cavity produced a gasp from the nurse who was assisting me.

Without the pressure of the blanket holding the bowels in place, several of the coils slid off onto the floor, leaving a gaping hole in his abdomen, about ten inches from side to side. This guy looked like a battle casualty, and my World War II training took over.

I had a quick flashback to my days as a medic and doing triage. Triage means spending your time on the patients who are salvageable and just making comfortable those whom you think are going to die. "Triage" has always been a dirty word to me; it suggests playing God.

With the nurse's help I got the bowel back where it belonged, covered the area with a massive sterile abdominal dressing, started an intravenous treatment of 1,000 cc of 5 percent dextrose in distilled water, and moved on to the next patient. *Save the ones you can help, don't waste your time on the doomed.*

Brother, age twelve, was crying. He had a compound fracture in his left arm. A bleeding wound obscured the ulna where it might peek through, if he moved. We quickly got a bandage on the arm, splinted it, and the nurse started to clean up the other lacerations of the arms and trunk.

By now, other help was arriving. The medical resident had been awakened and was working on the unconscious mother. A neurosurgeon had been called to examine her.

The fourth member of the family, Little Sister, was in the best shape physically, but not emotionally. She was only nine years old and lying in what looked like an abattoir. The victims were all her own family. She was frightened, sobbing, and in pain. She had been injured too, suffering multiple contusions, scrapes and lacerations. She had to be X-rayed, cleaned up, sewed up, and lovingly held and reassured. But what kind of reassurance might one give about a dying father, an unconscious mother, and a brother bleeding from an arm bent at an impossible angle?

The police were there and helped pin down what had happened to the family. They had been traveling down Highway 99W on the outskirts of the city in their two-door sedan. The kids were in the back seat. The car was sideswiped by a passing vehicle on a rain-slicked road and crossed the center divider, only to be hit head on by a car approaching from the other direction. The car rolled over and both doors flew open. Dad was thrown out of the rolling vehicle, up against the edge of the sidewalk's curb, and skidded along the edge of the curb many feet, shredding his abdominal wall. Mom flew out of the other door and banged her head somewhere along the way. Because the sedan was a two-door, the kids stayed in the car, which limited their injuries. There were no seat belts in cars in those days.

An orthopedic surgeon arrived to take care of Brother. Because the surgery resident on duty was already in the operating room doing a major case and couldn't get away, it became my responsibility to call the chief of surgery, Dean Seabrook, to look at Dad. I explained, when he came, that I was sorry to have had to call him, as it appeared hopeless. This great man looked at the patient and said, "We'll try."

While surgery was being prepared, the surgeon and I closed all the multiple lacerations on the kids and turned Little Sister over to the nuns for safekeeping. The nuns took over, loving and calming the little girl. It was obvious that these women cared about kids.

Brother went to surgery with the orthopedist, and Dr. Seabrook and I took Dad to the operating room. Four hours later we emerged, spent. Dad was back together but, because of the horrendous contamination of street dirt in the wound, we worried about infection.

It took months, more operations, the cleaning out of abscesses, and tons of antibiotics, but he lived. Never underestimate the will to live; this man had it. He never gave up, and neither did his surgeon.

Mother, who awakened the next day, was okay in a week and almost never left her husband's bedside.

The kids got well, except that Little Sister didn't really believe that Dad was okay. Hospitals in 1950 would not admit kids as visitors. The theory was that because kids carried infections, not the least of which were the childhood diseases and polio, exposure to children might create an epidemic in already sick people. Because she was banished, she thought her dad was dead but we just wouldn't tell her. Several times I passed Little Sister, seated forlornly in the hospital lobby, waiting. I always stopped to speak to the little girl. It was heartrending that she didn't understand, despite many reassurances, that her dad was still alive and would be home, someday.

Finally, one night, a sympathetic nurse and I conspired to sneak Little Sister into Dad's private room. Both of our jobs were endangered by this prohibited trip, for if we had been caught by the nuns, we might have been fired. The nuns rose to the occasion when life was on the line and situations were acute, but hospital rules were not to be broken. Beware, if you crossed the fine line of insubordination.

We made it in and out with Little Sister without being caught. Our careers were still intact. The reunion scene made the risk worthwhile. A week or two later the nun who was night supervisor, walked down the hall behind me. I heard a whispered voice say, "Are you having any little guests tonight?" With a chuckle she disappeared into a patient's room.

Kile told me that all the staff knew about our escapade and wondered what would happen. He said, "If the two of you had gotten into trouble, the entire medical staff was ready to go to bat for you."

❧

To add to our sense of establishing roots in the community, Glad's dad and mother moved to Sherwood to be near us and the grandchildren. Donnel and Grace Crawford were really Glad's aunt and uncle who had raised her from the time she was six months old when her parents died. They became my mom and dad as well. We never had an in-law relationship. I had lucked into a new family—they became mine as well as Glad's.

Dad, who was retired, embarked upon a career of making Creekwood self-sufficient by supplying the family with vegetables and fruit. The family orchard had fourteen different kinds of fruit trees, a filbert grove and a chestnut tree. There were several types of berry vines and oh, what wonderful berries grew in that rich, loamy Oregon soil. Dad planted lettuce, squash, melons, cucumbers, beans, corn, tomatoes, and more. We bought a huge, top-opening freezer and began to put away food for the winter.

During the period when we were remodeling the house, we had also remodeled the barn, erecting five box stalls to accommodate our growing stable of horses. We had Magic, Sugar Sally, Little Joe, and Conga and her colt, Mayday Mischief. To add to our equine family, Conga and Sugar Sally were pregnant again.

If you have added up the names and the babies that were expected and found there were soon going to be seven equines living at our house, you would be right. Sugar Sally's little Shetland foal could live with its mother, as the box stalls were built for regular-sized horses, but because there were only five stalls we would one day have to face reducing the size of our horse population. Pets, to us, always became family and we hated to have to get rid of any of them.

Part of the process of getting Creekwood ready for occupancy was to buy a tractor. The decision of whether to park my bottom in my saddle on the back of Black Magic or to put it in the seat of my tractor, was a problem I faced on each of my days off. I thought I was a real rancher. I had a Stetson hat, a horse, a pickup truck with a horse carrier built on the back, and a tractor. Creekwood may only have been ten acres but it felt like a hundred to me, a city boy who had grown up in apartments in San Francisco. I was lucky to have Dad there as my mentor.

Tom, at the age of two or three.

Tom as a sailor in World War II, in dress blue uniform.

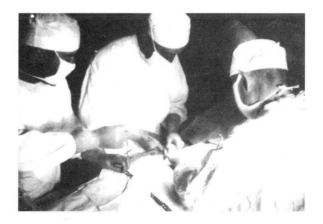

Captain Tom of the George Washington High School ROTC in San Francisco, 1937.

This is the real beginning of Tom's becoming a doctor. Here, he is a scrub nurse in the operating room of U.S. Navy Mobile Hospital II ("Mob 2").

ABOVE LEFT. Doctor Tom and Glad at his graduation from the University of Oregon Medical School. ABOVE RIGHT. Tom as a resident in General Surgery at St. Vincent's Hospital in Portland, Oregon, 1952. LEFT. This is Tom and Glad's first home, purchased new for $8,000 with a GI loan, 1946. BELOW. Glad and the children at Crater Lake, Oregon, 1956.

Don, Lee, Pam and their dad at the beach in Oregon, 1956.

Black Magic.

ABOVE. Don, Lee and Pamela with Glad and Tom at their twenty-fifth wedding anniversary. This was at their Palos Verdes Estates, California home, 1969.
OPPOSITE. Robert and Betty Young with Glad and Tom, in 1973.

James Brolin (Dr. Steve Kiley in the Welby show) with Tom in 1970, when big mustaches and long sideburns were popular.

From left to right: Tom, Glad, and Betty and Bob Young at the Sterns' Amelia Island, Florida home on Tom and Glad's fortieth wedding anniversary.

Moving day from Tualatin to Creekwood was scheduled for a Monday morning. On the preceding Saturday a few of our friends arrived with a truck, insisting that we needed help with some of our more difficult pieces of furniture—including the piano, a sofa, some chairs, and a table. Glad and I thought this was a dumb idea and argued that, after all, we had already engaged professional movers. Our friends were insistent; in fact, they pushed us aside when we protested, asking us if we didn't trust them or what? The piano and the other stuff left. That evening we went over to the new farm, ostensibly to play bridge with Kile and Louise in their travel-home, only to be greeted by all of our close friends in a surprise housewarming!

The piano was to be used by the country and western band hired for the evening. The party planners had created a wishing-well punch bowl with sterilized (I hoped) male urinals as flagons to drink the punch. Apple cider, the base of the punch, was spiked with large quantities of Scotch whiskey, which lent it a smoky flavor.

As the evening wore along, amid great hilarity among the guests, the band had competition from a Scots urologist from Portland. He had arrived at the party in a kilt. He spent the entire evening parading across the front porch with his bagpipes, mournfully piercing the peace of the neighborhood with the banshee-like screaming of Scottish airs. Being of the Scotch persuasion, the urologist took his piping very seriously, but no less seriously than he took Scotch whiskey; and he protested the combination of Scotch with apple juice. He drank his Scotch straight; and the more he drank, the more mournful became his piping. Somewhere around midnight the piper ceased his parading and sat in the corner for a minute to rest, promptly lapsing into a deep sleep from which he did not awaken until morning.

During the latter part of the evening, just before it started to rain, I and a friend, who had stabled Magic while we lived in Tualatin, illogically became concerned that Magic was alone in the stable and not enjoying the festivities. In order to rectify this oversight we went out, haltered Magic, and led him up the front porch steps toward the living room. Glad, who is very alert in cases like this, quickly saw the fallacy of our reasoning and halted us when the horse's two front legs entered the front door. She especially did not want his nether parts inside. She categorically refused to have a horse in the house. I was forced to leave the field, defeated by logic.

The return trip off the porch was accomplished less easily because, as the eleven hundred pounds of horse was ascending the stairs, one of the treads had given way beneath his hooves. Now he was reluctant to retrace his route by backing down the steps. We finally resolved the problem by marching the horse across the porch, in front of the bagpiper leaning asleep against the wall. Then, facing forward, he leaped down the stairs without touching the broken tread. Despite numerous attempts at repair, the tread never seemed completely satisfactory as long as we lived at Creekwood.

After the rain started, and when people started home, I had to get out the tractor and pull cars out of the mud in the orchard where they had been parked. In the morning there were still a couple of cars there whose ownership was unknown. These vehicles disappeared quietly during the day while the Hardestys were out. No bodies were found—except that of the urologist, who was resuscitated, fed breakfast and sent home.

⌘

A horse is an eating machine. The by-product of the machine accumulates on the floor of the horse's box stall and must be periodically removed, a job that fell solely to me. Once our horses were moved to Creekwood, I was forced to start a manure pile on the side hill behind the barn. The process was simple. I backed the tractor into the barn and, with a back-loading bucket, scooped up the manure from the box stalls. Then I drove the tractor out to the top of the hill and let the contents of the bucket drop. As the pile increased from the top, I was able to take the tractor and the bucket to the bottom of the pile and retrieve well-aged fertilizer. This was used by Dad to make our garden the best in the neighborhood; Glad loved the availability of this material for her flowers.

Try as they might, the two of them could not keep up with the production; hence I became a very popular guy with friends in Portland, who recognized that I would make a house call to deliver a truckload of aged manure onto their driveway for the cost of a free beer. Many of my days off were spent driving the horse van, clad in my oldest clothes, delivering horse manure. I imagined a newspaper headline—LOCAL DOCTOR DELIVERS THE GOODS: HORSESHIT.

I laughed to myself, believing that the difference in my appearance and my occupation was a good joke, as I drove anonymously through fancy Portland neighborhoods where my friends lived.

The Black Angus choir had to be reduced, painful as it was to sell its members with the soulful eyes to my affluent friends as beef. This was excellent meat and our friends bought a side of my beef to be kept in their freezers. We never did profit from the cattle, other than providing our family with free meat for our own freezer. This was the upside of our ranching days; the downside was insects.

❦

Somehow, as a kid, I had developed an unreasonable fear of insects. I was able to tolerate common flies and even liked ladybugs and the little jingle about their houses being on fire; but all the other bugs in the world gave me cold chills just to look at them. To this day, Glad has to be the strong member of the family when an insect invades our home. I'm okay with a can of Raid in my hands, but don't ask me to pick the bug up even after the loathsome thing is dead. We did not want our children to acquire their dad's fears, so Glad took special pains to try to coach them in the proper reaction to bugs, especially stinging ones.

"When there is a bee hanging around your head," she told them, "don't swat at it; just stand still and it will leave you alone. Actually, the insect is afraid of you and, if you frighten it more, it may try to sting you in self defense."

Sound reasonable? Yes, for the kids; but when I tried to stand still around bugs I would break into a cold sweat with goose bumps. I learned to control myself and just slowly walk away; but God, how I wanted to run!

The first test of her insect-training course came as a result of our trying to clean up the Eliza Coley family cemetery. We wanted to restore it as a matter of respect, but also we thought it would be a good conversation piece during martini time when we had guests for dinner.

Don and I were cleaning brush and pulling wild grapevines down from the trees where they made a nearly impenetrable network. I stopped for a cool drink, leaving Don and our number one collie dog, Markie, to carry on. Suddenly, the quiet of our bucolic glen was pierced by the yelling of our son and the throaty barks and growls of our faithful collie. The cacophony suddenly changed to screams and yips. When racing to the graveyard, I passed Markie going the opposite direction—and with good reason. He had been stung by yellow jackets all over his muzzle and eyes while attempting to rescue his young master.

The kid was standing immobile, while the yellow jackets (a species of wasp that doesn't lose its stinger, but can sting over and over again) did their number on Don. Later, we counted forty-odd stings. I snatched the boy out of the maelstrom and carried him, running to the house. After quiet had been restored and we were reasonably certain that Don was not going into anaphylactic shock from multiple yellow jacket stings, we asked him why he didn't try to escape.

He told his mother, "You always told me to stand still when there were bees around."

Well, a rule is a rule; but I counseled Don to make more realistic decisions in the future and to use his own good judgment.

About a year later Don and I were again cleaning brush in another area, when we inadvertently disturbed a paper nest of black hornets. Immediately, I was hit by one of these insects on the back of the head. When this vicious, stinging bug hits, it feels like a bullet. I yelled, "Run, Don, run!"

Being on a side hill, I quickly made a decision—go down the hill and jump into the creek, which I did, smelly water or not. I was hit by two more stingers on the way down, trailing a wreath of hornets around my head.

While sitting in the creek, I evaluated what had happened and realized that my son wasn't with me, and still had not learned to make resourceful decisions. Later, back in the house, while Glad was putting ice bags on my head and Don, who was not stung, was making sympathetic noises, I again counseled him about his decision-making. I pointed out that I had taken the best escape route and the way of least resistance, downhill and into the creek; whereas he had run uphill, which was slower, and he headed for the house, which was farther.

"But, Dad," Don explained, "I did that because the hornets were chasing you, not me."

Once again, I left the field, defeated by logic.

ᘒᘒᕢᕢᕢ

At the bottom of the hill, the creek divided the pasture. About three acres of lush grass covered the far bank, accessible to our horses over a rickety old bridge. The deck of this decrepit structure was about twenty feet from bank to bank. It finally gave way under the frequent pounding of horse's hooves. We called a pair of carpenters to consider rebuilding the bridge.

One Saturday morning Glad and I, the children, and the workmen had walked down the road in front of our place, crossed the highway bridge, and scrambled down to the pasture on the other side of the creek. All four adults and three children, none of whom could qualify as a bridge engineer, were discussing the mechanics of bridge construction when our collie, Markie, came to the edge of the hill. He evidently realized that we had ditched him and eluded his protective custody. He started to bark. One of the kids, not thinking of the route of Markie's travel, yelled, "Here, Markie, come on, boy!" The dog smiled and, enthusiastically desiring reunification with his family, raced down the trail, through the ferns and trees, zigzagging down the steep hill.

He hit the bridge at full speed and, within two strides, recognized that the distal portion of the span was missing. The dog leaped as high as he could, with forepaws beating the air, begging for flight, as Disney's Pluto might have done in a cartoon. The effort was not enough to keep Markie airborne, and he belly-flopped into the creek. An extremely bedraggled, embarrassed pooch made his way sulkily up the hill to dry out under a filbert tree, shunning the company of humans until he recovered his dignity.

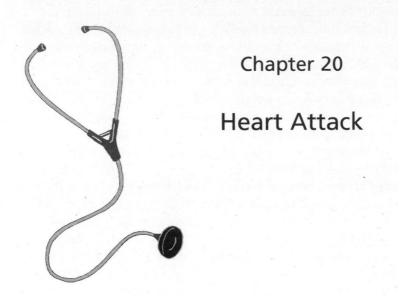

Chapter 20

Heart Attack

I will prescribe regimen for the good of my patients according to my ability and my judgment and never do harm to anyone...

— Hippocrates

Have you ever made a mistake so bad that you thought you had killed someone? I have, and his name was Phil. I had lost sight of the Hippocratic oath and its admonition, DO NO HARM.

Eleven point three miles from our Tualatin home just before we moved to Creekwood, past the Scarletts' place in Sherwood, was where Philip Doan lived. I know the mileage well because, somewhere between midnight and 4 A.M., four nights out of seven for two weeks, I had driven this route in response to a frantic plea for help from Mrs. Philip Doan, "Doctor, Doctor, Phil is having a heart attack!"

❧

I had thought a great deal about heart attacks since that dark day in August, three months before my fifteenth birthday, when I had arrived home from playing tennis all day and fooling around, to find my mother in tears and my father sprawled dead across the foot of their bed.

In the days of the deep depression that followed my father's death, and the near destruction of my soul when my mother died five months later from that lingering respiratory infection, I imagined myself reaching my father's age, sixty-two, also the victim of a heart attack. I worked my way out of that depression in the years that followed, and eventually into medicine, but I hadn't worked through the premonition I had as a teenager. I continued to imagine myself dying of a heart attack at the same age as my father. This fear of a heart attack was reinforced, later, when I was diagnosed as hypertensive.

I learned in medical school that, statistically, people of my body type were least likely to have lung disease and most likely to have heart trouble. These thoughts were not a part of my daily consciousness, but they lingered somewhere in the inner reaches of my mind, in deep, dark corners. The muscles of my chest wall tightened and my breathing became shallow when Mrs. Phil said "heart attack." I got out of bed a little faster and I drove the car at higher speed on my way to respond to such a call. The words "heart attack" gave me goose bumps then, and they do now.

❧❀❧

I knew Phil had heart trouble. He had high blood pressure and mild chest pain with exertion, but normal EKGs. These were the only tests available at that time. Today, we would study his condition with an exercise treadmill test, an echocardiogram and perhaps with cardiac catheterization.

Phil had awakened that first night, according to his wife, with severe chest pain. He had what is now known as unstable or resting angina pectoris. He called that night because of the prolonged pain, but it disappeared before I arrived at his house. I already had prescribed nitroglycerin sublingual tablets for his angina, which he had only with exertion. When he took these in the middle of the night, they did not seem to work until I was off the phone and on the road.

Sublingual medication is absorbed by the body after it is dissolved in saliva. What happens to a person like Phil is that fear dries the mouth, ergo no saliva, and it takes a longer time for the soft little nitroglycerin pill to work.

After that first night, Phil's wife called again two nights later. I jumped out of bed and drove to his house, only to find that Phil had taken his nitro and felt relieved. The attacks came over and over again during the next two weeks. Each time, the round trip cost me an hour in travel and house call time. Never having been a great sleeper, I found it difficult to fall asleep when I got back to bed.

I was tiring of the routine. Every other night was too much. During the day I checked Phil at the office and he seemed to be all right, but the pain would start again after the witching hour. With phone in hand, talking to Mrs. Phil, I felt like saying, "Give him his nitro and go back to bed. He'll be okay." But, remembering my father, I instead got up and drove the eleven and three-tenths miles to his house. I knew that next time they called, I would get up and go again. Perhaps I should have hospitalized Phil, but I thought each episode would be the last one, and that Phil would respond to some of the other medications I had given him.

On the night of my eighth midnight run to Phil's house, I finally blew up. He was sitting on the edge of his bed, grinning sheepishly and saying, "Gee, Doc, the pain is gone."

"Phil," I yelled, "this is going too far. I cannot be disturbed at night anymore. You have to give the nitro more time to work." Then, warming to the task of chewing out my tormentor, I finally laid it out. "Furthermore, Phil, I'm not sure you even have heart pain. This thing is a panic attack. You get a little indigestion or have a bad dream and you cry wolf. Well, damn it, Phil, I won't stand for it anymore!"

As I spoke, I thought to myself, *Hey, wait a minute! You're going too far with this yelling at a patient.* But, as so often happens, anger takes over from logic, and I pursued the subject as a result of my own frustration and fatigue.

As I continued my tirade, I watched Phil turning pale as I, in my anger, turned red. *Gee!* I thought, *I am laying it on a little heavy; the poor guy looks terrible.*

I said, "Phil, don't worry about it. I guess I'm just a bit tired."

Then Phil began to sweat and become short of breath. I worried that I had really stressed him with my behavior.

Suddenly he slumped over and fell forward; I caught him just before he hit the floor. This time he was unconscious, in cardiac shock, and had suffered a full-fledged grade-A number-one myocardial infarction—a heart attack. I thought, *My God, I've killed him!*

I quickly checked his pulse. It was rapid and weak. I didn't even bother with his blood pressure, knowing it would be really low, but ran to my car for the oxygen that I always carried. As I passed Phil's wife, I yelled, "Call the fire department! I'll be right back to talk to them."

The poor lady was so flustered by that time, she told me later, she didn't hear the last sentence and couldn't imagine where I was going, except that I was so mad that she thought I was going home and leaving her to deal with the fire department. She could not think of what to tell the firemen, other than that she needed a doctor because her husband had passed out and their doctor had run out and left them. She was deeply relieved to see me return with my small tank of oxygen. Only then did she struggle to the phone and make the call.

I started the oxygen, restored Phil to consciousness, and stabilized his blood pressure. When the ambulance came, I rode with my patient to the hospital. He lived, to my everlasting relief. Guilt would not have been easy to live with.

Once the episode of illness was over and Phil had returned to running his farm, in a limited fashion, the three of us sat down in the office one day and rehashed that worrisome night. I apologized for my abrupt behavior. Phil and his wife reassured me that they understood the circumstances and appreciated the fact that I was on the scene when the trouble occurred.

Phil said, "Doctor, I'm sure the attack would have happened, anyway. You just arranged for it to happen when you could take care of me." And he grinned.

⟲∞⟳

A few months after we moved into Creekwood, a phone call roused me at 1 A.M.

"Doctor, Lyle is sick. He says he has chest pain and he's sweating all over."

I told Mrs. Lyle Smith I would be right up. It was up, because their house was high atop the wildest reaches of Chehalem Mountain. Creekwood was at the base of the southeastern slope of the mountain.

Chehalem Mountain is, by Oregon standards, a mere hill. The mountain probably does not rise over two thousand feet above sea level. In comparison to the Oregon Cascades or the Rockies, Chehalem Mountain is a mere wrinkle in the earth's crust, heaved up from the surface when the continental drifts collided and the great volcanic peaks of the Northwest were formed. This little mountain separates the Yamhill River Valley from the great central garden area of Oregon, the Willamette River Valley. The Smiths lived over the top of the mountain and down a short way on the northwestern slope. This was a long trip in good weather.

Mrs. Smith asked, "Doctor, do you think you can make it? The snow is bad up here!"

I glanced out of the window and saw only a few inches of snow on the ground at our house, surely not enough to cause difficulty for my Pontiac with sawdust-impregnated snow tires on the rear wheels and sacks of sand in the trunk. I had not considered, in the ten miles or so of roadway to the top of the mountain, that the elevation changed about two thousand feet.

I reassured Mrs. Smith, bundled up, grabbed my bag, and headed up the mountain. My snow tires worked fine for about four miles. Above that, the snow had fallen on packed ice, left from the storm which had preceded the snowfall. My tires began to spin and I got stuck.

Time was important. Never mind trying to put on chains in this weather, a job I neither wanted to do nor was I very good at doing. I backed down to a wide spot, and with my back wheels on the gravel shoulder of the road, turned the car around and headed home to get my three-quarter-ton pickup truck with heavy horse hauling equipment on the back end. I was so proud of my old beat-up truck; I thought it would go anywhere.

I stopped just long enough to make a telephone call. I asked how Lyle felt. Mrs. Smith said that the pain came and went, was a dull, heavy feeling, and wasn't related to breathing. I had hoped that maybe Lyle was suffering from a respiratory infection, but the character of the pain his wife described was hardly reassuring. Somehow, I had to get to Lyle or get him off the mountain to a place were he could be treated. I told Mrs. Smith that I would be right along.

Before starting out again I called the fire department to have the ambulance go to the Smiths'. The bad news was that the ambulance had gone into the ditch earlier that night and was disabled. The Newberg fire department, ten miles west and actually closer than Tualatin, would not come because the patient was in Washington County and not Yamhill County; thus, out of their jurisdiction. We had a bureaucratic snafu, and to heck with anybody's health.

This time, when I took the truck, I made it another four miles up the mountain before I got stuck again. I was still about two miles from my goal. My level of frustration was climbing. I sat there in the warm cab of my truck and looked out on a beautiful but discouraging scene. The snow was falling heavily. The large fluffy flakes were pretty but what were they doing to my patient, Lyle Smith?

What should I do? If I don't go on, Lyle might die. Well, he might die, anyway, even if I get there. Or maybe this is a false alarm, like the one I thought Phil had.

The memory of my father's death flashed quickly through my mind. He had a heart attack—no one was there to help. I thought of my own potential for heart disease. Perhaps there would be a fatal episode one day, when I would want help.

If I started out on foot, it might take hours. I would be soaked, frozen, and have no way back. But my horse could make it. So down the hill I went, back home, saddled Black Magic, and loaded him in the truck (Sugar Sally in and Sugar Sally out wasted valuable time, but was necessary to load Magic).

Back up the hill we went, until the truck could go no further. I had made it about another mile this time, a result of having about eleven hundred pounds of horse in the back end. I unloaded the horse, tied my regular medical bag and my emergency bag onto the saddle, and we took off through the drifting snow.

Now, I worried about direction. Lyle lived on a side road. I wasn't sure I would recognize the turnoff. All of the familiar landmarks were obscured by snow. Mailboxes and their lettering were covered. Road signs did not even exist in this remote farming area. I passed one road to my right. I was sure that wasn't the correct turnoff.

The next road looked familiar, but I couldn't believe I had gone far enough. Suddenly, I glimpsed a bit of light off to the right. The light flashed on and off like an airport beacon, as the wind blew the trees. Mrs. Lyle had turned on the farmyard lights to guide me. Magic and I went the rest of the way at a gallop! We thundered into the open barn. I tied the horse and hurried to the house. I wondered, at the time, what the Smiths must have seen as I came into view covered with snow, riding a steaming horse whose snorting breath must have made it appear as if I were riding a fiery dragon.

Lyle was in the throes of a heart attack. He was in danger, due to an irregular pulse which I stabilized with intravenous zylocaine.

I remained all night and the next day, until the ambulance was repaired and able to get through to take Lyle to the hospital. The ambulance took me back to my foundered truck. I drove it over the recently plowed roads, back to the Smith farm, collected the Magical horse, and we went home.

Lyle lived.

❦

When I thought that I might be responsible for Phil's death, I was distraught. When he recovered, I hoped that scares like that were over for me. However, I realized that the fallibility of all of us in the health care field requires strict attention to detail and monitoring by each other. One time the local druggist was the one who narrowly averted professional disaster.

The pharmacist owned and operated the local drugstore. My partner and I had a symbiotic relationship with him; we needed each other. Without doctors in town, the drugstore couldn't make it. Without a drugstore, we would have had to stock a large supply of drugs to dispense to our patients. We certainly did not want that headache. Of necessity, we cooperated very well; but it was easy to cooperate, as we liked each other.

The Sherwood Pharmacy was also the repository of the state-controlled liquor store for the area. For a small-town doctor to buy booze was quite a challenge. Our patients probably would have realized that we occasionally imbibed, had they thought about it; but—out of sight, out of mind. What our patients did not want was to see us in the act. A patient getting a prescription filled and seeing one of us hauling off a jug of bourbon would most likely have conjured up a vision of the drunken doctor, reeling into the house to see a sick patient and thoroughly screwing up the case.

Only one of us partied at a time. We avoided being seen buying liquor at the Sherwood Pharmacy. Once in a while, one of our wives would go in and quietly buy a bottle. They were less recognizable. The bulk of our liquor purchases were wrapped in plain brown paper and marked MEDICINE.

The symbiotic relationship that we had was helpful to our patients, in that the pharmacist kept a good supply of the drugs we used most often. He also kept a small supply of drugs prescribed by doctors out of the area, from whom some of our area's citizens sought care. He kept a large supply of the medicines I used for Hannah Burkholter.

Hannah Burkholter was a very old lady and very sick. She had congestive heart failure. CHF manifested itself in many ways, including shortness of breath, swelling of the liver, dilation of the neck veins, and dropsy. Hannah had all these problems. She could not lie down in bed because her breathing was so labored; she could not walk because of the dropsy swelling in her legs, and she had some free intra-abdominal fluid (ascites) due to the congestion in her liver. The leg swelling was not the common garden variety of swelling of the ankles. Hannah's legs were swollen up to mid-thigh and the skin of her calves seemed as if it might burst at any time.

Treatment for Hannah was carried out entirely at home, where she was cared for by a concerned and involved daughter and son-in-law. Twice a week I made a house call to do a check on her cardiorespiratory system and to give her an injection of a mercurial diuretic agent called Salyrgan (increases urinary output and helps patients with CHF by reducing their internal fluid levels). Salyrgan was the most potent diuretic available. It had to be given intravenously and slowly because of its damaging effect to fatty tissues and skin.

Giving an I.V. injection twice a week to this poor soul was traumatic for both of us. She hated it because, no matter how careful I was, occasionally a drop of Salyrgan would escape the vein and the surrounding tissues would burn for hours. I hated it because it made Hannah suffer when I had to put the needle into those poor old scarred arms. Furthermore, we weren't getting anywhere. Hannah was gradually getting worse. We all knew that it was just a matter of time before I could no longer help, and she would die.

A new product was announced by one of the major pharmaceutical companies, a breakthrough in care for waterlogged patients like Hannah. It was not a mercury product, but a new synthetic diuretic called thiazide. It was touted as more potent, it could be taken daily and, wonder of wonders, it could be taken by mouth. I called the drugstore and asked the pharmacist to get some for Hannah. During my next visit I told Hannah and her family that I wanted to try something new, but not to get their hopes up too high; we would just have to wait and see what would happen. Meanwhile, we would continue with twice a week injections, as before.

I had tried enough new drugs that had not lived up to their promotional promises to be skeptical about this one. I told the family to weigh Grandma Hannah daily in order to measure her fluid loss.

When I returned in four days, Hannah had lost eight pounds. She was breathing better, the swelling in her legs had decreased, and she had reduced the number of pillows used to prop her up in bed from three to two. She thought she would try lying flat in a day or two.

The following week, Hannah was up and walking around the house. Her legs, although swollen, were slim by comparison to her former state. The family thanked me, over and over again, for prescribing the miracle pills. I told them to bring Hannah to the office the next week for her checkup and then we would begin to lengthen the time between visits.

A couple of months went by during which her condition was stable. Then her daughter called. She said, "Doctor, please come by on your way home tonight. Grandma is worse; in fact, she's a lot worse."

When I visited Hannah, she was, indeed, a lot worse. She was propped up on three pillows. Her legs were gigantic, and the skin had split (as I had previously feared that it would), and it was oozing a thin, yellow fluid. I injected Salyrgan and told the family that I would be back in three days, but to call if she became worse. Her daughter called on the evening of the second day.

"Doctor, Grandma is so much worse. I'm afraid we're losing her."

When I arrived, Hannah had very labored breathing, her legs were oozing badly, and there was a little blue discoloration around her mouth, attesting to her oxygen deficiency. When I listened to her lungs with my stethoscope, I realized that Hannah was drowning in her own fluids. While I was preparing a double dose injection of Salyrgan, her daughter told me that, because her mother was so bad, she had given her a second diuretic pill.

"Was I wrong to do that, Doctor? When you first gave her those diuretic pills she seemed to improve so much, but since we had her prescription filled again, with the medicine you changed her to, she seems to have gotten much worse."

Changed? I didn't change the medication. "Let me see the new pills."

When she brought the bottle, the prescription read the same but the white tablets were a tad larger than the ones I had prescribed, and the markings were slightly different. I kept my face from showing my anxiety and said, "I'm going down to the drugstore to get some of the original pills. I'll be back in half an hour." I took the pills and the pill bottle with me.

It was past eight o'clock and the store was closed, so I went directly to the pharmacist's house. Together we went down to the store and looked at Hannah's medicine. The pills in her bottle were certainly not what I had prescribed.

The druggist turned pale. He was visibly shaken. "I can't believe what happened. I recognize these tablets. They're a combination of cortisone and meprobamate that I got for a patient who goes to one of the doctors in Tigard."

"Good God, cortisone and meprobamate? What in the world is a stupid combination like that good for?" I continued, not expecting an answer. "Fill a script with thiazide and let me get back to Mrs. Burkholter to see what I can do."

Cortisone was one of the absolutely worst things that we could have put into Hannah's system. Cortisone causes salt retention which, in turn, retains water in the body. Hannah was drowning in her own bodily fluids. A drug that increased the water in her system could be fatal.

I gave Hannah a double dose of the proper medicine and returned in the morning to see how she had fared. She had improved physically but she was pooped from having a huge amount of urine during the night. She said, "Doctor, I had to pee every hour." I thought, *How wonderful! She's getting rid of all that water.*

The next day she was even better and, by the following day, she was out of the woods.

I never explained to Hannah or her family what had happened. They were all thrilled with the result and were glad that I had changed back to the original medication.

The pharmacist and I never discussed the episode again. He had made what was, possibly, the only serious mistake of his career and was paying for it, mentally. I felt sure he would never let it happen again.

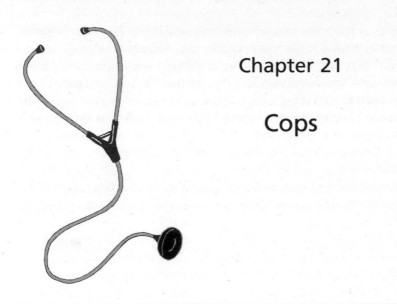

Chapter 21

Cops

Some people look young for their age. Eliza James wasn't one of them. She looked ancient and she was ancient. She was small and wizened, with thinning gray hair. Her red-rimmed eyes had slitted lids that made her look as if she had an eye infection, though she didn't. Despite appearances, Eliza was perky.

I once asked Eliza if she could be related to Eliza Coley whose headstone was in my backyard. Eliza James puffed out her cheeks and almost gave me a raspberry for asking such a dumb question. No, she wasn't related to no ghost and, furthermore, she didn't hold with that dumb story, anyway.

One afternoon Eliza was brought to the office by a neighbor. She had a pillow wrapped around her wrist (a darn good splint). Eliza had fallen in her yard and stuck out her hand to break her fall. I X-rayed her at the office and saw a typical Colles fracture of the wrist with displacement. The fracture would have to be reduced under anesthesia and a plaster of Paris cast applied. Eliza was sent to Tuality Hospital in Hillsboro.

Tuality was a well-organized, seventy-five-bed community hospital in the county seat of Washington County. There were about twenty physicians on the staff, mostly GPs from the Hillsboro, Forest Grove and

Beaverton areas. The emergency room was manned by local doctors on the staff.

There were no interns or residents at Tuality. At night, when a problem arose with a patient, the ward nurse evaluated the problem and called the supervisor. The two of them would then confer and decide whether or not it was necessary to call the patient's own physician. That physician had to decide if the problem could be solved over the telephone or if it would be necessary to go to the hospital. Occasionally, if the emergency was great and another doctor was in the hospital for his own emergency, waiting for an OB or surgery, or just making rounds, he would be asked to see the patient and call the patient's doctor. Only in a life-threatening emergency, or to deliver a baby whose arrival was inevitable, would one of us treat another doctor's patient without permission.

After office hours, I went to Tuality. I did a physical exam on Eliza and decided she would probably tolerate a general anesthetic very well. The hospital called an anesthetist to put her to sleep. When everything was ready, I attempted to reduce the fracture, but ran into a problem because the bone ends tended to slip when we tried to apply the plaster cast. If I failed I would face one of the problems a country doctor most hated, which was sending the patient back to bed without fixing what was wrong. In this case Eliza would have to be transferred to a hospital where an orthopedic surgeon was in attendance, or get one to come out the next day, and then submit the patient to another anesthetic and more expense. Eventually, I was successful. However, this meant Eliza was under anesthetic longer than usual.

Eliza was sent back to her four-bed ward about 9 P.M. The three other ladies on the ward were all reading and seemed not to be too sick. Each one greeted me with, "Hello, Doctor" when I entered the ward to check Eliza before leaving the hospital for home. Eliza was very drowsy when I left.

Sometime in the middle of the night, the ward nurse and the supervisor met to discuss Eliza's condition. Like many elderly patients she had awakened during the night, confused. She had tried to crawl out of bed over the side rails, which had been raised to prevent her from doing that very thing. One of the nice ladies in the ward turned her call light on and a nurse had come in to settle Eliza down and get her back into bed.

But then all hell broke loose. My dear, sweet, perky patient became loud and abusive. Nurse's aides held her down in bed while the supervisor phoned to ask me to prescribe a sleep medication to quiet her.

This was risky. Such medications in the confused elderly are often para-
doxical in their action and excite the patient. Paraldehyde, a vile tasting
liquid, was the safest medication under those circumstances. I prescribed
a dose for Eliza.

An hour later my phone rang, again. The nursing supervisor,
sounding exasperated, said Eliza was getting worse. She was shouting,
cursing, and throwing items from her bedside table. She had tried
reasoning with her and threatening to move her into another ward, to no
avail. Now the other patients in her room were awake and complaining.
The subject of leather restraints came up but neither the supervisor nor I
wanted to use them. The supervisor said they weren't particularly busy at
the hospital and suggested she move Eliza into an empty private room and
assign a nurse's aide to sit with her the rest of the night. This seemed like
a pretty good solution.

Again, the phone rang. It was 5 A.M. The nursing supervisor
reported that the aide sitting with Eliza had left the room for a break and
a cup of coffee. Eliza had once more crawled over the side rails and this
time had fallen on her head. The nurse reported that she now had a gash
over her eyebrow that would require stitches. What should she do?

"I'll tell you what to do," I replied rather testily, "put her back in the
ward, take the side rails down so that if she gets up she doesn't fall so far;
and if you can't watch her, perhaps the other ladies in the ward will. Then
get out a suture tray and I'll come over and take care of her."

Whew, was I angry! There was no excuse for this. If I had thought
she was going to be left alone, I would have ordered a private duty nurse.
It was now 5:30 in the morning and I decided I had better shower and
dress for the day, because it didn't look as if I'd have time to return to bed.

By the time I got to the hospital, there were two police cars in the
parking lot, not unusual for a hospital, but it was unusual to find four
Hillsboro city cops on Eliza's ward and everybody talking at once. They
reconstructed the story. It went like this: The three nice ladies in the ward
had worried about Eliza. During the night, when the nurses failed in
reasoning with her, they threatened her, saying, "We're going to take you
to another room where you'll have to be quiet."

After that actually happened, the ladies were shocked when Eliza
returned to the four-bed ward, bleeding from the gash in her head. They
assumed that the nurses had beaten her up. And so, one of the three nice
ladies used her bedside phone to call the cops.

It took at least an hour to pacify everyone, especially the three
ladies and the two nurses who were now mad at the three ladies. "They

called the cops, for God's sake! What kind of a hospital do those three old biddies think we're runnin' here, anyway?" asked the head nurse. The police were bored with the whole thing and accepted my reasonable explanation.

I put some sutures in Eliza's forehead and checked her over for other damage. I found none. She had no recollection of any part of the episode and couldn't understand what the fuss was all about. Later that day she went home, having returned to her usual self, a sweet, perky little old lady.

❧

The night of the first medical school class reunion I had time to attend, just as Glad and I were all dressed up and ready to go to Portland, the phone rang at Creekwood. The call was from the Sheriff's Department. A patient of mine, Bill Riley, had been suffering from psychological problems and had what was then called a psychotic break. He was delusional and violent. The caller reported that Bill was seated on a tree stump in his own pasture, wildly swinging an ax and threatening to bash anyone who came near enough. Would I come?

I demurred. I had plans. The night was to be a gala affair. We would be seeing classmates with whom we had become very close friends during our four years of mutually suffering the tyranny of the medical school professors. I told the deputy sheriff, "Call my partner."

The deputy on the phone said that Bill would only speak to his doctor and because I was his doctor, I had better come. The sheriff explained, "Doctor, if this guy gets wild enough, we might have to shoot him."

"Shoot Bill Riley? Are you guys the crazy ones? This is a perfectly law-abiding citizen who is sick and needs help. You hurt that man and I'll have all of you idiots shot." I was pretty excited.

"Doctor, now, just calm down. We can't leave him out there on his stump after dark. We don't want him loose in the neighborhood with his ax, so we can wait until just before dark; but if you don't have him calmed down by then, we're going to rush him. If he swings that big ax of his at us, we just may have to shoot him. You better come on over here right now, Doctor. We haven't got much time."

My God! Just before dark I want to be in the Benson Hotel in Portland, sipping a bourbon and soda with my classmates, and not in a muddy pasture trying to get an ax out of the hands of my crazy patient. Well, what the hell. I can't let them shoot Bill Riley.

"Okay! I'll come."

Glad went with me. When we pulled into the barnyard all gussied up in our fancy duds, but I with my old shoes on and my good ones in the back seat, there were three police cars, an ambulance with a straitjacket, neighbors, sightseers, and family. I was on center stage.

Bill was, indeed, now standing on a stump of an old Douglas fir tree in the pasture, occasionally swinging a single-bladed ax around over his head and yelling threats and cussing. He looked dangerous.

Trembling inside, but trying my best not to let Bill know that I was afraid, I walked out of the crowd and said, "Hey Bill, it's me. Can I come over and talk to you?"

"What fer, Doc?"

"Just want to talk."

"Whatta ya want to talk about, Doc?"

"Gee, Bill, I'd like to talk about your problem."

"I ain't got a problem, Doc. It's them."

"Who's them, Bill?"

"All of 'em, Doc, they've been tryin' to kill me."

"I won't let them kill you, Bill. Now, can I come over and talk?"

He agreed and I walked over to the stump. My heart was beating about twice its normal speed. I could feel the sweat under my collar and under my arms. I didn't want to be bashed by that sharp ax.

Mrs. Riley had explained before I started out in the field that, earlier in the day, some people had come to their farm and asked Bill if he wanted to sell it. Bill had become excited and scared and this was the result.

I reassured Bill that he was okay with me there, but that he needed rest. I suggested that he go to the hospital. No way would he do that. They would get his farm while he was away, or kill him, or both.

We started over. I told him if he wanted to hand me the ax we could talk better, because the ax was scaring me. He said he didn't want to scare me and handed it over.

At this point, the cops started to run across the field. Bill did not feel reassured by this. I could see a fracas developing if the cops attacked poor Bill, trying to get him in the straitjacket.

I yelled, "Stop! Stay there!"

The phalanx of armed men stopped dead in their tracks. I said, "You see, Bill, I'm in charge. These guys are going to do what I tell them. It's just you and me Bill; we make the decisions here. No one is going to make you sell your farm and no one is going to kill you. I want you to go to the hospital for a few days to get some rest. This has been pretty hard on you and your wife. So let's do it my way."

Bill understood that I was on his side. He permitted me to give him an injection of Thorazine, a powerful sedative, which settled him down. He was able to go to the hospital with dignity, not in a straitjacket. Later he came home with drugs that kept him on an even keel. He was functional from then on, though a little subdued.

When Glad and I finally got to the reunion, we were greeted by old friends who had specialized and were in city practice. When they asked me, "How are you doing—any exciting cases?"

I remembered an old definition I once heard of a country doctor. "A seedy-looking guy with manure on his shoes, straw in his hair, and a case to tell you about."

I replied, "Oh, nothing very much."

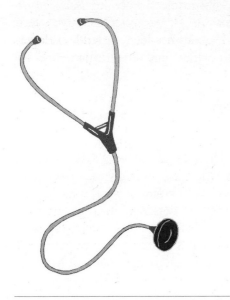

Chapter 22

Do-Si-Do

When I first arrived to practice medicine in southeastern Washington County, my partner said that "to get along in a small town, you have to become part of the scene. The first thing I'm going to do is propose you for the Kiwanis Club."

Glad is a musician. When Glad heard that every meeting of Kiwanis started with group singing, she cautioned me not to open my mouth. "If you sing, they'll probably throw you out of the club, and what will that do to your standing in the town where we plan to spend the rest of our lives?" She knew I couldn't carry a tune. She was uncharacteristically merciless.

I became a Kiwanian. Our club met in the Grange Hall at six o'clock on Thursday evenings. The Grange Hall, which stood behind the office was, except for the high school and the grade school, the largest building in town.

Dinner at those meetings was served in the basement dining room by the Grange ladies. It was where I had first met Mrs. Madigan. It was the best darn country food one could find. I adored the homemade dill pickles, and the fresh, homemade horseradish cleared my sinuses weekly.

Clearing my sinuses apparently did not help my singing ability, as I found that my Kiwanian brothers visibly winced when my rich, out-of-tune baritone voice offended their ears.

I took to arriving late so that I would not have to sing. Tardiness always resulted in a fine of one to five dollars and doing extra chores for the club.

❧

Six Corners, about twenty-five miles from Portland, Oregon, was the intersection on Highway 99W where a sign stated, SHERWOOD, ONE MILE. Hardly anyone ever saw that sign; not many motorists made the turn. Traveling sixty miles an hour, noses pointing west, waiting for a sniff of salty sea air, most travelers on 99W continued west to Highway 18, then onward to the Oregon coast resorts through the lumber mill town of Sheridan, about thirty-five miles west of Six Corners.

The six hundred souls who lived in the town increased by births and decreased by deaths each year in a fairly even number. There wasn't much that was newsworthy about the community.

The Kiwanis Club felt that the town hadn't reached its potential, so to stimulate business they had created the annual Harvest Festival. The festival consisted of a street parade of tractors and trucks, a flower show, and a carnival. Just what one might expect of 95 percent of the local festivals all over the country. As a way of attracting outside business or homeowners, the festival was a bust.

This was my first experience at living someplace no one had ever heard of. If non-Sherwood friends thought they knew where I lived, they assumed it was Sheridan, the town they passed through on the highway going to the Pacific Ocean coastal resorts. SHERwood...SHERidan—they both started with the same letters and each had a total of eight. Everyone had been through Sheridan and no one had ever been to Sherwood. Doctors in the lounge at St. Vincent's hospital in Portland marveled at my ability to make rounds all the way from "Sheridan" each day, a one-hundred-twenty-mile round trip.

When the mayor of Sherwood, at a Kiwanis Club dinner meeting, brought up the question of whether or not to continue the Harvest Festival, I went home and thought about our little town and how to put it on the map. I had recently heard about the Shrove Tuesday Pancake Race between Liberal, Kansas and Olney, England. They had national and international press coverage.

If waitresses in Kansas and England could run down the street, flipping pancakes and attract the press, why couldn't we in Sherwood, Oregon, have an annual, international archery shoot with Nottingham, England? And so an idea was born.

We called it the Robin Hood Festival. The idea caught fire. The Harvest Festival Queen was dumped for Maid Marian and her court. Floats in the parade were made to look like castles. The horses were draped as they might have been in Robin Hood's day. Black Magic loved it. He liked parades, anyway, and he seemed particularly pleased with his costume. Robin Hood and his Merry Men paraded through the streets in elaborate leather costumes made from deerskins donated by the local tannery.

The royal stag (actually a domestic elk, purchased for the occasion each year) was slowly roasted over an open fire on the high school grounds. My job was chief barbecuer. We made succulent elk meat sandwiches and the most popular delicacy, elk burgers.

Our entire family got into the action. Don, Lee, and Pamela all had Robin Hood costumes for the parade. Don rode a suitably draped Sugar Sally, while the two younger ones walked. Glad, who had been appointed the chaperone for Maid Marian and her court, drove a borrowed convertible with the Maid and her two attendants sitting high on the back of the rear seat.

An elegant trophy was created by a Portland jewelry store, archers were identified, and our team competed in an international archery shoot with Robin Hood's Merry Men in Nottingham, England. The scores were telephoned back and forth.

❧

Now, I may not have been a singer but I was a dancer. When I was thirteen, my mother decided that if I were to be a hit with the ladies, I would have to learn to dance. I didn't want to take the lessons but agreed to in exchange for the promise of a new tennis racquet. She arranged ballroom dancing lessons for me at a downtown San Francisco studio. The studio was in a dingy loft on Market Street, above the Crystal Palace Market. Everything that grew was obtainable there, and you could learn to dance upstairs.

The proprietor and sole instructor of this terpsichorean paradise was a slim, blonde woman. I stress…woman. Remember, I was still a kid. But I was supposed to hold her in my arms and dance with her. This lady seemed *old*. To a thirteen-year-old, everyone over twenty seemed old. She wore a white formal gown, made of silk or satin. It clung to her upper body while the skirt swirled as she turned. She smelled as if she had just powdered her shoulders. Every week I boarded the cable car on California Street, transferred at Hyde, and got off on Market Street. I went to the studio and danced. I never liked it, even though she smelled good. She was taller than I.

After dancing I would walk over to the Whitcomb Hotel and hang around, hoping to see a visiting baseball player. All the visiting teams stayed there when playing the San Francisco Seals of the Pacific Coast League.

Many years later, after we had moved to California, our older son, Don, who was thirteen, was invited to join the Palos Verdes Estate's Dance Cotillion, at the Palos Verdes Estates Country Club. All the neighborhood kids were invited. It was the way the ballroom dance instructor made a living. This was an afternoon affair, where the boys were required to wear a suit and tie and the girls wore party dresses and white gloves.

I sat down one day with Don to have a father and son talk. We were perched on the elevated brick hearth of our fireplace in the living room. No one was home but the two of us. It was an ideal time for a man-to-man talk. I wanted to broach the subject of the Dance Cotillion.

"Don," I said, "it's time for you to consider what it will be like to grow up…"

"Dad," he interrupted, "I'm not going to that dancing thing, no matter what you say."

Gee, I haven't even mentioned that. He must be prescient, I thought. "How did you know I was going to talk about the Dance Cotillion, son?"

"Dad, all the kids are talking about it and nobody is going, and I'm not either."

I must reason with the boy, I thought. *He needs to understand about girls.* So I said, "Don, you may not understand about girls now, but as you begin to mature you will have hormones develop in your body"—this was the skillful doctor talking, the counselor of numerous adolescents—"and these hormones will change you; you'll begin to develop a beard, hair will grow under your arms, and around your genitalia. Your muscles will become stronger and there will be urges in you to be with girls. When that time comes, you won't want to be a wallflower because you never learned to dance, now will you, son?"

"Dad, I'm just not going to do it."

"Son, you'll be sorry. Your mother and I always want the best for you and you should accept our advice."

"I know you want the best for me, Dad, and someday I suppose I'll learn to dance, but not now. I'm going to wait for my hormones to come in and then make a decision."

Logic, the bane of my existence, stopped me again.

I wish I could say that my son had a sterling character and braved the repeated pleading of his parents to go to the cotillion. He succumbed to bribery. Apparently, all the boys in the neighborhood had feet of clay, because the cotillion was jammed with reluctant young males. Don did not like it, any more than I had. The girls were taller than he.

❧

I had grown up during the big band era in San Francisco, so I had not counted on pattern dancing and do-si-dos. I was a freestyler. Once we started to square dance at the American Legion Hall, just down and across the street from the Grange Hall, I began to realize that I would never get the hang of it. Remembering what to do next, even with a square dance caller barking instructions, just left me cold. When everyone circled left, I went right; and when all joined hands to promenade, I went backwards. Then the group would have to stop and restart, to accommodate my missteps. I felt just like Seaman LoBelli, the miscreant marcher of Navy boot camp days.

About this time, we convinced the Mayfields to come square dancing with us. Carol did not seem to like us. We felt that she resented being uprooted from a comfortable city existence and moved into the country. She blamed us. She was from a family with money and social status. Square dancing, farming, and hobnobbing with people who wore overalls did not meet her personal expectations of life. Carol kept telling Pinky that he should get a better job.

Once I had asked Pinky if he would consider going to medical school. He had already finished college on the GI bill and had thought about pharmacy school, when his current job had been offered to him. His response to my question about medicine was that he was a born salesman, not a scientist, and he had better stick to what he knew. I had understood what he meant—he had a wife and two kids to support. There was a mortgage to pay, cars and bills, and he was trying to maintain enough of a life insurance program to sustain the family if they needed it.

He said, "There is no way I can go back to school."

❦

One year our monthly square-dancing evening fell on the night after Halloween. The group decided a costume party was in order. Glad and I were not into costumes, sewing was not her forte, and renting a costume meant making several trips to Portland.

I hit on an idea. I brought home two white scrub suits from one of the hospital operating rooms and with black paint we created circular stripes on the pullover tops and the pajama-like pants. Surgical scrub caps were likewise adorned and we went to the party as members of a Georgia chain gang. We had paper chains and beach balls painted black to round out the costumes. We did not realize the impact my costume would have on a certain patient.

Lazlo Hruby lived in Frog Pond, close to Wilsonville. He was a dairy farmer. Lazlo drank. His preferred beverage was not milk. Everyone know Lazlo had a problem, but his dairy farm prospered in spite of it.

Most of the complaints that were heard came from his wife, Reba. She told my partner that Lazlo must have a jug of illegal "corn" stashed in the barn. A couple of old boys up in the hills were known to have stills, and jugs of corn liquor turned up at parties from time to time.

Lazlo's modus operandi was to go to the barn after supper and milk his thirty or forty cows. When he returned in a couple of hours with his ten-gallon cans of milk to put in the cooling shed, he was roaring drunk.

Reba would not let him keep a bottle in the house. She broke what supplies he managed to bring home from legitimate sources. So Lazlo resorted to a stash in the barn, which Reba could not ferret out.

Once Lazlo returned to the house, his chores done, he would soon get sleepy and go to bed. Reba's complaint was his failure to remove his boots before climbing in between the sheets. No doubt Reba's complaint was justified, as the boots were the ones he had worn in the barn while milking and tramping through the inevitable cow manure.

When Lazlo was asleep, it fell to Reba to remove her husband's boots, but he was too much of a hunk for Reba to move around when he was asleep in his drunken stupor. This meant that many nights Reba had to crawl into a bed fouled by Lazlo's boots.

Lazlo was a mild-mannered man and would listen attentively to Reba and respond to her complaints with pleasant promises to reform. However, once he had unearthed his jug, promises went by the wayside. Reba resorted to threats. She threatened to quit doing Lazlo's laundry and to quit cooking his meals. She actually carried out these threats for brief periods, to no avail.

Finally, in desperation, Reba told her husband, "Lazlo, the next time you get in my bed with your boots on, I'm goin' out to the barn, get me a shovel, and mash you on the head."

Lazlo made it into bed for a couple of nights without his boots, but on the Saturday night of the square dance club's Halloween party, he regressed.

Reba told her husband to get up. He didn't. She told him she was going to the barn to get the shovel. He continued to snore. She went and got the shovel and tried to wake him up enough to see her brandish it. He just mumbled and rolled over, again smearing his muddy, manure-covered boots all over Reba's clean sheets. Reba snapped. She raised the shovel over her head, expecting to hit Lazlo on the head with the flat of it—or so she claimed when the police questioned her. Instead, the shovel became entangled with the ceiling light fixture. Reba lost control of it and hit Lazlo across the scalp with the sharp side of the tool.

He was a mess. There was blood everywhere. The white, glistening bone of the skull shone through the gore. Lazlo was unconscious. She knew that he was alive because he intermittently let out a huge groan. She made an attempt at resuscitation by pouring water over his head. This diluted the blood, making it appear that the bleeding was worse than it really was.

She panicked and called the fire department. The firemen, after surveying the situation, called the state police. Shortly thereafter, everyone repaired to the Sherwood Clinic. The firemen had phoned my house, where the babysitter had informed them of my whereabouts. The state trooper then tracked me down at the American Legion Hall, while the ambulance went to the office, two blocks away.

When we deposited Lazlo on the table in the office surgery, his appearance was appalling. The edge of the shovel had struck him a shearing blow from back to front. This had pulled his scalp forward from midcranium to the forehead and laid it over his eyes. He couldn't see, but his skull was not damaged. Covering his eyes were his scalp and his long, lank, blood-soaked hair. He was beginning to come out of his drunken stupor and he was mumbling, "Oh God, I'm blind, I'm blind, I'm blind."

The firemen and the state trooper, never having seen anything this grotesque, had simply slapped some sterile gauze pads over the wound and wrapped his head with roller bandage.

I removed the gauze pads, pulled the patient's scalp back into position, then wiped the blood from his eyes. Blinking from the light and from the tearing, he saw, first, the state policeman, then he saw me in my convict's costume. He cried, "I'm in jail! What have I done? You in jail too, Doc?"

I sutured Lazlo's scalp back into place and gave him a tetanus booster and copious doses of antibiotics. He would not file a complaint against his wife for assault, nor she against him for getting into bed with his boots on. The latter is probably not on the statutes as a crime, anyway.

All did not go well in the Hruby family from then on, although Lazlo Hruby improved. He drank less, but still drank a lot. He kept a jug in the barn and fell asleep in a drunken stupor almost every night; but he never, never again went to bed with his boots on.

The Robin Hood Festival continues to flourish, but it has not achieved the media success of the Shrove Tuesday Pancake Race.

The Sherwood Square Dance Club continued and flourished. After two more years, I revolted and we resigned.

Some people still believed I practiced in Sheridan.

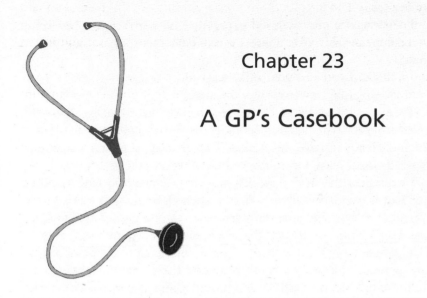

Chapter 23

A GP's Casebook

Lucille Oldenburger had cut her ankle by tripping over a piece of farm machinery in the Oldenburger barnyard. Lucille was a large woman of very sturdy proportions. As she sat on the end of the examination table, I could visualize her in the barn, pitching the hay into the manger for the cows and cleaning the stalls after milking. She was, indeed, a woman to be reckoned with.

Lucille was dressed in a housedress she had made herself. She was the archetypal farm wife. One hundred years earlier she might have worn a bonnet and had a dress like the ones Glad and Pamela had worn for the Oregon Centennial celebration the year before.

She was not a complainer. Lucille had grown up in a stoic German family and did not call the doctor unless it was urgent; in fact, she and her family generally treated themselves. Urgent, to the Oldenburgers, meant anything with unendurable pain, which I guessed had to be bad, worse than any pain I would care to put up with; or they might see a doctor for an illness or injury that threatened death. On this day Lucille thought she was dying.

The reason for her anxiety was the infected cut on her leg. There was a red streak running up her leg, ending in a swollen, tender lump in her groin. She said, "Doctor, I wouldn't have bothered you, but I think I have blood poisoning and my Aunt Mathilde died of that when I was a little girl. And, Doctor, Aunt Mathilde only lived a week after the blood poisoning set in."

Lucille had a very worried expression on her face and her voice quavered a bit as she spoke, entirely out of character for her usually stoic personality.

"When did you hurt yourself?" I asked.

"Last Saturday, a week," was the answer.

Today was Tuesday. I calculated the wound to be ten days old, plenty of time for lymphangitis and adenitis (inflammation of the lymph vessel and gland) to have developed. The incubation period for tetanus had passed, so, at least, I didn't have that to worry about.

I examined the wound, which was large enough to have required sutures had it been seen when it first happened, but now it was a pussy, oozing mess. It would require daily irrigation of a saline solution to clean out the debris while we treated the red streaks, the wound itself, and the swollen glands with hot wet-packs. I gave Lucille an injection of a large dose of penicillin, a tetanus booster, irrigated the wound, and applied a sterile dressing. I said, "Lucille, you have nothing to worry about. When your Aunt Mathilde died of blood poisoning, doctors didn't have the wonderful antibiotics we have today. If you'll follow my instructions and change your dressing after each time you apply the hot wet-packs, and come in again tomorrow for another injection of penicillin, I'm sure you'll be okay." Lucille left, greatly relieved.

I saw Lucille on Wednesday, Thursday, and Friday. There was some improvement but not enough to satisfy either of us. The wound itself continued to exude pus. The original culture of the pus showed a bacteria that was ordinarily susceptible to penicillin. Now I worried that we might be dealing with an exotic bacteria that hadn't showed up on the first culture. I knew that Lucille was again worried. The effect of the assurance I had offered, that she would not suffer the same fate as her long departed Aunt Mathilde, was waning.

Lucille was scheduled to come in during Saturday morning office hours but failed to show up. *Has she lost faith in me? Is she better and not coming in for that reason? Or has she just forgotten that the office was always closed on Saturday afternoon?*

The Oldenburgers had no phone. I decided that I would go by their place on the way home. If she had gone to another doctor or was mad at me for some reason, so be it; it was better to err on the side of safety than to be stubborn and wait for her to come to me. By that time her condition could be worse.

When I drove into the farmyard, Otto Oldenburger was coming out of the barn. He was carrying a newspaper that obviously held something of value because of the way it was carefully folded. He greeted me graciously and said, "Ah, Doktor, vee vas coming to see you later. Now I fix a little poultice for my Lucille." He proffered the hand holding the wrapped newspaper to demonstrate what he meant.

Well, now I knew one thing—the Oldenburgers had forgotten that we closed on Saturday afternoon. This relieved my anxiety about being rebuffed; I was still their doctor. I asked, "Otto, what do you have in the paper for Lucille's poultice?"

"Yah, Doktor, for my Lucille." He opened the newspaper and showed me its contents. Cobwebs! A great big collection of dirty cobwebs collected from the barn. I gaped. No wonder my patient hadn't improved! They were recontaminating the wound every day!

Otto said, "Doktor, in zee old country vee do zis. Spider webs make goot healing. After vee take off zee hot towel und zee wound looks fresh und zee pus is all gone, I put on zee spider webs to make it heal goot."

No wonder Aunt Mathilde died!

We went into the house where I took off the hot wet-packs that the Oldenburgers had applied half an hour earlier. The wound looked great. We had a long talk. I didn't run down the curative powers of cobwebs. Native healers in some parts of the world have some success with such things, but I disagreed with the site of their origin. There isn't any place dirtier than a barn that holds pigs, cows, and chickens. I pointed out that such treatments, which may have been of value in the days before antibiotics, were no longer as good as the offerings of modern medicine.

Lucille improved quickly, once we stuck to the regimen I prescribed. The Oldenburgers were abashed over what they perceived as their ignorance and their old country ways. I reassured them again, and said, "If you have any other tricks you brought with you from the old country, tell me about them. I'll bet some are good tricks and maybe I can use them in my practice." They felt better; so did I.

~~~

I delivered little Angeline Ferrar at Tuality Hospital. The birth was uneventful. Baby Angie was about as cute as they come. She was the Ferrars' first.

When Angie was five months old, her mother asked me to make a house call because Angie was sick and Philip wasn't home from work with their only car. She knew that the office would be closed shortly, and she really hoped that I could see the baby.

I dropped by after office hours. Angie had a miserable, runny nose with a thick mucoid discharge that she was having trouble handling. Because of her nasal congestion she wouldn't take her bottle and was quite fussy. I checked her ears, throat, and lungs and found them to be clear. The baby did not have a fever. I prescribed some infant nose drops to be used for a couple of days and an oral decongestant to be started the next day if she wasn't better. The Ferrars had an infant nasal syringe which I advised them to use to help the baby to breathe. Also, I suggested that they place her face down in her crib to facilitate nasal drainage.

My phone rang the next morning around six. It was Mrs. Ferrar. She was crying and shouting, "Angie isn't moving. She's cold and I don't think she is breathing. I'm afraid my baby is dead!"

I rushed to the Ferrar's immediately. Beautiful little Angie was dead. Her little body was cold, indicating that she had been dead for some hours.

I was shocked. It was the first and only SIDS (Sudden Infant Death Syndrome) in all my years of practice. There is no way to reconcile the shock of such an event. I wondered what I could have done or should have done. After the autopsy it became evident that this was one of those disasters that, if you are going to practice medicine, you are going to have to live with. My partner and other colleagues assured me that I had done no wrong. I was grateful that the baby's parents held me blameless and I finally put this case out of my mind.

But the bad memories never go away completely, and the ghosts of patients long gone, rise again and again. Recently there has been significant publicity given to research which has demonstrated that SIDS deaths can be greatly reduced if babies lie on their sides or backs rather than face down, as I recommended that night when I made a house call on little Angie Ferrar.

※

Raoul Fortier, age ten years, was brought to the office one day in June. He had a tummy ache. His mother, Maria, was from the Lucetti family whose oldest son, Eddy Jr., ran the family's bean field and truck gardens. She had married into the Fortier clan, who were successful farmers, and lived just a few miles away. Maria was almost tearful when trying to explain Raoul's symptoms. She said, "My poor little boy has cried all night with pains in his tummy. I should have called earlier; now, I'm afraid I may have waited too long and he's in danger."

I took the usual history. The pain had started the afternoon before and had continued during the night. Maria had taken Raoul's temperature and found it normal. This had made her think that this was a simple illness. In the morning, Raoul told his mother he'd had a loose stool during the night, reassuring his mother that this was a common, garden variety intestinal flu bug.

Raoul was supposed to go to work for a neighbor that morning to help get a crop in before it rained, but he stayed home. Later that morning he went to the bathroom and had another loose stool, but forgot to flush the toilet. An hour later Maria went into the bathroom and, to her horror, saw what appeared to be blood in the toilet bowl.

Maria was a very bright lady and a diligent mom. Wisely, she scooped some of the stool into a jar and rushed her son and the jar to the office. When I looked at the specimen she brought, I was sure I recognized the classic "prune juice stool," a definitive symptom of a volvulus (an intestinal obstruction due to a knotting and twisting of the bowel). The fact that Raoul's pain had subsided made the prognosis worse, for it probably indicated that a section of the bowel was dead. If so, time was critical. I had to get Raoul to the hospital immediately. He would require emergency surgery.

I stepped into the hall to call my nurse to come after the stool specimen and test it for blood, but I ran smack into my older son, Don. He had come to the office to get a package for his mother who was outside waiting in the car. Don had a glimpse into the examining room as I emerged, and saw Raoul and his mom. He said, "Hey, Dad, what's he doing here?"

"Don, I'm busy. I'm dealing with an emergency and I don't have time to talk. Furthermore, you know I don't ever talk about my patients with you." I was agitated, not only about the boy waiting in the exam room, but also about the number of patients that wouldn't get seen that day because I would have to go to the hospital. I let my irritation fall on Don's shoulders because he was nearest and because he was family and, as so often happens, we hurt those who are close to us when the problem lies elsewhere. Roughly, I said, "Beat it, Don. You've no business here." And I turned away.

But Don wouldn't be put off. "Raoul didn't show up for work this morning. What's the matter with him? Does he have a bellyache?"

Bellyache? How does Don know Raoul has a bellyache?

My mind began to function. Where did Don work? Why, sure, he was picking blackcaps (black raspberries) at the Jonathan farm. The kids started in the morning, very early before it got hot, and were finished before noon. The picking had begun yesterday.

"Son, why do you think he has a bellyache?"

"I told Raoul yesterday not to eat all those blackcaps—he'd get sick. Gosh, Dad, he ate more than he turned in!"

From the mouths of babes! The diagnosis was made. The prune juice stools were blackcap stools; the bellyache was from eating too many blackcaps. The pain had stopped because, like a green apple stomachache, in time it goes away. Raoul left, a wiser boy, and perhaps less a glutton.

∽∞∾

Sunday morning at Creekwood was family time. We usually had a leisurely breakfast and if I was on call I would take one or two of our children with me on hospital rounds. The kids would come into the hospital with me and wait in the doctors' lounge where there was always coffee, soft drinks, and morning pastries. I was not alone in taking my children on rounds with me, so there were often several kids waiting for their dads and trading stories about their parents, their schools, and life in general. Some of the regulars made friends and looked forward to seeing each other.

On the Sunday mornings that I was not on call, our family tended to be quite lazy. We would have a large breakfast and hang out with each other in pajamas or old clothes until it was time to go to church. We were not very faithful churchgoers and it didn't take a whole lot to distract us from going.

One of the distractions was the presence of the community's Lutheran Church about three hundred yards south of Creekwood. We didn't attend there, but many of our patients did; and of course, everyone knew that the doctor lived just up the road from the church.

One balmy spring Sunday morning when I was home just foolin' around, a car came careening up our driveway and stopped in front of the house. The driver began to blow the car's horn—continuously, raucously shattering the peace of a Sunday morning. A passenger emerged and met me as I came out the front door in my PJs and bathrobe with a mouthful of eggs and bacon. As he ran up the front steps I noted with some humor (I was pretty upset with this disturbance on Sunday morning) that my visitor tripped slightly on the uneven stair tread that was Black Magic's contribution to our housewarming.

"Come with me to the church, Doctor," cried my visitor, "Cora has collapsed; she is on the floor. We won't move her until you come, so hurry, Doctor!"

Cora, our receptionist? I thought she was a Methodist. Well, she does live across the street from the Methodist church, but that doesn't necessarily mean she is a member there. Maybe I guessed wrong.

"Cora Franklin, our receptionist?" I asked.

"No, Doctor, not Cora Franklin. She's a Methodist!" He spit out Methodist like it was a cussword; but this was not the time to get into local church politics. So, I asked, "Cora who, then?"

"Cora Bidwell," he answered, "and she's Lutheran, so hurry." Well, we had identified the correct denomination, and that seemed to be a reason to hurry. I put on some clothes and went over to the church.

When I got there I found Cora Bidwell lying on the floor, half in the aisle and half in front of one of the wooden pews. Luckily, for me, her upper end was in the aisle, so that I could talk to her. She was by now wide awake and wanting to get up off the floor. However, she was being kept there by concerned parishioners. Church services had been suspended and the crowd around Cora was steadily being exhorted by an officious member of the congregation to "Back up and give her air." The crowd didn't want to back up. They wanted to see what was going on. Cora's dilemma was probably more interesting than the sermon had been.

The common exhortation "Back up and give 'em air" has a good point. That is, back up and get out of the way. "Give 'em air" hasn't much going for it, unless the accident has occurred in a mine cave-in and there isn't enough air for anyone. Out of doors, in the chapel of a church, or anywhere that the crowd is able to breathe is okay for the patient. Cora had plenty of air; what she hadn't had was enough blood flowing to her brain just before she passed out. Because the service was long and Cora was very attentive, and because the pulpit was very high and she was in the second row, she had—by keeping her neck bent backwards—shut off part of the circulation to her brain by means of pressure on her vertebral arteries. When she fainted, her neck straightened out and full circulation returned, permitting her to return to full consciousness. Now she wanted to get up off the floor and go home. Cora was embarrassed.

I said, "Okay, but let me see you in the office soon for a checkup." She agreed.

I went home and Glad fixed a fresh batch of bacon and eggs.

Three weeks later I had another caller from the church. This came just after I arrived home from hospital rounds. Same story, third row instead of the second row. When the third episode occurred, church officials brought the patient to the house. Same story, first row.

It was time that the minister and I had a conference. I explained to him that, although this hadn't happened in years before, he should understand that his parishioners were aging. Some of the oldest, who had hearing problems, were moving to the front pews. Others, who were already in the front pews, had circulatory problems associated with aging. People were suffering from vertebral artery syndrome caused by craning the neck upwards. I asked him if he could think of a solution, such as lowering the height of the pulpit, getting a sound system, or eliminating the first couple of rows of pews. He didn't like any of the ideas. I also thought of suggesting that he shorten his sermons, but I didn't suppose he'd like that either; so I didn't suggest that.

There were two more bouts of syncope (fainting) before the first two rows of pews were blocked with ribbon and only opened on Easter Sundays when everyone came to church and two short services were held. The pastor was adamant about retaining the height of the pulpit.

❧

Andy McDermot lived near Wankers Corner, close to Lake Oswego and fast becoming suburbia. On a Saturday afternoon Andy's mother called, saying that Andy, who was eighteen, had a stomachache and a fever, and she was afraid he had appendicitis.

Andy's room was decorated as I imagined the room of most city teenagers would look, just like the boys on the television show *Ozzie and Harriet.* The college pennant was from Lewis and Clark College, which was nearby; and there was a collection of well-used sports equipment, including a baseball glove, a couple of well-scuffed balls and a new ball signed by Dick Traczewski of the professional triple-A Portland Beavers. Andy was a player and a fan.

I sat down on the edge of Andy's bed and talked to him. In answer to my questions he told me that the pain in the right side of his belly had been present for maybe three days. At first he had hardly noticed it, but today it had become unbearable. And he pointed to the right lower quadrant of his abdomen. He said he hadn't been nauseated until a few hours before, but he thought he could eat something and he had been drinking Coke and juices.

I took his temperature. It was 102.8 Fahrenheit, almost 103 degrees—a little high for acute appendicitis, unless it had ruptured and he had peritonitis. I examined his belly. It was not hard, as it would be with a ruptured appendix. I breathed a sigh of relief; but it was tender in the right lower quadrant where the appendix lies. When I pushed down on his abdominal wall and then let go quickly, there was no increase in pain as there would be if the peritoneum itself was irritated.

I stood back and looked at this kid. I thought, *He may well have acute appendicitis and he probably needs to go to the hospital and have a blood count, a urinalysis and an abdominal X-ray. Then, if the results are equivocal, perhaps exploratory surgery will be necessary.* But something nagged at my mind. (Sometimes I imagined myself with little men sitting on my shoulders. One might say, "Go ahead." The other often cautioned, "Wait a minute. Check again." Some people might call that intuition, others might say it's experience. Whatever it was, on that day the second little man won.) I decided to check one more time.

A physical diagnostic maneuver I had not tried, was to ballotte the kidney. This organ is hard to feel because it is actually behind the abdominal cavity. In fat people it may be impossible to feel at all. In a muscular, athletic young man like Andy, the only way to get a handle on the condition of the kidney would be to ballotte it. To execute this maneuver it was necessary for me to push my right hand firmly into his abdomen where I thought the kidney was and then, with my left hand, push deeply into the muscle area in his back, just below the ribs, and try to raise the kidney to where I could feel it with my abdominal hand.

Once my right hand was in position, I ballotted with my left hand, but instead of the firm muscle I expected, two of my fingers embedded in his back sank into a mushy substance. Andy screamed in pain. I withdrew my hand and discovered that my fingers were covered with pus. What in the world had I gotten into?

After repairing to the bathroom and thoroughly washing my hands, I rolled Andy onto his stomach and examined his back. There I saw the cause of all his trouble—a carbuncle (a multiheaded boil). The infection in these tissues had caused the lymph nodes in his abdomen to become swollen, inflamed, and very tender, simulating appendicitis. Lymph nodes themselves cannot be palpated, which often causes doctors to operate unnecessarily. Most swollen lymph glands are a result of a bowel infection and not from such an obvious source as a carbuncle on the back.

I was astounded that Andy had not told me about the infection in his back. I asked him why he had not.

He replied, "Doctor, I didn't see how a boil on my back that had been there for a week, could make me have a stomachache."

After I treated Andy and was driving home I reflected on those two imaginary guys, intuition and experience, who sat on my shoulders. I decided it might be because of them that doctoring was called "practicing medicine."

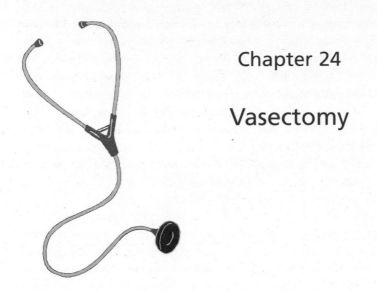

Chapter 24

Vasectomy

It was five o'clock on a sultry afternoon in July. There had been rain, earlier. Now steam was rising like fog on the macadam road in front of the Sherwood Clinic as the sun beat down. Cora left her cubicle and locked the front door. This was mainly a symbolic gesture. If anyone knocked, she would let them in so that we might avoid a house call later.

Our patients still did not have appointments. We saw everyone who showed up each day. My partner and I argued about this. I felt that many times patients got short shrift and were disappointed that we had too little time for them if they really needed more. His approach was always to increase the number of patients, whereas I wanted to spend more quality time with each patient. I consistently lost the battle to the specious argument, "If it ain't broke, don't fix it," the hallmark attitude of people resistant to change and therefore to progress.

Tonight, however, I did have an appointment with a patient.

There were two patients remaining in the waiting room, and both were put in examining rooms.

Helen, our nurse, was busy in the multipurpose room preparing the surgical setup on a Mayo stand. She placed a Bard Parker scalpel with a No. 10 blade on the edge of the tray. Then, in the middle of the tray, she lined up a pair of rat-tooth thumb forceps, two towel clamps, four mosquito hemostats, two Allis clamps, a pair of Metzenbaum dissecting scissors, a pair of suture scissors, a tiny self-retaining retractor, a tube of plain triple-O catgut, a needle holder with a small round curved needle, and a pile of sterile four-by-four gauze pads. She covered the tray with a sterile towel. Then she opened another package of towels and a surgical drape. She placed these on the side table. She also fixed a two-by-two gauze sponge on each of two ringed sponge forceps and opened a bottle of tincture of Merthiolate antiseptic solution. Everything was ready.

It was Friday, my partner was taking a long weekend, and I was alone in the office. At 5:30 P.M. I finished with the last patient. Cora and Helen went out by the back door; Blanche and Virginia had left earlier. I was now completely alone. I went into the lab, poured the dregs of the coffee pot into my mug, and sat down to wait.

At exactly 5:45 P.M., a car turned into the parking lot. The car did not hesitate in the patient's parking area, but drove directly to the rear of the building, where the doctors parked, out of sight from the road and only visible from the second floor windows of the Grange Hall next door. The Grange Hall was unoccupied on Friday evenings. The man hesitated, checked his rearview mirror, then quickly and furtively got out of his car and entered the unlocked back door of the clinic, calling out, "I'm here, Doc."

I hauled my tired feet off the desk and went to the back hall, leaving my coffee cup in the lab on my way through. Standing just inside the back door was the patient with the appointment. He was there to have a vasectomy.

I locked the back door and welcomed Theodore Stricke with a handshake. "Into this room, Ted," and I pointed to the multipurpose room. "Take off your pants and shorts and lie on the table on your back. Are you still comfortable with the idea? No last minute doubts?"

Ted looked pretty woebegone, but he stoutly answered, "No doubts, Doc. Brenda would kill me if I came home without having it done."

A week before, Ted, Brenda, and I had sat in the office and discussed the problems of birth control. The couple had four children. Brenda wanted no more. Ted didn't care. Brenda pointed out that he wasn't home all day looking after the kids.

The options for contraceptives were limited. Birth control pills were not yet on the market. Couples had a few basic choices: don't do it; use foam or a spermicidal jelly; adopt a rhythm method, or use male withdrawal prior to ejaculation, which method was frowned on for two reasons. One, it did not work because of pre-ejaculatory leakage; and two, it was sexually unsatisfactory. All the above methods filled the birthing suites of hospitals.

The real basic methods of the day were barrier and surgical methods. Barrier methods meant diaphragms or condoms. Men did not like condoms because they complained it was like "washing your feet with your socks on." Furthermore, condoms were not easily available.

Drugstores kept them in a secret drawer behind the counter. They were not being passed out in schools or advertised on the sides of city buses in those days. Men seeking condoms were too embarrassed to approach a female clerk at the store. They had to find a male employee, usually the pharmacist, and ask for a "box of Trojans, please." The pharmacist or a male employee would then wrap these items in a plain brown wrapper and surreptitiously hand them to the customer. In today's world, condom availability has changed.

Women did not like diaphragms because they had to stop and insert the device during the foreplay that preceded intercourse, or be prepared most of the time, both of which took away the spontaneity of lovemaking.

The surgical choices were tubal ligation and vasectomy. Both of these were surgical procedures, but vasectomy—unless a woman had a cesarean section and her tubes tied at the same time—was cheaper and easier. Modern technology, through the use of the laparoscope, has made tubal ligation much easier, and has changed the priority of the options somewhat.

After the conference, both Brenda and Ted signed release forms and the appointment was set up. Usually the procedure was done on Friday, so that the patient could rest over the weekend and go back to work on Monday morning, with no one the wiser. The husband could even look at the following weekend with a little joy. Guilt-laden wives often prepared sumptuous meals and lavished a lot of tender loving care on their "suffering husbands."

All this sneaking around in order to have a vasectomy bothered me. Vasectomy was not illegal.

The sneaking around had started with my partner, before I arrived. Everyone on the office staff knew that a patient was scheduled for after hours. Who was embarrassed? My partner, who had originally set up the charade? Certainly our nurse, who set up the surgical tray, knew what was about to happen and should have been scheduled to help me. I knew she was not embarrassed, and Cora wasn't, either. I thought the patients had been led into this sneaking around because of a concern that people in the community would find out that they had been made sterile. It made the entire procedure seem like some sort of illicit affair.

It always amazed me that men were so reluctant to have the simple vasectomy procedure done. Somehow, they felt that any alteration of their sacred male genitalia reduced their manhood and virility. Such ideas are even worse in some developing countries, where vasectomy is never used and governments resort to abortion. I saw the results of a study in Jamaica in which a woman who had her uterus removed for benign or malignant conditions was no longer sexually appealing to men, as she was considered no longer a real woman, despite the fact that she had a functioning and sensitive vagina perfectly capable of enjoying intercourse. Such women might even offer greater male satisfaction, thanks to their sense of freedom from having children.

Being alone in the office while doing an operation, even a minor one, worried me. This, too, had been a method established before my arrival in the practice. As a young, inexperienced doctor, when I first arrived I accepted most of what was handed to me. Now, after several years of experience, I had questions. The relationship between my partner and me had begun to unravel.

Ted lay on the table. I scrubbed his scrotum with soap and painted the area with the sponges of Merthiolate and placed sterile towels on either side of the area, then covered the surgical site with a sterile surgical drape. The drape had a built-in slit of about the size necessary to work through. The remainder of the area would remain covered and sterile.

Each side was done separately after an injection of Novocaine into the operative site. While I was working on side one, a period of about ten minutes, Ted began to sweat profusely. I asked him if he was all right.

He said, "I'm okay.... I guess."

Then he began to moan, deep down in his chest. The sounds were eerie. I asked, again, if he was all right or if I was hurting him. Again, he replied negatively.

Cheerily, I said, "First side is all finished, one side to go."

I injected the Novocaine and made the second incision. (Today's advanced methods require only one incision in the midline; the procedure has been greatly simplified.)

I hit a little artery and blood squirted up and out of the slit in the surgical drape, northward toward Ted's abdomen. Ted saw the blood. Now the moans increased. Suddenly, he went stiff, his face turned ashen, the sweating increased, and he started shaking all over with a full, convulsive seizure. His arms and legs were jerking and his body thrashing about on the table. He was in psychogenic shock. The blood had drained away from his brain, which caused him to have the seizure and faint.

Our modest office surgical table did not have a strap to hold the patient in place and, during the seizure, Ted flipped right off the table onto the floor. I was able to catch his upper body to keep his head from smashing on the cement floor, which was covered with only thin asbestos floor tile.

The convulsive motions stopped, but Ted was out cold. My sterile set up was in total disarray. I had contaminated my sterile gloves and that little artery was still pumping merrily away, shooting its bright red stream, making cheerful little red streaks wherever it fell.

This was not the first time a patient under my care had fallen from the operating table. When I was a resident, doing a thoracic procedure, the table had broken and my little patient (who was only about one hundred ten pounds) fell, but I was able to catch and hold her in my arms. Ted was six feet, two inches tall and weighed about two hundred twenty-five pounds. I tried to pick him up. No luck. I could get one end of him on the table, but when I tried to put the other end up, the first end fell off.

Also, there was a continuing problem. The little artery didn't know when enough was enough. The arterial blood was running on the floor, making it slippery. I decided if I did not straighten out this mess before long, my patient could suffer bodily harm. He was breathing peacefully, but he was in a dead faint.

I looked up from the floor and saw my Mayo stand and the tray of instruments intact. I grabbed a mosquito hemostat from the tray and clamped the little artery, shutting down its contribution to the confusion. *Now, what to do? Should I get an ampule of spirits of ammonia and hold it under his nose? Roll the oxygen tank from the corner of the room and start oxygen by mask? Then Ted would wake up, take one look at the mess and his open wound, and probably pass out all over again.*

I made the only reasonable decision. I took the tray off the Mayo stand and laid it on the floor beside me. While on my knees, with no sterile drapes, I finished the procedure.

I cleaned up the mess and woke Ted. He looked around and said quizzically, "What's going on? I'm on the floor?"

I told him, "Just as I finished, Ted, you fainted. I laid you down on the floor so you wouldn't hurt yourself."

He was satisfied with that as an explanation for his being on the floor of his doctor's office. I'm not sure many people would have been so trusting.

I sent Ted home with some antibiotic pills as a prophylaxis against infection. He was none the worse for wear. At about the time he was leaving the office, there was a noisy clap of thunder and the rain started, again.

After this experience, my partner and I had to rethink our methods for doing vasectomies. We bought a strap for the operating table. I still did not wish to be alone in the office doing this kind of procedure; however, my partner was unrelenting in his desire for secrecy.

Pinky was at the office one day and we discussed the problem. He volunteered to come in on the Friday nights when I had a "vas" scheduled (this only occurred a dozen times a year), and help me do it. He said, "I've missed being around surgery. We had so much fun together in the operating room at Mob 2, when we were in the Navy— let me come and help." He did, each time thereafter, and it relieved my anxiety.

Six weeks after doing a vas, we always checked a specimen of seminal fluid to be sure everything was okay before we gave the go-ahead for unprotected sex. Cases of anomalous division of the vas deferens had been reported, and even though we removed a segment of the duct while doing the procedure, anomalous ducts were always a possibility. In addition, the life of a sperm cell is about thirty days and some could live in the seminal vesicles or the proximal part of the duct even longer than that, so we checked the specimens.

Most men responded appropriately to the instruction, "Collect a specimen in a clean glass jar and bring it in within thirty minutes of the time that you've collected it."

One guy asked, "How do I get a specimen?"

I answered, "You know, by the mechanical friction method."

He thought about this briefly and said, "I don't know what you mean."

"Masturbate," I said.

"What?"

"Jack off."

"Oh, I don't do that."

"Did you ever do it as a kid?"

"Yeah."

"Well, pretend you're a kid again."

❧⚜❧

When Don was eight years old and a Cub Scout, I was asked to go to a Scout camp as camp doctor. This was a primitive camp in the coast range of mountains about fifty miles from home. The incentive for my going was that I could take Don along. This experience would be great for him and help him to decide to continue in scouting, which I thought would be a very good thing for our boys to do.

We arrived at camp at 1 P.M. on a Sunday afternoon, and were assigned to the first aid tent as our living quarters. We found out where the kybo (commode) and the mess tent were and, secure in our knowledge that all the basics were in place, went for a swim in the lake.

That night after dinner, when most of the boys were around the campfire, I went to the shower tent. As I started down the steps, I suddenly stopped in my tracks. An eleven- or twelve-year-old boy was standing under the shower, eyes closed, his hand around his penis and working it back and forth with great vigor. The kid was oblivious to his surroundings. I retreated. I waited a suitable period, went back to an empty shower tent, and took my shower.

I pondered, that night, as to what my responsibility was to that boy and the rest of the camp. Remember, I had grown up in a post-Victorian environment in respect to sex and bodily parts. When I was in grade school, everyone in San Francisco knew that a great football player at the University of California at Berkeley had died because he masturbated too much. It came out later that he had amyotrophic lateral sclerosis—Lou Gehrig's disease, an incurable, untreatable illness, which causes the body to literally waste away. But, in those days it was gospel, and actually preached from a pulpit, that the football player had died from playing with himself. Since then I had been in the Navy, gone to medical school, and had been in practice. I had learned enough to keep my peace. Also, I had learned that sexual experimentation among pre-teens and teenagers was usual and probably necessary for normal male and female sexual development.

The next night one of the scoutmasters went to take a shower about the same time as I had the night before. He returned to the staff area all in a snit. "Where's the doctor?" he cried.

"Here I am."

The scoutmaster rushed over and said, "We've got a terrible problem. I need to talk to you in private."

We walked out of range and, with his face all screwed up in horror, he whispered, "I caught one of the boys masturbating. I have two of the counselors guarding him. We must expel him right away. I want a note from you to his parents giving the reason why he is being expelled and what should be done to help him."

I wondered if he had found the same kid. If so, this kid was really pretty active, but his only crime was doing his thing in a public place where he was likely to be discovered.

"I don't think he should be expelled. I'll talk to him."

The scoutmaster was not satisfied. He went off to find the camp director and they both returned. The director said he could not countenance this kind of aberrant behavior among the scouts.

I began to boil. "What's aberrant about it? Didn't either of the two of you ever jack off as a kid?" Both of them seemed to have red faces—or was it just reflection from the campfire?

They didn't answer.

I went on. "This boy's only crime was being in a public place. It is no reason to attempt to disgrace him. I'll discuss it with him and ask him not to risk public exposure again, but I will not screw up his little psyche by causing him to be ashamed of his body."

I won the battle. The two of them could not face up to my indignation but, I fear, I did not change their minds. I worried about this kind of person being a leader of boys.

❦

Collecting the sample to check for sperm after a vasectomy wasn't the only problem about this procedure facing us as practitioners. A patient whose husband had undergone a vasectomy about a year earlier came to the office one day with symptoms of missed period and morning sickness. I checked her. She was pregnant.

Oh-oh!

The lady was a paragon of virtue in the neighborhood. She was a regular attendee at the local church and had been a deacon. She put up with a drunken, no-good husband and had carried his several children. No hint of scandal had ever involved this family, other than the drunkenness and shiftlessness of her husband.

This lady could not have been cheating. Could she? I had to ask the most delicate question, one I always hated to ask, "Have you had an affair?"

The answer was quick, explosive, and negative, "No," she said; with her face red and angry she cried, "you should know better than that. You failed when you did the vasectomy on my husband. It's your fault!"

This was bad news. I knew that the two sections of her husband's vas deferens, which I had removed and sent to the pathologist, had been anatomically confirmed. I knew that the sperm specimen I had checked under the microscope, at six weeks after the procedure, had no sperm in it. The lady was lying. But in my heart there was that tinge of doubt. There are few absolutes in this world. This was close—but absolute?

⚬⚬⚬

However, I had been down this street before. It had been only a short time before that a new patient had come in with a little different I-didn't-cheat-on-my-husband story. She said, "I can't be pregnant! My husband is impotent. We haven't had sex in three years."

"Madam," I replied, "you're surely pregnant. Do you wish to tell me how you got that way?"

The lady thought.

I waited.

Finally, she said, "He must have done it while I was asleep."

"That, madam, is the biggest cock and bull story I have ever heard. First, it is a lie that you could sleep through it; and second, it is a lie because if he had been unable to have an erection for three years and was finally able to achieve it, he would not have let you sleep. He would have talked about it all night." The lady must have taken her tale to another doctor, as she never returned.

⚬⚬⚬

My "paragon of virtue" patient, whose husband had a vasectomy, calmed down and said, "I need an abortion and you're gonna have to do it or pay for it."

Now this was a switch. She was attempting to blackmail me into doing or paying for an abortion on the basis of my presumed failure. I took a daring track. I said, "Fine, if the sperm test on your husband is positive, I will do it."

The poor soul had nowhere to turn. She was frightened and hoped for any solution. She sent her husband in for a sperm test. It was negative.

I never found out how, but she managed an illegal abortion, somewhere. Who was around our area, running an illegal abortion mill? Whoever it was probably did this lady a service.

She and her family continued as my patients but we never discussed this again.

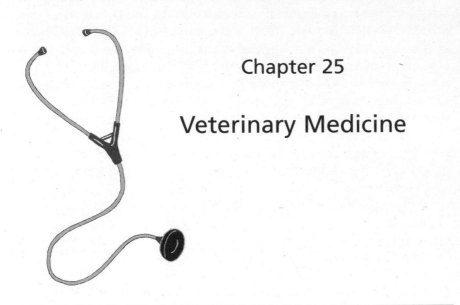

Chapter 25

Veterinary Medicine

Next door to the Sherwood Clinic was the home and office of our area's only veterinarian, Dr. Mervyn Chapman. Doc Chapman was a farm animal vet. You did not take your poodle or kitty-cat to him. If he had a specialty, it was fowl.

I learned quickly that Dr. Chapman didn't treat individual chickens, he treated flocks. In those days, when a chicken became ill, you didn't take it to the vet for a penicillin shot; that would have cost more than the chicken. No, you prayed that the entire flock didn't have what the sick chicken had. If you were interested in chicken health, you took your sick chick and a sample of healthy chicks to the vet, where they were all killed and autopsied. I never attended a chicken autopsy, but Doc, like any other scientist, was proud of his work and often called me over to see the results of an interesting autopsy. I wasn't interested but I went anyway. I liked Doc, and I understood his loneliness as the only practicing vet in the neighborhood. He had to have some one to talk to. Depending upon the results of the autopsy, the flock was either treated or not treated. If the disease warranted it, the entire flock had to be killed. Chickens had no rights or health benefits.

Large animals were different. For them, Doc Chapman's office was a huge barn that stood between the Sherwood Clinic and Doc's house.

Pickups and trailers holding sick animals arrived in Doc's parking lot daily. There were sick cows, lambs with scours (diarrhea), bull calves that needed to be modified into steers, and squealing piglets. The cacophony of sounds emanating from assorted animals in trucks and trailers lent a kind of cockeyed approach to human medical care, especially when I was working very hard to listen to a patient's heart, trying to differentiate cardiac clicks from other heart sounds, and there was a sick cow bawling outside the window. All of this added a zest to practice not obtainable any other way. You knew it just wasn't possible to go outside and say to that cow, "Please stop bawling for a few minutes while I examine this little baby's heart," or to the sheep to stop bleating, or to the pigs to stop squealing.

One day I decided to investigate why the pigs seemed to out-decibel all the other creatures under Doc's care. There were no patients in the office that spring day, so I strolled next door into Doc's barn, looking for the source of the noise. Doc had a box full of weaner pigs on the floor near where he was working. Weaner pigs are little guys who recently have been removed from their mothers' teats, and are ready to be put on regular feed. Neutering is performed at this time because, if the boy weaner pigs remain boars, they concentrate on things in life other than eating and getting fat. Worry and fretting over little girl pigs does not produce weight gain. Pigs are supposed to be eating machines and get their kicks out of life that way.

The little pigs in the box were all boys and they were to be neutered. No wonder they were squealing. This wasn't a vasectomy. These little males were having their sacred male genitalia unalterably changed.

It was the process of neutering that fascinated me. As a surgeon I never could have conceived a more efficient, but more barbaric, practice. The little pig's front feet were tied together. Then with his feet extended over his head, our squealing little patient (or victim) was hung on a nail by the string tied around his feet. Doc grasped the two hind feet and made two quick slashes of a scalpel; two testicles, with their shiny coverings, twinkled in the light coming in from the front door of the barn. With two more quick cuts the testes fell on the floor. Each of the spermatic cords were crushed with a hemostat, sealing the bleeding little blood vessels, and piggy was now released and returned to his little friends in the box. The wounds were not closed because, according to Doc, "They'd only get infected, and leavin' 'em open allows 'em to drain." The procedure was completed in less than two minutes, efficiently, and with a minimum of pain or distress to the animal, believe it or not!

◈

Veterinary medicine was not the exclusive purview of the veterinarian in Sherwood. My first exposure was with a lamb with scours.

I was making a house call at the farm of a family whose elderly mother was chronically ill and a shut-in. When I was about to leave after checking the patient, a young lady of the house—probably about ten years old—asked, "Doctor, can you check my lamb? She's sick."

At first, I thought this was a joke. But, observing the serious look on the young lady's face, I did not make a wise crack or plead ignorance. I said, "Sure."

Many times I had checked a toddler's teddy bear or a little girl's doll, at the office, in an attempt to mollify an anxious patient. But this was real. The lamb was sick.

"What are her symptoms?"

"She has scours, Doctor."

"What's that?"

"You know, she poops all the time and won't eat."

I looked at the lamb. It did look bedraggled. Its little backside was all dirty. I thought it looked wan. I said, "Do you have any Kaopectate in the house?"

Mother, who had trailed us to the barn, answered in the affirmative.

I then said, "Give the lamb one teaspoon of Kaopectate every hour for four doses, then one teaspoon four times a day until the scours stop. Let her feed from her mother as usual."

The little girl said, "I'm her mother; her real mother is dead. I'm bottle-feeding her. Shall I give her milk?"

I really didn't have any idea what I should say. *In a human baby I would try to replace her electrolytes, but how do you replace electrolytes in a lamb?*

I took a shot at it. I said, "Boil some rice, take the water that you boiled the rice in, add a little sugar for nourishment, and feed that to your lamb. If she doesn't get better in a day or two, take her to Dr. Chapman."

Two weeks later, when I went back to see Grandma, I was met in the yard by a happy little girl and her lamb. "Look," she cried. "See how my little lamb has grown!" Another therapeutic triumph.

◈

I had an even more meaningful encounter when Dr. Chapman was out of town at a veterinarian's convention. It was on a Sunday afternoon when I went to a farm to see a little child with croup. The mother had prevailed upon me to make a house call because of the difficulty her baby was having in breathing. When I drove into the farmyard in my red Pontiac, the farmer came out of the barn. "Doc, come here a minute." He beckoned me to the barn.

I could hear a calf bawling. I thought, *Not another animal with the scours.*

The farmer led me to the stall where the calf was bawling. The little guy did not appear to be older than a day or two. His mama was lying down with her head flat on the straw, her flanks heaving, and a low whistling coming from her nose.

"Doc," said the farmer, "she's down with milk fever."

"Hmm!"

"Can you fix her?"

"Me, fix her? I don't treat cows. I don't know what's wrong with her. She looks pretty sick to me."

As I stood there the calf came up behind me and butted me in the rear as if to say, "Do something, my mama is sick."

"Damn right, she's sick, Doc. Like I said, she's got the milk fever. She needs a calcium shot. Willya give it to her? Ya know, Doc Chapman is away and if she don't get a calcium shot, she's gonna die."

I looked down at this great big dirty, black and white animal lying on the straw covered floor, and recognized the same soulful, brown eyes that I had seen in the Black Angus choir.

"What do I have to do?"

"Just get two of them vials of that calcium gluconate and shoot it into her veins. That'll make her better."

Now, I thought, *here is an ethical dilemma. First, I was called to see a sick child, but I was waylaid to treat a cow while the child continues to suffer. Second, I don't really know if this guy knows what he is talking about, and if I give the cow a calcium gluconate shot and it dies, will I have killed her? Will he hold me responsible?*

"Hadn't I better get to the house and see the baby with the croup and then come back and look at the cow?" I asked.

"Now, Doc, you're out here. Why don'tcha fix my cow?"

Well, we have our priorities all lined up, don't we?

I went to my bag and got two vials of calcium, a tourniquet, and a 20 cc syringe. The farmer pointed to the foreleg where there was a vein.

I placed the tourniquet on the leg. When the vessel became prominent, I injected 20 cc of calcium gluconate right into that cow's vein. She never budged, but just continued her quiet, lowing sound.

I stepped back, folded up my case, wrapped the syringe and needle in a paper towel, and looked back at my patient. She raised her head, gave a big grunt, and got up.

"She's okay, Doc," exclaimed the farmer.

I went to the house, where I saw and took care of the sick child, and went home.

The next day I told Cora, "Charge for two injections, one for the cow, one for the child—and one house call for the child and one barn call for the cow! And ask Marcia to wash my tourniquet and the outside of my bag. I practiced veterinary medicine yesterday."

When Doc Chapman came back from the convention, he said the cow would have died in a few hours without the calcium injection.

⟳⟳

Another veterinarian moved into our area. Dr. Belknap was also a large animal vet, but specialized in horses. I met him the day I went out to our stable and only four noses poked out of the five box stalls. Little Joe, the half-quarter horse, half-Arabian, was in his stall, lying down and groaning. Now, that is a sight—a one-thousand-pound animal, lying on the floor in obvious distress. I walked around the horse. He made no move to get up. Every once in a while he drew up his legs, like a kid with the colic. I decided he must have a stomachache, so I called Dr. Belknap.

"Sounds like you're correct," advised Dr. Belknap. "This shouldn't be a major problem. Go to a feed store and buy five or ten pounds of bran mash and a quart or two of molasses, mix it in a big pan, and get your horse to eat the mixture. This should cure him."

I did as directed. The horse wouldn't eat. In fact the horse did not look as if he wanted to eat anything. This big old bay gelding was still lying down and looking bad. He was wheezing now and kicking a little, and in no mood for a breakfast of bran mash and molasses. I called the doctor, again.

"I'd better come over," he said.

Dr. Belknap did not arrive with a mere medical bag—he had a suitcase. He took the horse's temperature, rectally, with a thing that looked about the size of a little league baseball bat. When he withdrew it, he commented that there was no stool in the rectum. Then he got down and pushed around on the horse's belly with both of his hands, stood up and said, "Constipated."

My medical training indicated that mere constipation was not enough of a diagnosis. I wondered what kind of a horse doctor I had called.

Belknap produced a syringe and needle and a 10 cc ampule of prostigmin. He said he was going to give the horse that extremely potent muscle relaxant, which I knew is usually given to post-operative human patients who have bowel distention or urinary retention. An overdose would give diarrhea. Horse or human, it was absolutely contraindicated if there were a mechanical bowel obstruction. The drug could cause the rupture of the bowel by increasing contractions and peristalsis if the bowel were mechanically blocked. The irresistible force against the immovable object, and *boom!* a hole in the bowel wall—peritonitis and death.

"Wait a minute," I pleaded. "Is that all you're going to do?" I thought maybe he had an alternative treatment. I certainly would have voted for that.

"Nope, I've got this tube." He produced a six foot tube about the diameter of a garden hose. "I'm also going to give your horse a quart of castor oil."

I was not going to vote for that alternative. "Dr. Belknap, what's your diagnosis?"

"Fecal impaction or bowel obstruction," was the answer.

"Gee whiz, you're going to kill my horse."

"Not if he has a fecal impaction. Then I'll cure him."

"What if he has a bowel obstruction?"

While loading his syringe, the vet calmly replied, "Then, I'll kill him."

"Why don't we operate and find out for sure?"

"Then we'll surely kill him. Any horse whose abdominal cavity is opened dies of peritonitis. They don't have the ability to fight infection in that area. Even if we took him down to Oregon State Veterinary College in Corvallis and they operated in the most advantageous surroundings, there is a 90 percent chance he would die. Now, get me a funnel so that we can pour in this castor oil." (Modern veterinary medicine has overcome certain death for horses having abdominal surgery. Many vets operate successfully on horses.)

He pushed the plunger on the syringe and the prostigmin went into the horse's veins. When I returned with the funnel I used to pour gasoline into my tractor, we put the tube through Little Joe's nose, into his stomach, and poured in the castor oil. (At least, he didn't have to taste it.) I wished Stormin' Norman, my pharmacology professor in medical school, could have seen the nasogastric tube the vet used that day. If he knew that there was a tube that big he surely would have threatened his students with it, as the ultimate practical joke.

The veterinarian left, cautioning me to watch carefully and call him if trouble arose. I watched and waited. In about two hours, trouble started; and after three hours, I called. "Dr. Belknap, I'm in trouble. I will never again get this box stall cleaned. The horse has defecated up, down, and sideways. He has probably established a record for *Guinness Book of Records* for the number of pounds of horse manure produced in one hour."

Little Joe was cured. The problem had been that it was winter and the water in the watering trough was so cold that some mornings there was a crust of ice on the surface of the trough. Little Joe didn't like cold water and hadn't been drinking enough. (Possibly the Arabian genes held memories of the desert.) We solved the problem with a tank warmer.

Dr. Belknap was the official veterinarian at the new Portland Meadows Race Track, and he invited Glad and me and Pinky and his wife to go to the track with him one night. He gave Pinky and me tips. We lost every race. I thought Pinky bet rather too much, but I held my peace. Glad picked horses by their color, or by their demonstrated eagerness in the pre race parade. She collected her bets in six of the nine races.

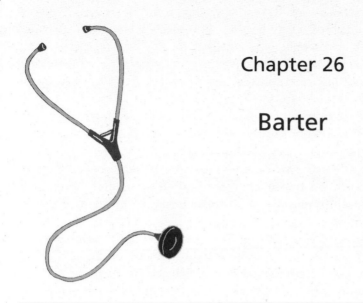

Chapter 26

Barter

Louise Sharpening brought her five kids to the office at least once a week for some ailment or injury. Richard stayed home and did a little hard-scrabble dirt farming. They were great customers, but terrible payers. In fact, they did not pay at all, so the frequency of the family's visits was of no great concern to Louise. Instead, the visits seemed to be part of her weekly social calendar.

When Louise became pregnant for the sixth time, I made arrangements to deliver her at Tuality Hospital. The hospital accepted her as a patient with the understanding that payment would be slow. The Sharpenings actually paid the hospital about five dollars a month, just enough to keep the collection agency at bay. They paid us nothing.

Caring for the family was part of our contribution to the community. Because we were the only two doctors in the area, we never turned down a patient. The Sharpenings had no other place to go, unless they traveled to Newberg or Tigard. However, the doctors in those towns were not interested in caring for our nonpayers.

Richard and Louise were not shiftless, they were just inadequate. Louise was a part of the goings-on in the Sherwood community. She knew everyone and talked all the time. And she talked about people. She happily talked about everyone and since she knew everyone, no one was safe from her gossiping tongue. On her weekly visits to the office, I learned whose spouse was sleeping with the spouse of somebody else. I didn't believe much of what she told me. Once she suggested that my partner was making too many house calls to the home of a comely young matron in the community. I never pursued that zinger. An affair with a patient was about the most self-destructive behavior that any physician (especially a small-town physician) could possibly have.

When little Richard Sharpening, Jr., fell out of a tree, we treated his fractured ribs. When Sally had repeated earaches and difficulty in swallowing, we took out her tonsils and adenoids. We gave the baby her immunizations. We took care of the Sharpenings' colds, coughs, tummy aches, rashes, cuts and bruises, and really didn't complain. With each illness, Cora dutifully placed the customary charge on the books. The debt grew and grew.

One day my partner and I sat down to review our accounts receivable. We found the Sharpenings owed us over two thousand dollars, a huge amount when you consider that an office call was still five dollars, and a tonsillectomy forty-five dollars. We decided this account was artificially elevating our financial statement.

With no hope of collecting it, we elected to charge off the bill as uncollectible debt and wipe the slate clean. Our bookkeeping system did not keep a record if there was no balance. New charges were created on separate statements. We both felt better at the end of that day, as we felt we were doing a worthwhile thing; however, we resumed charging the family on a regular basis, thinking that if the bottom line were doable, maybe they might make small payments. A two-thousand-dollar debt would be insurmountable, therefore discouraging to them. We continued to send monthly statements but neither worried about nor expected payments.

A few months went by and the Sharpenings' bill had grown again to about two hundred dollars when the father, Richard Sharpening, Sr., showed up at the receptionist's window with a checkbook.

"Cora," he asked, "what's our bill? I'm ready to pay it off. We're moving away."

Cora was flabbergasted. She asked. "You're moving? Where?"

"My uncle died over in eastern Oregon and left me about twenty thousand dollars and a one-half interest in his ranch. Aunt Myrtle owns the other half and wants me to come farm the place. We're going over there and start a new life. Lemme have my bill, Cora."

Cora went to the file, thoroughly rattled, forgetting all about the old bill that had been filed in an inactive file, and pulled out the current statement for two hundred dollars. "Here, Mr. Sharpening." She handed the bill to Richard.

"Well now, that's a lot, but I'll pay it." With a flourish, he took out his pen, wrote the check, and left.

Later, when we all reviewed the affair, we exonerated Cora of any guilt because, after all, only the current charges were on the books. She would have had to go to the old files and reconstruct the account to collect the back amounts. That would have been hard to do but it could have been done. Besides, if Mr. Sharpening thought two hundred dollars was a lot, what would he have said to a five-year bill of two thousand dollars?

We had fulfilled a civic duty, but we never again completely charged off an account.

⚬∞⚬

Times were not booming. Returned World War II servicemen were just beginning to get their lives together after time spent getting an education or working their way up in their companies. And the Korean War was going on. I had escaped further military service because of the amount of time I had spent in the Navy in WW II, but others were not so lucky. Farmers who had expected help from grown sons saw them drafted. Hiring farm labor was expensive and drove down farm profits.

Elmer Rupert was a farmer on the Sherwood-Hillsboro Road between Six Corners and our place at Creekwood. Elmer had fallen on hard times. He had too little help on his farm and an idea he had been pursuing had led to further problems. He had spent years trying to develop a purple potato.

Elmer had told me, "Doc, one day when I get them purple hybrids developed, restaurants are gonna holler for 'em. It'll be the biggest thing to hit potato farming since some guy in Idaho planted his first spud."

Elmer's wife became ill. After we had successfully treated her, Elmer came in to pay his bill. He asked to speak with me alone. When I entered the examining room I saw a flushed, sweating Elmer Rupert. Despite the heat of the office, he had not removed his heavy, wool, outer coat. The shaggy coat, hanging to mid-thigh, smelled like a wet dog; and with Rupert's pungent sweat permeating the room, the odors were overwhelming. Nevertheless, applying a preconceived principle of never damning the smells of honest labor, I took a deep breath and shook Elmer's hand. "What can I do for you, Elmer?"

Elmer was very agitated. He fumbled his words, trying to start the conversation, and finally came out with, "Doc, you've done good by my wife. I think you're a good doctor, no matter what."

The last part of the sentence caught my attention. "No matter what." *What is that all about? Should I ask what he means? Is it that his wife isn't better? Is it what someone else had said about me? Do I smell bad? No, that couldn't be the problem.* I started to ask, when Elmer gulped twice and blurted out, "No matter what you charge me."

I was holding the chart and billing sheet in my hand. I quickly reviewed it and said, "Well, Elmer, we did a lot for your wife, but if you think the fee is too high, let's talk about it."

"It ain't too high. Shucks, I just ain't got the money right now. You know those potatoes I was workin' on, tryin' to perfect the purple ones? Well, I got me a crop. They're just wonderful. Best potatoes I ever growed; but damn it, Doc, won't nobody buy 'em. There just ain't no market for purple potatoes. Here I am with a barn full of spuds and I can't pay my bills. And I can't pay you right now, Doc, but I'll pay you next year when I aim to plant regular spuds, again. How about you take these purple potatoes for your payment, Doc?"

Boy, if no one else wants to eat purple potatoes, I probably won't want to, either. Is he offering me a sack or a truckload?

I said, "Elmer, a sack would do just fine. Take one out to my place, tell Cora the retail price, and she will deduct it from your bill." One could not deny the ancient concept of barter for goods and services.

"Got two sacks in the truck right now, Doc. I'll put 'em in your car. You better take both, one for you and one for your partner. You can just credit me with one sack if you want."

Obviously he wasn't going to deliver them to my place, so I okayed two sacks for the trunk of my car.

My partner refused even to think about lugging one home. "My family won't eat purple potatoes," he growled. He did acquiesce to taking both sacks off the bill.

When I got home to Creekwood that night, I struggled into our cool, stone cellar with the two one-hundred-pound sacks of potatoes, secure in the knowledge that we had our winter supply of spuds.

Glad eyed the potatoes suspiciously, but agreed to try them. That night we had pot roast of beef with boiled purple potatoes. On the plate, this looked garish. The garnish of parsley did not seem to fit the color scheme and brown gravy turned the plate into a sea of mud.

One of the popular songs of the day was "The Purple People Eater." The kids categorically refused to eat purple potatoes, feeling that they were eating purple people. Two more attempts to serve the potatoes, utilizing different cooking methods, did not fare any better. Eventually the two sacks were disposed of in the canyon behind the barn, to be eaten by the denizens of the forest. They finally disappeared. Possums, squirrels, raccoons, and other denizens of the forest were a lot less finicky than our children.

⌖

After the experience with purple potatoes I should have realized that, in the area of barter, everything was not always as it seemed. A chicken farmer from Tonquin-Malloy came to the office with a proposal similar to the one offered by Elmer Rupert, only this time the bounty was to be chickens.

Well, a dozen Rhode Island Red fryers wouldn't be too bad, now would it?

The farmer said he would take them out to Creekwood and he painted a picture of how delicious these young fryers would be. I began to imagine twelve little bodies, all with their necks wrung and their feathers plucked, lying in a row on the kitchen counter, ready for the skillet.

Glad met me at the door. "Have you lost your mind? Is it not enough that we have five horses and a bunch of cows and seven rabbits to feed, but now you have sent home chickens. You take care of them. I am not being a mother hen to a bunch of feathered kids," and she stomped back into the house.

The children were hiding behind the door. When it was safe, they emerged to console me.

Lee pleaded, "We'll help, Daddy. Let us keep them."

Four-year-old Pamela exclaimed, "We just love them. We'll do everything."

Sure, just like they cared for the rabbits. Sometimes—when they remembered or weren't busy playing.

I had been a father long enough to hear their pleas for exactly what they were, a con game. They weren't going to take care of those chickens, though they meant well.

"Let's take a look at the chickens, kids."

We went out to the barn where the farmer had carefully left two crates of six chickens each. They were clucking and scratching against the slats of the crates, indignant at being confined. I opened one crate to get a better look and, suddenly, six chickens were running all over the yard!

We had a small building, just below the barn, that had been a tool house and was currently unoccupied. I told the kids to chase down the chickens and lock them in that building. We would figure out what to do with them after that. It took the four of us twenty-five minutes to round up those chickens. Pamela, trying to make good her promise to help, managed to scare off the last one three times, just as I was about to catch it. Finally, in order to finish the roundup, Pamela had to sit in the barn for five minutes until the boys and I finished collecting that last chick.

This may have been the beginning of her lifelong desire to obtain equality for women.

The tool house became the chicken coop, and for six months we raised chickens, acquired a rooster, collected eggs, and endured the odor. At the peak of the hot weather season, when the smell was unendurable, Glad and I took the kids to Portland for the day and Pinky Mayfield gathered up all the birds and took them to a place that slaughtered and dressed chickens. We told the kids we sold them to a farmer who needed the eggs. This was a little white lie that hurt no one. The chickens were anonymously put in our freezer and their appearance at the dining room table never elicited any comments. I believe the kids were as happy as Glad and I to be relieved of the chores and smells of keeping chickens.

Because the tool house was so fouled and impregnated with chicken droppings, we had the fire department come over and burn it. It was good practice for them and a godsend for us.

Markie, our collie dog, was the only one to come out ahead by the chicken experience. During the height of our chicken-raising period he came home, carrying a dead red fox. We quickly subscribed to the theory that Markie had interrupted Reynard near the chicken house, trying to steal a meal. He became the family's hero.

∽⚬≈≈⚬∾

Older doctors had told me stories of the hard times they had practicing medicine during the Great Depression, and how the exchange of food for services or services for services had helped them and their patients get through those difficult years. I hadn't objected to the chickens and potatoes—in fact, I had even enjoyed the experience a little. I felt that the barter system was okay when people really needed it. However, I was not prepared for the kind of pay for services that occurred with a stranger who had pneumonia.

A regular patient who lived down along the Tualatin River on Halcyon Road, a little east of Wankers Corners, called to tell me about a neighbor of his who was sick and needed attention. He explained that this man was a recent arrival in the area, lived in a shack, was pretty much of a recluse, did not seem to work, but was down sick with "lung fever." My patient felt that the neighbor really needed a doctor. The informant had been dropping in occasionally to see how this fellow was doing. The night before he had found the man in bed with a high fever and a terrible cough. He told his neighbor he would send a doctor.

"Thanks," I said.

Truly, I meant the thanks somewhat peevishly. The call had come about six-thirty in the morning. The caller wanted to get to me before I left for hospital rounds. Actually, he had called before I had gotten up. I was not exactly slothful, just tired. The previous night we had performed emergency surgery. I had gotten to bed for the second time about three-thirty in the morning. The first time to bed had resulted in thirty minutes sleep, so that my total rest for the night was three and a half hours. Now, I would have to get right up. Not only would I have a call to make before office hours to see the sick patient, but then I would have to hurry through my hospital rounds in order to make it to the office on time.

When I followed the neighbor's directions, I wound up on a mud track down beside the river. In a mixed grove of willow trees and cotton-woods, I spotted a one room shack with a tarpaper roof. A "Chic Sales" outhouse attested to the absence of indoor plumbing and, also, one of the reasons as to why the Tualatin River was polluted. Just think, we ate the crawfish and bass we caught in that river!

I knocked on the door. A voice boomed, "Y'all come in." I went in. Directly across the room was a wood stove and a table. To the left was an old dresser with a jumble of dirty clothes piled on top. Beside the door was a pile of wood for the stove. A chamber pot, which had been used and not emptied, was stationed at the foot of the bed that graced the right-hand wall. The man's head reared up from a pile of dirty blankets. His booming voice had a distinct Texas twang. "You must be the doctor? Come in all the way and shut the damn door."

If I hesitated, it was because of this man's appearance. He looked like my fantasy of a biblical Yahweh. He had a mane of wildly flowing white hair, a long, white, Rip Van Winkle beard, flushed cheeks, and wild, crazy, dark eyes—eyes that were shaded by bushy white eyebrows that would have made John L. Lewis look well groomed. In the days before the resurgence of beards and long hair, he was awesome.

As I hesitated the man rolled toward me, baring the under-surface of one of his several pillows. Beneath the pillows the pearl handle of a pistol peeked out.

He started talking loudly and profanely. "Come on, Sonny, get your goddamn ass over here next to the bed. Sonofabitch, Sonny, how in the hell are you gonna' take care of me from 'way over there in the corner of the room? Am I scaring the shit out of your poor peaked ass, Sonny, or are you just a lily-livered little puke who don't want to get your hands dirty? Gimme' a hand, boy."

Here I am—alone. Give him a hand? I would rather run for the door. What kind of a mess am I in this time, with a crazy old coot I have never met before, who has a gun? I wondered about how much money I had in my wallet. Probably not more than fifty bucks. *When he pulls out his gun, I will throw my wallet on the bed and get the hell out of here.*

Reason began to overcome anxiety. He did look sick; he had not yet reached for the gun; and my patient (his neighbor) had been calling on this old guy from time to time, so he was not a transient stickup artist. But he did look pretty crazy.

Into my head came one of those instant plans that is no plan at all, just a reaction. I stepped up to the bed, with my right arm extended to shake "Yahweh's" right hand. I plunged my left hand under his pillow, grabbed the pearl handle of the gun, and flung it over him into the corner of the room.

We both looked startled. I was scared of what his reaction might be. He looked over at the gun and then back at me and began to chuckle. "Cautious, ain't you, Sonny? Good idea to be cautious."

His demeanor changed. His language cleaned up. I guessed I had gained his respect and he no longer felt a need to try to bully me.

I checked him over and told him he had a case of early pneumonia. I wanted him to come to the office for a chest X-ray, and I started to write a prescription for penicillin.

"Well, I ain't gonna get no X-ray and I ain't got the money for the drug store, so why don't you just give me a damn penicillin shot and be on your way?"

I responded with, "If you can't pay, come to the office, anyway. I won't charge you for the X-ray and I'll give you samples of penicillin that will help you. But you're right, I'll give you an injection of penicillin now.

You come in tomorrow, when you're feeling better." I prepared and gave him the injection.

The old man thanked me. As I was getting ready to leave, he said, "How much is this call?"

"Ten dollars."

"Maybe I'll pay you, Sonny. What'll you give me for the gun?"

I did not own a pistol, but often thought it might be a good idea. I went over to the corner and picked up the gun. It looked like a pretty good weapon. It was a long-barreled .22 caliber pistol with a clean barrel and a good-looking sight. "What will you take for it?" I asked.

"Tell you what, Sonny, you give me ten bucks and take the gun, and we'll call it square."

I gave him the ten dollars and left. "Yahweh" did not come in the next day, so two days later I went to see him. The cabin was empty. I went to the neighbor's house to find the old guy, but the neighbor didn't even know he was gone. He must have been a drifter and just disappeared.

I took the pistol out behind the house and set up a target range of old bottles. After firing twenty-four shots without hitting one bottle, I gave up. I took the pistol to my friend, John Brown, who was not only the Tualatin grade school principal, but was also a captain in the U.S. Army Reserve and a member of a crack army shooting team. John took the pistol to the army firing range and tried it out. He reported back to me, laughing, "They must have made this gun for shooting around corners, because it sure wouldn't hit anything you pointed it at." He advised me to throw it away. I did.

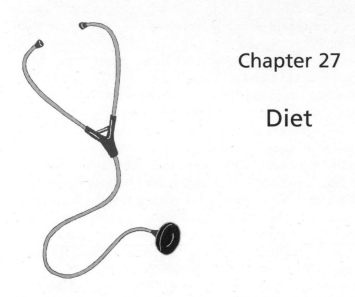

Chapter 27

Diet

The scales we had to weigh patients were the first thing a person saw when approaching the examining rooms at Sherwood Clinic. As the nurse escorted the patient back to a room she would stop and weigh those adult patients who had not been seen for a long time, who were to have a complete physical or who she perceived had a weight problem—either too much or too little. Audrey Hill was weighed at every visit.

Audrey had three kids. I had delivered the last one. We had become pretty good friends. She went through a lot during her pregnancy. She was considerably overweight, even for her large frame, and we fought the battle of weight gain together. At one time I thought we might have to do a c-section on her because of a soft-tissue dystocia (too fat to deliver), but little Roger (eight pounds, fourteen ounces) squeaked through with the help of forceps. With a difficult pregnancy and a very difficult labor, some patients think well of their doctor; but a few learn to hate him. I was fortunate. Audrey and I liked each other.

I gave Audrey plenty of time after her pregnancy to nurse her baby without my nagging about her weight. I had done a vasectomy on Jake, one lonely Friday afternoon, so there weren't going to be any more kids. One day when she was in with the baby for a well-baby checkup and I thought the time was right, I told Audrey that it was about time to settle down and think about losing some pounds. I advised her to come in someday when she could leave the baby at home, and the nurse and I would set her up in a program of weight reduction.

She didn't come.

A month went by. Late one Saturday afternoon, Audrey's husband, Jake, called me at home. He asked me to make a house call to see one of the older kids who was wheezing. He sounded somewhat apologetic for having to make the call. I sensed he thought it was the mother's responsibility, but he said, "Audrey is getting supper and is real busy."

I had one other house call to make, so it was about an hour before I arrived. The family was eating dinner when I knocked on the door and walked into the kitchen. The sick youngster was in a bedroom. Audrey led me in to see him. I checked his lungs, his nose, throat, and ears, and prescribed a medication for his asthma. I had a sample of the drug in my bag, enough to last until Monday, so there was no urgency to go to the drug store to have the script filled. Audrey led me back to the kitchen and, on the way she asked, "Will you stay for supper, Doctor?"

Glad had taken our kids to a birthday party in Portland and had told me, before she got in the car, that there were leftovers in the fridge and I should help myself. When I thought about my lonesome house and the probable meager pickings there and I looked at Audrey's sumptuous board, I made the only reasonable decision. I said, "Thank you, Audrey. I'd love to stay." The family made a place for me and I sat down.

If Norman Rockwell were drawing a picture of a farmer for the cover of *Saturday Evening Post* he might have used Jake Hill as his model. Jake's tall, lean, hard body was covered with clean bib-overalls. His face was tanned up to the point at which a billed cap had covered his forehead. There were crow's feet at the corners of his eyes from squinting at the sun and from smiling. He did a lot of both. Jake was a well-to-do farmer and it showed. The table was laden. There were three vegetables and a big bowl of salad with mayonnaise. Audrey said, "Try the mayonnaise, Doctor. I made it myself." Also being passed, family-style, were a platter of roast chicken with stuffing, a platter of sliced roasted meat, and mashed potatoes with gravy, as well as oven roasted potatoes on the meat platter, freshly baked bread, and crocks of homemade butter at each end of the table.

Every delectable platter and bowl was passed to me. When I refused the mashed potatoes and gravy, Jake said, "You'd better take some of that, Doc. Audie makes the best mashed potatoes in the county. She uses cream when she mashes them."

How could I refuse? I had never tasted potatoes like that. Glad prided herself on her mashed potatoes made with skim milk, but this was something else. I had seconds.

Pies followed the main course and I looked around the table in wonderment. This was not an obese family. Audrey was the only one who was overweight. Did all the kids get Jake's genes or was I missing something? If this was an example of dinner at the Hill's, the entire tribe should look like porkers. They did not!

I was a good guest that night and certainly didn't bring up the subject of weight, but I resolved to do so at the next opportune moment.

I didn't see any of the Hill family, again, until it was time for Audrey's annual pelvic and pap smear. When I finished the exam I broached the subject of diet once more, by saying, "Audrey, I can't remember having a more wonderful dinner than the one I had at your house, but I can really understand why you can't lose..." I did not get to finish the sentence. The roof fell in.

Audrey exploded, "Damn you, Doctor, you saw my family. You ate my food. That's what I do. I cook. I cook for Jake and the kids and, in the summer, I cook for a couple of hired hands. I like to cook. I eat what I cook and I'm damn well sick and tired of your carping at me all the time about my weight. If I want to be fat, it's my business. If I ever want to lose weight I'll tell you; and then, and only then, will I talk to you about a diet. And, oh yes, you can tell that skinny little nurse of yours that if she ever weighs me again without my asking to be weighed, I'll walk out of this office and never come back!"

With that parting shot Audrey grabbed her purse and left.

Whew! I really had opened a can of worms with that lady! Apparently she saw her life slipping away in the kitchen—food and the stove were her life preservers. In no way would I try to take this away from her. She was a fine person and, as far as I knew, had no reason to think so badly of herself that she would become this obese. I didn't know what had led her into this self-contempt.

Three years went by without a mention of weight. One day Audrey came in and asked the nurse to weigh her on the way to the examining room. I picked up her chart from its holder on the door outside the room and, seeing her weight on the chart, I hesitated before going in. I called Helen, who was not the nurse who had weighed her three years earlier, but who knew the story because in big red letters across the top of her chart it said, DO NOT WEIGH THIS PATIENT!

Helen told me it was okay—she had asked to be weighed. When I entered the room Audrey smiled and said, "I'd like you to put me on a weight reduction program."

I wanted to ask, "Why, what happened?"

I didn't need to—Audrey volunteered the information. "We're going to change the way we eat at our house. My oldest daughter has been gaining. She came home from school the other day crying because some of the kids called her 'Fatty.' That's what they called me in school when I was a kid, and I don't want my daughter going through life like I always have, ashamed of my body."

At the end of a year Audrey had lost over fifty pounds and looked great. Her daughter grew taller, lost her baby fat, and never had another problem.

I never arrived at the Hill's farm at dinner time again, but I'll bet, if I had, I would have seen an even happier family.

❧

Overweight patients were not the only ones I treated with diets. My diabetic patients caused me great concern.

Violet Finney was a twenty-year-old patient of mine who had suffered from juvenile diabetes mellitus since the age of nine. Childhood, or brittle, diabetes (now known as IDD, insulin dependent diabetes) was tough for a youngster to handle. In addition to a strict diet, Violet had to take one or two insulin injections each day. We had often discussed the complications of the disease. She understood that she could suffer from cardiac and vascular complications, blindness, severe infection, kidney failure, and many more diseases if she did not take good care of herself. However, Violet demonstrated youthful nonchalance about her condition with an attitude of, "It can't happen to me." Teens usually don't visualize themselves sick or dying; instead, there is a mindset that what is happening now is important and, without experience, looking at the future seems unimaginable.

I had cared for Violet through high school and I perceived that controlling her blood sugar levels was becoming harder and harder. I'd guessed that she was cheating on her diet and maybe drinking alcohol. She seemed to be fudging on the number of urine tests that she did in order to adjust her insulin dosage. We talked about this. She denied straying from her regimen. She told me she was dating, wanted to appear normal to her friends, and didn't want anyone to know she had diabetes.

I felt sure that dating and her desire for secrecy was the pressure which had probably caused her to stray from her strict program.

When she didn't come to the office on the day I had asked her to come, I called her. When I got her on the phone she told me quite brusquely that she had changed doctors.

When a patient of mine changed doctors I always found it a little hard to take. It wasn't a matter of the lost fee, but a sense of professional pride. Did I not professionally satisfy Violet or her family? I thought I had done well. In frequent office sessions she had learned about her diabetes. She knew that she had the responsibility for her own life, that I couldn't be with her all the time, but I would be her coach.

While Violet was on the phone, I swallowed my pride and offered to send her records to her new doctor.

"My new doctor doesn't believe in all that stuff you make me do, but has a way of treating me so I can be normal and happy."

"Violet," I asked, "who is your new doctor?" I was worried. This sounded like she was going to some kind of an irregular practitioner. If she stopped taking her insulin or stopped the rigid control of her diet, she could get into serious trouble.

"He doesn't need my records, Doctor. Thank you for all your trouble in the past. I'm moving on, now." She hung up.

I did the legal thing. I wrote Violet a registered letter. In general, the letter stated that, because she had a serious illness and would not follow my orders, I would have to resign from her case. I would give her five days from the receipt of the letter to obtain the services of another doctor. I would be glad to refer her to another doctor and forward her medical records. I also stated that she should feel free to return to my care if she felt she could follow my instructions.

I had done the legal thing. I was covered. The fact was that she had fired me and she was in the hands of a quack practitioner.

Even though I had resigned, I hoped that she would return to my care or to the care of someone who would wish to use the records I had about her case, before she was irreparably damaged by her new health care provider.

Weeks went by. At first, I anticipated that she would call and ask me to take her back or another doctor would call or send for records. After some time, Violet's case drifted out of my mind.

It was five in the morning on a summer day that the phone rang. It was Violet's mother. "Doctor, something terrible is wrong. I can't awaken Violet. Will you come quickly?"

I forgot all about the legal stuff and had my car flying over the back country roads. The sun was rising and I can remember the sweet smell of the new cut hay. I also thought of the sweet smell of the breath of a very sick diabetic patient with a high blood sugar in the last stages of keto-acidosis. I hoped that wasn't what I was going to find, but the coma her mother described was a threatening symptom.

When I arrived at the Finney farm on the far side of Chehalem mountain, Mr. Finney was waiting in the yard. "This way, Doctor," he said, as he led me quickly into the house.

Violet lay on her bed, a skeleton of her former self. She had lost pounds and pounds. Violet was dead.

She was the victim of an unscrupulous practitioner who had identified himself as a chiropractor and who had sold the gullible youngster a story that diabetes was the result of poorly aligned vertebrae. Her parents told me that he took her off her insulin and her diet. He told her she no longer had to test her urine for sugar and, when her urinary output increased and her weight decreased, he told her that it was the poison leaving her system. He realigned her vertebrae three times a week until she died. Violet was a victim of an unscrupulous charlatan. A genuine, ethical doctor of chiropractic would not have done this to Violet.

I reported the case to the coroner's office and went home. The coroner took no action to put a stop to the perpetrator of this horrible practice.

⌖⌖⌖

During the years when I was in training at St. Vincent's, the interns and residents met and decided to request permission from the sisters to remodel the basement of the house staff's quarters into an outpatient clinic for the poor. Because many of us had decided on careers as gener-alists, we felt we needed exposure to the common problems we would encounter in everyday practice. This is the premise that modern Family Medicine training programs utilize to train residents in the specialty of Family Practice. We were ahead of our time in recognizing the need to train young physicians to deal with problems other than those seen in the hospital setting.

In remodeling the building we did the labor ourselves, with help from our families, and with donated materials. We painted, sawed, and nailed on weekends, taking the precious time usually devoted to our home lives, and worked to create a new environment in which to learn. It was in our new clinic that I met Emma.

Emma was blind, grossly overweight, hypertensive, and exceedingly morose. When I took her history I found that five years previously she had experienced a hypertensive crisis. Her blood pressure had risen to very high levels and she had suffered a stroke. Subsequently she lost vision in both eyes. Emma was only in her late thirties. Just before this life event, Emma's fiancé had examined his relationship with her and decided it was to his advantage to plow other fields. When her great love ("the only man I ever cared for") took off, he left a lady who, as a result of this tremendous emotional trauma and the hypertensive crisis, became blind, fat and depressed.

Emma's quality of life had improved with support from the Braille Institute and the San Rafael, California, Guide Dogs for the Blind Foundation. The addition of reading in Braille and a dog companion brightened her life. Emma was mostly homebound because of the disability and because of her enormous bulk. She vigorously embraced a church, and her zeal for God was restoring her personality.

Emma was brought to the clinic by a church member. She was assigned to be my patient. She told me that she had gallstones.

The treatment for gallstones was surgery. There were no drugs or electronic devices for the elimination of gallstones as there are today. The treatment for gallstones was, pure and simple, to take out the gallbladder. However, I was not able to confirm the presence of gallstones through X-ray, because of her massive size. The X-rays would not be strong enough to penetrate the many layers of fat without having X-ray burns on her skin. Her history, and what meager findings I could obtain from palpating her abdomen, certainly suggested gallbladder disease; but performing elective surgery on this lady in her present obese condition seemed out of the question. The prospect of mining through layer upon layer of fat, in order to expose the gallbladder, made all of us who examined her decide that a conservative course of treatment was best. Further, because of her history of stroke, we wished to have her general health in an optimal state in order to minimize her surgical risk. The obvious plan was to put this lady on a gallbladder diet and weight reduction program, putting off a definitive diagnosis and treatment until X-rays would be more revealing; but surgery would probably be her ultimate cure.

Because transportation for her was so difficult and because I was infused with the desire to help this lady, I began to make house calls to review her diet. I really wanted to be the surgeon to take out her gallbladder, as I needed this kind of surgical experience. Surgery residents competed with each other for cases like Emma, where we were the physicians of record and assured of the responsibility for performing the operation. Her attacks of abdominal pain occurred frequently and, on many occasions, I went to her house at night or on weekends to give her an injection to ameliorate her pain. We did not make much progress in weight loss, but it appeared that she was losing a little. We had no scales large enough to weigh her.

I once suggested to a church member that she take Emma to a wholesale feed store in her neighborhood, where they were accustomed to weighing sacks of grain, and ask them to check Emma's weight. The church member refused on the basis that it would be insulting to Emma. Maybe she was correct; I didn't have the nerve to suggest it to Emma, directly.

This period, while I was taking care of Emma, was a transition point in my education. This was the time when I graduated from being an intern to becoming a general surgery resident.

❧

A friend of ours had given little Don, on his first birthday, a collie puppy whom we named Marquam MacDougall O'Donnel, shortened later to "Markie." The puppy grew so big, so rapidly that his exuberant enthusiasm was a challenge to Glad, who tried to push a baby in a stroller with one hand while hanging on to the dog's leash with the other. She and I decided to take the dog to obedience school. We were so proud of the progress Markie made in his schooling that, with the encouragement of our instructor, we entered him in an obedience trial. This occurred on the one day off I was going to have in over three weeks. It was to be my only family day—and here I was going to a dog show!

Glad said, "If you're going to do this, we're going to make it a family outing and we'll all go."

I said, "No, having you and Don in the audience will distract Markie. You know how he adores Don. I don't want the dog running out in the crowd to lick Don's face." So Markie and I went alone.

Remember, this is now an adolescent Lassie dog. He loved everybody and, being raised with a child, he loved kids in particular.

I showed the dog in obedience trials at the dog show. He worked well in the ring, obeying all the commands on leash perfectly. Then came the big event, walking at heel, off leash. I took off the leash, commanding the dog to heel. We walked around the ring together in front of the judges. As we passed the far corner, I heard some kid call, "Here Lassie, come here, Lassie," and then, tittering from the crowd.

I kept saying, "Heel, Markie," but when I looked down at my left side, there was no dog. Now, there was outright laughter in the audience. The dog was out in the audience, licking the face of a three-year-old.

We decided obedience training had failed. He preferred loving, and so be it.

Many people admired the dog. He was a big, rawboned collie with a white blaze on his face, and ears that stood straight up. Conformation standards required a compact dog with tipped-over ears, but we didn't know that. So, with the encouragement of friends, we entered Markie in a dog show. He was in the novice class for collies under one year. He won his class. He had good hindquarters, a fine big chest, and a lush coat and soulful eyes. So, now, we were encouraged and took him on the road to an out-of-town dog show.

It was while I was on the road for a weekend with Glad, Don, and Markie, that Emma got sick. She called the hospital. A fellow surgical resident, who was covering for me, had her come in, rather than making a house call. (He was ahead of his time.)

Emma was having a difficult attack of the abdominal pain I had ameliorated so many times with medication. But my colleague elected to operate. He, too, was eager to take out gallbladders.

When I arrived back at the hospital on Monday morning, I was informed that Emma was on the surgical ward, post-op. The nurses told me she was doing well. I went to the door of the four-bed ward. Emma was at the far end, reading the newspaper.

Reading? The newspaper? Emma is blind.

As I entered, she looked up and greeted me by name. I had not spoken.

Emma can see! Does this mean that during all of the months I treated her, she was faking?

Why?

A friend of mine at the hospital had once told me that she had seen Emma on a downtown street, with her guide dog, looking into a shop window. I had passed this off as a day when she was feeling well and had gone out. As far as the shop window was concerned, I just supposed that she was resting there. Now, all of a sudden, this was coming back to me, as well as other peculiar things she had done. Had she been sighted all the time? What a bummer!

Emma was having other problems at this point. She was halluci-
nating. She told us that she was being commanded by Jesus to do certain
things. She yelled and carried on for two days. She became abusive,
striking nurses, cursing her fellow patients, and throwing her bath water
on the floor. This was not a tiny, perky, little Eliza James who was raving
and needing restraint; this was huge Emma, and she was more than a
handful for the nursing staff. She insisted that her actions were being
governed by outside entities. In a nutshell, Emma was crazy, but she was
no longer blind.

Members of her church wanted her discharged, but we felt that it
was important that she be examined by a psychiatrist. He filled out
committal papers for admission to a psychiatric institution for her own
protection. The diagnosis was dementia praecox (schizophrenia). Her
intermittent blindness was diagnosed as conversion hysteria.

Actually, she was unable to register in her brain what her eyes saw.
The emotional trauma of her lost love had shut her off from the world.
The high blood pressure had been real enough; but the doctors who had
treated her at that time had misinterpreted her inability to see. The process
of having been anesthetized, along with the shock of surgery, dislodged
her coping mechanisms. This allowed her to see permanently, but
returned her emotionally to what had probably been a psychotic experience earlier in life, when she lost her fiancé. The church group threatened
to sue me because I called in a psychiatrist, claiming that her restored
vision was one of God's miracles. I have wondered—if she became blind
once again, would that have restored her sanity?

Incidentally, Markie did not do well in the show. He came in third
out of three in his class. This ended his career as a show dog. Markie lived
to a ripe old age as a beloved family retainer.

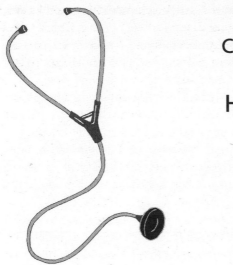

Chapter 28

Hillpoint

Frank Kramer lived on the break of the hill where Pleasant Hill became Parrett Mountain. For over a year, whenever I passed Frank's house, I wondered if he would ever consent to sell me his property. Because the farm wasn't on the market I was afraid to ask for fear I would insult him; but it was obviously the most desirable piece of property in the area. Instead, I made inquires about another piece of land across the road and down the hill a short distance, but this property was tied up in probate and not available. That piece of land wasn't nearly as desirable as the Kramer place, either, as it looked west into the Yamhill River Valley instead of east to the five snowcapped peaks visible toward the rising sun. Besides, I would have had to be part goat to farm it, as most of the place was straight up and down. No, it was the Kramer place I coveted.

We were happily living at Creekwood with our three children, four horses, two ponies, a polled Hereford cow named Mrs. Hahntahbler and her yearling son, four collie dogs, three cats, and eleven rabbits whose number was expected to expand momentarily. Our ten acres and small house with only two tiny bathrooms wasn't going to hold us much longer. We wanted to have more pasture and a larger house with three or four big bathrooms. We dearly loved Creekwood and the life we had there, but we had outgrown it. So, in addition to Pleasant Hill, we searched the neighborhood for some land where we could build our dream house. It seemed as if we were going to live the rest of our lives in Sherwood.

About ten o'clock on a beautiful, early summer's day a call came to the office that would change our lives forever. Frank Kramer had collapsed on a road near his home while changing a tire on his pickup. The local ambulance was rushing him to Tuality Hospital in Hillsboro and Mrs. Kramer wanted me to come. Would I?

Frank was suffering a massive heart attack, but he was a tough old bird, of good farm stock, and as he often said during his recovery period, "You didn't think I was goin' to make it did you, Doctor? All the time you was rushin' around, stickin' needles in my veins and makin' me breathe oxygen, I knowed I was too tough to die. You understand? I'm too tough too die, so you quit worryin' 'bout me and take care of them as really needs it."

The old guy may have been too tough to die but he was "bad sick." His old heart was never going to be the same; and it came as a great shock to him, weeks later, when he finally realized that he could no longer do farm work. He had angina pectoris (cardiac chest pain) with as little exertion as trying to run his tractor to till the orchard. About the only thing I could do for him was to advise him to cut down on his exertion, take the drugs I prescribed for him—including nitroglycerine whenever he had chest pain—and, if he couldn't find a hired man to do the work, then he would have to retire.

"I won't have no hired man on this place. Had one once; weren't no good. Lazy guy. Wouldn't do farmin' the way I wanted. Drank, too. Nope, guess I'll have to sell the place and move to town. You wanna buy it? Heard you been nosin' around 'bout buyin' some land. You interested?"

I caught my breath and swallowed a smile. *Heck, yes, I want to buy his farm. But I have some questions. Maude, his wife, isn't present. Would she want to sell? They have lived on the place their entire married life. This is a pretty big place for a gentleman farmer—over fifty acres; and besides, how much would he want for it?*

And then Frank said the words that became my greatest stumbling block to accepting his offer, "Doctor, I'd like you to git the place. You've done a lot for me. I guess, down deep I knowed I wasn't too tough to die. No sir, you saved my life. I'm beholden."

I said, "Frank, I'll have to think about this. I very much appreciate your gratitude and your offer but give me some time to think. We'll talk, again; and you'd better talk to Maude about selling the place, whether it's to me or some one else."

Glad was excited when I told her that Frank wanted to sell, until I told her about my ethical dilemma. "I'm beholden" put me on the spot. As a physician, I couldn't, in any way, unduly influence a patient in order to acquire an asset. If Frank Kramer felt beholden to me, I could accept a small gift such as a book, a plant for the yard, or any one of the many things that grateful patients give their doctors; but after advising him to retire, and then knowing in my heart that I coveted his land, to have him offer to sell it to me challenged my sense of right and wrong.

Did I suggest retirement, subliminally wanting him to sell his farm to me? If that were true, I was being a scoundrel. What to do?

Glad and I hashed it over, far into the night. Our final answer to ourselves was that I had done no wrong, but to avoid the appearance of impropriety I would, after determining that Maude was in agreement, suggest that Frank name a price. If I felt it was reasonable, I would then tell Frank that he should hire a licensed appraiser of his choosing, and we would pay either the appraised amount or the Kramers' asking price, whichever was higher.

The asking price and the appraisal were within a few dollars of each other and the sale was completed within a few weeks. The Kramers moved into town where Frank lived several more happy and comfortable years.

Glad and I now began to assess what we had done. We had acquired fifty-four beautiful, rolling acres whose apex was at the point of Pleasant Hill. We promptly named the farm Hillpoint. In addition to the acreage we had a huge old barn and a fifty-year-old farmhouse, which was the kind of house a well-to-do farmer might have built around the turn of the century. However, it would not serve our family any better than the house at Creekwood, where we were currently living. We would have to build.

In addition to pasture and crop lands, there were three orchards. The family orchard occupied almost two acres and contained about every kind of fruit and nut grown in that part of Oregon. There were two prune orchards. The upper orchard was gnarly and said to be as old as the house. The young orchard, forty-five years its junior, was bright and clean-limbed but, according to Frank, not yet in its prime.

The largest structure on the premises was the prune dryer. When I moved to Oregon from California I supposed all prunes were really plums and only became prunes when dried in the California sun in the San Joaquin Valley. Not so! Prunes of the kind we grew in Oregon were prunes by their species, and they could be dried, canned, or eaten fresh.

Frank Kramer had dried them, the cannery in Sherwood canned them, and everyone ate them fresh off the tree.

The ingenuity of the design of that big, old, out-of-date prune dryer fascinated both of us. The structure was built on a side hill with the receiving dock on the upside of the hill. When Frank Kramer had dried prunes for himself and his neighbors, the prunes were put on trays of window screen. The trays were then inserted into one of five chutes, all slanting downhill toward their ultimate destination, the shipping dock located at the bottom of the hill. Upon arrival there the prunes were dry. As each tray was removed the entire lot slid down a notch, making room for a fresh tray to be inserted at the top of the line. Beneath the structure was a huge, wood-burning furnace with heat ducts which pointed up in this hollow building, bathing the trays of prunes with just the right amount of heat; so that a tray could pass through the process in thirty-six hours. The wood-burning furnace had to be tended day and night during the prune-drying season, in late September or early October, with the fire being banked to give just the correct amount of heat. Because of the impracticality of the process—the cost of firewood had escalated and, most important, there was nobody to tend the fire—we decided to sell our prunes to the cannery.

During the late summer I found myself on the tractor every spare moment in order to keep the orchards in shape for the picking. I gleaned knowledge from other farmers in the area and from Glad's dad as to what had to be done, but I wondered how in the world I would manage this every year and still carry on a busy medical practice. I was able to make a deal with another farmer (whose string bean crop would require picking at about the same time as our prunes), to go to Portland's Skid Row at 5 A.M. on the days we would be picking and gather a crew of workers. The bean farmer had an old school bus he used just for this job; I rented seating space for our prune pickers.

All the men we picked up on those mornings were probably alcoholics. I had never dealt with this population in my practice and really didn't know what to expect. According to my friend, the bean farmer, some of the men would be drunk when the bus pulled up at the street corner in Portland. These guys gathered in anticipation of being hired for the day in order to get enough money for another jug of wine. He told me that we would have to feed them a hot lunch, because it would be the only real food they would get that day. He made it clear that some of the would-be workers wouldn't work, but would just sleep all day, so they should not be fed under any circumstances, as it showed weakness on our part. If it got around that we were an easy mark, they would take advantage of us. I was also warned that they expected us to refrain from asking their names and they had to be paid in cash at the end of each day. They received so much a bucket for the prunes they picked up after we had shaken the trees to make the prunes fall. He also recommended that I carry a pistol when I handled the payroll, laying the pistol on the table in clear view as a deterrent.

Wow! All of this was pretty daunting!

When the prunes were ripe I took two weeks of vacation. Each day Glad would make a huge pot of beef stew and haul it up to Hillpoint from Creekwood before noon. We stopped work and invited everyone to eat. Some wanted to continue picking, as this was their chance to get enough money to satisfy their habit for several days. We made them stop working but, as it is said about horses, "You can lead a horse to water but you can't make him drink," so it was with some of our pickers. Apparently food revolted them and they would not eat.

None of them wanted to work two days in a row. Therefore, it was with interest that I noticed one guy show up every day for the better part of a week. On the day of his fourth visit, when it came time to take the workers back to the city, I noticed that two of our bright new buckets were missing. Now, I'd heard that a good bucket could be sold, downtown, for enough to buy a jug of rotgut wine. As the guy who had been there for the fourth time was about to get on the bus, I said to him, "Two buckets are missing. Can you find them for me?"

Without saying a word to me, he got on the bus and yelled, "One of you S.O.B.s has stolen a couple of buckets. I'm gonna get offen this bus and me and the boss (that was me) are goin' in that house for a minute. When we come out I want those two buckets settin' here on the ground and no more'll be said. Iffen they ain't there, I'm gittin' on that bus an' I'll drag each one of you S.O.B.s off till I find the buckets; and you don't wanna be the guy I find with 'em!"

We walked into the house and closed the door. I thought about all the time I was spending doing this farm work and how much time I had to spend each day after the pickers left, loading the crates of prunes onto my truck and going to the cannery where I had to wait as long as three or four hours to get my load of prunes checked in. I said, "Hey, how would you like to be my crew boss and work steady for a few days?"

The guy looked kind of funny and said, "I don't usually work steady."

"Want to give it a try? I won't hold you to anything. I just need a little help for a while."

"I'd have to stay here," he said. "Iffen I go back downtown to stay I prob'ly ain't gonna be back."

I guessed the man to be in his mid-forties. He had a shock of jet-black hair brushed straight back. He was stockily built but not a bit fat. His clothes were reasonably clean and he didn't have the peculiar stench that I had noticed in the other pickers with alcohol and tobacco breath and of being unwashed. He was obviously cut from a different cloth than most of the men we had encountered on Skid Row.

He told me his name was Bob Wilston and that he would curl up in the empty farmhouse for the night and go after his stuff the next day if I would take him to Portland and bring him right back. I sensed a new feeling in Bob.

We went out to the bus and our two buckets were on the ground by the bus's door.

After a trip to the cannery I took Bob home with me and Glad gave him dinner. I left him in the old farmhouse for the night, wondering, as I drove home, if I was creating a peck of trouble for myself.

That night the bean farmer called to tell me that the old school bus had broken down and he wouldn't be making the Portland run in the morning. Because it was so near to the end of his picking season, he decided he wouldn't repair the bus. Now, that was a bummer! We had another week's picking left. I couldn't haul pickers in the back of the horse van, so it was Glad's Mercury station wagon or nothing.

At five the next morning we went to our usual corner and got a load of workers—one in the front seat with us, three each in the second and third seats, and two on the open tailgate. When our seat companion in front said he thought he was going to throw up, we stopped and put him on the tailgate. We reached Hillpoint without incident. Bob was waiting for us. Glad had brought a thermos of coffee and a roll for him.

I would not have been surprised if he had left, but he hung in and was by far the best picker we had, in addition to running the crew.

My vacation time was over and I had to return to work the next day. What to do about the pickers? Bob could look after them in the orchards but how were we going to haul them out from Portland? Glad said, "I'll do it and be back in time to get the kids off to school."

I answered, "You can't do that alone. It isn't safe."

"I can do it and I will do it. There's safety in numbers. And besides, that one guy with the buckets was the only trouble we've had. I notice you have even left your gun at home."

She did it, every day and without even the slightest trouble, except that there were always more pickers wanting to get in the station wagon than we had room for. Maybe riding in a car seemed better that in an old bus or truck, or maybe they liked to ride with a pretty girl. Whatever the reason, she was able to pick the best ones standing around waiting for a ride; and we had only one who conked out under a tree and slept all day. We fed him, anyway.

When the picking season was over, Glad and I and her dad talked it over. It was clear that we needed a hired man. Should we ask Bob to stay on? This was a challenge. There was an old wood stove in the house, but he would need some other necessary furnishings and transportation. If I let him use the house, what about the risk of fire with an irresponsible drinker in the place? If I let him use my truck was there danger to himself or the public, and would I be financially responsible if he got into trouble? So far, in the short time I had known him, he had been reliable and sober. The three of us decided that I should talk to Bob, lay out my concerns, and see what his reaction was.

Meanwhile we were busy with the architect who was designing the house we planned to build at Hillpoint. This would be our dream house—it would probably qualify as anyone's dream house. It would sit just below the highest point of the property, adjacent to a thicket of Douglas fir trees that Frank Kramer had kept as the family firewood lot. We resolved never to destroy one of these beautiful things just to keep warm. We would get our firewood elsewhere.

The view had Oregon's most beloved snow-capped peak, Mt. Hood, featured from every room in the house. In addition, there were vistas of Mt. St. Helens, the Three Sisters, Mt. Adams, Mt. Jefferson, and even a glimpse of Mt. Rainier, near Seattle, on a clear day.

I had left the truck at the farm and I knew Bob would have to use it to get groceries and to dispose of some of the rubbish he was cleaning out, now that the picking was done. I knew I had to talk with him, but I was concerned about the confrontation, possibly making him angry, and losing him as a worker. I procrastinated.

One evening, just before dusk, I was driving through the middle of town, returning from a house call, when I saw my truck parked on the street in front of one of the two local saloons.

Crisis! *Bob is in there, drinking. My worst fears have come true. What should I do? I could go in and confront Bob, but wouldn't that be so demeaning to him that we would part ways? But, maybe we should part ways. If this is to be his pattern of behavior, can I afford to keep him?*

I parked my car and thought, *I have to go into the saloon and get my truck keys. Leaving this guy on the highway with a vehicle would be akin to abetting homicide.*

I had never been in the saloon. Drinking establishments were not the places where one of the town's two doctors should be seen.

I felt strange as I opened the door. There were two men sitting at the bar, each with a beer sitting in front of him. They were staring at the back bar, as solitary drinkers are wont to do, lost in their own thoughts. The bartender was reading a book. A book, for God's sake. Not shooting pool, not dispensing advice to his customers, not polishing glasses, not with a smoke hanging from his lip. Just reading a book. Bob was not there. Perhaps he was in the men's room.

The bartender asked, "Whatta'll ya have?"

I would have liked to have said, "I'd like to have Bob Wilston tied up in a sack so I can haul him away from here with the least amount of trouble." Instead, nonplused, I said, "Draft please."

The bartender drew my beer and said, "You've never been in here before have ya? My name's Ben." He stuck out his hand for a welcoming shake.

I thought, *If the bartender is this friendly to everyone, he'll know Bob. By now Bob should have come out of the bathroom.*

I said, "I'm Tom…" Before I could finish, he said, "Ain't you the doctor?"

I mumbled a yes, not wanting the news broadcast. The two guys at the bar looked up, bleary-eyed, and one said, "I needed a doctor last week but I guess I'm okay, now." And he went back to staring at the back bar. I wondered if he thought I had come in to solicit business and this was his way of rejecting me.

The bartender went on, "Doc, you took care of my aunt awhile back. Did a good job. The beer's on me. She told me she fell out of bed while she was at the hospital and somebody called the police and the nurses got mad. Any truth to that? Aunt Eliza gets a little goofy sometimes. But anyway, you fixed her wrist good."

I remembered Eliza James and her broken wrist and the fuss that ensued after she fell out of bed while at Tuality Hospital. But I didn't want to talk about Eliza; I wanted to find Bob Wilston.

When I started to ask the bartender about Bob, he interrupted again, asking, "Doesn't Bob Wilston work for you?"

I said, "Yeah, and where…," but the loquacious barkeep kept talking.

"Bob came in here today for the first time and really hung one on. He was pretty damn drunk. I told him he'd better quit. 'Okay I'm broke, anyway,' he said. 'I'm too drunk to drive and iffen I wreck the doctor's truck, he'll skin me.' So I asked Pete Mitchell, who was sittin' around here doin' nothin', to run him home. That was about an hour ago."

Whew! I breathed a big sigh of relief, finished my beer, and went home. Glad said, "Where'd you get the beer?" I answered, "Oh, just down at the saloon." She said, "Sure, you…in the saloon. That's a joke." And she promptly forgot all about it.

The time for procrastination was over. The next day Bob and I sat down to talk. I told him I needed a hired man and I thought he might be the man for the job. Was he interested? I said I knew he had a problem and what did he think he could do about it if he took the job.

"Doctor," Bob said, "I ain't worked steady for a good many years. I move around a lot. I like you, Doctor, but you won't like me after a while. 'Bout the first time I don't show up for a couple of days, you'll can me and I'll be off again. I ain't gonna change. I'm a drunk. When I get a few bucks ahead I get drunk like I did yesterday and I don't quit till I'm broke. I didn't have enough money yesterday to stay drunk. So here I am back on the job, but the next time, who knows when I'll get back? I'm no good, so don't put your trust in me."

"Do you like working here, Bob?"

"Sure I do. You're a good guy and your wife's an angel. I like this old house. It'd be good to find a place to hole up for the winter, but I don't think I can do it."

"Bob, you showed me something yesterday when you wouldn't drive my truck when you felt you weren't capable of doing it safely. That attitude means, to me, that maybe you don't think enough of yourself, that maybe there's more substance to you than you think there is. I can't reform you. I won't even try. But, I'll put up with some of your problems, up to the point where you become irresponsible; and if that happens, we part ways. I'm willing to try it, knowing what I'm getting into. You do the job and I don't care what you do on your off time, so long as it doesn't hurt others. Whatta you say?"

"Doctor, I really do appreciate your confidence. It's been a long time since anyone has said anything like that to me. I'd like to take the job and I'll do it for six months. If I get itchy then and I want to move on, well, I guess I'll have to do it. I think I'll ask you to squirrel away some of my money in the bank so later, iffen I need it, I'll have a stake. I'll try to stay off the booze, but I'll fall off the wagon; and when I do I may be gone as much as a week. Don't come lookin' fer me and you dock my wages while I'm gone. That's okay. When I feel I got to go out drinkin', I won't take the truck; you got no worries on that score. If you want to try it on these terms, I'll do my best."

We agreed. Bob kept his side of the bargain. He was a good worker and a very capable person, more than he ever let on. He never talked about himself and I never asked. He went on several binges, twice for as long as a week, but he stayed the promised six months and then was off. I didn't ask where he had been when he returned the next picking season to help out with the harvest and then, he left once more.

We never saw or heard from Bob again. He came to us in a time of need and helped us over a major crisis, and when he dropped out of sight, we were a little disappointed. However, the need for a hired man was almost over. Although we didn't know it at the time, our life in Oregon was coming to a close. Frustrations in the practice were growing, our relationship with my partner and his wife were deteriorating and, although the architectural plans for Hillpoint were finished, we would never build the house.

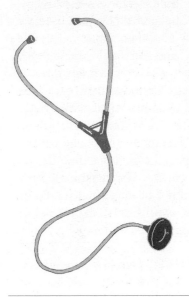

Chapter 29

Life, Death, and Friendship

When our outside telephone gong rang on a Saturday afternoon about two o'clock, the patient said, "Doctor, I have a terrible stomachache. I don't think I can stand it much longer. Can you come?"

I knew the caller. I had seen the old gentleman before. He'd had an occasional minor farm accident and, about a year before, a kidney infection. I had never been to his home, but I knew he lived up on Parrett Mountain, far past the place where Pinky Mayfield lived with his family. I also knew he lived alone and was quite reclusive. I asked, "Can you meet me at the office, Mr. Zellner?"

The message came back in a way that I couldn't ignore, not this time, not ever, in taking care of people. "Doctor, please come. I'm too sick to come down the mountain."

Sure, once in a great while I got stiffed on a phone call like that when some nut got a pain in the big toe and thought it was a calamity. For the few times that happened, I was rewarded over and over with the knowledge that by going I had relieved someone's pain and maybe, on occasion, saved a life. So, when this call came on a Saturday afternoon when I was home with the family, I controlled any irritation I may have felt by knowing that this was what being a doctor meant.

Don, Lee, Pamela, Glad and I were at Creekwood, out in the riding ring with the horses. I was working on training the colt, Mayday's Mischief. Don was on little Spunky, the Shetland colt, while Lee was galloping around the riding ring on Spunky's mother, Sugar Sally. Glad was leading Pamela on my big black horse, who had a pained and fearful expression that seemed to say, "For heaven's sake, don't let her fall off!" He walked as if there were cartons of eggs set around to booby-trap him. Pamela, whose little legs stuck straight out from his broad back, tried to kick this big, black horse like Daddy did when nudging his heels into the horse's ribs. All the while she was yelling, "Get up you ole black debbil!"

I really hated to leave. This was a special time for the family and our friends who, with their kids, were due out from Portland in about an hour for riding and a potluck supper. The kind of day when we invited people by saying, "You bring a hot dish and we'll furnish the rest."

However, if I leave now, maybe I could be back in time to greet our friends.

First, we had to secure the horses. Glad couldn't manage four horses and the kids by herself. We left the saddles on, tossed some hay into their feed bins, and put them in the barn. That way, the horses would be ready to ride when our friends arrived.

I cleaned up a bit and drove up Parrett Mountain. When I came to Pinky's, I glanced over, as one does when passing a familiar place, and prepared to wave if I saw someone. There was no one in the yard—but there was a sign. I read the sign, but I couldn't believe it. My momentum had carried me past the house, so I stopped the car and backed up. What I read confirmed my first impression, FOR SALE BY OWNER— INQUIRE WITHIN.

Thoughts streamed through my mind. *Carol is sick of the country life and wants to move back to the city, or they found a better house and can afford it because of Pinky's success with his territory, or his company had transferred him, or he decided to go back to school after all. But why didn't he talk with me about it before taking action?*

I couldn't possibly have, in my wildest dreams, guessed the reason for his silence on the matter.

Pinky was the brother I never had. But he hadn't mentioned this move to me. I was shocked. Don't brothers confide in each other? I'd find out about this as soon as I could.

When I reached Zellner's place, there was just a lane and a mailbox to point the way. As I parked the car, I realized that Mr. Zellner wasn't the only one in trouble. A half dozen Guernsey ladies were standing behind the fence, close to the barn door, mooing their heads off, protesting their neglected and very full udders. The old man was really in trouble if he couldn't get out to milk his cows.

I knocked and entered the house by the kitchen door, calling out for Mr. Zellner. I was guided to his room by his moaning and a faint cry, "Hurry, Doctor."

When I entered the bedroom, the patient was lying in his bed with his legs drawn up, his face pale, and he was alternately grunting and moaning. I had seen this man tolerate pain with great stoicism during his prior farm accidents. His appearance was alarming. This was a very sick man.

I asked the usual questions about the history of his illness while preparing an injection of morphine to relieve his pain. Gus said, "It come on sudden-like, Doc, and kept gettin' worse. I wouldn't a called you up here, Doc, iffen I felt I coulda made it down the hill. Doc, I ain't never had nothin' like this, before."

A sudden onset of pain such as this usually meant a perforated abdominal organ or a vascular accident, such as a blood clot. I found out that he had thrown up, had not had a bowel movement that day, but was still able to pass urine. However, when I touched his abdomen, he screamed with pain. His belly was as hard as a board. There were no bowel tones. Listening to his abdomen with my stethoscope was almost eerie in its silence. Usually there are gurgles and creaks, like a ship rocking at the dock, but his was ominously silent. What I learned from this was that Mr. Zellner needed to be hospitalized immediately, and a surgeon called in consultation. Blood counts and X-rays of the abdomen would have to be done, but it seemed that, ultimately, the solution was going to be exploratory laparotomy—that is, opening the belly to see what was wrong; and the sooner the better.

While I waited for the ambulance I gave my patient a second injection of morphine, as the first one hadn't helped much. "Pain is the antidote for morphine," our pharmacology professor, Stormin' Norman, had told us and boy, was that ever proved here!

I called a neighbor to ease the suffering of the ladies out in the barnyard and I asked Mr. Zellner if he wanted me to notify someone that he would be in the hospital—maybe a sister or a cousin. He said, "There is no one."

Gustavus Zellner wanted to go to Tuality Hospital in Hillsboro, so the surgeon I called had to drive out from Portland. When he arrived and reviewed the X-rays and lab results and checked Gus, he agreed that abdominal laparotomy was our only choice. I had given Gus more morphine than I had ever used on a patient and still he had violent pain. His mind was clouded, but he continued to moan almost constantly. I reasoned that the blessed relief of a general anesthetic would be welcomed by him. More diagnostic tests could only prolong his agony and kindness dictated that we should proceed quickly. Waiting would not help. We decided to operate immediately.

Before Gus underwent his anesthetic, he asked only one question. "Do you think I'll be all right?"

Both the surgeon and I answered in medical double-speak, suggesting hope, promising nothing. I had grave doubts about the success of any surgical procedure for as violent an illness as this one was proving to be. *What the devil should I say in a case like this?* If family had been there I could have shared my concerns with them, but there was no family. *Does Gus really want to know what I think?* I hoped against hope that he had a treatable condition but, deep in my heart, I thought it was hopeless. Does a dreadfully sick man, already confused by morphine, want to know my innermost fears; or was it better to offer hope, as I did, but with no promises?

We made a vertical, midline abdominal incision. Upon opening the peritoneum and looking into the abdominal cavity, we were presented with the most ghastly sight it had ever been my misfortune to see. Gus Zellner's entire small bowel, from the jejunum to the cecum, was gangrenous. Instead of the usual pink snakes writhing in peristalsis, there was a mass of motionless, dead coils of blackened bowel. The main artery to the bowel had thrombosed (obstructed with a blood clot), and with no blood supply for the twelve hours or so between the onset and the present time, a dry gangrene had set in. The thrombosed vessel could not be reopened, but even if it could have been, the bowel was dead. And so Gus would be, soon.

All we could do was close the abdominal wound and wait. Our patient was doomed to spend a few hours or, at the most, a day before all of his various organ systems would fail and he would die.

Now we wondered what to do. Do we awaken Gus and tell him about his condition and expose him to the pain, or keep him under heavy sedation until he expired? The surgeon pointed out that it was my decision, as the family physician, and he returned to Portland. *Thanks a lot!*

Does a person have the right to know he is dying? There is no family to notify. Does Gus have a will? Probably not. What will happen to his little farm? Gus's last words were, "Will I be all right?" Did that mean he would want me to let him awaken so I could tell him he was dying? Should I have told him of my fears about his chances before he went under the anesthetic? Was Gus religious, and would he want to make peace with his God? He had declared that he was Protestant on his hospital admission form. His hospital admission form identified no next of kin. The form gave, as a person to be notified, the neighbor who was milking his cows. This gave me a person with whom to share my burden.

I called the neighbor. He was appalled at the news. No, Gus did not attend church. No, he didn't know if Gus had a will, but he did know that Gus had a mortgage on the farm.

Remember, it was Saturday night, so the bank was closed and wouldn't open until Monday. By then, Gus would be gone. No help in getting any more information from the bank. I asked the neighbor for a suggestion. He didn't have one, except to say he would take care of the cows and the milk until something definitive could be worked out. He was sorry and said goodbye. This left only me to make the decision for Gus. It was one of the loneliest times of my life.

If I were the guy in this position, what would my choice be? What would I want if it was me, lying in this bed? Well, I have a wife and children to say goodbye to. Gus does not.

I agonized back and forth—*Let him wake up and tell him the bad news or keep him asleep and spare him the pain. If I let him awaken, maybe he would give us some last wishes regarding his property; or maybe there is someone who, if Gus knew he was dying, he would want to have notified. Practically speaking, the State of Oregon would search his papers in order to probate his estate, and possibly discover the whereabouts of any relatives.*

Day became night. I sat in the doctors' lounge. Another doctor came in and I presented my problem to him. No help. He said, "Sorry. I hope I never have to face the same problem."

The nursing shift changed, and still I sat there. The head nurse came in and asked if I had any orders to change for Gus Zellner. I finally made my decision. I told the nurse that there would be no change in my orders. "Keep Gus under deep sedation until he dies." It happened some twelve to fifteen hours later. He suffered no more.

Gus had asked, "Will I be all right?" His answer had become no, but he never heard it. Was I right in doing what I did? I have had to live with my decision.

❧

When I returned home, late that night, our guests had already departed. Glad had, once again, been forced to entertain by herself. She never complained. We had recognized the pitfalls of a doctor's life and we both had accepted that there would be many times when we would each have to go our own way because of the exigencies of practice.

That night I was too tired to find out what was going on in Pinky's life. I made the call to Pinky on Sunday, but there was no one home. On Monday I called from the office, not expecting to reach him, but hoping to leave a message with Carol. Surprisingly, he was there. In answer to my question about the place being for sale, he said, "Yes, it is."

"But why?" I asked. "Are you in any financial trouble? Can I help?"

"No trouble," he said.

"If you're not in trouble why are you selling your farm?"

His answer took me completely off guard. "I've asked for a transfer out of this territory. We aren't happy here, so I'm taking the family and we're moving away. As soon as I can, I want to get out of this kind of work."

"My gosh, Pinky, I thought you were doing so well in this territory. Where do you intend to go?"

"Don't take this too personally, but I'm not going to tell you where we're going and I don't want you to try to find out. You see, I want you out of my life."

"What in the world have I done?"

"You haven't done anything. It's me. You see, you have everything I want. You're a doctor. I could have been. If I had taken the time when I got out of the service and finished school on the GI bill like you did, I could be where you are, now. As it is, I never will be. I have the intellect, but now I'm committed to my family and I can't take the time to go back to school. Being around you constantly reminds me of my failure. I just don't want to be around doctors. I'm going to find another career where I won't see doctors and, although it's not your fault, I don't want to see you anymore."

I said, "But Pinky…." He was gone. Pinky had hung up! I didn't see him again. Losing Pinky was like the death of a loved one. I felt guilty, but for what I didn't know.

I mourned over my lost friend and I wondered what I could have done, or should have done. I worried, too, over my not having awakened Gus Zellner. When I first saw Jimmy, a short time later, I wondered if he would be the cause of another heartache.

❧

Jimmy Ricci was married to Angela Carbonis. Jimmy's real name was Angel, but to avoid problems within the family, trying to differ between Angel and Angela, he asked his friends to call him Jimmy. He never said why he picked Jimmy; I guess he just liked the name.

When I was a young guy working in the laundry of the United States Marine Hospital in the Presidio in San Francisco, I folded sheets off the mangle with a guy named Joe Brown. I'd worked with Joe Brown (nobody ever called him Joe, only Joe Brown) for three months before I found out that his real name wasn't Joe Brown. It was said by the old hands in the laundry that Joe Brown would fight anyone who used his real name, Richard Burchett. I could understand why neither of these men wanted their real names used, but I never figured out why they chose the names they wanted people to call them.

On the day Angela Ricci brought Angel (Jimmy) Ricci to the office with violent abdominal pain I looked at Jimmy, and a picture of Gus Zellner flashed through my head. Not again!

Jimmy was younger than Gus, with a history of gradual instead of sudden onset of pain, but the violent symptoms were the same. In addition to the pain he, too, had a board-like belly, but he didn't scream when I palpated his abdomen. Also, there were active bowel sounds, too active perhaps, suggestive of a bowel obstruction.

I thought back to my first weeks of practice and the botched case of Emil Wishong, when I had moved ahead too fast and scared my patient away from definitive therapy. I remembered the words of my surgical colleague who had said, "When you have an interesting case, don't play all your cards at once. Sometimes it's more than the patient can stand."

I asked Jimmy when he last had a bowel movement. "Day before yesterday," was the answer, and, "Doc, there wasn't much."

I did a rectal exam with a gloved finger and found the rectum empty, highly suggestive of a bowel obstruction. I contemplated doing a sigmoidoscopic examination, but I was going to take a little time before I showed Jimmy that foot-long shiny chrome tube that I would have to use. Also, I thought I needed further confirmation of my working diagnosis of bowel obstruction before rushing Jimmy to the hospital for surgery. My choices for diagnosis included a perforated abdominal organ, diverticulitis with perforation and abscess formation, or cancer of the bowel.

It is an old adage in medical circles that problems run in threes and, once you have two similar cases, wait for the next shoe to drop. I don't believe I'm superstitious anymore—but I don't walk under ladders, I toss spilled salt over my left shoulder, and I knock on wood to forestall adversity. I hoped Jimmy had rapped his knuckles on a chunk of wood and we were not facing another case like Gus Zellner. Jimmy made my decision about doing some tests a whole lot easier by asking, "Doc, do I need some tests or something? Can I have something for this horrible pain?"

"Yes, to both of your questions, Jimmy. You need to go to the hospital." I asked Marcia to give Jimmy an injection of Demerol for his pain.

Jimmy elected to go to St. Vincent's in Portland. Inwardly, I breathed a sigh of relief at his ready acceptance of the need for further tests. His white blood count was high and his red blood count was low. The low red count might be the result of prolonged microbleeding from a tumor of the large intestine. The flat X-ray of the abdomen confirmed that the bowel was obstructed but it did not reveal the reason. Putting the low red count together with the obstruction certainly made a case for tumor of the cecum as the most likely cause. I didn't need to do the sigmoidoscopy, because the bowel was obviously obstructed, and he needed surgery for that.

I called in the same surgeon who had worked on Gus. True, he wasn't a genius in dealing with tragedy, but he was a darn good technician. He had reinforced what I already knew, that dealing with the patient's family and giving them support was really my responsibility as the family doctor.

We set up three pints of blood, one to be given as soon as it was typed and cross-matched, to overcome his anemia; and the other two were to be held in readiness, to be used during surgery, in case they were needed.

I talked to Angela about the possibility of this being a life-threatening problem and she said, "Please tell Jimmy everything. He will want to know." She also pointed out that Jimmy was Catholic and would like to see the priest to hear his confession before we went to the operating room. While we waited for the blood to be typed and cross-matched, I sent for the hospital padre, but I also called Father O'Hara in Sherwood. Father O'Hara had bailed me out of difficult circumstances before and I wanted him to talk to his parishioner if he could get away. He could, and showed up before we went to surgery.

Sharing the responsibility of support for Angela and their three grown children with the priest lifted a heavy burden from my heart. Father

O'Hara and I discussed how we would tell Angela and Jimmy about cancer, if that was what we were dealing with. Father thought Jimmy had enough faith in God to handle anything. I said I was pleased that he thought this, but my experience was that even some of the seemingly toughest patients didn't really want to know and avoided the issue, living more comfortably with denial than with the brutal, hard facts. People that really wanted to know usually asked straightforward questions like, "Do I have cancer?" and "How am I going to get along?" Gus Zellner had asked, "Am I going to be all right?" I wondered again if I should have awakened him and answered his question.

Inside Jimmy's abdomen we found a huge mass in the cecum, the part of the large bowel that is continuous with the ileum or small intestine. We took a biopsy and sent it to the pathologist who reported back that Jimmy had cancer. The growth was so large that it was stuck to the back of the abdominal wall, the urinary bladder, and to the adjacent loops of the small intestine. The cecum was totally obstructed and, because it was stuck to everything else, it could not be removed. Instead, we did a bypass procedure, linking a free loop of the ileum to a more distal segment of the large intestine. This procedure would reduce the pain and allow the bowel to evacuate, but would not in any way cure the cancer.

We took another biopsy for the pathologist for future study and closed Jimmy's abdomen with a heavy heart, fearing that he did not have long to live.

Jimmy's problem was different from Gus's. Death would not come quickly. We would use palliative radiation therapy as soon as his wound was healed, and there would be an interval of good quality of life. Perhaps Jimmy would get as much as a year. Then he would suffer pain, loss of appetite, and the inexorable spread of the cancer that would eventually kill him.

The day after surgery, Father O'Hara and I met with Jimmy and Angela at his bedside. Jimmy said, "Have I got cancer?" We openly discussed this with them. Angela and Jimmy took it well, but they were stubborn. They both resisted the thought that death was inevitable. They both embraced denial as a way of coping.

With the obstruction bypassed, Jimmy returned home after a few days. He began his radiation treatments in about a week after discharge from the hospital. I made arrangements to see him in two weeks, then monthly for a while, to check his blood count and general health.

At one month Jimmy felt and looked great. At three months Jimmy was the picture of health, running his farm with Angela at his side, enjoying things they had not done before. Even though the two of them resisted the idea of dying, they realized they'd had a close call and decided to open up their lives. They vacationed in California, went to football and baseball games, and began to make a little wine from a patch of grapes near their orchard.

At one year, Jimmy was not only still alive but seemed extraordinarily healthy. I was pleased, but astounded; so I called the pathologist at the hospital and asked him to review the case. He still had a portion of the biopsied material, made new slides, and examined them carefully. Nothing had changed. This was cancer. I didn't mention to the Riccis that the slides had been reviewed. Their confidence was too beautiful to interfere with. I kept my own counsel.

I did ask the pathologist for another opinion. The pathologist volunteered to send the slides off to experts at the National Institutes on Health in Washington, D.C., and the M.D. Anderson Cancer Center in Houston, Texas, for review. There was unanimity in their opinions. This was cancer.

At eighteen months, Jimmy and Angela suggested that he didn't need any more checkups. They pointed out that they had known from the beginning that nothing bad was going to happen to Jimmy. "Doctor, we appreciate your concern and everything you have done, but it is quite obvious that the cancer is cured; and thank you very much."

I didn't argue. I corresponded with Jimmy and Angela for two years after we moved to California. Jimmy was still healthy.

All the things that happen to people are not yet explainable by science or reason. Was the radiation curative instead of palliative? Did they deny the inevitable, or was their faith great enough to take care of them? The disappearance of tumors like this is just not explainable. Was it their faith? I didn't try to explain their success; I just accepted what was dealt to them. When what is dealt is good news, so much the better.

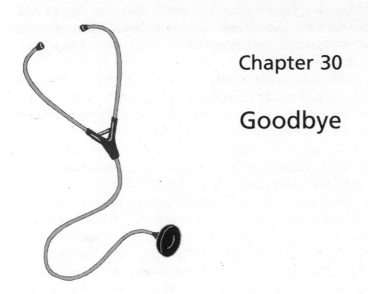

Chapter 30

Goodbye

The years I spent in Oregon represented a decade of the ultimate joy for a general practitioner—caring for a large and loving practice of devoted patients. My goal had been to settle in a small town and devote my life to the patients there. I would deliver babies and then deliver the babies of the babies I had delivered. One day the town would have an "Old Doc Day" and I would retire.

Alas, this was not to be. The partnership that had begun in 1952 failed in 1960. It is said one should be more compatible with one's partner than with one's wife. But the partners had a falling out, and because he had been there first, it was my contractual responsibility to move on.

When the decision to leave was announced, the farewells started. In the office or in patients' homes these were often tearful, hugging affairs, with promises.

"You will come back and visit, won't you?"

"Of course we will, all the time."

We weren't sure we would have the money to return. We would be starting all over again, and this time without a ready-made practice to walk into. But it would be my practice. There wouldn't be any arguments about how patients would be treated or whether there would be appointments. It would be done my way.

"Sure, we'll come back."

The fifty-four-acre farm we had christened Hillpoint, that was to have been our ultimate home, would have to be sold. The acrimony surrounding the breakup of the practice would make it uncomfortable for us ever to move back permanently.

"Yes, we'll be back," we told them.

We knew it would be only for visits.

We sold Creekwood to two ladies who raised dogs. Sugar Sally, the kids' Shetland pony and her colt, Spunky, were sold to the couple who had bought our first home in Tualatin. The two Saddlebred colts, Mayday Mischief and Mayday Madcap, went to a man who showed horses and had a reputation for taking good care of his stock.

I could not sell my big black horse, Bourbon's Black Magic. He was fourteen years old and probably in his prime, but it wouldn't be long before he would begin to show his age. I went to the barn and talked it over with my pal. He put his head on my chest while I scratched his ears and, with tears in my eyes, I told him we would be leaving. I promised him retirement and the good life. I believe he understood. I arranged with Shelby Smeed, an enthusiastic fourteen-year-old horsewoman, to care for Magic on her parents' large farm. She would ride him, occasionally, but mostly his life would be one of retirement. He had earned it.

We took the cats and two of our three collie dogs with us and we arranged for the third one to become a farm dog, a good life for a collie.

The parties went on and on, becoming less gay and more sad as the time for departure came closer. Of course we would keep up our friendship with Jane and John Brown, our friends from college. We would see the Harvey Bakers at medical meetings. The Hites, Drummonds, O'Callahans and McGraws had become close friends who would be a part of our lives, always.

The day we closed the door at Creekwood and took Magic to the Smeeds, and the rest of our animals to their new homes, caused the tears to flow from all our eyes.

I had often remarked that I was a Californian "by birth and inclination." In 1960, I set out to prove that. Glad and I and the children formed a caravan and headed south. We traded our farm and horses for a swimming pool and palm trees. We traded a practice of farmers and almost-farmers for an urban practice of aerospace scientists and airline people. For our children, we traded country schools for the sophisticated schools of an upscale California neighborhood. In our new life and location in California, we looked forward to the same joy of patient care and the independence we had wanted in the Oregon practice.

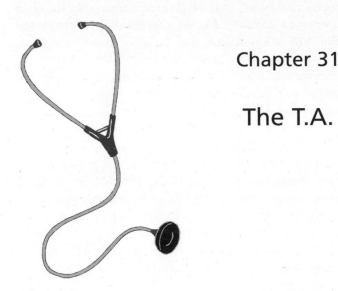

Chapter 31

The T.A.

Becoming the technical advisor for the *Marcus Welby, M.D.* television show and using the show for a treatment modality was the farthest thing from my mind the day I received a call from Bill Delay, the head of public relations for the American Academy of Family Physicians (AAFP), asking me to meet with David Victor, the executive producer of the show.

The AAFP, a national professional association of physicians, had been interested in having the Welby show promote the concept of family practice. By a strange coincidence, the birth of the new specialty of Family Practice occurred in 1969, the same year the first episodes of *Welby* aired. They hoped the producers would air an episode demonstrating Family Practice Residency programs, showing how physicians who entered this new primary care specialty were being trained. When Bill Delay asked David Victor to do this, David logically asked, "Where can I find such a program so I can see how it works?"

As an active member of the California state chapter of the AAFP, I had long been interested in medical education. I felt the highest honor accorded a physician was to be asked to teach other physicians. I had been very proud to be on the preceptor panel of the University of Southern California School of Medicine. In this program, I took a medical student into my home and, literally, into my life for six weeks. The student lived with us, went to my office with me, and saw patients with me. As the term of the preceptorship neared its close, I often allowed the student to see patients before I did and report to me, and then we would see them together.

One of the students was a woman. Heide was not only female; she was a beautiful female. I worried that men might be hesitant to be seen by a woman and I worried about Heide possibly being hesitant in dealing with male patients.

I didn't have long to wait before I sensed a crisis building. A male patient who had a history of a urethral discharge from his penis came to the office. The proper diagnostic procedure would be to obtain some of this fluid by prostate massage. This somewhat uncomfortable procedure is done by inserting the gloved finger in the rectum and firmly pressing on the prostate gland until a drop of fluid appears at the tip of the penis, and then placing a glass slide at the urethral outlet and asking the patient to milk any remaining discharge onto the slide so that it could be examined under the microscope.

This is a daunting task for any young medical student, as the patient is often embarrassed and in pain during the examination. I remembered the first time I had performed a prostate massage. I had not explained to the patient exactly what I was going to do, other than perform a rectal exam. I was pretty green, and had not known exactly what to say. Professors in medical school hadn't taught the art of medicine; they were too busy with the science. Once I inserted my gloved finger and pressed down on the prostate, the patient began to yell and tried to run away from me. Uncertain of how I should act in this circumstance, I followed the patient across the room, keeping my finger inserted in his rectum, until he hit the wall and stopped; whereupon I completed the exam. I have always been grateful that this happened before video surveillance of students was instituted as a teaching device. Our race across the room, united as we were, finger to anus, would have made the outtake (blooper) archives of the medical school, forever.

I didn't want Heide to suffer the type of ignominious experience that I had suffered. I called her into my office and asked her to be seated so that we could discuss the patient that she had started to work up. I intended to explain that she shouldn't be embarrassed because this was a member of the opposite sex and she would have to handle his genitalia; and asked her to be sure to position the patient on the examining table so that he wouldn't try to get away—or to request that he bend over and hold onto the table, for the same reason. "Now," I said, "do you feel you can do this?" I was worried that something might go wrong and I was prepared to let her avoid the procedure if she said she was at all concerned. I asked, "What about it?"

Without a second's hesitation Heide said, "I've already done it, Doctor. I made the slide and it's under the microscope for you to look at. I don't believe he has gonorrhea. An antibiotic and a couple of trips in here for prostate massage and he'll be fine." She grinned. She knew that *she* had gotten *me* over a crisis.

After several years of having a medical student in the office from time to time, some patients expectantly asked, "Will you have another young doctor this year?" They seemed to be pleased that their own doctor was qualified to teach, and I thought they liked the extra attention.

Soon after the specialty of Family Practice was created, Dr. Will Snodgrass, also a member of the AAFP, had invited me to come to Santa Monica Hospital to create a residency in family practice. Santa Monica Hospital had been a teaching hospital for many years. When this respected institution put its prestige and experience behind the offer Dr. Snodgrass had made, I felt honored but concerned over what taking on such a position would do to my life and to our family. We were comfortable with our lives. I loved my practice and the patients I took care of. In order to take on this new challenge, what would I have to give up?

The position at Santa Monica was half time, offering me the ability to continue my private practice in Manhattan Beach, only twenty-five minutes away. This was also my escape hatch. With the half-time deal they offered, I could keep my patient base in my own office. If the new residency flopped, I could go back, full time, to the comfortable surroundings of private practice.

To start a whole new residency program would be a real challenge and, even though I wasn't sure it was going to work, I felt excited at the prospect of being in on the ground floor of a new field of medicine that had the potential to become the largest specialty in the country. (Family Practice has now become the largest specialty in the USA and around the world.)

So it was, that when David Victor asked Bill Delay where he could see a functioning family practice residency program, Bill said, "Real close to where you live in Beverly Hills—just down Wilshire Boulevard in Santa Monica."

I told Bill I would be happy to meet with David Victor. Two days later, Mr. Victor called. We set up a late afternoon meeting at my office at Santa Monica Hospital, to be followed by dinner with our wives.

David and Florence Victor arrived at the hospital about three-thirty in the afternoon. Glad was already there. I showed the Victors the family practice office where the residents saw their own patients. We had only three residents; we were just getting started. Eventually we would have twenty-one. They practiced as they would, someday, in their own offices; except that, now, they were being supervised.

At the restaurant I asked David how he happened to have created the *Welby* show. He explained that he had always wanted to be a doctor but, growing up during the Great Depression, there was no money for college. He applied for many different types of scholarships and when he was awarded one in journalism, he took it. After doing newspaper work for a few years, he left New York for Hollywood and began his career as a screenwriter. His first big show was *Young Doctor Kildare,* which he developed for television. He produced this show starring Lionel Barrymore and a very young, budding star, Richard Chamberlain. Since then, he had produced a number of episodes of the *Man from U.N.C.L.E.* series, starring Robert Wagner and David McCallum, and other network shows. I was delighted to be in the company of such a celebrity.

Before meeting David Victor, if I had thought about it at all, I would have had a mental vision of any big Hollywood producer smoking a giant cigar, surrounded by starlets, all throwing their bodies at him for a chance to be in movies. Instead, Glad and I were in the company of a quiet, intelligent man, interested in the real world of medicine and accompanied by his charming wife, Florence.

David wanted to know about me and asked some fairly searching questions, not revealing that the reason for his interest was to determine if I was the right person to become the technical advisor for the show.

We suddenly realized that it was after eleven o'clock, the restaurant had closed, and the waiters were standing around, politely waiting for us to leave. We had talked for five hours.

Two weeks later to the day, Gath, my receptionist, told me that a Mr. Victor was on the phone. "Said he was from Universal Studios and that he had dinner with you a couple of weeks ago. Do you want to take the call?"

"Sure."

David Victor asked me to become the technical advisor to the *Welby* show. I would be required to review every word in the scripts and numerous script revisions, in order to ensure absolute medical accuracy. I would also be called upon to work with writers from time to time, to develop medical input into a dramatic scene or into an entire script.

Occasionally I would be called upon to come to the studio to teach one of the actors how to move and handle instruments or behave with patients.

Before I made a decision, he wanted me to come to the studio to meet the stars, Robert Young, Jim Brolin, and Elena Verdugo. In addition, he wanted me to meet the producer, David O'Connell, and the person I would have most contact with, Nina Laemmele, the executive story consultant. Boy, what a name that was! The Laemmeles, Carl and Carl, Jr., had been giants in the early development of the motion picture industry.

I didn't seem to have any hesitation about doing it. I was so excited at the prospect that I almost said yes while talking to David Victor, although he had warned me to think it over before I answered.

When I simmered down and went home and talked to Glad about it, she warned me not to become overly excited. I had several interviews to get through, not the least of which was one with the fabled Robert Young.

Upon reflection, I wondered if I really wanted to get into the Hollywood scene. Two high school classmates of mine had gone to Hollywood and I wasn't sure that I wanted to emulate either one of them.

Judy Turner, who later went to Schwab's Drugstore in Hollywood and sat at the soda fountain in order to be "discovered" as the "Sweater Girl" and become Lana, lived around the corner from me in San Francisco. She was a cheerleader at Washington High School at the same time I represented the school as a debater and thespian. A copy of the *Washington High School Eagle,* the student newspaper, ran an edition with two headlines. The first stated, TOM STERN IN SPEECH CONTEST FOR WASHINGTON. The second read, JUDY TURNER GOES TO HOLLYWOOD.

She was the prettiest girl in the school and, I thought, perhaps the prettiest girl anywhere in the world. I was proud to let her in free when I worked as the doorman at the Balboa Theater. We had a little scam worked out. She would arrive in front of the box office around the end of the first half of the double feature, when the incoming crowd was the thickest. The instant I saw her I would begin to tingle, my hands and feet would become cold and my face red and hot. Her smooth complexion drew my first glance, but then my eyes wandered to the sweater, as did the eyes of every male who ever encountered the living Lana. She would hang around until a number of people were going through the door and handing me their tickets. Instead of a ticket we would touch hands and she would give me a little squeeze. I became slightly short of breath as she passed through the door. I always turned to watch her progress through the lobby, as the magic of the undulations of her skirt were a sight to see. I could hardly wait until I was off duty and I could sit with her in the balcony. I was sometimes rewarded with a kiss, but I never deluded myself into thinking that Judy cared about me. I was a free pass to the movies, that's all.

A few years after she became a star, I ran into her while dancing at the Rose Room of the Palace Hotel in San Francisco. Lana was with a hunk from the movie scene. By now she had become a star. When she saw me, I got a hug and a sisterly peck on the cheek. She remembered. I was so sorry, later, to hear of her misfortunes in marriage and her tragic life. No, I thought, if becoming part of the Hollywood scene was to become vulnerable to Lana-like misfortunes, I didn't want any part of it.

Hal Mendelsohn, who became Hal March, the M.C. of the infamous *$64,000 Question* television show, was also a classmate. While in the drama class Hal and I competed for several roles. I hated him! He was better-looking, all muscle, had a car, a family, money in his pocket, and an attitude that said, "I'm the best there is." I was orphaned, living in a furnished room, and trying to work my way through high school. And I didn't have a great opinion of myself. Nevertheless, we each won our share of leading roles. When it came time for the senior play, the highlight of a high school thespian's career, I won the lead.

After graduation I went looking for a job, while Hal realized my ambition and enrolled in the famous Pasadena Playhouse, the acting school that produced so many great stars. I got a job in a hospital laundry sorting the dirty linen as it came down from the wards. I didn't know it at the time, but this was the beginning of my medical career.

His acting career flourished. He was seen in a number of motion pictures and TV shows; but it was the *$64,000 Question* that catapulted him into stardom and later, when the show was found to be fraudulent, into oblivion. He died at an early age from lung cancer. This was also not a life I wanted to emulate.

Glad and I reached a decision. If the job were offered to me, I would take it. But we also agreed that I was a doctor first and foremost and our life would be as it had always been, with my patients and my family having priority for my time and attention. However, Hollywood looked as if it might be fun. It also appeared that I could make a contribution to Family Practice, our new specialty of medicine, and to the public by making the shows medically accurate.

On the appointed day I went to Universal Studios and, sure enough, there was a pass for me at the front gate. I was told to drive in and park by the bungalow that housed the *Welby* show. When I went upstairs to David Victor's office, I was introduced to the producer, David O'Connell, who said, "Welcome to 'The House of David.'" Both Davids explained that we would meet Nina and Bob Young at the commissary. Since this was off-season and they weren't shooting, Bob was coming in just for this meeting. I guessed Glad had been correct—that meeting him was going to be the big deal.

When we entered the commissary I tried not to gawk, but it was difficult. On my first day in the movie business I met Telly Savalas, Anne Jackson, the cast of the show *The Mod Squad* and, of course, Nina Laemmele and Robert Young. I had nothing to fear from Bob Young. A more cordial and gracious person I had never met. I tried to behave rationally but I found my voice quavering and, being afraid that if I spoke I would squeak, I shut up and listened. At the end of lunch David Victor said, "Will you do it?"

I found my voice and answered, "Yes."

I signed a contract mailed to me from Universal. It was less a contract and more a statement of what I would not get from them. I would be paid for each episode I worked on when it had aired. No air, no pay. I would receive no residuals and my name would not appear in the credits, per company policy.

Darn.

When Nina called in a couple of weeks, she said that the first script would arrive shortly, and I was to call her within a week with problems and corrections. When the script arrived by messenger (mail wasn't fast enough—nothing is done cheaply in Hollywood), and I started to read it, I began to get nervous about what I had let myself in for. My God, what I did and said was going to the TV sets of millions of people. I would be, or my work would be quoted as accurate medical care. I began to think of getting backup. Working as I did at Santa Monica Hospital, I had the entire teaching staff to call upon to review my work. On the other hand, would asking for advice expose me to faculty criticism and perhaps bring negative comments about my fledgling residency program?

For many years I had had the privilege of lunching daily with three of the finest doctors I have ever known. We had become fast friends; they kidded me a bit when I told them about my new position in Hollywood, but they had offered to help if I needed assistance. One of these friends was an internist. He was a small man of keen intellect and a wry sense of humor. I asked him for a consultation on my first script. Jack took it home with him, promising to read it overnight and report the next day at lunch.

When the four of us gathered at noon, Jack was very serious. He had the script with him but said he didn't want to discuss it until after we had eaten. He didn't talk much during lunch and seemed preoccupied. I fidgeted and worried about what Jack would say. Finally, when we had finished our coffee, Jack reached behind his back and pulled out the script. "I don't know how to tell you this," he said. "The shock may be too great."

"Jack, tell me."

Jack, with his droll sense of humor declared, "I hope this won't affect you too much, but the magnitude of the medical problems facing your television patient are beyond the capacity of even a famous doctor such as Marcus Welby to correct, and he will surely die. You're going to lose your first patient on prime time television."

Everyone howled with laughter, and I was on my way to becoming a real technical advisor to Hollywood's most popular television show.

⟡⟡⟡

There was a light knock and the door opened slowly. Gath, my receptionist, said, "I'm sorry to bother you, Doctor, but there is an important phone call; it's Robert Young."

Gath was my right hand in my Manhattan Beach, California office. Her name was Agatha, pronounced uh-GATH-uh. Anyone who called her AGG-uh-thuh received an irritated look. Only a favored few were allowed to call her Gath. She was in charge of the appointment book and therefore ran my life during office hours. She did this well, but resisted competition for my time. Calls from Universal Studios were not among her favorite interruptions.

There were times when being the technical advisor for *Marcus Welby, M.D.* had its bad moments, and this was one of them. I'd been at it for just over three years and I still wasn't able to control when and how much time I needed to devote to the endeavor.

Seated across the desk from me, in my private practice office, was Monica O'Neal. Monica was a patient with a serious problem. Monica was very seriously, and somewhat tearfully, telling me how she got the ecchymoses (black eye) around her left eye. The eye was a beauty, with swelling of both lids extending onto the cheekbone. Monica wasn't a raving beauty under any circumstances. Her face was all circles: a round nose, puffy round cheeks worsened by her swollen eye, a round mouth that seemed to be in a constant OH, and a round chin that sloped off into a second round chin that she didn't need. She had the pudgy body of a person who drank too much and didn't pay a lot of attention to how she looked.

This was an office visit I really wanted to control. I didn't want to interrupt Monica, because for years I had hoped to gain her confidence sufficiently to have her open up regarding the spousal abuse I thought she had been suffering. On the other hand, keeping Robert Young waiting wasn't a good option either. I guess I took the easy way out. I said, "Excuse me for just a moment, Monica. I've got to take this call."

I could envision the set on the sound stage on the Universal Lot, with the entire crew standing around waiting for Bob Young to wrestle with a word of dialogue which he felt he couldn't say with the proper dramatic flourish. The two of us had worked together long enough for Bob to develop confidence in my ability to change awkward medical content into words that flowed. However, any interruption on the set stopped the work of forty or fifty union workers—besides the directors, producers, and actors—which increased the cost of production. In addition to Monica sitting across from me, I had four more patients waiting to be seen before the office would close; and after the office closed, I still had three house calls to make and needed to visit my hospital patients before going home to Glad and our three kids.

On the other hand, shooting at the studio didn't stop until the day's schedule was completed. We had ten working days in which to shoot each weekly segment of *Marcus Welby, M.D.* The director would keep everyone on the set, even if it took most of the night, causing the producer a great deal of financial pain due to the overtime which would have to be paid. He would then confront the director, who would become a grouch on the set, resulting in nervous actors who might forget their lines, necessitating more than the usual retakes, delaying production further…and the band plays on.

So, with all that in mind, I picked up the telephone and said, "Hi, Bob."

"Oh boy! I'm glad I could catch you. I hope you're not too busy to help me. Are you?"

"Never too busy for you," I lied. "What's the problem?"

"I'm supposed to ask this patient if she can urinate okay. I can't ask a lady if she can urinate. I'm an actor; but ask a beautiful actress if she can urinate? Not me! The next thing these writers will want me to do is talk about bowel movements. What would you say to this patient if she were in your office?"

I thought, *I'd probably ask her if she could urinate okay.* But if Bob couldn't do that, we'd have to take another tack.

So, I said, "I'd ask her if she had any burning or pain when she urinated. But there's that U-word again. Gee, Bob, why don't you try to say it that way? After all, urination is a normal bodily function."

"That's it, Tom! I'll say, 'Are your normal bodily functions okay?' Will that do it?"

"Nope. There're too many bodily functions. Not specific enough. You can't ask her if she can make her water either, it's too folksy for Welby. And really, it's sort of a male thing, the sort of question I might have asked one of my patients when I practiced in Oregon farm country. You better stick with urinate."

I wondered how long this problem of Bob's was going to take. Monica was fidgeting in her chair. I'm sure she wondered what in the heck was going on. Was she seeing her doctor or some kind of a weird Hollywood writer?

"Tom, not on prime time in living color. I won't do it."

"Bob, try saying, 'Do you have any burning when you go to the bathroom?' It's not very specific, but I think it will do the trick."

"That's great. Thanks. Bye."

Robert Young, great star that he was, had his contract written so that he could make script changes on the set when he felt that the words as written were not what he felt he could deliver. Lesser stars did not have that prerogative and directors could ignore their complaints. No director argued with Bob Young. He was easy to work with and a consummate professional.

Monica, sitting in her chair across the desk from me, had her right eye wide open and bright while her left was doing the best it could under the swelling. "Was that really Robert Young? I think he's wonderful, and I love his TV show. Do you really work with him all the time?"

"I try to help out with the medical part of the show. Let's get back to you, Monica." I didn't want to lose the moment. She needed to talk about her home life and what I perceived as her problem with spousal abuse. "Now tell me again, how did you get that mouse on your eye?"

"I fell."

"Cut the bull, Monica. Who hit you?" It was time to talk tough to her. It was time for her to let it all out and stop the destructive behavior, of which the black eye was only a superficial symptom.

Monica began to sob, again. She was ready to talk and the story rushed out all at once. The story that I had tried to get her to tell me for months spilled out in great sobbing gulps. "My husband did it. But I had it coming, Doctor. I'm a drunk. I didn't go home last night. When I got home this morning and he asked me where I had been, I slapped his face and he punched me in the eye."

I didn't know if I could help Monica but she had opened up a little. I had to try. "Monica," I asked, "tell me about your drinking. How much? How often? And maybe, if you know the answer, why?"

Monica looked grim. Her eyes clouded up, again. She looked away, "Doctor, maybe we shouldn't talk about this. I like to drink. I'm not sure I want to quit."

"You've already said the magic words. You've admitted your alcoholism. You said 'I'm a drunk.' You may be ready to kick this thing. What makes you say that you like it so much?"

"I like it because of what it does for me. If I'd been raised in a family like a TV show, maybe like *Father Knows Best,* then maybe I wouldn't be like this; but my father was a drunk and he died in a drunken barroom brawl. My mother couldn't really raise us properly, so I left home when I was seventeen and I haven't been back. I don't even know if my mother is still alive or what happened to my sisters and brother. Look at me. Don't you see I'm just a mutt? I'm not pretty. I'm fat. I don't say the right things. But when I have a couple of drinks I feel like I'm the prettiest, wittiest, smartest, cutest gal in the bar. I feel like I'm attractive to men and, if a guy shines up to me, I might just take him on like I did last night. But when the guy looks at me in the morning and he's sober, I know he's thinking where did he get this mutt, so I go home and collect the black eye that I earned. But I still remember how good I felt last night and how good I looked to myself, full of booze, and peeling off my clothes like maybe I was Marilyn Monroe. I can't quit. I like to feel that way, even when I know it's wrong and the guy is disgusted with me in the morning. How could I live with myself without liquor and the good feeling I get when I'm drinking? How could I?"

Wow, I thought, *this poor woman has a deeper problem than I first realized. Her self-image is rotten; this has to change. It is going to take some startling and dramatic event to get to her.*

I asked her to go over and sit on the couch in my office while I got both of us a cup of coffee. Then, I drew up my chair near to the couch and, once we were both relaxed, I explained to her that she could learn to live with her problems just like every other drunk who got off the sauce. I also told her that help was available from organizations such as Alcoholics Anonymous, and that I had another patient who was a member of AA who would be glad to be her sponsor. I said, "You need some professional help. You need to look at yourself objectively and find out your true worth and change your image of yourself. I know just the woman to help you. She's one of my patients."

Monica hesitated and then said, "Doctor, do you really think I could do it? Besides this one lady who is your patient, do you know any others with my problem who have succeeded in staying dry?"

I answered, "I'll give you a good example without breaking any confidentiality—Robert Young. It's not a secret; his story has been in the newspapers. Bob Young has many of the same feelings of insecurity that you do. He doesn't consider himself an alcoholic. Instead, he says he has used alcohol inappropriately to overcome his depression and fears. No matter how you say it, the problem's the same. He's done pretty well, don't you think? He isn't perfect and slips once in a while, but only briefly, and then he gets back on track. Do you think you could use him as a model?"

"Have Robert Young as my model? Why, I don't know anyone as important as he is and I could never imagine him ever talking to someone like me. I don't think it would work."

Then I dropped the clincher. I told her that if she would join AA, clean up her act and stay dry for six months, I would take her out to the studio and we would have lunch in the studio commissary with Robert Young. All the stars ate there, and she maybe could see Telly Savalas, Jim Brolin, Lee Majors, and who knows how many more.

At that point, with shining eyes, she agreed. I called my patient, Mamie Byrd from AA, who came right over. The two women left together arm in arm, Mamie saying, "We'll do this one day at a time." Later I explained to Mamie how I had convinced Monica to permit me to get AA involved. Mamie looked a bit dubious at my tactics but she said she would certainly help Monica achieve her goal.

We didn't have our lunch at the studio within the six months goal. It took longer, but it did happen. Monica saw a marriage counselor and finally resolved her abusive marital problems with divorce. When we went to lunch, she was all dolled up. She had lost weight, she was witty and cheerful, and her mouth now seemed to say, "Hey, look at me!" To me, she was one of the cutest gals in the commissary that day.

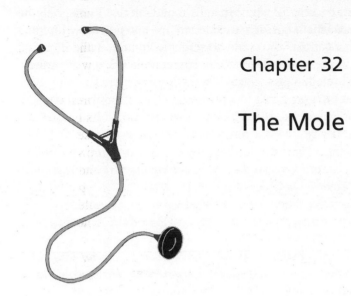

Chapter 32

The Mole

Shortly after I opened my practice in Manhattan Beach in 1960, nine years before the beginning of the Welby show, a local surgeon from Torrance called and invited me to lunch the following week. I had met the man briefly at South Bay District Hospital in Redondo Beach, where we both admitted patients. I hardly knew him, so why was he inviting me to lunch?

In my previous practice experience in Oregon, where I had taken all of my training, including my year as a general surgical resident, I had known most of the specialists at the hospitals and the medical school. Sherwood, of course, didn't have any specialists or even any other doctors besides my partner and me. At Tuality Hospital, in the county seat where we hospitalized many of our patients, we saw specialists only if we could finagle one from Portland to make the trip. Now I was in the big city, and I guessed I must have become a target for specialists seeking to obtain patient referrals. With my small town practice experience, I didn't know that specialists had to market themselves. Maybe they didn't, in Oregon.

❧❦❧

The day after the surgeon from Torrance called, Dr. Ewings called. Hector Ewings was a local GP who, when he found out that I was going to open a practice in Manhattan Beach, tried to lure me into practice with him. He said he wanted a partner who could do surgery with him. I told him that wasn't appealing to me, as I wanted to cut down on the amount of surgery that I did because I felt that procedures were becoming more complex; and I jokingly said that the gray hair I had prematurely acquired was the result of complicated surgical cases. Nevertheless, Ewings said, "I have a patient who needs to have her gallbladder out. You want to do it with me?"

Sure, I thought. *I should be able to get at least forty or fifty dollars for an assistant's fee and because I am just getting my practice started, I could use a little extra income.*

"When is the case scheduled?" I asked.

"Day after tomorrow, 8 A.M. at Torrance Memorial. Be on time. Do you know how to get there?"

What kind of a question is that? I have been to the hospital and applied for staff privileges, so I must know where it is. Is this some kind of a put-down because I refused to join him in practice? He seems like a crusty old guy, but he is probably just being sure I know where I'm going and assuring himself that I will be on time.

"I'll be there and I'll be on time."

When I walked into the surgeons' lounge, Hector was already there. He introduced me to the other doctors. We scrubbed up and entered the operating room where the patient was already anesthetized. The scrub nurse helped us on with our gowns and gloves; then Hector walked around to the left side of the table. *What's this?* I thought. *Most people operate on gallbladders from the right side of the table.* The scrub nurse introduced herself and asked, "What kind of sutures will you be using, Doctor?"

"Just a minute. You've got this wrong. Dr. Ewings is operating." *If that's true, what am I doing on this side of the table?*

Hector spoke up. "This is your case, Doctor. You're on temporary staff here and the surgery department wants to get a look at how you do. They'll be dropping in from time to time. Let's get started."

"Hector, I don't want to do this case. First, I no longer want to do surgery of this magnitude and second, I can't operate on a patient whom I have never met and didn't have a chance to work up. You come over to this side of the table and do this case yourself."

"I don't do gallbladders. Never have. You gonna keep this poor patient asleep while we argue about this or are you just gonna do your job and get this gallbladder out? You've got a reputation to establish in this community. Don't start off on the wrong foot with the doctors of this hospital."

I operated. No one came in to check on me. The case was easy to do and, when I was finished, I still felt very angry but relieved that it was over. While we were dressing Hector said, "You can charge seventy-five dollars for this case."

"That's hardly a large enough fee for a gallbladder removal. How come so little?"

"She's my patient. I charge the surgeon's fee."

I thought, *Welcome to the big city.*

☙⚬❧

Ken Maynard was the surgeon who had invited me to lunch. I often kidded him about his name, which was the same as that of a cowboy film star of my childhood. The cowboy Ken Maynard always wore a white hat. You could tell he was one of the good guys. Dr. Ken had a good reputation at the hospital and, even though he didn't wear or own a hat, he was a good guy; thus I was pleased to meet him for lunch.

Ken had been trained on the East Coast, and reminded me in some ways of a close friend and surgical colleague I had left behind in Oregon. He had glasses whose lenses closely resembled the bottom of a Coca-Cola bottle. His prematurely graying hair and professional demeanor apparently allayed the fears of patients who may have been concerned about his vision.

His approach was a very soft sell. He told me he would always be available for consultation in emergencies as well as for regular consultations in his office. He also pressed the right button when he said, "I'll never refer any patient of yours to another specialist without first informing you and gaining your permission."

When Ken indicated he knew the needs and sensitivities of a general practitioner, I recognized him as a kindred spirit and mentally agreed to refer to him and see how it would work. The first few cases would also give me an opportunity to observe his work.

I didn't have long to wait. Within a couple of weeks of our lunch, Ken called to ask me to assist him in surgery. The patient was Mamie Byrd, on whom we were to do a wide excision and lymph node resection for the diagnosis of malignant melanoma. He felt that it was important for me to be with him in surgery in order to gain firsthand knowledge of the patient's problem, as neither she nor her family had a family doctor and he was going to refer them to me if I would take them. This whole scenario was better than I could have hoped for. I would not only get a new family in my practice but I would have a chance to observe Ken at work without putting a patient of mine at risk, in case he wasn't a very good surgeon.

Ken was not only good, he was terrific. We cemented a relationship that lasted throughout my practice years in California. He and I thought alike. I anticipated his movements so that we operated like a well-oiled machine; so well, in fact, that Ken often asked me to assist him on his own patients when the referring doctor was not surgically inclined. He also assisted me when I did surgery on my patients for those procedures for which I felt surgically qualified.

❧◆◆◇

Mamie Byrd was the Alcoholics Anonymous member who later supported Monica O'Neal in her struggle to stay dry, so that I could fulfill my promise to take her to Universal Studios to meet Robert Young.

The day Monica went to the studio commissary she also met the cast of *Marcus Welby, M.D.* because I took Monica to the set myself. I even obtained permission to take her to the "back lot." Going to the back lot to see the Welby house, or Alfred Hitchcock's Bates house from the movie *Psycho,* was not a privilege accorded everyone. Universal Studios was pathologically afraid of fire. It happened that, on the day of Monica's visit, the studio was shooting nearby and had the fire trucks in attendance and was, therefore, more amenable to visitors.

❧◆◆◇

On another occasion, after a call from the American Academy of Family Physicians asking me to entertain the president of that prestigious national organization, I was faced with a physician and politician overblown with his own importance. He demanded to be escorted to the Welby house so that he could be photographed, Welby-style, descending the front stairs carrying a medical bag as did Robert Young in the opening of each episode.

The studio refused. The Academy president was furious and accused me of being ungrateful to the Academy for the position they had obtained for me. I wanted to point out that all the AAFP had done was to try to put David Victor and me together for their own purposes and that the question of my becoming technical advisor had been born in David's mind only when we had met; but I kept my peace. He also suggested that he would inform the Academy of my poor attitude and see about my removal. What a jerk!

I took the man to lunch (a terrible mistake), where he met David Victor, the show's executive producer. He made a scene in the commissary, indicating that he would have the sponsorship by the American Academy of Family Physicians revoked if he was not treated better. I was embarrassed to the point of wanting a hole to crawl into. No hole being available, I tried reasoning with the bully but to no avail. Finally David Victor, being a gentle person and not wanting any more adversity, went to the studio officials with the problem and finally obtained permission for him to visit the "Welby House". This necessitated a substantial delay while a still photographer was found and a guard with an appropriate fire extinguisher was located to accompany us. Later, the AAFP president complained that he was going to miss his plane (which would take him out of our hair). Everyone pitched in so he would not miss his plane. We did not want to be stuck with him any longer than necessary.

This experience had its good points. I made sure that before I was asked to entertain anyone at Universal Studios again, the person or the organization knew the guidelines for a visit ahead of time. I never suffered a similar experience.

⚬❀❀❀⚬

Mamie Byrd's mole was just above her left breast. Ken Maynard, the surgeon, did a wide excision. This meant he cut away the skin for an area three inches in diameter from the center of the lesion and covered the open raw area with a skin graft taken from the thigh. Mamie went home after several days in the hospital. Ken asked me to make house calls every other day to change the dressing and keep the grafted area moist. During these home visits I met Hugh Byrd and their three sons.

I really admired Mamie. She had accepted her diagnosis with aplomb. She didn't complain about the pain during her dressing changes and refused my offer to prescribe pain medication for her. She faced the world with the joy of being alive instead of the melancholia of knowing that life-threatening tumor cells could be lurking in her body and they might erupt at any time, anywhere in her system.

One afternoon after office hours, when I was making a house call at the Byrd home, Hugh asked if I would stay and have a drink. We were all becoming friends, so I accepted. When Hugh served us he didn't even ask Mamie if she would like one. I spoke up out of turn, as usual. I said, "Mamie, if you would like a drink, I believe you've recovered enough from your operation that it shouldn't bother you."

The Byrds laughed heartily. I guess I looked somewhat discomfited that whatever I had said had evoked such gales of laughter. Mamie said, "I'm sorry. We shouldn't have laughed. We weren't laughing at you, but were laughing at the fact that I'm a recovering alcoholic and I'll never be recovered enough to have a drink."

She told me her story. After her third son had been born, ten years earlier, Hugh had been forced to travel frequently, back and forth to Washington, D.C., for the aerospace company he worked for. Mamie was left alone a lot. She was originally from the South (I had guessed that from her accent), and had been raised in a family with several servants. She wasn't prepared for the details and responsibilities of raising three little boys almost by herself. She began to drink.

At first Mamie drank at night after she put the boys to bed. She thought it helped her to sleep. Then she began to drink in the late afternoon, in order to get through the day. The drinking became worse. She told me that sometimes it was so bad that the children in diapers had raw, sore bottoms from being left without being changed. When Hugh came home she would snap out of her troubles for the few days he was around and have only a few drinks at night, which he thought were sociable and fun. He didn't know the extremes to which her drinking had gone.

Finally, Mamie was totally unable to care for the boys, who cried so often and for so long that a neighbor called the police. The police found her in a drunken stupor. They called the Department of Social Services, which took the boys and admitted Mamie to the drunk ward at the county jail to dry out. Hugh was called home from his trip. He got the children back under the proviso that he not travel in his work. This was a time in the aerospace industry when people with Hugh's talents were rare, so he was able to change jobs and stay home.

Fortunately, Hugh and Mamie had heard of Alcoholics Anonymous. They went to their first meeting within a few days of contacting her sponsor, who was another recovering alcoholic. Mamie had been almost dry ever since, slipping only a couple of times the first year.

Now I realized that she had refused my offer of pain medication because she understood she had an addictive personality and didn't want the stress of having to deal with taking her own medication at home. While in the hospital, when the nurses had controlled the dose, she was willing to accept the relief; but at home she chose to accept the pain instead.

My admiration for this woman grew as her story unfolded. I was impressed with the high-mindedness she exhibited, regardless of the severe adversity under which she functioned. I went out of my way to serve her and her family as well as I could. When, a year later, she came into my office to tell me she had two more moles that were growing, I worried that these might be malignant. After I had removed them and the pathology report was negative—not malignant—we were both overjoyed.

Early in my career in the *Welby* series, we had an episode in which a young minor league baseball player, who had tremendous prospects of becoming a major leaguer, discovered a mole on his leg. The young man fought having a biopsy because he was frightened.

As I reviewed the story outline (a synopsis of what the script is going to be, a sort of promise to the executive story consultant and to the network representative that a finished product will be acceptable), I thought of Mamie and her bravery.

When the episode was produced, we agonized through forty eight minutes of, "Gosh, oh gee, I don't want my leg operated on." The story continued with the biopsy of the malignant melanoma and emotional thrashing around of, "Oh my, I'll never be able to play baseball again," and the almost inevitable dramatic conclusion that all's well—and the kid goes on with his career.

It was not one of my favorite shows. Usually we tried for realism and some of our patients on Tuesday night on ABC died (as did my first-ever patient on prime time) or had poor outcomes. This particular episode was not a favorite because, in my own practice, Mamie was a living model of the stoicism and courage that a real patient could exhibit.

But that isn't the end of the story about malignant melanoma on television, or about Mamie. During the eight years I treated Mamie and her family I saw innumerable demonstrations of her courage. The boys grew and became typical teenagers, placing the same stresses on Mamie that other mothers experienced. Her parenting skills seemed above average. However, there was one discordant note in the family's dynamics—Mamie and Hugh no longer seemed as close, but that was more covert than open.

Mamie grew moles (nevi) like no other patient I had ever seen. This was of concern to both of us. I insisted that she have frequent examinations; I looked for the danger signals that might indicate that a mole was undergoing malignant metamorphosis. During those eight years I identified one hundred twenty moles that were suspicious and removed all of them. One was malignant! That one was referred to Ken Maynard for definitive treatment.

Mamie handled this news with her usual dignity and grace. My admiration for her showed itself in a number of ways, including spending more time with her than with the usual patient, discussing personal things such as the lives of our respective children, and frankly telling her how much I thought of her bravery and character. I thought that showing her I really appreciated her bravery would help sustain her courage; and I felt this would be particularly helpful, in that she and her husband seemed to be drifting farther apart.

The day of reckoning came when Mamie booked a full hour appointment. All my patients knew they could book up to an hour if they had a particularly knotty problem on which they wished me to spend extra time. Mamie had never done this but she always got extra time, anyway. She came into my private office, sat in the chair beside my desk, looked at me intensely for a moment, then got up, went to the door, and closed it. I did not miss the significance of that act. By her action she told me that the conference was confidential and serious. I wondered if one of the boys was into drugs or if her marriage to Hugh was in big trouble. The second thing I divined from her taking the initiative to close the door herself, instead of asking me to do it, was a signal that she wanted to be in charge of this session.

Finally, I noticed that Mamie was all dolled up. She seemed as if she had dressed with great care, not wearing the usual attire that made living at the beach comfortable. She really looked nice.

She said, "I'm in love with you!"

"What?"

"I'm in love with you, my darling. I've loved you for a long time and now I want to show my love. I want to fulfill my dreams by making love to you."

"Mamie, this is a joke, right?" I knew it wasn't a joke but I guess I thought that, maybe, I could avoid the reality by not acknowledging the seriousness of the situation.

She reached across the desk to take my hand. I pulled away as if she were brandishing a red hot poker. I said, "Good Lord, Mamie, you know

I'm happily married. I love my wife and family. You should never have done this." I can imagine what my face must have looked like. Horror! Shock! I looked at Mamie. She looked stricken. She had made her pitch and it had failed. Now she felt foolish. It didn't look good on her.

I began to think about the ramifications of her declaration as we both sat there, glumly staring at each other.

Is this the way doctors I had heard of used their position of authority to take advantage of their female patients? Is this the transference that psychiatrists frequently have to deal with? Or is this just a dumb mistake on my part, being over-zealous in my attempt to make Mamie secure in her troubles, and show her the admiration I felt she had coming. Good Lord, am I a part of the chasm that developed between her and her husband, Hugh? Or did that chasm contribute to her need to find affection elsewhere?

She broke the silence. "I guess you don't care."

"Of course I care. I care a lot about you as a patient and as a friend; but good God, Mamie, I don't love you, and I'm not going to bed with you."

Again we sat in silence. I realized that she had probably misinterpreted my admiration for her being able to kick the booze and rationally dealing with her malignancies, as something else—something I had never intended.

I thought, *I can no longer take care of her.* Ethically, I could no longer be this woman's physician. Continuing to see her would put me at risk of being the innocent victim of a scandalous situation, in addition to the implication of exercising inappropriate control over her.

Again Mamie broke the silence, anticipating my concerns, saying, "Doctor, you mustn't worry about a scandal, or that I will ever tell anyone what I've done. I care for you too much to ever hurt you." She began to cry softly.

My mind was spinning. My first thought was to get up and comfort her. I had never seen Mamie cry before. *NO! I can't do that. I can't touch her lest my intentions be misinterpreted. What should be my approach to her?* I had never faced a problem like this.

I handed the box of Kleenex across the desk to her and said, "You know that we'll have to plan for your care elsewhere." She agreed but said she hoped that I could care for the rest of the family. I indicated that I would have to think about it and asked her to leave. She waited a few moments, dabbing her eyes with Kleenex and gaining control over herself so as not to be a spectacle as she left.

After she had gone Gath asked me what the charge would be. She had booked an hour but stayed only twenty minutes. I said, "No charge." And I told Gath what had happened. Gath said she had seen it coming, and why weren't men smart enough to read the signs?

Later, after going home and telling Glad the entire story, I decided what my relationship would be with Mamie. I worried about even seeing her, again. I didn't remember anything in my practice that had hit me quite so hard or had thrown my equilibrium off so much. When Glad and I were married, it was for life—without a few days off here and there. It would stay that way and I never wanted anything to cast shadows on that original vow.

I asked Gath to call Mamie and suggest that she come in to the office. When she entered my office, we left the door open—WIDE open. I offered her the following solution: I would continue as the family's doctor, seeing Hugh and the boys, but I would not in any way provide for her care. I would not make house calls under any circumstances; I had a fear of being trapped into a situation that might prove embarrassing. It was true that she said she would never cause me any trouble, but I was no longer sure of her stability and worried that she was a little crazy. I also told her that we would never speak of this again. She agreed to my plan and I did not see her again for two years. I took care of the boys who were almost grown and required little attention. When she had another mole she wanted removed, she pleaded with me to at least take care of that condition. After much consideration, I said I would do only that part of her care. I instructed my nurse that I was never to be alone in a room with Mamie.

We never again spoke of the incident. She was true to her word.

❧

It wasn't quite the same as on *Marcus Welby, M.D.* when young Dr. Kiley was confronted with a loving patient. The character, Stephen Kiley M.D., played by James Brolin, was unmarried. He was an avant-garde character for the times. He was supposed to represent modern youth, and he rode a motorcycle everywhere he went. Brolin and Young played against each other beautifully, a study of two professional men trying to understand the foibles of each other's generation. This story line was used by the motion picture industry for years. It was perfected by television producers, and by David Victor in particular. He had produced *Young Doctor Kildare,* starring two doctors. The younger Kildare was played by

Richard Chamberlain, and the older Doctor Gillespie played by Lionel Barrymore.

Brolin and Chamberlain were raw talent when they began these series; both went on to successful careers, while Barrymore and Young were at the end of the line and never again did anything significant. Both were great talents at the time.

Welby and Kiley made house calls, as I did. In one episode, Kiley made house calls to a character played by a very beautiful English actress, Dana Wynter. Dana had long, jet-black hair, setting off very white skin. She was tall and almost painfully thin, magnificently cast as a sickly wife, suffering from tuberculosis and husband neglect. As Kiley made numerous house calls over the several weeks during which this story unfolded, he became smitten with the charms of his patient as she, too, became smitten with him.

As this plot developed, it was obvious that even Welby recognized that there were too many house calls to this patient and asked Kiley about it. The visits didn't stop until after a big love scene. This love scene was hardly torrid. In the early seventies, the TV screen had far less skin showing and explicit sex than today. And, remember, Bob Young had trouble saying "urinate" on prime time (would that it were the same today!).

My concern, never voiced to the producers, was: who paid for the extra house calls—the cuckolded husband or the family's health insurance?

❧

There is an ending to the malignant melanoma episode that no one dreamed of. When Bob and Betty Young were flying cross country on TWA, a stewardess came up to Bob, who was sitting in the first class section, and said, "I would like to speak to you for a moment, Mr. Young."

Now, Bob Young had a sense of what he felt was the proper respect for his privacy. Autograph seekers had plagued him for forty years. After all, his was hardly a face one would miss, even in a crowd. Bob Young was a man of great dignity but also a man who had dealt with insecurity every day of his life. Unless he knew the person requesting an autograph or was in a social group where the autograph seeker was also invited, he might very well growl "no," and turn away. This could be embarrassing when we were together in a public place. Many times I have apologized to a well-meaning fan—who was terribly disappointed. On the other hand, at a party where everyone was invited, Bob would be the most gracious guest there.

What rushed through his mind that day, on the airplane, I will never know. Did he think, *This is a stranger invading my privacy;* or did he think, *This young lady is a crew member and therefore within my boundaries for congeniality?* At any rate, the stewardess talked on. "I would like to speak to you, Mr. Young, because you saved my life."

This was not a conversation that anyone could turn away from. Bob looked at her, smiled, and asked, "How was that?"

The TWA stew lifted her foot and pointed to a large scar on her calf. "That was where they took off my melanoma," she said. "I had this ugly mole and, after I saw your show about the baseball player with the mole that was malignant, I went to my doctor. He biopsied it, found it was a melanoma, and removed all of it. He told me that, because I had come in to see him while the growth was still in its early stages, this had saved my life. *You* saved my life, Mr. Young. I have wanted to thank you and now I have the opportunity. I'm so grateful!"

What greater applause could an actor receive from his audience?

When I mentioned those words to Bob Young some years later, he said, "The only actor I know who gets greater satisfaction from his role is Ronnie Reagan. He's doing a good job being president because he is enjoying life in the best role he's ever had."

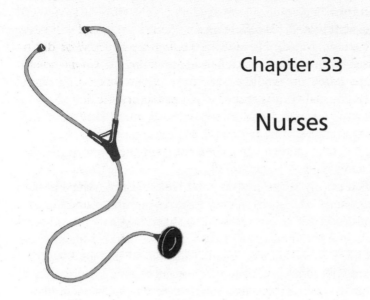

Chapter 33

Nurses

When David Victor recruited me to work on *Welby*, I asked him how much of my time the job would take. I was concerned because I was already heavily committed to my practice and to teaching, and doing the administrative duties as director of the family practice residency at Santa Monica Hospital. David explained that I would have an assistant who would be on the set whenever they were shooting. The assistant was Connie Izay, a nurse who worked in the intensive care unit of a nearby hospital.

I had learned the value of nurses early in my career. I had been an intern for only three days at St. Vincent's Hospital in Portland, Oregon, when I had to take my first night on call. This was the first solo experience I had as a real doctor. I was anxious. Of course, I could summon backup. My superior, the resident physician on call, was sleeping in the house staff's quarters and would support me for any emergency. He had been out of medical school for two or three years in contrast to my two or three weeks. Weren't we an experienced pair? To me, the resident seemed to be a fountain of knowledge.

This was a time in my career when I wanted and needed to look sharp. I didn't want to call my backup too soon but, even more, I didn't want to call too late and harm a patient. There is an old adage in medical circles: "If your personal physician is on the staff of a teaching hospital, don't get sick at the beginning of the academic year (July and August) when the house staff is new." We were green.

The phone rang, awakening me while I slept a restless sleep in my bed in the house staff on-call quarters. The charge nurse on Ward 4 South told me a lady had died and would I come over and pronounce her dead. This was purely a formality, in that the nurse knew perfectly well she was dead, but protocol demanded that a person with an M.D. degree, no matter how inexperienced, preside and write a terminal note in the chart. This ritual was meant to guard against someone popping up on the gurney in the morgue and saying, "Where am I?"

As I pulled on my white trousers and buttoned my white intern's tunic, my hands shook. Dead was not my forte. In the first place, I didn't like "dead." I presumed it meant medicine had failed. Really, it did not; but at that point in my career, it seemed so. Second, I had to make sure that the patient had really expired; if I failed and she popped up, I thought I might be popped out of my internship for incompetence. Finally, I felt I had to do this alone because this was a simple task. My backup would not respond favorably to a call for help on something like this. Nope, I was on my own.

Arriving at the bedside I found a very elderly woman who had died of cancer of long standing and who had suffered a great deal. This was a person who probably had longed to die and was finally relieved. Her dry skin was drawn over her cheekbones, stretching her lips away from her teeth in a grinning rictus. I wondered if the lady had really been laughing at the moment she died because by dying she had finally beaten cancer. There was an odor surrounding the bed that I would forevermore associate with death.

With trembling hands I placed my stethoscope on her cachectic, bony chest. No heartbeat. *But,* I thought, *could I be missing a faint pulse?* I took a wisp of cotton and touched her eyeball, which already had the glassy, dry look of the dead. There was no blink of the eyelid. From my medical bag, I took a small mirror and held it under her nose and mouth. There was no fogging of the glass. Still afraid to make a decision, I was about to get my stethoscope out and listen to her chest once more; but the nurse who had stood by patiently, said, "Doctor, she really is dead. Don't worry, you have done all you can." She gently nudged me aside and pulled the sheet up over the patient's face.

Night nurses are a special breed. If they have worked nights for a long time they have become wise and philosophical, having had the quiet to meditate. Often they are, by nature, quiet and reclusive. Their competence comes from having to make decisions on their own without a lot of supervisors or doctors around to assume the responsibility. This nurse was typical of the night breed, helping me overcome a rough spot in my fledgling medical career.

I left the patient's bedside, went to the chart room, and wrote my terminal note. When the nurse came in, I said, "Thank you." I had taken the first step in learning that an experienced nurse is a doctor's best friend.

❧

Connie Izay, at Universal Studios, knew everything about the technical equipment that was needed to do a doctor show on television or in motion pictures. She had done this sort of job many times before. Connie and her actor husband, Victor, were show-biz people. She was eminently qualified to handle almost any situation that might arise on the *Welby* set; and I would always be available by telephone if she felt she needed consultation. Connie had the responsibility for the medical equipment while it was on the set. This might include an anesthesia machine, a Bennett positive breathing apparatus, pumps, intravenous setups, all the stuff in the operating room or in the emergency room, and the X-rays that the actors would look at while making a diagnosis. X rays were our downfall.

Because of union rules, Connie couldn't move any of the equipment while it was on the set; instead, she had to instruct a "grip" (laborer) to do it. This included placing X-rays into the viewing box. Of course, the grips didn't know if an X-ray was right side up or upside down; and, in one specific case, whether the X-ray of the chest was placed backwards or forwards.

Shooting a television show or movie is not done in sequence as it appears on the screen. The shooting is done through an interminable series of retakes and different angles until a "take" is finally achieved.

Picture a scene with Bob Young and Jim Brolin standing in front of the X-ray viewing box examining a chest X-ray and consulting with each other on the diagnosis. Bob has his left hand on his hip and is pointing at the X-ray with his right hand. Of course, as a veteran actor, he does this purposely, thereby stealing the scene by reducing the other actor to a motionless body and directing the focus to himself. In the script he might say, "Now, look at this side view," and he pulls the first film out of the box, tosses it on the table behind him, and slides another pre-positioned film into the box. The second X-ray film, despite Connie's precautions, has been picked up the wrong way and winds up incorrectly placed. Connie has to stop the action, which does not endear her to the director. They try it again and the X-ray is placed correctly, but the director finds a subtle motion by one of the actors that he doesn't like and says, "One more time."

Connie is human. Connie is subject to the calls of nature. During the short time she is gone, the director stops the action and orders a retake. The grip puts the X-ray in the viewing box, but despite having done it six or seven times before, this time he does it wrong. Everyone makes the right moves. The director loves it and says, "That's a take." Everyone breathes easy and the crew starts breaking down the set, getting ready for the next scene; thus a gaffe is born.

When Connie returns the set is already in disarray. She asks, "How did it go?" She is reassured by the assistant director or the script girl or whoever is around that it was great. Some Tuesday night in the future the public is treated to a new episode of Welby looking at a goofy X-ray. Maybe a critic puts a laugh in his next column of the newspaper, but the really important people, the public, don't see it or care about it. They simply enjoy the show. Who cares?

I cared!

For the five years when I was employed by Universal Studios, technical advising was only a small part of my daily life; but it was the most public aspect. Particularly when the *National Enquirer* ran a story about the "Reel Doctor and the Real Doctor." I spent a week of prominence in grocery store checkout lines. It made me the butt of a series of colleagues' jokes.

Most doctors do not watch "doctor shows" on television, but my colleagues at the hospital did, hoping to catch me in a gaffe. And catch me they did—with the chest X-ray inserted backwards into the X-ray viewing box. When I entered the doctors' lounge on the morning after the show, the "gotcha team" was ready for me. I passed off the mistake as a case of "situs inversus," a congenital condition in which all of the body's organs are on the opposite side of where they belong. This didn't wash with my doctor friends. It was weeks before the kidding stopped.

One morning I went to the X-ray department to see a chest X-ray of a hospitalized patient of mine. When the technician put the film in the viewing box, I instinctively reached up and turned it around so that the heart was on the left side where it belonged. I heard tittering from behind me, which erupted into outright guffaws. The entire X-ray department and some of my clinical friends were there—waiting for me to do just what I had done! The film wasn't my patient; it was from a rare case of situs inversus that the radiologists had saved and brought out for this special occasion. To the onlookers this was funnier than forty people emerging from a telephone booth.

Within a year, another episode of *Welby* got me in trouble. It featured a malpractice case that aired on the *Welby* show on Tuesday night. That episode closed with the idea that Marcus Welby might be convicted of malpractice, and to see the startling conclusion the viewer would have to watch the *Owen Marshall* lawyer show on Thursday night.

Because David Victor was the executive producer on both shows, he was able to tease viewers into watching ABC on both Tuesday and Thursday nights.

The lawyers for the plaintiff showed an X-ray of the spine in the courtroom scene which closed the *Welby* episode on Tuesday. This film had been improperly hung, upside down, so that the ribs were lower than the pelvis.

When I sat at home and watched on that Tuesday night, I gasped out loud during the scene. Glad was alarmed, thinking perhaps I was ill. I was ill all right, knowing what I would face the next morning in the doctors' lounge at the hospital. After the chest X-ray fiasco, I knew my colleagues would be all over me on Wednesday morning.

As I approached the doctors' lounge I designed my defense, which was to be an offense. I walked through the door into a den of M.D.s waiting to slay the lamb. They had tasted blood the last time and they wanted more.

There was a hush as I entered the room. An orthopedic surgeon, who loved to play "gotcha," cleared his throat. I didn't let him get started but immediately began talking. "How did you guys like the new orthopedic technique we introduced on the network last night? You may have noticed the X-rays of this case and wondered about them. Well, we hung the patient up by his heels and stretched his vertebrae. That released the extruded intervertebral disc substance and relieved the pain of his ruptured disc. As usual, the lawyers didn't understand the technique, and we got sued; but watch Thursday night at 9 P.M. on channel seven when we win the case on the *Owen Marshall* show."

This was such a goofy concept that the doctors were left temporarily speechless and I departed, without anyone else getting in a word. As I closed the door I glimpsed a row of would-be hecklers, mouths agape, silent.

Despite the two mixed-up X-rays, Connie Izay was a wonderful person to have on the set. Her ingenuity was often taxed when she had to train an actor to do "doctor" things. Sometimes she had to ask me to come in and do the tutoring, but by and large she coped.

One day when I was at the studio for a production conference, after we had looked at the dailies in the studio's viewing theater, I still had some time before my first patient was scheduled at my Manhattan Beach office. I went over to the set.

When the red light went off, indicating that they weren't shooting and it was safe to open the door, I went in. Bob Young, Connie, and a baby were in conference on how to shoot the next scene. The script called for Welby to give mouth-to-mouth resuscitation to a tiny baby. This probably could have been handled by using a doll, but the director wanted realism, so they had hired a living, tiny baby.

There are strict laws governing the use of children in making movies or TV shows. The amount of time they may spend in front of the camera, under the lights, or even on the set is controlled. For practical purposes, when working with a baby, unpredictable crying is also a problem. When a baby becomes really fussy and needs to be fed or take a nap, the director had better have two babies available or go to another scene and wait until the baby is ready. Changing the set takes time and time is money. This baby was on the set and ready. He was a cute little guy, rosy-cheeked and happy. The reason he was happy was that Bob Young was playing with him, buttering him up for the big scene. Playing with a baby wasn't all that strange to Bob. He and Betty had four daughters, so he was coming from a position of experience.

Bob had rehearsed the scene earlier using a doll, with Connie as his coach. Now they were ready to shoot. The baby was placed in a crib with its side bars down. The lights came on, the shot was numbered, and action started. I held my breath. How could Bob make it seem that he was really doing mouth-to-mouth without the baby crying? One movement from this supposedly unconscious baby and the shot would be ruined and a retake necessary. I noticed Bob was standing so that only his left side was facing the camera, giving the best profile of him for the viewers to see. The consummate actor, I thought. But that wasn't the reason at all. Bob had his right hand under the crib sheet, playing with the baby as he had been doing before, and baby was still loving it, not moving or making a sound. Bob was now bending over and making the blowing movements that Connie had taught him, simulating mouth-to-mouth resuscitation, but doing it four inches away from the baby's face. The camera angle made it look as if it were real! The scene was a take on the first try. The only time the baby cried was when Bob handed him back to his mother. The professionalism of the nurse and the actor had made the day.

Elena Verdugo was the actress who played Consuela, the sole employee at the Welby-Kiley office, doing the work for two doctors. She was nurse, receptionist and bookkeeper; she made the coffee. Connie guided Elena in her role, although it's unlikely that Connie had ever worked in a doctor's office or made the coffee.

The show took a lot of ribbing in the press and on the late night talk shows about having only one patient a week, and each of those had some sort of crisis. I always pointed out to our critics that we couldn't afford more help, in that it cost two hundred forty thousand dollars a week to see that one patient; and we couldn't afford any more at those prices. To put the cost in perspective, my own office was run on five hundred dollars a week; and we saw about one hundred patients in the office, at home, and in the hospital.

⚬⚬⚬

One employee for a solo practitioner's office wasn't really unusual. When I first arrived in Manhattan Beach, California, my office space was in a little house converted to a doctor's office, located on one of the main streets. After I signed a lease, Glad and I began to refurbish the interior with paint. We commissioned a sign painter to paint a shingle to hang on the little front entryway to the office. The day I climbed a ladder to hang it up I was proud to see my name on the main street of Manhattan Beach. Although I had practiced for eight years in rural Oregon, I'd had a partner. This was to be my first experience as a solo practitioner.

While I stood atop the ladder, an attractive young woman, most notable for her jet-black hair, piercing black eyes, long legs, and the deepest brown tan I had ever seen, spoke to me. She asked, "Are you the doctor?" After I had climbed down and answered, she continued, "I've been watching this office to see if a doctor was going to move in. You see, I'm a nurse and I want to work here." She spit it all out, hardly taking a breath. "I've been working as a stewardess for United Airlines, flying to Hawaii, and I want out of the rat race. I want to stay home—maybe take some night classes, live a normal life in one place, and maybe find a husband. How about a job as your office nurse? I have good references. You're just starting so I'll work cheap for a while; and, as you grow, I'll expect to have my salary grow with you. Will you hire me?"

All of this came out before we went inside. Well, her job certainly explained the tan; laying over in Honolulu would do it. I said, "Come in and meet my wife." The three of us talked it over. Carol went home, got into jeans, and returned to help us paint. I had acquired a nurse-receptionist, and she didn't mind making the coffee.

After a week of painting and checking in the equipment I was able to purchase on credit, we were within a day or two of taking the CLOSED sign off the door and being able to take care of patients. Carol had brought her uniform to the office. "I want to be ready," she said.

There was a loud knock on the door to the street. Glad looked out and told us that a man was standing there and looked as if he really wanted to come in. Carol quickly slipped into her uniform while Glad called through the door, "Just a minute, please."

The man said he had seen the CLOSED sign but, because he had seen people moving around inside, he hoped he could see the doctor. Carol filled out the appropriate forms with name and address while I put on my tie. This was an exciting moment.

Sherwood, Oregon was a very small town. We served about eight to ten thousand people who lived on the rural mail routes. As one of the two doctors in town, everyone knew me. I could go to a local restaurant with an empty wallet and the owner would say, "Well, I'll see you tomorrow, Doc. Pay me then." Now I was about to embark on my new medical career, competing with the other twelve thousand doctors in Los Angeles County. I had walked away from a successful practice to this funny little building on the main street of a beach city in Los Angeles County. Could I make it?

I had a family to support. I'd better make it!

This well-dressed man standing in the waiting room could be the beginning of an entire new base of referrals. If satisfied, this first patient would go home and tell his wife and friends about the excellent new doctor in town. I went into the examining room.

"Good afternoon. How may I help you?"

"Doctor, I think I've got the clap."

Gulp!

How am I going to build a practice on the visit of this first patient? He probably won't even tell his wife he has been here.

"What makes you think you have gonorrhea?"

"Well, Doctor, I met a girl in a bar about two weeks ago and we made out. You know, it wasn't any big deal. I wouldn't have done this if I'd been home; but I travel, you see, and I was up in Flagstaff—I live in

Phoenix. So, anyway, after about ten days I began to feel a burning at the end of my dick and pretty soon a yellow discharge showed up; and here I am. I couldn't go to a doctor in Phoenix; I'm too well known there. My expense account covers my travel so I just got on a plane and came over here. This is the first town I came to after I left the airport and your doctor sign is the first one I've seen."

Now wasn't that wonderful? My first patient, a traveling salesman from out of town. This was hardly the practice builder I was looking for. I treated him and collected seven dollars and fifty cents for the visit and two dollars and fifty cents for the shot of penicillin Carol gave him.

Carol was a great asset; she stayed until she met Mr. Right, or in this case Dr. Right, a prominent obstetrician. Phyllis followed Carol but, before Carol left, she recruited Gath to be my receptionist and we were a three-person-office.

Babette, who became my office nurse after Phyllis departed due to the arrival of a baby, was available because she was dissatisfied with her previous job. Her previous employer was a stickler for the time his employees spent on personal activities. When he bought a stopwatch and timed her trips to the ladies' room, Babs gave notice.

I gave her a stopwatch for Christmas one year as a joke. She turned the tables on me and timed my postprandial naps when I closed the door to my office, put my feet up on my desk—using a thick medical book as a footrest—and snoozed. When she thought I'd had enough of a nap, she brought the timer from our lab into the office, set it on my desk just out of reach, turned it on, and left the room. She was a bit of a martinet but I appreciated her.

A patient suffering with body lice came to my office one day. I treated him with the usual body shampoo and lotion, with apparent success. Babs was upset with the thought that a lousy patient had been in the office. Lice offended her sense of cleanliness, and she spent hours cleaning up after he left. The patient returned after a couple of weeks with itching eyelids. Babs put him in an examining room. When I was ready for the patient with the itchy eyes, Babs confronted me conspiratorially in the hall and said, "I think he has lice on his eyebrows and on his eyelids."

Indeed he did. Instructions for the medication we had used on his body clearly stated, "Keep out of the eyes."

What to do? We got out a textbook that identified this problem and explained that the only way to treat such a patient was to pick each louse off the area with a pair of tweezers and destroy it. Babs got the job. She protested; she really hated it. Lice grow from eggs called nits. The nits attach to the root of the hair and are hard to see and hard to remove. New lice kept appearing around his eyes. Our patient had to come in every few days for a month for nit-picking and Babs became the office's chief nit-picker.

Phyllis was my full-time nurse for several years and my off-and-on nurse along with Babs for many more years. The off-and-on part had come as a result of Phyllis and John having two daughters. The on times came as a result of my needing help to fill in. It was during one of the off times that she had her big trouble.

One morning at about 10 A.M. during my second year with *Welby*, I received a call at Santa Monica Hospital. It was Gath. She told me that John had called. Phyl was sick and he wanted me to phone him at home. When I called John answered and said, in his understated way, "She's pretty sick, Doc."

I asked to speak to Phyl. He said, "I don't know if she can talk. I'll try to get the phone to her." In a minute I heard a quavering, little voice say, "I'm awful sick. I've never felt this bad before in my life."

I took off out of the parking lot, burning rubber. Phyl was not a person to have nervous fits or to exaggerate. If she said she was sicker than she had ever been in her life, she meant it. Driving like mad down the San Diego Freeway I kept thinking, *What am I going do if a cop stops me?*

When I practiced in rural Oregon most of the sheriffs and state troopers knew my car and I was able to speed around the back country roads without fear of getting a ticket. I guess the officers always thought I was on an errand of mercy. I didn't think the CHPS officers would be so understanding.

⎯⎯⎯

Some months earlier in the city of Torrance, I had been stopped by the police. It was Sunday, and as usual on Sunday I was playing tennis at the home of my friends, Jack and Barbara Cameron. A pregnant patient, whom I knew to be carrying twins, called to say she was in labor. *Gosh,* I thought, *she isn't due for a month; these are going to be pretty small, premature babies; her labor may be precipitous. I'd better hurry.*

I told her to rush to the hospital and I would be right there. The patient only lived a short distance from the hospital but I was a good fifteen or twenty minutes away, in Rolling Hills. I took off with tires squealing and pebbles flying. At the bottom of the hill, hitting about sixty in a thirty-five-mile-an-hour speed zone I crossed into Torrance, where the law was waiting for me.

When the patrolman pulled me over, I jumped out of the convertible and ran back to his car. This disconcerted the officer, who was not used to this kind of behavior from a suspect about to get arrested; so he, also, jumped out of his car and tugged at his gun. Fortunately his quick-draw holster jammed, which gave me time to yell, "I'm a doctor. I'm on an emergency!"

He finally got the gun out, looked at me, and didn't shoot or point the gun. I guess, dressed in tennis shorts and T-shirt, I didn't look too formidable. "You're a doctor?" he asked. He seemed nonplused. I was driving a convertible with the top down; and in my tennis clothes, I did not appear to be on an errand of mercy.

"Yes, and I'm in a hurry to deliver a baby."

"You don't look much like a doctor," he opined. "Where are you going in such a hurry?"

"Look," I said, "the mother is having twins at South Bay Hospital and I've got to get there—right now. If anything happens to those twins it's going to be your fault."

"Twins? At South Bay Hospital? That's in the next town. Are you gonna go sixty miles an hour clear over there? Hell, you'll get yourself killed and God knows how many others you'll take with you. You follow me. I'll get you there, but I'm goin' in with you and there better be a lady having twins or you're goin' to the slammer. Now stay close behind me."

We went all the way with flashing lights and siren at full blast. Staying behind the cop wasn't the easiest thing I ever did. I had visions of a car running a red light and getting between the patrol car and the convertible and my ending up dead or mangled.

When we arrived at the hospital the officer, true to his word, followed me into the OB department and was reassured by the nurses that, indeed, I had a patient in labor with premature twins. What the nurses didn't tell the cop was that her labor was just beginning and, in fact, I stayed at the hospital thirteen hours more before I delivered a pair of six-pound babies.

❦

The police were not around when I rushed from Santa Monica to Manhattan Beach to see Phyl. I made the trip in under twenty minutes. It would have been a record for A. J. Foyt.

John was waiting for me at the door. I spent about thirty seconds examining Phyl, went to the phone and called an ambulance. I almost wished that I was back in Oregon where I had carried an "everything" bag in my car. This bag had contained, among a great many other things, intravenous setups. I needed one right away to try to stabilize her blood pressure. It read forty over zero—which meant profound shock.

Phyl was going in and out of consciousness and, each time she faded, I desperately hoped she wasn't going to die. I had no idea what could be the cause of her problem. She had diarrhea, had vomited blood, was in shock, and had a huge, red swelling on her upper left arm near her shoulder.

In the hospital it took all the resources we had to finally stabilize her blood pressure. I called in two specialists, who were as confounded as I.

I did not leave the hospital that day. As I sat by her bed that night, I watched the I.V. drip into her vein and agonized about why her life was slipping out of her body, seemingly due to some unknown and vicious microbe.

Why Phyl? Phyl, who is so kind to all of our patients, the person who is always calm in emergencies and whom everybody loves.

By the next morning, we were afraid her kidneys were failing, not an unusual circumstance in light of her low blood pressure. The huge swelling on her arm was getting worse; in fact, it was so bad that the skin was beginning to slough away as if gangrene were starting.

Her blood tests were off kilter, not telling us anything that we couldn't tell from observing her. What was the relationship of the diarrhea and the bloody vomiting to the swelling in her arm? The blood loss hadn't been sufficient to have caused the profound shock she had suffered.

I decided to call yet another specialist, this one a specialist in infectious disease. When the ID saw her he asked her the key question, "Have you had an insect bite?"

She was fully conscious then and answered, "No, but I did have a stinging sensation in my arm for several hours last night before my arm began to swell."

"What were you doing when you first noticed the stinging sensation?"

She said, "I remember very well, because I was carrying my groceries into the house and it stung so much I had to shift the bag to my other arm and the bananas almost fell out."

The infectious disease specialist said, "That's it! Bananas are the key. I have read about cases like this but I have never before seen one. You were bitten by a South American brown spider that arrived in a shipment of bananas. You're lucky to be alive."

Phyl got well. Her kidney function returned to normal in a few days and she was able to leave the hospital. The big problem remained. Where was the spider? John and the girls had moved out of the house. I called the Los Angeles County Health Department and found a bureau that took care of insects, but they were more interested in fruit flies than they were in brown spiders from South America. After much cajoling and threatening they finally sent out a bug hunter.

The bug hunter turned up an awful lot of insects, including a pot full of black widow spiders and a thing he called a Jerusalem cricket or water bug. I thought this was the worst looking bug-creature ever put on this earth. It had a shiny round head with a number of appendages emerging from various parts of its four-inch-long body. The bug man assured us that it was harmless. But no brown spider was ever discovered. John had the house fumigated and the family moved back in.

This was such a dramatic story I thought it might become a *Welby* episode. It had all the visuals that a dramatic doctor show needed. The patient was the doctor's nurse. We could have Consuela bitten by the spider, and Welby could be the hero. Instead of calling the health department, we could have Kiley look for and, in this case, catch the varmint; but not before it threatened to bite the little daughter of Welby's best friend at the yacht club or whatever.

One of the show's writers, Charlie McDaniels, and I were having a cup of coffee one night after we had been talking about some rewrite on a current script. I told him about Phyl and her spider bite, including the stuff about having Kiley chase the spider in my TV scenario. I pictured a scene zooming in on Kiley capturing the long, multilegged, hideous creature. He thought it would make a great show, so we decided to collaborate on writing the script. I would be the creative writer because the story came from my practice and Charlie would put the whole thing into usable form. A script like this would be worth twenty-five or thirty thousand dollars and we would split it fifty-fifty. I just knew we would win an Emmy.

We spent long hours writing first the story outline, for which we got approval from Nina Laemmele, and then writing the script, for which we never got approval from the powers-that-be. The final stage in the approval process was the network. In this case, the network turned the script down on the basis that it was unrealistic and couldn't possibly happen in real life!

When was TV ever real life? My career as a screenwriter ended—but not my relationship with writers.

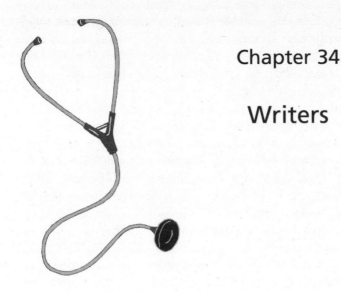

Chapter 34

Writers

I found out I was in trouble soon after I took the job with *Marcus Welby, M.D.* I had assumed that all my various activities would somehow fit into available time slots in my week. I knew I would spend about twenty hours each week at the Santa Monica Hospital Family Practice Residency program, about twenty-four hours at my private practice office plus making hospital rounds and house calls, two to three hours at the studio, as well as a few hours at home reading scripts and talking on the phone to Nina Laemmele. However, my new job was like a spiderweb, spinning its way into every facet of my life.

I was accustomed to a sixty-hour week, as all family physicians were, but I was used to some degree of order. Of course emergencies and obstetrical patients were a constant source of interruption, but they were all in the context of patient care. I had already become a teacher who had to prepare and give lectures, an administrator preparing budgets and managing personnel, a surrogate father to the young doctors in the residency, and now I had to deal with the egos and pressure of people trying to stay on top in Hollywood. Sixty hours a week was a joke. Everything in Hollywood was an emergency—meeting a deadline, soothing a fragile ego, or creating a dramatic event.

Patients just visiting their doctor, as Emanuel Blinsky was doing one day, didn't expect drama. Emanuel was a small, balding man of very serious mien and outlook. He walked around with a worried look on his face and, I suppose, rightly so; for he had a number tattooed on the inner side of his wrist and he spoke with a German accent. I didn't know this about him that first day when he arrived in my office as a new patient scheduled for a complete physical.

His appointment was for two o'clock. At ten after two, I was enmeshed in the web the *Welby* show spun about me. I was sitting at my desk, facing away from the door, talking on the phone with a writer from the studio who was working on a script. Gath was fidgeting because I was starting to run late. I had been on the telephone a long time and, as she watched Mr. Blinsky in the waiting room, she noticed he looked worried. She didn't know he looked worried all the time. She thought that if she put him in my office I would get the hint and end my conversation. However, I was concentrating on the problem which the writer was presenting to me. I didn't notice that Mr. Blinsky had arrived and was sitting in the chair across from my desk.

Emanuel Blinsky, a survivor of the Holocaust, had walked into my office just as I was trying to insert a medical scenario into a dramatic plot that the writer had created. I said, still facing away from the door and Mr. Blinsky, "I guess what you're telling me is that the old lady has to die, is that right?"

There was a pause while I listened to the answer. Then, I said, "Have you thought about how you want to get rid of her?"

Another pause, and, "You want me to figure out how to do her in? Well, she is known to be diabetic, that's why she's seeing the doctor. How about if she mistakenly takes an overdose of insulin? That could be swift and sure.

"Oh, if you don't want it to seem as if the doctor is in any way involved, then I think we should give her a stroke. Elderly diabetics are likely to have…" I heard a noise. It sounded somewhere between a growl and a moan. When I turned, I saw my new patient sitting across from me, his face chalky white, his breathing rapid and shallow. He seemed to be trying to get out of his chair, but he was unable to do so. I thought, *This man is having an attack of some kind.* I told the writer, "I'll call you back," and hung up.

I quickly got out of my chair and went around the desk to the patient. As I tried to take his wrist to feel for his pulse, I asked, "Sir, are you all right?"

The man pulled his arm away from me and hissed. "Don't touch me. Zis is Amerika. Zis does not happen hier. I vant to go. You Nazi! You animal!" He struggled to his feet, but seemed too weak to take a step.

Gath came rushing in, hearing the commotion, and steadied Mr. Blinsky. Suddenly I returned to lucidity and out of the world of Hollywood fantasy and recognized what I'd done. This poor man, hearing one side of a conversation that he shouldn't have had to hear at all, was in the same state of shock as radio audiences had been in 1938 when Orson Wells had broadcast his famous "War of the Worlds" drama about Martians landing and taking over the earth. Mr. Blinsky thought he had been listening to me plan a murder!

I told the poor man the true story. He listened but he looked doubtful. He really wanted to get the hell out of my office, until I got an idea that saved the day. I reached into a drawer in my desk and pulled out a script I had been working on. I said, "Look, Mr. Blinsky, I work for a big Hollywood studio." The script had Universal's name on it and then, among the list of people to whom it would be circulated, there was my name highlighted in yellow. Mr. Blinsky calmed down. We had a cup of coffee and chatted. He told me about his past and the memories that my conversation had evoked.

To be in the presence of one of the courageous survivors of the Holocaust was an honor and a thrill. It brought my own memories back to me and my fear of the Germans—no, not all the Germans, but the Nazis.

After my parents died, I shared a furnished room in a boarding house with a Jewish boy. He had been smuggled out of Germany immediately after *Der Kristallnacht.* When Hans and I talked, it was almost always about his experiences. He couldn't seem to focus on anything else. His entire family was gone. He had been brought to America by a relief organization. What he told me did not assuage my grief at the death of my parents from illnesses, but it did point to the horror of having a parent cruelly shot and killed right before his eyes. He didn't know what had happened to the remainder of his family, except that they had been taken away in trucks while he hid under a pile of rubbish and animal dung until it was safe to emerge. Hans told me over and over that the Nazis would win the war and they would come to America and we would all be subjected to the horrors suffered by the non-Aryans in Germany.

I didn't want to believe him. *This is America,* I thought. But then I would see pictures and read stories of the German-American Bund, saluting swastikas and making threatening statements about how

Adolph Hitler was the Fuhrer. It seemed to be gathering strength in my country. I was scared. Without a parent to talk to or any adult with whom to share my concerns, I resolved that if the Nazis came to America, I would kill myself. What a hell of a state of mind for a fifteen-year-old. When I met a survivor, like Mr. Blinsky, it brought my personal hell back again and shamed me, as I compared my own situation in those days with what he had gone through. I vowed that, as far as his health care was concerned, this man would never feel fear again if I could help it. I finished taking a history from him but postponed his physical to another day. I thought that, perhaps, his blood pressure would be too high on this day.

I took care of Mr. Blinsky as long as I practiced in Manhattan Beach. I always wondered what had made him strong enough to withstand the ravages of his early life and still be in such good health.

I lost track of Hans from my teen years. I wished that I had seen him later to have told him how proud I was of my country.

When Harold Peary, the first "Great Gildersleeve," came to me as a patient it was a dramatic event. The Great Gildersleeve himself was a dramatic event. While in the waiting room before his appointment, he entertained the other patients. In fact, no one wanted to leave the waiting room and come in to see me. That was a switch. The patients were late and the doctor was on time.

Harold Peary was an event just walking down the streets of Manhattan Beach. He played the character he had made famous on radio and on TV every day of his life. Maybe he really was the character and there wasn't any other Harold Peary. He would stop and talk to everyone he met and he signed autographs until all the citizens of our town who wanted an autograph had one; then only tourists accosted him. He told me, "When they stop recognizing me or stop asking me, I'll know I'm done." They never stopped.

Gath and I resolved that my various occupations had to be kept separate. We decided that when I was with a patient, the time was sacred unless there was a medical emergency, not a Hollywood emergency. The studio was encouraged to make telephone appointments or the writers could make appointments to come to the office on a scheduled basis. My life and my practice were better served when I better organized my life.

There was more to learn about how to deal with writers for the show. I had no idea where they got plots for their stories until Nina Laemmele called me one day to ask what I knew about bone marrow transplants. I answered honestly, "Nothing."

She told me that one of the writers had seen a six-line write-up in a section of *Time* magazine, entitled, "Milestones." It stated that one of the first blood marrow transplants had been performed in Texas. He wanted to base a *Welby* segment on this new treatment, but he didn't know anything about it nor did he know how to find out about it. Nina thought the idea was a good one, as it demonstrated that the show was up-to-date; and would I please find out about blood marrow transplants and help the writer insert accurate medical information into the script?

Jeez! Bone marrow transplants would not be anything I'd ever want to know much about, nor would Dr. Welby or I ever perform one. This would be a job for hematologists.

We did the story. I spent hours talking to hematologists and researching the subject in the UCLA Medical School Library. I learned more about the subject than I would ever want or need to know. I consoled myself by hoping that there would be a question on the Family Practice Board Certification Examination (which I was scheduled to take). There wasn't. *Marcus Welby, M.D.* was ahead of the examiners of the American Board of Family Practice.

Writers, I found, would do almost anything to make a dramatic point in a story. This was okay on two other shows for which I reviewed scripts—*Medical Center,* starring Chad Everett, and *The Bold Ones,* starring E. G. Marshall as the doctor. These two shows were not designed to be medically accurate, although the one I did for *Medical Center* entitled "The Family Practice Man" was accurate. However, *The Bold Ones,* written and produced by Lee Siegel, was a futuristic, anything-goes vehicle.

A writer for the Welby show once did a script about a patient who had been badly burned. This girl had a twin sister. They played it as a bad-sister, good-sister routine. The good sister was burned and the bad sister was needed to provide skin for a graft. She wouldn't do it. The big dramatic scene, as written, had the burned sister near death from infected burns; and if the bad sister didn't let them take her skin to graft onto the good sister, she would die before morning. High drama? You bet! Accurate? Not by a long shot!

I called Nina Laemmele and told her it wouldn't work. I said, "It's not possible to graft skin onto an infected area. The graft wouldn't take and it would worsen the infection."

Nina replied, "I asked the writer about that and he told me he had the script checked by the physician who heads the burn unit," and she named a most respected hospital in the San Fernando Valley. It seemed to imply, "Who in the heck are you to argue with this far more experienced physician?" She continued, "I'll give you his name and you can check with him if you wish; but remember, we're on deadline. The writer was late with the script and we have to get this one into production."

I called the famous burn specialist. "He's out of town," said his office.

"When will he be back?" I asked.

"Not for a while," was the answer. "He's out of the country."

I called Nina back. "We've been suckered." I told her. "You can't let that script run like it is. It's just plain wrong."

Nina's response floored me. "We'll have to go with it as is. I talked to the writer and he was pretty upset. Swore he had the scene checked by the expert before he left town and he'd be dammed if he was going to change it on your say-so. Taking out the part about needing the graft before morning or the sister would die would just plain ruin the dramatic effect. If you still want to change it, you'll have to get your own expert to back you up."

We hung up. Damn, I was mad! I thought, *Screw you, I quit! Shoot, I can't quit. I'm under contract. Now what do I do?*

If ever a guy had been given a vote of no confidence, it was me. *All right, I'll get my own expert. I'll show up this writer for what he is, a guy who will go to any length to put over a dramatic point despite our demand for accuracy. Then Nina and I will have an agonizing reappraisal of my role because if I don't have the final say about things like this, I can't continue to be their T.A.*

I got my expert. He backed my stand. The script was rewritten using pigskin as a temporary covering for the burned area and the bad sister came through later. They both became good sisters and lived happily ever after.

So did Nina and I. After our agonizing reappraisal we reached a working agreement—that I had the final medical say, and that if in doubt, I would check with experts.

Diabetes was a hot topic in the sixties, when new treatments and new drugs as a substitute for insulin were emerging. We did a show on the subject. Of course, the diabetic patient on the show didn't fare well. Patients on a dramatic show seldom do well at first. If they did, there would be no drama and then no one would watch.

Other doctors often complained that we didn't show the practice of medicine as it really was: a lot of patients with colds, boils, or with the God Only Really Knows (GORK) diagnosis. Nor did we indicate that in most cases the illness, whether treated or not treated, goes away in one or two weeks.

A typical GORK case comes in. The doctor examines the patient and then says, "Have you ever had this before?" If the patient says yes, the doctor says, "Hmmm, you've got it again. Did it go away the last time?" And if the answer is yes, "Well, then, it'll probably go away this time, too." Then the doctor writes an Rx for a harmless pill.

Doctor shows on television don't work that way. There has to be a problem and there has to be a diagnosis; the public doesn't want its doctor heroes wandering around scratching their heads. So, we had this loony diabetic patient who would not accept the fact that he was diabetic and needed insulin and needed strict dietary control. Furthermore, he had a Type A personality, he had a stressful, high-paying job, and he drank.

All of this was fairly realistic. The writer wanted more. He wrote a scene in which the patient was warned by Welby that he needed more strict control and that he would have to lay off the sauce. Things become tight in the patient's life and, in the big scene he takes a drink. Boom! The patient is out cold in diabetic coma. But in real life it can't happen that way. Alcohol is sugar. Excess sugar in the blood can cause diabetic coma, but only over time.

Take my own patient, Frank Aston. Frank was sixty years old. He'd had diabetes all his adult life. He was well controlled with diet and insulin. Frank was a smart guy and he'd been around the block with his disease and knew that people on insulin sometimes find that their normal dose of insulin is too high. This may be due to a variety of causes such as excessive exercise, vomiting or fasting, febrile illness and many other reasons. He also knew that one of the first signs of an insulin reaction is dizziness or lightheadedness and, in order to abort an insulin reaction, he must get some sugar into his system in a hurry. A sugar cube, hard candy, or a glass of orange juice might do the trick; and when he was away from home he always carried some hard candy with him, although he seldom needed to use it.

One Sunday morning Frank went to early mass so that he could get a project done at home. He was going to paint the ceiling in the living room. He wanted to finish it in one day and get the mess cleaned up because his wife, Ethel, was away at their son's house for the weekend and wouldn't be back until about six o'clock, and he wanted to surprise her. Frank was old-fashioned and used a brush for painting; he didn't cotton to a newfangled roller.

Frank started his job standing on a ladder, brush in his right hand, and the bucket of paint on a shelf on the ladder. With his head craned back to see the ceiling, it wasn't long before he began to feel lightheaded. "Oh, oh," he says to himself. "Too much insulin this morning," and he climbed down and went out to the kitchen for a glass of orange juice.

If Frank had been thinking about his recent trip to Rome and his visit to the Vatican and the Sistine Chapel, he would have recognized that Michelangelo didn't stand on a ladder to paint that famous ceiling but lay on his back on a platform during those years it took him to do his remarkable art. If he had been standing on a ladder all that time he surely would not have finished the job; he would have been too dizzy. Remember those patients at the Lutheran Church in Sherwood when we lived at Creekwood? Frank didn't know about this and so, when he felt better after his orange juice, he went back up the ladder. He didn't realize that the act of coming down and straightening his neck was the act that dispelled his dizziness.

This sequence of events went on all day. Get dizzy. Come down and take some sugar, go back up. And it happened all over again. He thought, while he was still lucid, that the extra work he was doing obviated his need for his afternoon dose of insulin; so, he skipped it. As his blood sugar rose, he was now eating sugar cubes by the handful, his consciousness was being affected, and his senses were becoming clouded. He was getting goofy. At about five-thirty in the afternoon he lost consciousness and fell off the ladder. His blood sugar level was at twelve hundred—about ten times normal.

When Ethel came home she sent for me and we got him off to the hospital. He was in the hospital three days before I could get him straightened out. It had taken him a whole day of abnormal behavior to get into the shape he was in. The loss of consciousness came on gradually, and only after some bizarre behavior that would have been noticed by his wife, had she been home. He didn't just abruptly collapse, as did the patient in the show.

When I spoke to Nina Laemmele, she again said that the writer of this piece had checked with an expert and had been informed that it was medically correct. This time, because of our previous agreement, she wondered if the expert could have misunderstood the problem. I called the same diabetologist the writer quoted. He was a really nice guy who certainly hadn't understood the problem, nor had he seen the script. The writer, seeking the most dramatic impact he could engender, had left out a little in explaining the sequence of events to his expert. He had asked,

"Will alcohol cause a patient to go into diabetic coma if he already has high blood sugar?"

The expert had answered, "Yes, it would." What he hadn't been asked was how much it would take and what the interval would be between the ingestion of the alcohol and the onset of coma. When I explained that the TV patient was supposed to take a drink and then, BOOM, pass out, he laughed and said, "Of course, you're right. You've got a tough job. I wouldn't want it."

We repaired the script so that further drinks were implied and, using fade-outs, a time lapse was created. Everyone was happy. Even the writer thanked me.

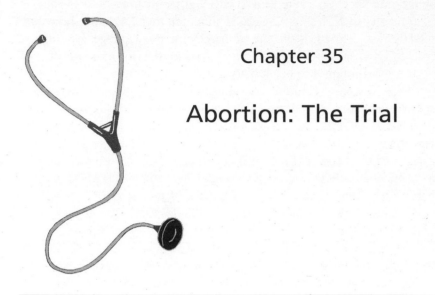

Chapter 35

Abortion: The Trial

When we still lived in Sherwood, abortions were performed in back alleys. It was unusual to find professionals who would perform the procedure and jeopardize their licenses to practice.

A Portland chiropractor advertised in the *Oregonian* with a picture of crossed hands, captioned, "The Paws That Refresh." Everyone knew those paws would do an abortion if a woman presented herself properly. Properly meant she had three hundred dollars, wasn't connected with the police, and was willing to come to his office twice. The first visit was to pay the three hundred bucks and be screened. The second visit was to have the abortion. Screening was less for medical reasons and more for screening out police traps. Women who thought they were pregnant, but actually were not, still got the full treatment. At least all these women lost was the money.

To put that three hundred dollars in perspective, consider that the Sherwood Clinic charged thirty-five dollars for a dilatation and curettage for a spontaneous, incomplete miscarriage, and fifty dollars for a normal delivery, which consisted of pre- and postpartum care and one year's well-baby care, including immunizations. The abortion business was profitable.

In the 1950s, abortions were absolutely illegal. People who were caught doing abortions were sent to jail. Well, sometimes!

The city of Newberg, Oregon is about ten miles west of Sherwood, down Highway 99W. It is the site of the George Fox College, a small and excellent Quaker school. Newberg was also the location of one of Oregon's most infamous abortionists, Elmer Pitt, M.D.

The Newberg Community Hospital was a nice little country hospital that should not have been in the abortion business, but was dominated by Dr. Pitt who was part owner. The other doctors in town had to close their eyes to what was going on, or be refused hospital admission privileges in their town. If they did not wish to put up with the shenanigans at Newberg, these doctors had to take their patients to McMinnville, twenty miles west. Some did that. The bulk of the citizens of Newberg, not concerned with the inner workings of the hospital, wanted very much to stay at home when they needed hospitalization, so the hospital flourished. My partner and I would have liked to admit some of our less seriously ill patients to this hospital, as it was closer to our office than the two hospitals we used, but we refused to be tainted by association with the infamous Dr. Pitt. We would not send or treat patients there, despite having to travel more than twice as far to Hillsboro or Portland.

An attractive, well-dressed new patient came to our office on an October day and asked to see me. She looked about thirty-five years old. Actually, she was twenty-nine, but worry about her condition made her seem older. She was dressed in a tailored suit, a little out of character for women going to the doctor's office in Sherwood. Sherwood women dressed well on occasion, but going to see the doctor was not usually such an occasion; they might be in jeans, a house dress or shorts. Millie had golden curls in a stylish hairdo. Her address was Lake Grove, a suburban community of Portland just west of Lake Oswego and east of Tualatin, a sort of buffer zone between the very posh community of Lake Oswego and the "Crawfish Capital of the World," Tualatin. Lake Grove was semi-posh.

Millie said, "I'm pregnant, and I am going to have an abortion."

My mind began turning somersaults. *Is she asking me for an abortion? I don't do abortions. Is this a setup by the State Board of Medical Examiners? What is she doing here, anyway?*

"Yes?" I inquired, softly.

"You see, I'm not married." And Millie told me her about her problem.

It turned out she was a schoolteacher; she taught at a high school in another county. If this news got out, it would end her career. She had gone to Doctor Pitt in Newberg. He had examined her and said she was pregnant, but she didn't trust him. What she wanted from me, first of all, was to know if she really was pregnant; and next, a promise to take care of her in case something went wrong after her abortion, since I was a legitimate doctor whom she had heard about and could trust.

Wow! This was the kind of problem no doctor wants to have. I didn't know if I was sympathetic to her idea of abortion or not. Certainly, there had been times when I thought abortion could have been a good idea for the good of the patient.

Every July we had one or two teenagers deliver, as an aftermath of the big Sherwood High School Homecoming Celebration the previous November. Precedent called for a bonfire and rally, followed by a snake dance all around the streets of the town. The school officials and the town fathers decreed yearly that the bonfire should be extinguished by the local fire department at 9:45 P.M. so the children could be home by 10 P.M.

Well, the children didn't go home. With their passions aroused and their juices flowing they went off in cars, or to hay lofts, or into the woods, and did what came naturally. Nine months later they delivered the result of the bonfire and the snake dance. When these poor little girls came to the office around Christmas, a little while after having missed a period, I often wondered what should be done to help them; but the law was rigid. Abortion was illegal, and I was not about to risk my career by becoming an abortionist.

When Millie said, "It would be the end of my career," I decided to accept her as a patient. Her career was as valuable to her as mine was to me. At that moment, I suppose, I recognized a woman's right to make her own decisions.

I examined Millie. She really was eight to ten weeks pregnant. I collected urine for a Friedman Pregnancy Test and sent the specimen to the lab at St. Vincent's Hospital in Portland. The results were positive, confirming my physical diagnosis.

When Millie returned for the results of the test and I told her that they were positive for pregnancy, she said that she had an appointment with the abortionist for the next day.

I counseled her very seriously. "Millie, if there is the slightest problem, come right back to see me. Don't wait until you are really ill."

A week passed. Millie returned. The cervix, or neck of the uterus, showed the tell-tale signs of recent dilation. The uterus was smaller and she had a moderate infection. I successfully treated the infection with antibiotics, and I repeated her Friedman test. The results came back negative. Millie was finished with her problem and her career was saved, at the expense of an unborn fetus. At that time in history, the fetus wasn't an issue. We didn't think of the fetus as a real baby. Times have changed.

She returned to the care of her own doctor and I thought I would never see her again until the district attorney from Yamhill County appeared at my office several weeks later.

The D.A. was from Newberg, the county seat of Yamhill county. He explained his visit. For some time the authorities had attempted to pin a rap on the infamous Dr. Pitt but, because many of his patients were local, no one would inform on him.

After extensive planning, the D.A.'s office and the sheriff's department had figured out a way to catch him. A sheriff's car watched Pitt's office and, when a woman of childbearing age left, she was followed. If she left the county it was surmised that she had come to his office for no good purpose. Within a few days officers questioned her. Among the many women they interviewed, they turned up five cases of women who had undergone illegal abortions and were willing to tell their stories before the grand jury. Since these proceedings were secret, Millie was one of those who agreed.

I guess I never really understood these women who were willing to testify. Each had sought out an abortionist because they were, or they imagined they were, in trouble. He had done what they asked of him. Now, they were willing to become state's witnesses against the very person who had pulled their chestnuts out of the fire. If the case against Pitt was successful, then no other women would have the same opportunity to control their own lives as had these five.

In their minds, was the law applicable only to others and not to them? It was a time when abortion was an illicit operation, performed by unsavory people with dirty instruments, for large fees. And there, perhaps, was the rub. Money! The fees were disproportionate to other fees in the offices of legitimate doctors. Abortionists had a real scam going. Perhaps the women felt they had been taken advantage of, financially, and were willing to right the injustice.

Millie had told the authorities about my role in her case, hence the district attorney's visit to my office. The D.A. said that one of the five cases was almost air-tight and would be the only one brought to trial. He wanted to check with me to see if I would be a friendly witness if subpoenaed before the grand jury. I told him I would do what was right before the law and he left, assuring me that I would probably not hear from him again after my grand jury appearance. He was sure he would not need to try the case involving Millie in open court. I certainly hoped that Millie would not be involved because of the attendant publicity.

My only experience in a courtroom had been in a few cases in which patients had been involved in personal injury claims and I had testified on their behalf. Even this type of trial was unpleasant, and I wanted no part of anything as adversarial as this, a criminal trial.

My appearance before the grand jury was a straightforward matter without opposing counsel present. The D.A. asked the questions and I answered them simply and truthfully. One juror asked a question about why I hadn't attempted to stop my patient from going through with the abortion. I guess my answer, not thought out in advance, established my own thinking for the rest of my life. I said, "I believed that the decision was hers to make and I didn't want to interfere." Years later, when abortion became a political and moral issue, I took a very active role in counseling patients regarding the alternatives and the emotional as well as the physical complications.

A month later the D.A. was back. The grand jury had finished its job. Five indictments were brought before them and all five cases were declared true bills. Pitt was indicted on all five.

The Yamhill County D.A. told me that he had never tried an abortion case, so he had sought consultation from Charlie Johns, a lawyer in private practice in Portland. Mr. Johns had been the Multnomah County prosecutor who had successfully prosecuted the chiropractor with the "Paws That Refresh," and had put him away for a jail term. The D.A. said he had outlined his case and strategy to Charlie Johns and was given minimal advice. He went on to say that the enterprising Mr. Johns then had called Dr. Pitt and, in effect, said, "I hear you're in trouble. I know all about the case and the Yamhill D.A.'s strategy. I think you would do well to hire me to defend you."

Was there a rule against this sort of behavior? Not legally, only morally.

Because of his betrayal by the lawyer, the D.A. decided to substitute a different case. He had five indictments; but which one should he select? He decided on his second most airtight case, Millie and me. We would have to go to court as state's witnesses.

Millie was upset. She had been promised that this would not happen, but now she was under subpoena to testify in this case. If she didn't answer the subpoena, she could be held in contempt of court. She didn't need this kind of publicity.

While all this was going on, Pinky and I discussed it and he asked if he could accompany me to the trial. I thought having a friend in the courtroom would boost my morale, so I agreed.

Charlie Johns was a gallus-snapping, shirt-sleeved, country lawyer. He acted dumb but was sharp as a tack. I thought, *If I am ever prosecuted, I'll take Charlie Johns for my lawyer!*

During the two days I was on the witness stand I hated his guts. He was Clarence Darrow, Melvin Belli and Gregory Peck (as the lawyer in *To Kill a Mockingbird*) all rolled into one, wandering around the courtroom, sparking the ladies on the jury, flattering the men, and making a fool out of me without a murmur of protest by the D.A.

He fiddled around with testimony regarding the integrity of the urine samples for the two Friedman tests until he finally broke the chain of evidence and had the results of those tests disallowed; and he had already begun to discredit me.

He had walked up to the witness chair and asked, "Well, now, Doctor, do you know what an endometrial polyp is?"

"Yes."

"And, Doctor, one of them polyps in a woman's womb will cause her to bleed, sometimes, won't it?"

"Yes."

"And, Doctor, if a woman was to have one of them polyps endo…? …endometrial, wasn't it?, and she bled some, wouldn't you be tempted to remove it?"

"Yes, if she wasn't pregnant."

"Well, Doctor, if you did remove it, would you do that by performing what you doctors call a D and C?"

"Yes."

"After doing a D and C would the neck of the womb have tenaculum marks on it, like you described on the womb of that lady over there?"

"Yes." I thought, *Where is he going with this line of questioning? There never was the slightest suggestion that Millie had a polyp.*

"Do you think your patient could have had a D and C between the second time you saw her and the third time?"

"Yes." *Do I think she'd had a D and C ? I know damn well she had! That's what this trial is all about. It was the D and C that Pitt used to remove the tiny fetus from her uterus.*

"Do you think the D and C she had, between her visits to you, could have been for a polyp?"

"No."

"My goodness, Doctor, why not?"

"Because of her pregnancy."

"But, Doctor, you said that test you talked about, where you have to kill a poor little rabbit, was what made you so sure she had been pregnant. You remember, of course, that we established that the test you said you performed is not a part of this trial?"

"Yes."

"Well, Doctor, even so, isn't it true that sometimes one of those endometrial polyp things will also make that little bunny give you a positive test?"

"Never."

"Doctor, did you say—*never?*"

"Yes." *Please, Mr. D.A., object to this.*

"Well now, Doctor, knowing you to be a learned man, I didn't even think to carry one of those heavy medical books into court to read to you about that test. I was just sure you would know about that."

"Mr. Johns, that test is never…"

"Now, now, Doctor don't get yourself in any deeper. I'll just forget that question."

Please, Mr. D.A., help me. Object, throw a fit, do something!

Charlie Johns sighed, and—with a little gesture to the jury indicating, too bad about that doctor, he's so dumb—proceeded with a new line of questioning.

Never did any doctor, or Charlie Johns, believe that an endometrial polyp could cause a positive Friedman test. Only the jury believed it. And I looked incompetent. The trial ended with a hung jury.

The D.A. prosecuted again, and once more I spent two days on the stand; but the lawyers and judge conferred ahead of time, and the Friedman test was ruled out completely. We were warned that even mentioning it would result in a mistrial.

The second trial also ended in a hung jury and the Yamhill County District Attorney's office gave up. However, the State Board of Medical Examiners had become interested and held a hearing on the abortionist's case. Elmer Pitt pleaded nolo contendere. This was not a guilty plea, but one that said, "I will not contend." The result? Dr. Pitt had his license suspended for one year. He spent that year traveling in Europe. He returned to the same old place, doing the same old thing, one year later. I paid dearly in frayed nerves and frustration for his actions.

Pinky thought the entire process was a farce. He said, "If that's the way people feel about abortion, maybe Dr. Pitt is right and he should be doing them. All he got was a slap on the wrist. He was already rich enough to vacation in Europe for a year." Pinky shook his head in disbelief.

After the trial, Millie resigned from the school system and applied for a government job in another state. I hope she went on to a successful career.

Abortion became an issue for me, my patients, and the world in the years to come. Even Marcus Welby had to deal with it, in a most unusual situation.

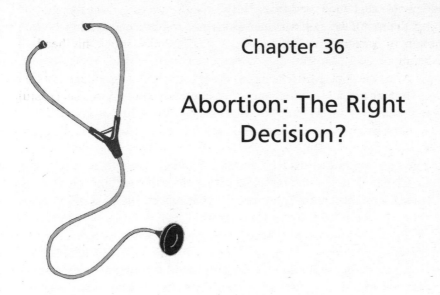

Chapter 36

Abortion: The Right Decision?

During the spring of 1971, Dr. Marcus Welby walked into the front door of the Welby house and found his daughter Sandy waiting in an examining room. This was his home, shared with Dr. Stephen Kiley, and it was their office.

The close association of the two doctors had started lewd rumors among the Hollywood columnists and the series competitors that the two guys were gay. Anyone who watched the series could refute this claim. Stephen Kiley, as the junior lead, was on the prowl for the ladies— sometimes to the embarrassment of strait-laced Welby and the even more strait-laced star, Robert Young.

Bob and Betty Young had married while Bob was still an aspiring actor in the nineteen-thirties and Betty was a singer and actress. Betty decided to give up her career, stay home, be a wife, have children, and support Bob's career. She never wavered in her fierce devotion to her husband. She probably sacrificed an opportunity for success for herself, but I'll bet she never regretted it. At a time when celebrities' affairs made headlines, Bob Young was never implicated. Whether Bob actually felt that way himself or whether Betty kept him on a short leash, I don't know but, observing the two of them together over many years of their lives, I'd be willing to bet on his devotion. Oh, there was a rumor or two, especially about a woman he referred to as "Elly."

Bob, one day, called Elinor Donohue, his juvenile lead in *Father Knows Best,* "Elly."

Elinor said, "Mr. Young, you're the only person who ever called me that."

Bob then asked, "Is it okay?" And then wistfully added, "I once knew a nice lady in Hawaii with that name." When Elinor agreed, Bob called her Elly, evermore. Elinor told me that he used the name affectionately.

When the four of us, Bob and Betty and Glad and I, were visiting in our Florida home on the occasion of our fortieth wedding anniversary and the discussion naturally turned to what made a durable and loving marriage, Bob related a fascinating incident regarding an experience he had with Hedy Lamarr. They were starring together in a picture.

Hedy had been made famous by a nude scene in a movie entitled *Ecstasy.* Her nudity was extraordinary for the times. Actually, it wasn't a big deal. I was a teenager at the time and wasn't tremendously titillated, thus attesting to the fact that it wasn't a big deal. Nevertheless, Hedy had become a star partially because of that scene and a whole lot because of her remarkable beauty. A number of people have ascribed a great acting talent to her but, to me, she was always a beautiful stick. Stick or not, her sexuality was undisputed. According to Bob Young, Hedy had a reputation around the picture industry that she had bedded every leading man she had worked with.

Bob told us he had heard around the studio that Hedy was telling anyone who would listen that she was going to get that stiff-necked Bob Young into bed before the end of the filming of the picture. Bob became upset when he heard about these remarks. He went to Hedy and clearly informed her that she was not going to bed him during the filming of this picture or any other time, and that she had better quit trying or she would embarrass herself.

"Boy," he said, "did she ever get mad! During the big love scene, hugging her was like squeezing a box of saltines!"

According to the show's story line, Marcus Welby's wife died after a stillbirth some years earlier when Sandy, her only child, was twelve years old. Sandy was devastated that her father, with all of his knowledge, hadn't been able to save her mother. Nevertheless, Sandy was devoted to her dad. When the two-part episode entitled "The Basic Moment" opened and Consuela told Marcus that Sandy was waiting for him in an examining room, he was surprised because Sandy should have been with her husband in South America, where he was the engineer on a road-building job. It turns out that Sandy is frightened, "I had a rash and a fever a couple of weeks ago and now I'm scared. Could it have been German measles? And, Daddy, I think I'm pregnant. We're living in a little village up in the mountains with no health care, so I thought I'd better come home and see you. Daddy, what should I do?"

Marcus Welby is overjoyed at the prospect of becoming a grandfather but he is worried about the possibility of Sandy having had German measles (rubella) during the first few weeks of her pregnancy. Rubella babies are often born with severe congenital defects. He says, "Sandy, dear, I want you to see Steve Kiley, my associate; but I'll be right there all the time."

❧

My patient, Margie, when she had come to me for care ten years earlier at my Manhattan Beach office, was first seen by Phyl, my nurse, who said to me, "You'd better come see this lady right away. I think she has Graves disease and she looks as if she's going to explode."

Graves disease is a goiter in the neck accompanied by overactivity of the thyroid gland. A typical case includes bulging eyes, high blood pressure, rapid pulse, heat intolerance with sweating, and weight loss. Margie had all of these symptoms and she was having a lot of trouble breathing. When I entered the examining room to see her I could almost feel the heat emanating from her body and, with her eyes seeming to be almost ready to pop out of her head, I could understand Phyl's remark about her being ready to explode. I was most concerned about her breathing difficulties, which appeared life-threatening. When I listened to her lungs with my stethoscope, the wheezes of bronchial asthma were apparent. Upon questioning, Margie related that she had a history of asthma which, in the past, had been controlled with an inhaler and asthma pills.

But, she exclaimed, "Now these medicines seem to be making me worse!"

Of course they were. Bronchial dilators all contained ephedrine or ephedrine-like products that tend to raise the blood pressure, speed the pulse, and aggravate an overactive thyroid gland; this, in turn, creates a situation that worsens the asthma. To treat Margie, I had to slow up the thyroid so that she would be able to use the bronchial dilators that would help her breathing.

Then, when her thyroid and her asthma were under control, I would refer her to the surgeon, Ken Maynard, for removal of the goiter. This surgery was fraught with potential danger, such as damaging the nerve to the vocal cords (thus interfering with speech), or inadvertently removing all or part of the parathyroid glands that were sometimes embedded in the substance of the thyroid gland itself. Sound complicated? Sound like the plot for a doctor show on TV?

According to Murphy's Law, *What can go wrong, will go wrong,* and in Margie's case, it did. On her first post-operative day she suffered a kind of seizure, or tetany. When the hospital called to tell me she was having seizure-like symptoms, I ordered an I.V. with calcium for her and rushed out of the office with my heart in my mouth, worried that Margie was in grave danger from the loss of parathyroid tissue.

When I reached the hospital Ken Maynard was already there. Her symptoms had subsided but she had developed the pathognomic diagnostic symptom of hypoparathyroidism, Chevostek's sign. This is a twitching of the facial muscles, most noticeable at the corner of the lip when the patient's face is tapped lightly on the cheek with the examiner's finger. Ken suggested that the rapid infusion of calcium I had ordered over the phone may have saved her life. We were sick over this complication and asked the pathologist to go over her goiter specimen with a fine-toothed comb, looking for parathyroid tissue.

It took the pathologist three days to make the necessary slides and examine all the tissue that was needed to confirm whether or not the parathyroid glands were in the specimen. Margie held up a lot better under the strain than Ken and I, as she did not fully comprehend the lifelong significance of living without parathyroid tissue. The seizure she had suffered could be the first of many during the rest of her life unless her condition was rigidly monitored and controlled with replacement calcium.

Luckily, the pathologist reported that there was no parathyroid tissue embedded in the thyroid gland we had removed. Margie had no repeat episodes of tetany and we supposed that what she had suffered was just swelling in the area of the parathyroids, temporarily shutting them down. But the positive Chevostek's sign persisted.

After Margie went home, I frequently checked her serum calcium for possible signs of returning hypoparathyroidism; and I always tapped her cheek looking for a Chevostek's, which continued to be positive. She had no more trouble with her thyroid except that she was going to have to take thyroid medicine for the rest of her life. Her problems with asthma subsided, but the nagging question persisted of the damned positive Chevostek's.

One day, when she came into the office, I proudly dragged out a new medical journal and said, "Look at this little article that Ken Maynard found for us in this obscure medical journal. Three per cent of normal people have an asymptomatic positive Chevostek's sign."

Margie squealed with delight. She had never completely come down from what I thought was a thyroid high, but was actually her own ebullient personality. "You mean that I'm finally okay? I'm going to be well and happy, and if I take my thyroid pills I'm going to stay healthy? What a lucky girl I am! I've got my husband, two kids, and now I don't have a worry in the world."

I was about as happy as she was. There is nothing that cements a relationship between a doctor and a patient as well as the successful conclusion of a critical illness, and, boy, had we just concluded a tough one. It felt good.

We had no idea that a couple of years later Margie, her husband Howard, and I would be sitting in this office discussing the problems she was about to endure with an unexpected pregnancy.

❧❀❧

A few years before I started with the *Welby* show, I decided to give up delivering babies. Although this was the happiest part of my practice, it seemed that deliveries always occurred at inopportune times. Our kids were teenagers and needed my support, so giving up delivering babies was my contribution to family harmony.

My new practice mode was referring my patients to an obstetrician in whom I had a great deal of confidence, Lonnie Priest.

Lonnie and his partner had assumed the care of my pregnant patient, Maybelle Barkley. Maybelle's husband, Bill, was also a patient of mine. The Barkleys were really excited about the upcoming birth; but current practice did not permit husbands to be involved in the birth as they are now, in Lamaze training.

Maybelle's labor started at about eight in the evening. Bill called to tell me about it and to alert me, as I would be taking care of the baby when it arrived. This was their first baby and he was very excited.

I didn't think too much about the delivery, knowing that Lonnie would call me when the baby was born. I would go to the hospital and check the infant at a convenient time if the birth was uneventful or immediately if there was a problem. Maybelle delivered about four-thirty the next afternoon. It had been a long labor, but this is often true with a first baby. Mother and infant were resting comfortably so I told the nursery I would be over after office hours to check young Mr. Barkley. I had an appointment for a haircut at five-thirty and planned to check the baby on my way home.

My haircut was about half over when my beeper went off. The barber handed me the telephone and waited while I called my answering service. The operator at the exchange said, "Mr. Barkley wants to talk to you. He sounds upset. Shall I put you through?"

I told her to go ahead and within seconds I was listening to Bill Barkley. "Doctor," Bill said, "I'm mad! I'm so goddamned mad, I'm going to kill the sonofabitchin' doctor that mistreated my wife. I'm gonna get my gun and I'm gonna kill him. Do ya unnerstan? Kill 'im!"

"Whoa, Bill, what are you talking about? Maybelle's fine. I'm going now to check the baby. They told me he's fine, too. What's the matter?"

"You don't know. You weren't there. Doctor, that poor woman suffered the tortures of the damned. I stayed up all night and I could hear her screaming, her and the other ladies having babies; and that goddamned doctor didn't help her, he just let her yell! Well, he's gonna pay! I'll make that sonofabitch yell before I kill 'im!"

"Hang in there, Bill; everything went well. Doctor Priest told me so when he called right after the delivery. Everything's fine at the hospital, but you're pooped. Why don't you sleep on it and see how you feel in the morning? I'll call you first thing. What time do you get up?" I reasoned that Bill was suffering from sleep deprivation and a type of psychotic break associated with emotional trauma, but that a good night's sleep would calm him down.

Bill was now yelling so loudly that I wasn't sure he heard what I was saying, so I changed my approach and I yelled, too. I shouted, "Bill, now shut up and listen to me! Do you hear me? Listen to me! I'm coming over. I'll be there in five minutes. Don't you leave the house until I get there. Stay put! I'm coming over. Do you hear me?"

The line was quiet for a few seconds and then Bill said, in a slow, thick voice, "You can come if ya want, but you won't stop me. Nobody treats my Maybelle like dirt. I'm gonna kill that bastard."

I pulled the sheet away from my neck and got out of the barber's chair. The barber said, "Hey, I'm not finished; I'm only half through."

"I'll be back," I said.

I picked up the phone, called my answering service, and asked them to put me through to Lonnie Priest. When he answered the phone from home, I said, "We've got a real problem with Bill Barkley. He's having a psychotic episode and he's temporarily not accountable. I want you to take your family and go out to dinner and to a show or to a friend's house; but don't go home, to your office, or to the hospital. Call me at home after a couple of hours and I'll keep you informed. Now, I gotta go. Do what I tell you, okay?"

"For heaven's sake, tell me what this is all about."

"Can't. Don't have time. He says he wants to kill you. I've gotta get over there right now. Bye."

I hung up and started out the door. The barber said, "Hey, wait a minute; when are you coming back?"

"Don't know."

As the door was closing I heard him say, "You look like hell, don't you want me to at least comb...." The door closed and I didn't hear the rest. I was into my car and burning rubber for Bill Barkley's house. When I got there I didn't bother trying to find a parking place. I double-parked, grabbed my medical bag, and ran up the stairs to the front door. I tried the door. It was locked. I pushed the doorbell and waited. I wondered if Bill was still home; or, if he was home, if he would let me in, and if I got in would I be his victim instead of Lonnie Priest?

The door opened. A woman stood there. She glanced at the bag in my hand and said, "You're the doctor? I'm so glad you're here. Bill is wild. I'm their neighbor. I was bringing over a dinner for Bill. I knew how much sleep he has lost, so I thought a nice dinner and a night's rest would be good for him; but, my gosh, when I got here he was yelling at someone on the phone—maybe it was you—and he says he's going to kill somebody. He's usually such a quiet man; I can't believe what I'm hearing. Is Maybelle all right?"

Finding Bill in the house wasn't going to be a problem. I could hear him alternately grumbling and shouting. Now that I was here I began to have misgivings. *Maybe I should call the police. What if Bill is mad at me as well as Lonnie? If I called the police what would they do, arrest him? Then what will happen to this nice family? I'd better try to see what I can do, but carefully.*

I followed his voice to where he was and quietly said, "Bill, look at me and relax and tell me what's troubling you."

The neighbor was right behind me. She didn't seem to be frightened, just concerned. This bolstered my courage, so I went over to Bill, put my hand on his shoulder and again said, "Relax, Bill, and talk to me."

He stared at me for a moment, wild-eyed, sweating, and breathing hard. We locked eyes and I repeated, "Bill, relax. I want to help you."

The tension went out of his face. The wrinkles left his forehead, his cheeks sagged and his eyes closed. He said, "Doctor, I'm so tired. Help me!"

We talked awhile but not about killing anyone. He ate a little. Then I asked the neighbor, if I gave Bill a sedative, would she check on him through the night. When she agreed, I injected Bill with a potent dose of Thorazine, waited until he went to sleep, went to the hospital, checked the baby, saw Maybelle, did not burden her with the trouble with Bill, and went home. Glad said, "What's the matter with your hair? You look as if you had half a haircut!"

Bill was fine the next day and we never spoke of the incident again, except for a brief conference with Bill and Maybelle together, for me to assure them that this was, probably, a one-shot deal that would never recur.

Lonnie was grateful and so was his wife, who had gotten a night away from the stove. The next morning I revisited the barber, who was confounded by the strange antics of his customer.

Again, I ruminated about the dangers of medical practice.

❧

Ray, the husband of the mythical Sandy, Marcus Welby's daughter, suddenly comes home from South America. When he hears that Sandy has told her dad and Kiley that she had rubella he tells Sandy that she is faking it; that she is afraid to have a baby and that's why he has come home—so they can go through this thing together.

Welby can't remember if Sandy had rubella as a child. "There were so many babies, so many kids with measles, mumps, chicken pox, and rashes that I can't trust my memory. I'm not sure, Sandy, what childhood diseases you had."

Steve Kiley tells Sandy that he will get a blood test to see if she has ever had rubella. He also tells her that if the test is negative she's home free. However, if it's positive, all it will tell is that she's had the disease, but not when.

The rubella antibody test is positive. Sandy has had rubella, but when? Was it during the first weeks of her pregnancy or was it as a child?

Now the agonizing decision has to be made. California Law permits therapeutic abortions up to the fourteenth week of pregnancy. There isn't much time. Ray is against it. Marcus Welby thinks that perhaps this pregnancy should be terminated, but he realizes that he is too close to the problem. That baby in Sandy's body is his grandchild, his only grandchild, so he makes no recommendation. Ray is absolutely sure that the baby will be all right and doesn't want to interrupt the pregnancy. Kiley lays out the problems of the possibilities of abnormalities if the pregnancy goes to term; but, as an ethical doctor, he can give the information only to the parents and they must make the decision.

Suddenly, Sandy is in trouble. A spontaneous miscarriage threatens. If she miscarries, the problem is solved.

This is the end of the first part of the two-part segment of the show—*to be continued.* Whoever believes that the problem is going to be solved that easily hasn't watched much television. If she miscarries, what are they going to do for forty-eight minutes next Tuesday night?

⋐⋙⋑

My patient, Margie, who had the goiter and is now blissfully happy with her life in order, unexpectedly becomes pregnant. She and her husband, Howard Hancock, come to the office for a conference to discuss the conduct of her seven week pregnancy. They are pleased, even though they have two kids in their preteen years. I explain that I won't be doing the delivery but that I will refer them to Doctor Lonnie Priest. Margie isn't happy with the idea because, she says, "You're my doctor. I have confidence in you. I don't want anyone else."

This is pretty heady stuff for me. I am hearing one of the greatest rewards that a doctor can get from a patient, but I knew this might happen when I decided to give up obstetrics in my practice. So, I am adamant; I can't do it. I will take care of the baby and Margie until the beginning of the third trimester, when she will have to start seeing Dr. Priest.

Three days later Margie calls and tells me that she has a rash and a very low fever and she wants to know what it is. She asks, "Shall I come to the office?"

"Yes," I tell her. "But come to the back door so that if you are contagious you won't infect the other patients."

When I see Margie, it's pretty definite that she has rubella. She has the typical rash and the telltale symptom of enlarged lymph nodes on her head behind her ears. As with Marcus Welby's daughter, Sandy, Margie needs a rubella antibody titer. Hers is negative. The antibodies haven't had time to form. Another test in two weeks will definitely confirm the diagnosis, if there is a fourfold rise in the titer. I am convinced that we are dealing with rubella, but making that diagnosis is so devastating that I want to be absolutely sure. I am more fortunate than Dr. Kiley. I can confirm the diagnosis and present concrete findings for my patient and her husband to consider.

We wait two weeks. The titer comes back high. Margie had rubella during the first few weeks of her pregnancy. She and Howard come in for another conference. These are intelligent people, easy to talk to and without conflict in their marriage.

This is different than the setting for the *Marcus Welby* episode. The time is several years earlier and therapeutic abortion is legal only to save a mother's life. I explain the possibilities and percentages for fetal abnormalities, and then I offer a solution. I will give Margie a couple of sleeping pills containing barbiturates. After she takes these pills (actually a small dose and not harmful) Howard is to take her to the emergency room of the hospital where he will tell the staff that she attempted suicide due to her despondency over the possibility of having a baby with severe congenital abnormalities. The emergency room doctor will test her blood and find barbiturates in her blood. The next day I will refer her to a psychiatrist who will determine that she is suicidal, confirming this with the emergency room report of sedatives in her blood stream, and recommend a therapeutic abortion to be performed by the OB consultant, Dr. Lonnie Priest.

The Hancocks are stunned with the knowledge. They had known that there might be a problem but they hadn't recognized the magnitude nor the extent of the problem. Because Margie is still only in the tenth week, we still have a little time. The Hancocks decide to go home and think it over. I encourage them to do this and also to consult with the pastor of their church.

To be continued.

❧

The two *Marcus Welby* episodes entitled "The Basic Moment," featuring Marcus Welby's daughter, aired in the months near the time when the Supreme Court made its decision on *Roe versus Wade,* which gave the states the right to regulate abortion. The show demonstrated its currency by airing a contemporary topic. I hadn't realized the impact this would have on me when I attended an award ceremony in Anaheim.

The Orange County chapter of the California Medical Association wanted to give *Marcus Welby, M.D.* an award at their annual meeting at the convention center in Anaheim. They wanted Robert Young to come and receive the award. If he was not available they would opt for Jim Brolin; but they definitely wanted one of them. What they got was me! It was during the off season. We weren't shooting, Brolin was away, and Young was spending time at his other home in Rancho Santa Fe, north of San Diego. He didn't want to come to the event.

My appearance was scheduled for just after dinner, about 8:30 P.M., so that the video would make the local evening news. The story wasn't big enough to hold over until the next day, so if it didn't show right after it happened, it was dead meat. The medical association officials were gracious, even with their disappointment about not having a celebrity to receive the commendation, and hosted me at dinner. After dinner we went into the auditorium for the *Marcus Welby* presentation as well as some other presentations. A large crowd of about seven hundred physicians sat patiently through the proceedings, alternately yawning and falling asleep, while digesting drinks and a big dinner. The podium for the VIP guests was on the left edge of the very large stage at the Anaheim Convention Center. There was another podium and microphone on the other side of the stage. It had been used by scientific speakers during the day.

During a moment's hesitation, while the doctor who was master of ceremonies looked over his notes and looked over to me and nodded, indicating that I was on next, a man popped out of the audience and vaulted onto the stage, grabbed the other microphone, and said, "I'm Joe Campanella and I'd like to speak to you for a few minutes about abortion. Is that okay, Mr. Master of Ceremonies?"

This is where the M.C. made his first mistake. He agreed.

I had felt sorry for him. He had wanted to have a bona fide celebrity and was disappointed, but here was a real movie star gratuitously popping out of his audience. The assembled doctors seemed to throw off their postprandial somnolence and a shifting of seats occurred as the doctors woke up.

I watched Joseph Campanella take over the stage. He was an accomplished performer and, with a dominating stage presence, took over the audience. He started out with a reasonable approach to the issues surrounding abortion, but soon lapsed into the jargon of a right-to-life zealot.

About fifteen minutes into his unscheduled presentation, some members of the audience began to boo. The doctors may have felt that after a day of sitting in this auditorium listening to six or eight hours of scientific lectures followed by cocktails, a banquet, and an evening meeting, they didn't want to hear any more on this subject or any other subject. Within minutes, the audience began to trickle out of the auditorium.

I didn't blame the doctors in the audience. Nor did I blame the M.C.—he had a tough job. In the operating room he was in his element and in control, but in his current role he was being badly used. The speaker had usurped the entire stage and didn't allow the frantic M.C. to get it back. The microphone cord attached to the mike Joe Campanella was using must have been twenty-five feet long, but the mike at the M.C.'s podium was fixed in place. The M.C. asked Mr. C. to cease and desist. He was ignored. He got up and took a few steps across the stage to take Campanella's mike away from him, but with his long cord, Joe was able to dance away. This put the rather bulky surgeon in the unenviable and undignified position of having to chase the younger and more agile actor around the stage. The M.C. retreated to his own side of the stage and resorted to glowering as his only offense.

It was now 9:30 P.M. Not only was I going to miss the late news, but I was in danger of having made the trip in vain, as the audience was departing in droves. Those who remained shouted derisive comments at the speaker. A few loyal anti-abortion advocates remained and cheered the usurper. Bedlam reigned! Finally, an official of the medical society called security. The cops came and, once they appeared, Campanella went peacefully. We were one hour late. The TV cameras had already gone. Joe Campanella had provided them with far more newsworthy pictures than I would have.

I received the award in an almost empty auditorium, for now even the anti-abortionists were gone, having followed their leader into the hall. The only people left were either bored to desperation or, I fear, sound asleep.

ာထာ

In the continuing saga of Marcus Welby's daughter, we left her last week with a threatened spontaneous miscarriage. Wouldn't that have been the easy way out? But, if that had happened, why would the audience turn on their TVs next week? No, she had to overcome that threat, develop anemia, get into a controversy about whether or not to have an amniocentesis, and ultimately decide what to do. Ray, her husband, tells her, "It's your decision." By innuendo and suggestion, he indicates that he thinks she ought to go on with the pregnancy. He had called her a coward when he first returned from South America. Although he never says it again, Sandy knows that if she decides on abortion, their marriage will never be the same.

Marcus Welby, the counselor for all kinds of patients, has to distance himself from this case; he's too emotionally involved. Sandy is on her own. She really has no choice, has she? She knows her husband's feelings; her dad won't or can't help her. She says, "I'll keep the baby!"

⌘

We left Margie and Howard Hancock, my patients, wondering what they should do. I have offered them a way out if they choose to take it. Margie is wavering, worried about the consequences of bringing a child who might have major physical problems into the world. What would the impact of that be on the family?

Howard is a successful business executive as well as a reserve military officer, accustomed to being a leader and overcoming adversity. I'm not privileged to sit in on their private deliberations. When they come back the next day, Howard announces, "We have decided to have the baby. We can't abide the thought of circumventing the law." I can guess who dominated the decision-making process. Now, Margie chimes in, "We want you to do the delivery."

I tell them, "I've given up OB. I don't do deliveries anymore. I'll refer you to Dr. Priest, in whom I have the greatest confidence."

Margie is crying. With tears trickling down her cheeks she says, "Doctor, it's hard enough for me to go through with this at all. I don't want my baby delivered by a stranger. I want you to be there. We have confidence in you. Please?"

I've always been a sucker for a woman in tears. I've also always been a sucker for flattery. I waver. I think to myself, *This is a tough case to foist onto someone else. Margie is a healthy woman at this point, so the delivery shouldn't be a problem. I'll have to take care of the baby when it arrives, anyway.*

"Okay," I say, but I think to myself, *This is the very last time. I promise myself—never again! No matter what the circumstances.* I tell the Hancocks, "We've been through a lot together. One more time should be just fine."

⌘

The pregnancies of Sandy and Margie progressed quite well, although there was considerably more emotional stress in the *Marcus Welby* gravidity than in Margie's case. Of course, fourteen million people weren't watching Margie, and we weren't selling soap or toilet bowl cleaners.

Sandy delivered. The baby had the stigmata of rubella, a cardiac anomaly. The condition, patent ductus arteriosus, is usually correctable by surgery after the baby is several months old.

Margie delivered. The baby appeared normal.

Sandy's baby developed congestive heart failure, requiring emergency surgery. This was on prime time and guaranteed to boost the ratings. The audience watched, engrossed. The baby would be all right— this is TV. But it's not all right. Marcus Welby's only grandchild died on the operating table. The story ended with the baby's parents vowing to have another baby; and the audience was left with the good feeling that all is right with the world.

Margie's baby was physically strong and seemed to be very healthy. After a couple of weeks, Margie brought the baby in for a checkup. She said, "I'm worried, Doctor. Jonathan doesn't respond to noise. When there is a loud bang in the house, and there are plenty with the two older kids and their friends in and out all the time, he doesn't cry. Could his hearing be impaired?"

We sent Margie and Jonathan to a famous hearing clinic in downtown Los Angeles. After a protracted period of testing, Jonathan, at the age of three months, came home with hearing aids. He was stone deaf.

Life was going to be difficult for Jonathan and his family. The entire family was primed to support the baby. Howard was the first to suffer. His gung-ho, macho attitude took a fall. Business wasn't going well. He was referred for psychiatric counseling. The sibling's grades were falling off. Margie wasn't there all the time and no longer was there a house full of kids. Jonathan's trips to the hearing clinic and training sessions for the hearing-impaired took all Margie's time.

As Jonathan grew up he became a problem child. He was in trouble: drugs, stealing, and a school drop-out. He was out of control. The other kids didn't seem to rise to their potential. The Hancock's marriage was shaky.

Margie and I got together again when Jonathan was nineteen. I was no longer in practice in the Los Angeles area but, because of the close friendship we had during those troubled years, we met for lunch. We talked about Jonathan and her whole family.

Margie cried. She said, "When I decided to go through with the pregnancy, I'm not sure it was the right decision."

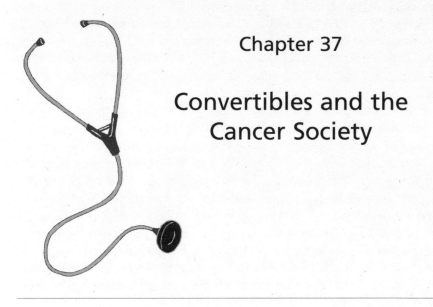

Chapter 37

Convertibles and the Cancer Society

Anyone who thinks that the only thing doctors do is to take care of patients hasn't had a doctor for a husband or father. Ask my family.

"Where's Dad tonight, Mom?"

"He's going to be late tonight."

Second kid: "Why, Mom?"

"The hospital staff is meeting and he has to be there."

First kid: "Will he be home tomorrow night to play catch with me?"

"No. He has to go to the county medical society meeting."

"Oh. How about this weekend? Will he be home then?"

"Well, this weekend he's going to a continuing education symposium. He has to go so that he can give his patients the best care."

One kid now says to the others, "Let's go out and play."

"What will we play?"

"Oh, I don't know. Lets play Go to a Meeting."

Honest to God, that happened in my family. Whatever happened to Cowboys and Indians?

Nina Laemmele called soon after I had submitted some new dialogue for a medical sequence in one of the weekly Welby segments. The medical dialogue hadn't been quite accurate, and I had expanded it.

She laughingly said, "When you write stuff for Jim Brolin, don't let it run more than two sentences. He can't memorize!"

When I started as a technical advisor, I wasn't sure how I should present dialogue; whether it should be sterile fact for Nina and the writer to put in proper form, or if I should actually write the dialogue. To begin with I tried the first method. After all, who was I to presume that I could function as a Hollywood script writer?

Also, I wasn't sure about the actors. Did they throw themselves into the roles they played and feel as though they were the doctors they were playing, or were they simply Robert Young and James Brolin, playing themselves and memorizing lines to be said in front of a camera? I heard Bob Young say, often enough to be believed, that he never really felt like a doctor; instead, he felt himself to be an actor privileged to play a role about a profession he considered to be one of the two highest callings— medicine and the clergy. After watching the two of them, over time, I realized that they indeed played their roles, but each with his own inimitable style. So when I said that Robert Young was *Father Knows Best* with a stethoscope, I wasn't demeaning his acting ability, I was only referring to his style.

Trying to write to fit the actors' styles was a bit daunting, but I found they were adaptable to my style, as they wanted to sound like doctors. I soon reached a comfortable state where I wrote the medical language as I would say it in conversations with other doctors or, as the case might be, with patients.

James Brolin, as Dr. Stephen Kiley, played second banana to Bob Young as Dr. Welby. Jim, at twenty-six, was a Hollywood hunk— handsome and brawny, but a little stiff as an actor, especially when compared to a polished performer like Robert Young. He had done some movies before coming to *Welby*, the most notable being *Capetown Affair,* co-starring Jacqueline Bissett, done two years before *Welby* aired in 1969. I never argued with Nina about Jim and his memory but it seemed okay to me; besides, he was a nice guy.

The Los Angeles chapter of the American Cancer Society asked both Jim and me to appear at their annual luncheon and speak to the members. The group was courteous to me and listened attentively while I gave a short talk, but they saved their enthusiasm for the Hollywood star.

Jim hadn't really prepared what he was going to say, he rambled on a bit about what it was like to be an actor, and then opened the meeting for questions. This was just what the doctor ordered as far as the audience was concerned. They peppered Jim with questions, so he ran overtime. Jim and I had made previous plans for me to take him to the airport on my way to my office. I was fidgeting, not only because of his need to be on time for his flight, but because I had a full set of patient appointments scheduled for the remainder of the afternoon.

I finally went to the podium, apologized to the audience, and explained that we had to leave. The Cancer Society people were having a lot of fun, and now I sort of sensed that I had become a pariah. Pariah or not, I dragged Jim away.

The luncheon was held in the Coconut Grove of the Ambassador Hotel on Wilshire Boulevard. In order to leave the hotel and get to the valet parking in front of the building, it was necessary to pass through the arcade shopping area.

When Jim and I rounded the first turn in the arcade, two female tourists, hoping to see a movie star, had their wishes fulfilled. Eyes bugging, heads turned, they walked smack into one of the store windows. This wasn't a simple knock on the head. The glass broke and the ladies tumbled into the store amid shards of broken glass. The scene became chaotic. There was blood everywhere. The ladies screamed. Passersby offered all kinds of advice. Some one cried, "Call a doctor!"

I said, "I am a doctor," but no one paid any attention, even though I was down on my hands and knees in the debris, trying to render first aid. One citizen tried to move me over, exclaiming, "I've had a first aid course. Let me in there!"

Finally, Jim Brolin approached and the crowd thought they recognized a real doctor. One spectator said, "Make way for Dr. Kiley."

At this point I heard sirens. Somebody had called the police and an ambulance. When they both arrived order was restored. The carnage wasn't as bad as it had seemed. I had effectively stopped the bleeding and the wounds weren't going to be too bad; in fact, the ladies now wanted Jim's autograph. He obliged. At least they got something to show for their horrible experience. I wonder what they told their bridge club in Dubuque?

While the parking attendant went for my car I went into the men's room to wash off the blood. There were two men in the john. One was wearing the uniform of a cleanup man from the hotel. He was telling the other, who was wearing a suit, "Did you see the mess I'm going to have to clean up out there? There's broken glass and blood all over the place. Two smartass guys pushed two broads through a plate glass window. I guess they got smart with the gals and a fight started."

At that point the man in the suit looked at me, washing the blood off my hands and said, "Boy, guys like you ought to be locked up!" And he slammed the door as he left.

The janitor suddenly got real busy over in the corner. I felt no compunction to try to straighten him out as to what really had happened; he wouldn't have believed me, anyway. This looked like fodder for the tabloids: TV DOCTOR AND REAL DOCTOR ATTACK WOMEN. I thought I'd better get out of there.

My car was a gray 1967 Lincoln convertible with red leather upholstery. Pretty wild car for a general practitioner? It wasn't quite as extravagant as it seems. My across-the-street neighbor worked for a division of the Ford Motor Company. My neighbor was able to purchase, at cost, a new Ford product of his choice every six months. Because my neighbor was addicted to Lincoln convertibles, I owned two such cars, bought at ridiculously low prices, over a six-year period.

The parking attendant brought my convertible as Jim and I talked about the departure time of his flight. We decided it was good that we had left the luncheon when we did, in order to allow time for the unexpected to happen. Now we were on our way, and it seemed as though we had enough time to get to the airport.

The trip on the surface streets to the Santa Monica Freeway was uneventful, but when we reached the freeway and I settled down in the left lane, the fast lane, the trouble started. A car filled with teenagers pulled alongside of us and the kids began to point and wave. They had sighted a movie and TV star! Sitting in the seat of my open convertible! Jim laughed and waved back. They were like puppies.

We never should have encouraged them. Their waving and pointing attracted the attention of the people in the car behind us. The occupants of this car, with out-of-state license plates, were tourists. What a lark! They would have a wonderful story to tell when they got home, so they hung on our tail. Meanwhile, the puppies were having a ball and holding tight to the right side of the Lincoln. There was also a car in front of us going about seventy, as we were. We rapidly approached the off ramp to the San Diego Freeway that would take us to Century Boulevard, the airport exit.

We were boxed in. Puppies beside us, tourists behind us, and a speeder in front. I waved to the puppies to indicate that they should move over and let us go by. They waved back. I put on my right turn signal. So did the car behind us, letting us know that wherever we went, they were going, too. I leaned on my horn so that the guy in front of us would move over and let us pass. He had decided that this was his piece of the road, and he didn't move. When I honked my horn again, all I got was a middle finger raised up in the air in a symbolic gesture recognized the world over as—screw you! I wasn't surprised; he was an L.A. driver.

We missed our exit. We were stuck in a four-car unit. A break occurred when the speeder turned off to go up Bundy. As soon as he turned I speeded up to about eighty-five, scooted across to the right lane, and hung in there until I got to Lincoln Boulevard. Then, without a signal, I scrambled off the freeway and left our tormentors behind. I felt like a stunt driver in a cop show on TV.

Lincoln Boulevard did lead to the airport, albeit on slow surface streets; but at this point we decided they would be safer. I pulled the car off on a side street, put the top up and resolved never again to drive a celebrity in an open convertible.

We made it to the airport with about five minutes to spare. Fortunately, Jim Brolin was an athletic fellow, and I learned later that he made his flight. I was twenty minutes late to my office and suffered the rest of the afternoon trying to catch up. I decided not to try to explain to my patients that I was behind because two women had walked through a plate glass window at the Ambassador Hotel, and that I had been boxed in on the freeway by carloads of celebrity-seeking gawkers and one rude L.A. driver. Instead, I had Gath tell people that I'd had an emergency. Most patients probably wonder why their doctors run late in their offices. If they were to ask, I wonder what stories would be told?

～✿～

It was through my activity with the Cancer Society that I was introduced to the Hollywood scene some years before my association with Welby. One of my patients, who was a luminary in the local branch of the Los Angeles chapter, invited me to a society luncheon held at the Pen and Quill Restaurant.

The Pen and Quill was owned and operated by a famous journalist and may have been, for a while, the best eatery in a city that had a lot of places to eat but not many that were high class. Take, for instance, a joint down by the beach where one could get "the best steak in town." When it opened, wanting to cater to a young, high-rolling beach crowd, it applied for a license under the name of the Oar House. The city fathers thought of the play on words and turned down the application at an open meeting where the applicant was present. This individual (who was infuriated by what he considered the stodgy attitude of the council) shouted for all to hear, "Well then, FRIGATE!" The mayor, without hesitation, responded, "That's fine." And Frigate it became. But it was not a place where the Cancer Society would hold its luncheon.

There wasn't an event in town where someone didn't hit on the doctor for a donation. So it was, on the day I attended a luncheon at the Pen and Quill, I was also inveigled by my patient to buy ten dollars worth of raffle tickets. The myth that we all had a lot of money was accepted by all fund-raisers. These people didn't realize that I had the same expenses they did: a big mortgage, an insurance program, and three kids who went to school, played in Little League, took piano lessons, and went to the orthodontist. The whole family was unable to take a vacation because, if I wasn't in the office seeing patients, the money stopped coming in.

The first prize offered at the Cancer Society Luncheon was a trip to Hawaii, the second prize was a three-day golfing vacation at a famous resort near San Diego, and the third prize was two tickets to a Hollywood opening. I was lucky I didn't win either of the first two prizes (that would have required time away from the office). I did win the third prize, the Hollywood opening. It was the first time I had ever won anything. Glad and I looked forward to going to the opening of the movie *Star*, with Julie Andrews, Omar Sharif, and a new young talent, Richard Crenna.

Glad and I planned what we would wear to the black tie event. She bought a new formal gown. I had an old tux that I had worn before World War II when I worked as a doorman at the Balboa Theater in the Richmond district in San Francisco, the place where Lana and I had a tryst. It had been let out a couple of times but it was still wearable, even if it was shiny and a wee bit tight. On the appointed day I had Gath schedule a limited number of appointments so that I could get home early and be ready for our big adventure in fabled Hollywood.

Upon arriving home, having first stopped at the car wash to make sure that our Lincoln convertible was clean when we drove under the awning at the theater and gave our car to the parking attendants as instructed in the formal invitation, I found Glad absolutely wretched, in the bathroom throwing up. She had a GI virus. We couldn't go! I was unperturbed about not going to the party; I was more concerned about poor Glad's misery. She assured me that the worst of it was over, but she felt as weak as a kitten and couldn't go.

And then the idea struck both of us—Pamela, our fifteen-year-old daughter. We called the ice arena where Pamela and her brother Lee were practicing for an upcoming local ice show, and told Lee what was going on and to bring his sister home immediately.

Everyone helped in getting Pamela ready except me. I was having enough trouble with my starched tuxedo shirt collar and the bow tie. Fortuitously, Pamela had just gotten her first formal gown in anticipation of her first high school prom date. It was a pretty, form-fit blue sheath that announced to the world that my little girl was becoming a woman. To go with the gown, her mother had gotten her a white fur stole; rabbit, I guess, but we hoped it would look like ermine. Her hair was quickly teased into the stylish beehive of the day and we were ready to be off. We told Glad and Lee that after the show we would go to the party for a while and be home early.

When we arrived in front of the theater on Wilshire Boulevard there was a line of cars waiting to unload onto a red carpet that led into the theater lobby. We didn't feel out of place arriving in our Lincoln convertible with the top down amid the Mercedes, Cadillacs, and Bentleys. When we arrived at the red carpet and showed our invitation, the parking attendant assured us that our car would be driven safely to the Metro, Goldwyn, and Mayer Studio and would be available to us after the party by asking for it, just with our name. He said, "You will be driven to the studio by our limo service."

We got out of our car and started walking down the red carpet. Crowds of people who attend Hollywood openings in order to catch a glimpse of their favorite stars were held back by red velvet ropes. After we had taken a few steps, there was a smattering of applause. Pamela whispered, "Dad, what's that for?"

I said, "Because you're gorgeous and these people think you're a star." I was right, for once the applause started, it began to build, and as we entered the theater our faces were almost as red as the carpet. We made it safely to our seats because, once inside, it appeared as if the insiders were celebrity-savvy and they knew we didn't qualify.

The lights dimmed and the show started. We hadn't expected an intermission; but when the lights came up we followed the crowd to the lobby. The bartender poured champagne for me and a Coke for Pamela.

The crowd was lively. It seemed as if everyone knew everyone else. Because we knew no one, we slid to the edge of the crowd and stood beside a wall, watching the passing parade. Pamela would say, "Oh, look, there's Marlo Thomas!" or, "That tall guy is the Rifleman!" Or I would grab Pamela's arm and surreptitiously point to a movie star or maybe an athlete like Wally Moon of the L.A. Dodgers.

Suddenly, there was a very short, round man standing in front of us. I'd noticed him a few seconds before, scanning the crowd. It seemed as if he were looking for someone. He had passed us by, but apparently noticing this beautiful and very young girl holding the arm of an older man, decided she must be a starlet on the rise; and if that were true, probably I was some kind of a bigwig. He put on the brakes, came back, and—breathing right into my face—said unctuously, "Well, hello there." And he stuck out a pudgy, wet palm for me to grab.

I wondered what he wanted or for whom he had mistaken us, and said, "How do you do? It's a good show, don't you think?"

He turned to Pamela. Having addressed the bigwig, he felt it necessary to compliment the starlet. "What are you doing, my dear?"

Pamela, not connecting at all with this guy, said, "I'm in school."

"Ah," said the hunter; for hunter he was, looking for a comet whose tail he could grab and perhaps ride to the top, "Pasadena Playhouse or Hollywood High?"

Pamela, looking nonplused responded, "Palos Verdes High School."

He got the picture and disappeared without a word. Later, at our table at the party, one of the Hollywood people told us that this person was an aspiring agent without any clients. He had worked in the industry for several years and, unable to make it on his own, had decided that perhaps he could make it on the talents of others.

After the movie ended (which we enjoyed but the critics panned) all of the theatergoers were driven to the Metro lot in stretch limos, dozens of them. The critics may have panned the picture but they couldn't pan the party. Money for the party hadn't seemed to be a concern. A huge sound stage had been constructed to resemble Maxim's of Paris in the late 1800s. Pamela and I discussed what we should do. By now it was eleven o'clock on a school night. Time had passed and we hadn't had any dinner. We decided to stay and see what was going to happen.

We were the first at our table. The center of the table contained, in addition to a bouquet, bottles of bonded bourbon, scotch, gin, vodka (all name brands), and two bottles of very good French wine. I poured myself a pretty good jolt of bourbon and soda and a wee one for my daughter. Two more people showed up at the table. One explained that he was a writer and the other a sound engineer. When they learned that I was a physician and Pamela was my daughter, they introduced us to the other guests as they arrived.

The next couple was Rudy and Mrs. Vallee. Mrs. Vallee was much younger than Rudy. She explained to Pamela that her husband was a famous bandleader and actor in his time, famous for his rendition of the "Maine Drinking Song." It looked to me as if drinking was something Rudy Vallee was all too familiar with. He arrived at the table wobbly and soon became incoherent. The next guest was a grandmotherly type of woman who was neither a drinker nor a Hollywood type; she was the mother of one of the stars, Richard Crenna.

We got caught up in the evening and forgot all about its being a school night as the various celebrities dropped by the table to pay their respects to the star's mother. Richard Crenna danced with his mother and then invited Pamela to dance. She nearly swooned, but made it to the dance floor and had a wonderful time. Miss Andrews came over to chat but I didn't muster the courage to ask her to dance. I've always regretted it. What a lovely lady! Pamela and I danced, and never was there a prouder father.

When dinner was over and the last musical selection had been played and the orchestra had put their instruments away, we claimed our car, with its top down. The fog had rolled in and the leather seats were wet. Despite attempts to dry the seats, we arrived home at 5 A.M. with very wet bottoms and very sleepy, to a very cross Glad, who wanted to know why in the world we were so darned late. All our daughter could say was, "Mom, I danced with Richard Crenna."

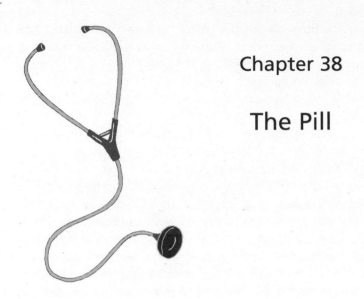

Chapter 38

The Pill

During the third year of the Welby series, in an episode titled "In Sickness and in Health," a character, Mrs. Jamie Bell, asks Welby and Kiley to prescribe birth control pills for her, but conceals the fact that she is separated from her husband because she doesn't want the doctors to think she is a wanton woman, about to go out on the town seeking male companionship. Horrors! How would that play today? Today she would be in bed with her clothes off in the first act. Remember, this was 1972 and, although we had been through the 1960s sexual "freedom," prime time television hadn't yet surrendered its standards. Neither had the public.

❧

My patient Jennie Saurer turned eighteen the day after she graduated from high school. Two days later she got her first job as a typist in one of the large aerospace companies located in the area. Six months after that Jennie fulfilled her young life's dream: she had enough money to make a down payment on a new car. When she drove away from the dealership in her new Toyota Corolla she was the happiest woman in Manhattan Beach. When she signaled and stopped, preparing to make a left turn off Sepulveda Boulevard to go home, she became another statistic of the most common accident that occurs in Los Angeles County: she was rear-ended.

I saw Jennie in the emergency room of the hospital soon after her mother called me. Jennie was lying on an examining table, trussed up in a neck brace, weeping noisily. When I asked her if it hurt she responded, "My beautiful new car. It's ruined."

"I'm sorry," I said, "but can you move your legs? Where does it hurt?"

In order to answer my first question, Jennie waved both legs in the air and said, "My neck hurts. I wish you would take off this stupid brace. I want to get out of here and see about my car."

Jennie was an attractive young beach girl with sun-bleached hair whose roots were dark enough to suggest that some of the color had come out of a bottle. She was dressed in a print minidress, and pantyhose which the nurse removed, revealing surfer's nodules on the insteps of both feet. These are fleshy bumps found on the feet of all surfers. They had scared me to death when, as a novice in beach medicine fresh from Oregon some years before, I had imagined that the first couple of surfers I examined had some kind of a tumor. When I finally asked one of these patients about them I was told that they were calluses from "hanging ten."

Since X-rays of her neck seemed normal and her checkup was otherwise unremarkable, I thought she was more distressed about her car than the pain in her neck. No doubt she had a flexion-extension (whiplash) injury but, since it didn't seem serious, I sent her home with instructions about neck care and some muscle-relaxant medication. I saw Jennie a week later. She reported she was fine and cheered up because it appeared that her beloved Toyota could be repaired just like new.

Two weeks later Jennie returned, complaining of neck pain radiating from her head down or from her neck up; she wasn't sure which. But, she said, it had come on about a week before and she thought it was related to the accident. My examination of her neck at that office visit seemed to be negative but, because of her continued pain, I decided to refer her to an orthopedic surgeon for a consultation. I wondered if Jennie or her family had been contacted by a lawyer and now suffered from "litigationitis."

The orthopedist who treated Jennie called, two weeks later, and told me he had hospitalized her for over a week and had even sent her to UCLA for a new type of X-ray, but he was still without a diagnosis. The day after her trip to Westwood, her pain abruptly disappeared and he had sent her home.

A week later the orthopedic surgeon called back and said, "Jennie's back in the hospital with neck and head pain, again. I don't have the faintest idea what to do next. I wish you would check her and see if there is something else wrong that could be causing her trouble. Will you let me know what you find? I'll continue to call on her every day but I'm returning her care to you."

Thanks a lot! This orthopedic surgeon had the best reputation in the area for solving neck problems and he doesn't know what's wrong? How am I going to find out? Well, I thought, *the only thing I can do is ignore her accident, start from the beginning, and do a thorough and complete history and physical examination.* The next day was my afternoon off so I gave up my regular tee time with my golfing partners and devoted my afternoon to Jennie.

I started the history by asking Jennie about her chief complaint and present illness. She explained that the pain seemed to be in her head and radiated to her neck. It had come on a couple of weeks after the accident. When the orthopedist had put her in the hospital the first time she lived on pain pills that seemed to help. Then suddenly the pain had disappeared, only to reappear in a week. Next, I took a family history. She told me that no member of her family had migraine or a history of headaches. Her own past history was also not helpful, as she had never been really sick. Then I said, "Jennie, have you any allergies, nasal congestion, sinus attacks, or dental problems?"

She answered, "No."

I asked her, "Do you take any over-the-counter medications or prescription drugs that I don't know about?"

"No."

"Do you take laxatives, vitamins, uppers or downers, or birth control pills?"

A long pause. "Well, ah…ah…no."

"Whatta ya mean, 'Well, ah…ah…no.' Do you or don't you?"

"Doctor, I just started taking birth control pills, but please don't tell my mother." (Today her mother would have stuffed her purse with condoms.)

"When did you start the pills?"

"About a week before you sent me to the other doctor. I went to the free clinic in Santa Monica. They checked me over. I'm okay."

"Did they warn you about the side effects of taking the pills, such as blood clots in your legs, missing your periods, or headaches?"

"No."

The little diagnostician who sat on my right shoulder, called experience, tapped me on the head to get my attention and murmured, "Birth control pills cause headaches."

I said, "I can see what happened. You started the pill and the headaches started. You went to the hospital and, after three weeks on the pill, you stopped taking them for a week, as prescribed. For that week the headaches went away; but then you started the pill, again, and the headaches came back. You're taking them now, aren't you?"

When she answered yes, I knew I was on the right track and that Jennie could go home. The headaches would be gone. Did I think Jennie was a wanton woman? Of course not. In fact, I was able to find a contraceptive pill with a lower dose of progesterone that she was able to tolerate, and with her Toyota in good running order so was her life.

⚬⟩⟨⟨⟨⚬

My patient Stella Coustakis was deaf. Stella lost her hearing following viral encephalitis when she was three years old. She was a lipreader who had never learned to sign; consequently she sometimes appeared to be slow when spoken to, if she was not facing the speaker. Her voice was the typical nasal, unemotional voice of the hearing-impaired. She was a physically handsome woman—although her facial expressions lacked animation. Stella worked for one of the large aerospace companies in the area.

I had been dealing with a lipreader for a couple of years because one of the family practice residents at Santa Monica Hospital was hearing impaired. This young doctor had never informed people of his affliction as he feared this might keep him out of medical school and a good residency position. When he first came to the residency I had many complaints about his attitude. He was considered surly and withdrawn. Frequently, he didn't answer people who spoke to him. Of course he didn't; he didn't hear them. It was only after a long talk between us that he finally confessed to his obvious impairment. Once this was known, his coworkers were careful to speak directly to him, and his reputation for grumpiness disappeared.

Stella was not grumpy, but she didn't make friends easily; she was shy and consequently lonesome. Because I knew this, when she came in to see me for birth control pills I was really surprised. She said, in her odd voice, "Doctor, would you think it awful of me if I asked you to give me a prescription for the pill? I'm twenty-eight years old, I've never had a lover, and my sister says that, because of the way I am, I probably never will be able to attract a man. She's younger than I, but she's already married, and she says sex is wonderful. She wants me to experience it, but she says I need to be on the pill. Will you give me a prescription even if I'm not married?"

This was the saddest story I could imagine for this nice young woman. I certainly didn't agree with her sister that Stella had nothing to offer to a man; I was sure that the right guy would come along and I told her so. And besides, I asked, "If you don't know any man who is interested in you, how are you going to experience sex? Mind you, marriage is not a requisite for taking the pill, nor is it my prerogative to know what you're going to do. But I consider you a friend, as well as a patient, and I'm interested."

She hesitated and then responded, "I want to tell you how fortunate I am. Because I have never had sex I am lucky to have found a nice fellow at work who has agreed to help me. He is going to come by my apartment on his way home, several nights a week, and teach me about sex. My sister says that after I've learned, I'll become more aggressive with men—and that will help me to get to know other men."

I thought, *My God! What kind of a sleazeball is planning to take advantage of this naive young woman? The lecherous S.O.B.!* Then I mentally calmed down. This wasn't my business. I wasn't about to inflict my morality on the rest of the world, especially not on Stella. Maybe her sister was right. I didn't really think so, but maybe I had undue confidence in Stella. I liked her, I certainly didn't want to see her hurt, and I felt that a relationship like the one she was proposing was doomed to failure. There was a pause in our conversation and I quickly realized that if I didn't respond immediately my silence could be construed as disapproving. I said, "You'll need a checkup before I prescribe a contraceptive. I'll have my nurse get you ready."

After the checkup and my discussion of how to use the pill, Stella left. I put the incident out of my mind. Stella showed up two weeks later. When I entered the exam room I noticed more animation in her face than I had ever seen before. She was obviously distraught. I thought, *Oh-oh, the deal has blown up and her feelings are hurt.* I was prepared to be sympathetic and supportive.

Stella said, "I threw up on my friend."

"You what?"

"Doctor, I was so nervous. He kissed me a lot and took my clothes off and I liked that; but then he took off his clothes and, when

I saw his thing, I threw up. It was so big and, when I thought he was going to stick it in me, I got scared. He got right out of bed and went home. The next day at work he asked me if I wanted to try it, again. I said sure. So, he came back last night and I did it again. When he left he said he wasn't going to put up with this. He told me to go to the doctor and get something to stop this throwing up. He said if I did it again, he wasn't going to come back. He said the smell of my vomit made him sick and, when he looked at me, that was all he could think of—and how the hell could he make love to me with that on his mind. Can you help me?"

I excused myself and left the room. I ran to my private office and, with the door closed, exploded with laughter, not at Stella, but at the lecherous S.O.B. covered with vomit. *Poor Stella. What an embarrassing thing for this poor woman to go through. I'll try to do something for her.*

I went back to Stella's room and we talked. I told her that, having done a pelvic exam two weeks earlier, I could assure her that penetration by her friend wouldn't hurt. I explained that it wasn't unusual to be nervous when doing something new and that some people respond to acute stress with an upset stomach. I gave her a prescription for a tranquilizer and told her to take it an hour before her friend arrived.

Stella was back in a week. The prescription hadn't worked and her friend had left and wasn't coming back. She said, "But I'm lucky. One of the girls at work recommended another fellow and he agreed. He's coming in a couple of days. Maybe his thing won't be so big and I won't be scared."

I assured Stella that most of those "things" looked alike and they were all about the same size. "We'll try another medication. This prescription is a sedative but also stops people from vomiting. You'll be all right this time."

The medication was Thorazine and maybe I gave her too large a dose. Stella went to sleep before her new friend arrived. This guy, after trying once, never came back, and Stella gave up. A tragedy? No! A year later she met Mr. Right and when she was in love, did what comes naturally. She never even thought about that big "thing," and she just made love. She married the man.

❧❧❧

Welby and Kiley prescribed contraceptive medication for Jamie Bell and they didn't consider her wanton; maybe a little mixed-up, but I made sure they informed her about the way to use the pill and the risk in taking it. I insisted that the writers put that into the script.

Jamie was separated from her husband and morose about her life. Her best friend, a swinging fashion model, encouraged her to get out of her slump and meet some guys. The implication being that a little extra-marital sex would be good for her.

Jamie Bell finds a guy to fool around with in the second act. His name is Sten. I thought this was a hoot and wondered at the time if this was the writer's double entendre. Sten is the name of a British rapid-fire gun and Sten was surely a "gunner." He provides Jamie with a case of gonorrhea and a pelvic infection that threatens her life and her ability to have children. In the last act, Jamie's husband forgives her by taking responsibility for the trouble in the marriage. They get back together and, supposedly, live happily ever after.

ைைை

When Peggy Pepper came to my office I saw a tall, rangy thirty-year-old dressed in stretch pants and a tight T-shirt, heavily made up, and sporting the latest beehive hairstyle. Peggy was a real-life patient and was not as lucky as Welby and Kiley's Jamie.

She was a new patient. The chart indicated that she had come in for a prescription for birth control pills. Peggy had left blank the part of her office admission questionnaire which indicated her marital status. I supposed this meant she was single. Her home address was listed as Inglewood, a good half hour's drive from my office and a drive which would pass a number of other doctors' offices. My natural curiosity caused me to wonder why she had come all the way to Manhattan Beach for a simple exam and a prescription for a contraceptive, so I asked her why and if she was referred to me.

"Yeah," she answered, "by a girl at work."

"Who? I'd like to thank her."

"Shit, I forgot her name."

Shit? The free speech people in Berkeley and San Francisco who were advocates of foul language hadn't really penetrated Manhattan Beach. Had they made it to Inglewood? I went on, "What type of contraception have you used in the past?"

"Rubbers, ticklers mostly. It makes the john—my boyfriend, John—happy."

I thought, *Wow, this girl is a hooker. Why does she want to switch from the safety of condoms to the risks of venereal disease by going bare?*

I remembered chatting with the hookers in Honolulu during World War II when, as a hospital corpsman in the Navy and serving on the Navy Shore Patrol, I accompanied the doctors on their biweekly rounds of the whorehouses to check the girls. I drew blood tests for syphilis while the doctors did pelvic exams, looking for gonorrhea. I usually finished before the others and sat around talking to the residents of the houses while they waited for the lines of servicemen who were standing in the street to re-start when we were finished. Jokingly, or maybe seriously, I was always offered a "freebie," but I never partook. Our presence had caused all activity to stop, which annoyed the hookers as well as the long lines of guys out in the street.

Few people knew that the U.S. Navy controlled prostitution in Hawaii, and brought women from the mainland to the Islands for that purpose. I remember a headline in the *Honolulu Advertiser* the day after a pay raise for servicemen was activated. The raise for a recruit went from twenty-one dollars a month to fifty dollars. The whores raised their fees from two dollars to three dollars, and the article in the *Advertiser* stated that the whorehouses would remain closed until they lowered their fees back to the original two dollars. They did it the same day.

I thought, *Maybe it's none of my business what this woman does, but as her physician I have to talk to her about the risk. If she gets up and leaves, so be it!* "How come you want to change, Peggy? You know you're taking a risk; your john may not be clean."

She took a hard look at me, hesitated, then said, "Okay, Doc, I'm a working girl, but I'm not a streetwalker; and I've got a high-class guy who's gonna set me up in my own place and I'll be his girl. Now, what's wrong with that?"

"Nothing, if you're sure of the guy; and if he is the only guy and you're his only girl."

I went ahead with her exam and prescribed her medication with all the usual words of caution. She came back in three months for a checkup. As we got to know each other better she told me she hadn't wanted a doctor where she lived, or where she might run into a cop, and had just picked me out of the phone book.

A year or so later Peggy called, said she had a stomachache, and needed to see me right away. I suspected the worst and I was right. She had a PID (pelvic inflammatory disease), probably due to gonorrhea (I wouldn't know that until I cultured her drainage), and needed to be hospitalized. I asked, "What happened, Peggy? Did you get a new boyfriend?"

"No, I've been straight with the sonofabitch, but he hasn't been straight with me. He thinks he's a real gunner, but all he's got is a water pistol, the S.O.B. How the hell can I afford to go to the hospital?"

Gunner, eh? I thought of the *Welby* segment and Sten. But Sten was imaginary and this was real. "Do you have any hospital insurance, Peggy?"

"Whores don't have a union. How the hell would I get insurance?"

"Peggy, I'll take care of you for nothing but you'll need to pay the hospital. Will your guy help out?"

"Help out? That S.O.B.? He'll kick my ass out of there if he finds out I'm sick. You've got to take care of me in the office. Once I'm okay, I'll leave that bastard."

"Peggy, you've got to go to the county hospital. This is too serious to be cared for as an outpatient. I'll call over there and get you admitted."

"Oh shit. The county hospital. How the hell did I get into this mess? What am I going to do when I get out and I have nowhere to go?"

"Get a new line of work, Peggy—get a new line of work."

She got well and called to tell me. She also said she was leaving town. She had, indeed, gotten kicked out of her apartment. She didn't say where she was going or what she was going to do. I never saw her or heard from her again.

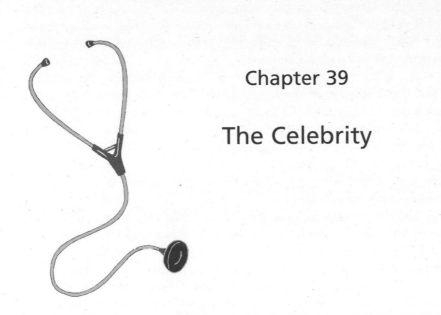

Chapter 39

The Celebrity

As a high school kid I wanted to be a celebrity. Because I was insecure as a teen, perhaps more than the usual adolescent, I sought recognition. But when I finally elected medicine as a career, I was no longer interested in fame. My purpose in life was to be focused on humanity and service.

Being the *Marcus Welby, M.D.* technical advisor didn't make me famous. The stars were famous. My experience with Jim Brolin on the Santa Monica freeway is a case in point. I have never been able to imagine what it would be like to have (or to suffer) the instant recognition of everyone in the Western world. Robert Young had that kind of recognition and, to some degree, so did Jim Brolin. Both of these actors had distinctive, handsome features. When you saw Robert Young you knew immediately who he was. But if you saw Max Gale or James Sikking walking toward you, you might think, that face is familiar, I wonder if he is an actor?

Bob could not walk down a street, dine in a restaurant, shop in a store, ride on an airplane, travel on a cruise ship, or do anything in a public place without having people stare, ask for an autograph, point, whisper, or criticize every action.

Some celebrities are able to tolerate this type of intrusion into their privacy better than others. It's well and good to say that fame is the price stars pay for all the money they earn and that they should be responsive to their public. Living in a glass house isn't all that great, even if no one is throwing rocks at it. My brief periods in the spotlight were not enough to test my tolerance for recognition.

Being the only doctor in "show biz" in the South Bay beach cities of Manhattan Beach, Hermosa, Redondo, Torrance, and Palos Verdes Estates made me the butt of a great deal of humor among my colleagues, but it didn't translate into public recognition. Newspaper stories about the strange development of my career informed the patients in my practice about what I was doing, but I sensed that they were sort of proud that their doctor was in the public eye. I don't believe that I gained or lost a patient due to my outside activities.

The doctor who was the technical advisor to the movie *M.A.S.H.* actually had a bit role in the picture. He was in several of the scenes doing surgical procedures. In these scenes his face was always covered by a surgical mask, but he enjoyed the opportunity to play at being an actor. His medical specialty was thoracic surgery. Since he was a handsome, young single guy, a movie career seemed appealing to him; so after the movie he joined the Screen Actors Guild, took acting lessons, hired an agent, and sought a career in film. He probably wasn't a very good actor—he never got a decent role. Whereas he was sought after socially when he was a single, good-looking thoracic surgeon, when he became just another out-of-work actor he was no longer popular with hostesses. He had given up his career in medicine for the tenuous opportunities offered in theater and it didn't pan out. Rumor had it that he turned to drugs and died.

When David Victor asked me, half seriously, to take a minor role in one of the *Welby* episodes, I thought I should reject the idea out of hand; but the role he offered was appealing. We were finally getting around to the concept that had gotten me involved in the first place—they were going to showcase a family practice residency program. If I accepted I would be cast as the somewhat grouchy old residency director (certainly authentic typecasting). David anticipated my hesitation and before I could answer he said, characteristically, "Think it over tonight and give me your answer tomorrow."

That night at home I did think it over. I considered the same points I had thought about when I accepted the T.A. job. I worried about getting too heavily involved in the Hollywood scene and I reviewed in my mind what had happened to the people I had known—Lana Turner, Hal March, the *M.A.S.H.* technical advisor—but I also thought about the appeal of the role of being a family practice residency program director on TV, a role I was filling in real life. Being a program director means being a teacher, advisor, mentor, leader, and surrogate father. I could demonstrate this to the public.

☙❦❧

After dinner that night, when the kids were in bed, I sat down to think about whether or not to take the role and dabble in the art of acting. I began to remember a few of the experiences I'd had with some of the young men and women who had come my way in my present role of residency director.

There was the first year resident who came to me during the Fourth of July picnic Glad and I held each year for the residents and their families. He told me that, after only four days as a doctor, he wanted to quit. I said, "Jodie, for God's sake, why? You've gone through all of these years of education—college and medical school; you have been a doctor for four days, and you want to quit?"

He answered, "I don't think I'm good enough for this; I want to get out of medicine altogether."

I grabbed him by the arm and led him into the house. When he was seated in my living room, I said, "Let's talk this out, Jodie. You've too much invested in your career to make a judgment like this so quickly. What happened to you?" I sensed he had suffered some traumatic event which had brought him to this kind of rash decision. Possibly he had been on call and was pooped. He certainly seemed depressed. Fatigue could cause people to behave strangely; and I remembered Bill Barkley, Maybelle's husband.

Jodie said, "Doctor, it's the dying. I can't stand it when people die and it might be my fault. When I'm on duty and people die and I'm helpless to do anything about it, it tears me up inside. When I was in med school and working on the wards, the residents were responsible; but now I'm a resident, I'm responsible, and I can't take it. I'm going to quit!"

We talked it out. Jodie told me he had been on call and three people had died on his shift. He admitted he was tired but didn't think it was fatigue that had brought him to this decision. "I just don't think I'm ever going to be able to handle this kind of emotional trauma," he said.

I called the senior resident in from the picnic. He was vehement that what had happened on Jodie's call was not his fault. He had done a fine job, all anyone could have done. People die despite everything medicine has to offer. Death doesn't necessarily mean failure. Failure is in not providing for patients during their last days, controlling their pain, and supporting them and their families. The senior resident and I reassured Jodie with that information. We counseled him to have a couple of beers with us, get a good night's sleep, and we would talk about it again the next day.

When Jodie and I spoke about this again, I found him in a much better mood, and we decided to give it more time before making any decisions. I told him that he and I would talk about his cases and his feelings in depth over the next few months and re-evaluate his future as we went along. We did just that. Jodie developed a greater sense of security in himself and eventually conquered his personal concerns. If anything, the experience had made him stronger and he remained an extremely sensitive and exacting physician.

And then, there was Carlton. Carlton was gay. We didn't learn about that until he was in his second year of training, when I decided that each resident should be given a complete physical examination by a member of the faculty in order to be sure these young doctors were healthy; also they would have a living template of a physical exam on which to base their own practice.

Each of the residents was assigned to a faculty member. I did the first exam and it went off without a hitch; but on the second day of doing physicals my most senior faculty member stormed into my office, raging at me, "You lunatic! This idea of yours to do physicals is crazy. I won't do it. It's crazy. You're a damn fool. You've got to stop this thing right away! I won't do any more!" He literally was sputtering.

I said, "Jim, calm down. What happened?"

"I can't tell you. Just don't ask me to do another physical on a resident."

"Let's see, you were assigned Carlton, weren't you? What happened, did you find out that he's gay?"

"How did you know that?"

I said, "I guessed. But, so what? Did he tell you?"

Jim wouldn't answer, except to say, "What he told me is confidential."

"Sure it is, Jim; but, if he told you, he wanted you to know. Maybe he wants out of the closet. That might be the best thing for him. I'll bet in a couple of days everyone will know because he'll have found a way to tell people. This isn't going to interfere with his work or his health, so let's you and I forget we talked about it."

I was wrong, in one sense. Ten years later Carlton died of AIDS.

Becky was a transfer from another program. She was never at peace with herself, the staff, or the faculty. At first impression the woman was a troublemaker. The nurses couldn't stand her. The appointment clerks threatened to quit. No one could please Becky. I had to call her to my office more than any other resident to answer complaints about her relationships with the other residents and the staff, but I never had a complaint from a patient. When it came to the care she gave her patients, Becky wouldn't compromise. She bedeviled the appointment clerks to work in her patients against the rules for fair time allotment we had established for the clinic, and she drove the nurses to exasperation, expecting special care for the people she was treating. Becky demanded perfection and the world never quite lived up to her expectations.

Antonio was seeing a patient in the family practice ambulatory center. I went into the examining room with him after he reported his findings and treatment plan to me. He had advised me that he had seen a thirty-eight-year-old woman with an inflamed pharynx, a fever, and swollen glands. He wanted to do a streptococcus screen and treat her with penicillin. Sounded good to me. When I checked the patient her physical findings were as he stated, but there was something else. By her verbal responses and by her body language this patient exhibited typical signs of depression, more than one would expect simply from the acute illness.

After we left the room, I asked Antonio if there was anything else wrong with the patient.

"Of course. She's depressed as hell," he responded.

The specialty of Family Practice takes the position that the whole patient needs to be treated and that behavioral problems should be accorded the same vigor as physical problems. So, I said, "What are you going to do about that?" I assumed that I would get an answer such as, "I'll ask her to come back for a recheck for her sore throat and then I'll try to find out if I can help her with her depression."

Instead, he answered, "I'm not going to open that can of worms."

Antonio and I had a series of talks and, at the end of them, we decided that maybe family practice wasn't the best place for him in medicine. At the end of the year I helped to place him in an emergency medicine residency where he would not have the depth of involvement with patients demanded of him in our field.

Charlie was the program's free spirit. He had long stringy hair, and wore a peace medal, sandals, and a shirt open down to the navel (unless I caught him and made him button up). I wasn't strict on dress code, but I did feel that a doctor's professionalism is reassuring to patients and a part of that professionalism is appropriate attire.

I didn't wear a tie in my private office in the summer. I have always hated ties as part of the male uniform. To me it has always been a soup-catcher, an adult-male bib.

Charlie rode a Harley hog and lived an avant-garde life in Topanga Canyon. I accepted him into the program as a second year resident to fill the slot of Antonio who, by then, was gone. I had funding for Charlie for one year only; but that was okay with him. He had avowed that his purpose in joining the program was not to become a family physician. He was using the experience to prepare for missionary work in Africa.

One day Charlie came to work with his feet in bandages. When I asked him what the problem was he replied that it was from his organic garden. That seemed strange to me so I asked him to explain.

Charlie said, "I had to plow the garden yesterday."

"What's that got to do with it?" I asked.

"Well, you can't plow an organic garden with your shoes on."

"Oh? So what happened to your feet?"

"Well, the garden is the site of an old dump and it was full of broken glass and tin cans."

I hoped Charlie's organic garden wasn't being grown in a dump that had been used for toxic waste. He won first prize that year in the Santa Monica pumpkin-growing contest.

Charlie was a fine doctor and, with his indomitable spirit, a lovely human being. Near the end of the year, when it was time for Charlie to leave, he came to my office and said, "I've changed my mind; I want to be a family physician. I want to sit for the board exams and do the whole bit. So, I want you to take me for another year."

I said, "I can't, Charlie. I haven't the funding for another position, and you know all of our spots are filled."

Charlie replied, "I'll work for nothing. I'll do you a good job and I'll help teach, as the other senior residents do. You won't be sorry. Please, this means a lot to me."

"First of all, Charlie, you can't work for nothing. I can't have two classes of residents. Furthermore, you would have to do something to support yourself and it would take so much of your time that the year wouldn't be fruitful for you." I was tempted, though. I liked Charlie a whole lot and I admired his *joie de vivre*. So, I said, "Tell you what I'll do: I'll go to the administration and ask for enough money to fund you for another year if you will promise to do something for me." I was pretty sure that the administration would back me for another resident.

"I'll do anything."

"Okay, Charlie, here's what I want: Wear your hair short." His face fell as I continued, "Wear a necktie every day, get rid of your sandals and wear shoes, and, most important, be a role model for the junior residents."

He never hesitated. He said, "I'll do it."

And he did all of it. On July first, the first day of the new academic year and not one day before, Charlie showed up, as promised. I won't say that he acted like Andy Hardy or Tom Swift all year but he did what he had promised, took his board exams, and went off to Africa—still a free spirit, but a neater looking one.

⚬⚭⚬

When I returned from my evening reverie I realized how much I enjoyed medicine and teaching and that I couldn't do anything to alter my lifetime goals. The next day I told David Victor no. He said, "You'd have been great in the part, just the kind of an old curmudgeon I wanted."

The studio wanted me to take an active role in the promotion of the show despite the disastrous results I'd had at the Anaheim Convention Center with Joseph Campanella. It wasn't long before I received a call from Southern Methodist University asking me to speak at a large alumni meeting. Concurrently, I received a call from the local ABC television outlet, in Dallas, to do a guest appearance on an early morning talk show. I was pleased to be asked to do something such as this, the honorarium was good, and I'd never been to Texas.

The timing wasn't great, as the TV appearance was the same morning as the evening speech at S.M.U., necessitating my arriving in Dallas the night before. I then would have almost a full day to kill before the speech and I still would have to wait over until the following day before returning home. Not so good for a busy doctor. The TV studio announced they would have me picked up at my hotel at four o'clock in the morning. "Four A.M., for God's sake. Why so early?"

"Doctor, the show is on from 5 to 7 A.M., and with the time it will take to get you there, plus your time in makeup, we feel an hour before showtime isn't too early."

Makeup? Must be the big time! "What time will I go on?"

"We don't know exactly—sometime between five and seven."

Don't know exactly? Must be flying by the seat of the pants! Not the big time. "The restaurant at the hotel won't be open that early. What about breakfast?"

"Not to worry, Doctor. We'll have coffee at the studio and after the show we want you to be our guest at Brennan's for breakfast."

Gee, it is big time, after all. Brennan's, the famous New Orleans restaurant, had just opened a branch in Dallas. "Okay for 4 A.M. I'll be ready."

I hadn't slept well. It was hot. In fact, when I got off the plane, upon arrival, I thought I'd never been so hot before in my entire life. Coming from Oregon and coastal California, I wasn't used to the humidity. Where I came from, when the sun went down the temperature went down. Not in Texas, not even in an air-conditioned hotel. I was hot and uncomfortable, and perhaps somewhat anxious about my debut on talk-show television. When the car came to pick me up at 4 A.M., I was bleary-eyed with fatigue and anxiety. The cheerful crowd at the studio and a couple of cups of steaming coffee didn't do much to relieve my tension, but the coffee did help to wake me up.

When I went into makeup, a bored, bleached-blond guy in a smock wiped my forehead with a towel that contained a powdery substance and said, "Try not to sweat, dearie."

Dearie?

I went back to the control room and watched the two anchors on camera grinning and giggling while reading the news from teleprompters. This patter was interspersed with a guest during each half-hour segment. It soon became obvious that I was destined for the last segment, between six-thirty and seven. For this I had gotten up at three-thirty and had sat for two and a half hours waiting for my turn? I was grumpy when the makeup artist came back at 6:30, looked at me and said, "I asked you not to sweat." He swiped at my forehead again with the towel.

I griped, "You wouldn't have had to do that, again, if I had been on sooner."

As he left, mincing his way out of the room, he said, "They keep the best for the last. More audience near seven o'clock, dearie."

Dearie?

During the break for the weather and five minutes of network news, the woman anchor came in and asked, "What would you like to talk about?" Without waiting for an answer, she then proceeded to tell me what we were going to talk about, which included my role in the show, did directors really pay attention to what I told them or was I just window dressing, and where and what was I going to speak about that night. When I told her that the title of my presentation at S.M.U. was "What if Marcus Welby Practiced in Texas?" she asked what would be the difference between Dallas and Los Angeles. She seemed to be satisfied when I said that he would be a Cowboys fan instead of a Rams fan and that he would be a Dallas Texans fan instead of a fan of the L.A. Dodgers. Fortunately, on camera, we got somewhat deeper into the differences between L.A. and Dallas.

During my ten or twelve minutes on camera, under the lights, I began to sweat again; but "Dearie" didn't return to wipe my brow. After the first couple of minutes, when I stopped shaking, the interview was quite positive—a good plug for the show and a good plug for the new specialty of Family Practice. Of course, the studio people were quite complimentary about my performance. Well, you wouldn't expect them to tell me I stunk up the place; but they seemed sincere and I got over my grouchy start as we breakfasted in style at Brennan's.

After breakfast, the PR guy from the local studio and his assistant asked me what I wanted to do. Was there a place I would like them to drop me off? I said, "No, nothing special. I guess I would like to be dropped at my hotel. I'm pretty pooped, you know, and boy, it's hot. If I don't get out of this suit I may sweat to death."

They agreed, but first said they wished to take me past the place where President Kennedy was assassinated. I pointed out that the cab driver the night before had taken me there and that I had seen the grassy knoll and the book repository, that it was hot and I was tired, and that it might be better if we just went back to the hotel.

"Nonsense," said my host. "Cab drivers don't tell you the real story. It's really not much out of the way. We want to show you the place." And they did. It was the same as when the cab driver had done it. The next day on the way to the airport to go home the second cab driver insisted on going past the spot and pointing out the sites, as did every cab driver and host I had in Dallas during the many trips I made there over the next several years. There must have been such a sense of guilt among the people of Dallas during those years that taking visitors to the site was a type of pilgrimage for them, a way of atoning and apologizing.

On the way back to the hotel my hospitable host continued to point out other city landmarks—the last one before reaching the hotel was the famous department store, Nieman Marcus. Now there was a place I said I would like to visit. My host pointed one block ahead and said, "There is your hotel. Why don't I let you out here? You can enjoy

Nieman Marcus and have only a short walk back to your hotel when you're ready." I thanked him and went into the store. Oh, blessed air conditioning!

At first glance Nieman Marcus looked like any other department store in a large city. It looked like the Emporium in San Francisco; Meier & Frank in Portland; Stix, Baer, and Fuller in Kansas City and St. Louis,;or May Company in Los Angeles. But I wasn't going to be content to simply look at the areas of the store that looked like all the rest—I wanted to get to the part where they showed those wonderful items that came out in their Christmas catalogue every year. I wandered around the first floor, thinking I might pick up a little gift for Glad. I knew she would get a kick out of having something from the fabulous Nieman Marcus. It needed to be something with a label on it, but cosmetics wouldn't do. I went to a counter where the store displayed scarves and, as I picked up a scarf to look at it, I inadvertently bumped the elbow of a woman who was also checking out the scarves. I said, "Excuse me."

When I spoke the woman turned toward me, studied my face for a moment, and let out a shriek. I really didn't think I had bumped her that hard, so I quickly said, "Oh, I'm so sorry. I hope I didn't hurt you."

She shrieked, again, "My God, I saw you on television this morning! You're from Hollywood!" By now people were looking our way. She went on, "You're the *Marcus Welby* guy." Looking around and recognizing that her audience was growing, she announced in a loud voice to one and all, "This is the doctor from *Marcus Welby!*" And then she said, "May I have your autograph?"

Autograph? Me? She must think I'm someone else. Once, someone took me for Caesar Romero even though we really didn't look much alike. But she says she's seen me on television. But I didn't take the role on the series. I'd never been on television. Oh, my God, she's serious! She saw me this morning being interviewed and after only that meager performance she wants an autograph? I've never given or asked for an autograph from anyone. How do I do it?

The lady had thrust a piece of paper in my face and was saying, "Please make it to Joanie." I had nothing to write with. As I looked around helplessly the salesperson at the scarf counter rescued me by handing me her pen and a piece of paper saying, "I'm next."

I signed both of the scraps of paper, writing, "Yours truly" and my name, probably quite a dumb thing to write, but I wasn't experienced in this sort of thing. Hearing a noise, I looked up to behold a frightening sight. I was surrounded by at least two dozen people, each holding something I could write on—jostling each other for position to be next in line to get the signature of a celebrity, many of whom I'm sure had not the faintest idea who I was, and if they had would have promptly gotten out of the crowd.

I learned fast. Before I was finished, I was smiling and talking to the people and answering their questions. When it was over and there were no more autograph seekers, I decided to forgo the pleasure of touring the store and risk meeting another observant early morning television watcher. I bought Glad a leather purse and hurried to my hotel. As I entered the elevator I noticed a sign that read, THE HOTEL MANAGEMENT WISHES TO APOLOGIZE FOR THE INCONVENIENCE CAUSED BY THE FAILURE OF THE AIR-CONDITIONING SYSTEM. IT WILL BE REPAIRED PROMPTLY. SHOULD YOU WISH AN ELECTRIC FAN BROUGHT TO YOUR ROOM, PLEASE CALL THE DESK.

In the middle of the afternoon, lying on my bed clad only in a pair of undershorts, with the fan turned fully on me but with sleep escaping me due to the heat, I pondered the life of a celebrity. My experience that morning, after I overcame my surprise and trepidation, had been kind of fun. It had been nice having people interested in me even if for the wrong reasons. Wouldn't it have been nicer if they had wanted my autograph because of some outstanding feat of medical science I had just performed or because I was the finest doctor in the...and I guess I drifted off to sleep.

The next morning, when I arrived at the airport, there was a long line in front of the metal detector at the airport security station. One of the security officers came out from behind the machine and took me by the arm saying, "I'll take you through this closed line so you won't have to wait. I saw you on television yesterday morning. *Marcus Welby* is my favorite TV show."

Who said fame doesn't pay?

As a teenager, when I sought fame as a way of bolstering my depleted self-image, I didn't know I would eventually enter the most important of all professions. When I was accepted to medical school I resolved I would try to bring credit to medicine and work in its best interest. I wasn't aware of the opportunities that would open up for me in pursuing that goal. In 1972, the 3,000 member California chapter of the American Academy of Family Physicians honored me by selecting me as their president. My installation was held in the hotel where the scientific meetings were held that year, the Westin Century Plaza in Los Angeles. The hotel property backs up to the Metro lot where my daughter and I attended the fabulous opening of the motion picture *Star.* Because the academy booked so many rooms, the hotel gave us the presidential suite for my use. On the morning we occupied that prestigious suite of rooms, President Nixon had just moved out. Glad and I felt like royalty. The luster has worn off after these many years, as the glory of sleeping in the same bed as a sitting president has declined, along with that president's image.

At the end of *my* presidency I received a visit from the executive director of the American Academy of Family Physicians National Headquarters in Kansas City. He brought an offer to join the headquarters staff as the head of all the educational activities of the national association. The Academy's primary mission was twofold: provide and accredit continuing education for its members, and support existing residency programs while helping to create new ones. I was floored with the magnitude of the offer and the opportunity to became a national pioneer and leader in the development of our new specialty that had been created only four years earlier, in 1969. But I would have to leave everything: my patients, the residents, the *Welby* show—and our kids.

We had a family conference. As a family we had always settled issues pertaining to all of us in a somewhat democratic fashion, with Glad and I as the convenors and benign despots. In other words, each person got to speak and their ideas were considered, and then the despots made the decision.

Pamela said, "You'd be leaving us. We'd have no home. You can't do that." Of course Pamela was in college and came home for a square meal once in a while, and to get her laundry done.

Lee said, "Dad, you're a Californian, your father was born in California. You can't leave California. I'm a Californian; don't expect me to go to Kansas City." Lee was working, had an apartment in West L.A., and came home less often than Pamela. I pointed out to him that he was born in Oregon, as was his mother, so it was true that we were West Coast people; but it might be fun to see what the rest of the world was like.

Don had already left home. He and his wife were doing graduate work at Michigan State in Lansing. By phone, Don thought it was a good idea; Kansas City was a lot closer to Michigan than California was.

It took us a year to make up our minds but, in the end, it boiled down to where I could do the greatest good. Should I remain in California, taking care of individual patients, and each year teaching residents and students to care for people, thereby increasing—in a positive way—the number of lives my efforts would impact? Or should I move to the national headquarters of the American Academy of Family Physicians, where there would be an opportunity to exert influence on the way health care was going to be delivered in America, forever?

In the end I chose Kansas City.

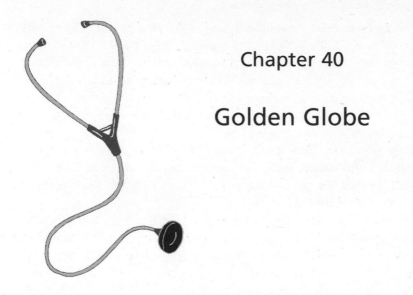

Chapter 40

Golden Globe

Betty Young phoned Glad and said, "Glad, Bobby and I are so sorry that you're leaving us. Bobby has so much faith in Tom, he is just beside himself, but we know that it's something you want to do and we wish you all the best. You know, the show has been nominated for a Golden Globe Award. Bobby doesn't think we'll win but we're going, anyway. We have four tickets. As a going away present, will you go with us? Will you?"

Glad told me she was almost speechless, but not quite. She was able to say, "We'd love to, Betty."

Betty explained that it was a black tie dinner affair at the Beverly Hilton Hotel, gave the date and time, and then said, "It will probably be better if we arrive in one car—parking is such a problem, even though they have attendants to deal with it. And we'll go to a party or two in the hotel after the awards dinner is over, in order to avoid the autograph hunters that hang around outside. You know how Bobby hates that." She suggested that we drive our car from Palos Verdes Estates to the Beverly Hills Hotel, park there, and meet them in the bar. She said, "You remember, it's where we had lunch a few weeks ago; Bobby knows the manager and will tell them you're coming."

❧⚘❧

You bet we remembered the Beverly Hills Hotel and the imaginary red carpet that was rolled out when we said we were meeting the Youngs. We also remembered the quiet graciousness of the lobby and dining room. Yes, and we remembered the fuss when an enthusiastic autograph hunter (probably a tourist) came to our table and asked Bob Young for his autograph. Bob gruffly refused. The maitre d' hôtel, alert to what was going on, hustled the tourist away amid the complaint, "I only asked him for his autograph, for Christ's sake; I didn't want to have lunch with him." I really didn't understand the fuss, either. Remember, by then, I'd been to Texas and Nieman Marcus and was happy to deal with autograph seekers; but then, the guy hadn't asked me.

The Beverly Hills Hotel, like so many of the posh Beverly Hills bistros of the day such as Chasen's and Scandia, wanted to keep their restaurants as retreats for the rich and famous. I recall having to go through Universal Studio's public relations office to obtain a reservation at Chasen's when entertaining a visiting dignitary from the American Academy of Family Physicians. The food was okay, but maybe the most fun at Chasen's was the mime doing a Charlie Chaplin bit on the sidewalk as we exited our car. This was a show to spend time watching, but not too much time; your reservation might be canceled if you were late.

The luncheon that day at the Beverly Hills Hotel was memorialized for Glad and me with a gift from Betty. She always had a little gift for each special event. Her thoughtfulness that day was a portable backgammon set that, she explained, we could use when we traveled. She told us that she and Bobby never got on a plane without one. She knew that Bob and I occasionally played backgammon in his trailer on the set and maybe she hoped that, with a little practice, I would improve my game and make it more interesting for him. The Youngs arrived driving their own black Oldsmobile Tornado. It was the only time I ever saw them when they weren't driven in a studio-provided limousine.

❧⚘❧

Preparations for the momentous night at the Golden Globe dinner occupied an inordinate amount of our family's time. Glad proudly wore a stunning creation Lee had spent his hard-earned money for and had brought to her before the affair. Wonder of wonders, it fit! Both Pamela and Lee were devotees of film and TV and advised us who to look for. I had to find my old tux, get it cleaned, buy a new shirt, and find my cuff links. Both children, home to help us get ready for the big event, were standing in the driveway when we left in our freshly washed Lincoln convertible, waving goodbye and telling us to have fun, with joy and a bit of envy shining out of their eyes.

After all the fuss, while driving north on the San Diego freeway, I began to wonder if we were going to a show biz party or a presidential inauguration. Despite my association with a few Hollywood folks, the only major event I had ever attended was the opening of Julie Andrews in *Star,* but on this occasion we were part of the scene, sponsored by the Youngs, an entrée I hoped would smooth our path. As a farewell to Hollywood, this was one hell of a party to bow out on.

The only Hollywood parties that Glad and I regularly attended was the cast party every fall at the end of shooting of the *Marcus Welby, M.D.* show. Thinking about those cast parties made me wonder if perhaps they weren't more fun than this stuffy, formal, Hollywood extravaganza was going to be.

The cast parties each year featured an hour-long film of outtakes. This was probably the funniest TV never shown to the public. It couldn't be shown because some of the language would not have been allowed on the network. A blown line often resulted in, "Oh sh...!" Or a botched medical term sometimes resulted in a tangled tongue that caused such glee on the set that production had to be stopped long enough to restore order. Changing a medical word to a lay term so that the actor could pronounce it was done a lot. Some of the dumb, funny dialogue by the stars and the weekly guest stars, which didn't show the persona they wished presented to the public, had to be cut; but it did wonders to relieve the boredom of filming.

❧

When we had been sitting in the bar of the Beverly Hills Hotel for about thirty minutes, the Youngs' driver came in to tell us they were ready and it was time to go. We had been early. I was nervous about being late as I didn't want the Youngs kept waiting. Glad used to kid me, saying, "I'll bet you were a premature baby, and you are spending your life being ahead of time." While waiting, we had a Coke. I thought a real drink might have quieted my butterflies, but later it became obvious that a before-the-party drink wasn't necessary.

Betty was dressed in the style she affected, a one-of-a-kind dress, all flounces and lace. Bob was splendid in his tuxedo. As Betty predicted, there was a traffic jam in front of the Beverly Hilton Hotel. No one was allowed to leave their vehicle until it arrived in front of the red carpet that ran into the lobby between velvet-covered ropes. There were crowds, outside the velvet ropes, who applauded as the guests exited their cars. This time I wasn't nonplused by the applause, as it was obviously for the star of the show. There were cameras and reporters along the route into the lobby, but Bob waved them off and we proceeded to our table.

The room was arranged in round tables that seated ten guests. Our reserved table was an ideal location on an elevated area off the center of the room, but out of the crowded pit. The view of the proceedings from our location was unobstructed. We were the first at our table. As I looked around the room I saw the cast of *Jesus Christ Superstar* just below us in the pit, and at the next table the entire cast of the *Mod Squad.*

There were place cards on the table. Glad and I were seated together. On my left was Julie London, who played the role of a nurse as the star of *Emergency;* and to Glad's right, Julie London's husband, the musician and composer Bobby Troop. Betty Young was on Bobby Troop's right with her Bobby to her right. Next to him was Mrs. Peter Falk and Columbo, himself, on her right. Finishing the table were the producers of *Columbo* and *Emergency* and their wives. Glad and I were the lucky ones—Julie London and Bobby Troop were ideal dinner partners. Peter Falk lived up to his reputation of being a grump and rude. Without eavesdropping, I'm sure Bob Young out-grumped him, while remaining a gentleman.

When Julie London arrived, she did so in a manner that everyone assumes is the norm for a Hollywood star. Julie was dressed in a tight-fitting, beaded white sheath. With one hand she was dragging a full-length sable coat along the floor. I whispered to Glad, "Horrors, she'll get it dirty!" She leaned over toward me and said, "Don't worry about it; she probably has two or three of them and will wear a different one tomorrow night." With her other hand Julie was waving and greeting folks along the way. When she arrived at the table she looked at my place card and said, "You're the REAL doctor on *Welby?* I'm the nurse on *Emergency*. We'll have a lot to talk about. Let's have a drink." She seemed a little tipsy. I decided she must have been to a party before the party.

I looked at this woman and thought, *She looks delicious.* What a gorgeous creature she was and, with that dress, every movement she made caused a ripple, somewhere. Glad, on the other side, was involved with Bobby Troop as they shared a love of music. The Youngs were busy accepting congratulations (about the nomination and success of the show) from numerous people who dropped by. The two producers at the other end of the table talked business all evening and Peter Falk was gone most of the time. Maybe he went to the bar. That wouldn't have been necessary, as the drinks at the table were plentiful. Julie and I had several. Because she had a head start, I thought she showed it more than I, but isn't that the usual impression? (You're acting funny, but I'm okay). At any rate, I was having a very good time and so was Glad. I noticed that Glad and Bobby were exchanging addresses and phone numbers. Had I been a suspicious man I might have begun to worry, but neither of us had ever worried about the loyalty of the other. With the foundation we had in our marriage we never had cause to worry about each other. About a week later a package in the mail for Glad turned out to be a signed copy of a piece of piano music written by Bobby Troop.

I told Julie about my practice and about the residency at Santa Monica Hospital. She made an astute remark. "How come," she said, "you didn't start the Family Practice residency at St. John's Hospital where Welby practices? The opening of the show even shows stock shots of St. John's."

I answered, "That's one of the incongruities of television. *Welby* is a dramatic show, not a docudrama; but by showing a real hospital this does suggest a real relationship. However, St. John's Hospital has a policy excluding family doctors from their staff. All their doctors are from the limited specialties. On the other hand, they are happy to have the positive publicity of a picture of their hospital on prime time every Tuesday night and, apparently, glad to have Welby and Kiley, a pair of family doctors, admit patients to the hospital on television—even if not in real life."

"Gee, can't you get the producers of the show to switch? How come they used St. John's to begin with when they could have used Santa Monica Hospital and been authentic? You've been telling me your job is to make sure that the medical scenes are authentic; how come they don't want the entire show authentic?"

"Julie, I'm not even going to try to get them to change. Their intro is established; it's a hallmark for the series. They used St. John's because the guys who started the show knew about St. John's and knew nothing of the politics of the hospitals in Santa Monica."

"Bull," she said, "I'd change it." We each took a sip of the drinks in front of us and glanced around the room.

Had I been starstruck I suppose I would have surveyed the scene more intently than I did. All the stars were there. I saw Carol Burnett across the room and the beautiful Angie Dickenson a couple of tables away; but I never had been tempted to try to meet celebrities. Though I have cherished a couple of chance meetings with sports stars.

❦

I wonder what percentage of Americans pass through O'Hare Airport in Chicago at some time in their lives? I have been there dozens of times. People who fly Delta Airlines a lot have been heard to remark, "To get to heaven it's probably necessary to go through Atlanta." Well, on most airlines, to get to hell, it may be necessary to go through O'Hare. Some say, "When you're at O'Hare, you're already there."

Perhaps one of the most memorable times at the Chicago airport was the night when, on my way from visiting Don in Lansing, Michigan, I missed my dinner flight to L.A. Because my plane was delayed in Lansing, I was to be on a night flight with no meal service for the remainder of the trip. I did what thousands of airline passengers do every day—I bought a hot dog and a Coke. The snack bar didn't have regular chairs and tables; instead, there were several tall stand-up tables where a customer could put the food while applying condiments such as mustard and catsup. Then, if desired, a person could stand there and eat. Not a very restful place for a tired traveler. I took my hot dog over to one of the communal stands that was free at the moment, and slathered the wiener with mustard. As I was taking my first bite I realized I was being joined by another diner. I didn't look up, but I couldn't avoid seeing that I was staring at the belt buckle of my dinner partner. I also saw that he had a hearty appetite and was holding two hot dogs in each hand, plus a large drink. I could not restrain myself and glanced up to see a grinning face, somewhat over seven feet toward the ceiling.

The grinning face of Lew Alcindor, later to become Kareem Abdul-Jabbar, was recognizable to any Los Angeleno who had any sports knowledge at all. I was a sports fan and followed UCLA basketball. I hesitated before speaking, as the newspapers had repeatedly stated that Alcindor was a shy and perhaps very neurotic person being shielded from the public by John Wooden, "The Wizard of Westwood." His shielding of Lew Alcindor was thought to be more directed toward his wishing to preserve his star for basketball, rather than aiding in the development of the young man's personality. The Lew Alcindor who was grinning at me didn't seem remote or shy.

I said, "Hi."

Alcindor said, "Isn't much of a dinner, is it? You through with the mustard?"

"Sure, take it." I thought I was lucky to have arrived first, as when he got through painting all those buns there wouldn't be any more mustard.

I took the bit in my teeth and decided to talk a little basketball. "I sure admire the way the UCLA team is going this year. What's your prediction for the season?"

"We're going to take the national title."

Well, the kid wasn't shy. And he was right.

That same year I was the president of the California Chapter of the American Academy of Family Physicians. We were very much interested in improving health care in the inner city and supported the development of medical services in under-served neighborhoods. When the Martin Luther King Hospital opened, I was invited for a tour of the facility. I was hosted by Dr. Ludlow Creary, chairman of the Department of Family Practice at the Charles Drew Graduate Medical School in the Watts community. As Dr. Creary, a young intern named David Satcher (now the Surgeon General of the United States), several others from the hospital, and I rounded a corner in the hall, we ran into another touring group. There was no question that this was a more high powered group. The dean of the medical school and an L.A. supervisor were there, as well as the chiefs of several medical services and a very big guy who was obviously the star attraction, Mr. Muhammad Ali.

The big guy was grinning at the confusion resulting from the two groups bumping into each other. Dr. Creary rose to the occasion, saying, "I would like you to meet each other," and mentioned both of our names. We both stuck out our hands in a gesture designed to say hello to each other in the accustomed way, but it wasn't going to happen the usual way. I put out my hand with my elbow straight and my fingers pointing toward Ali, while he put his hand out with his elbow bent at a right angle and with his fingers pointing up and curled a little. Whoops! We both saw that we had misjudged the other and we both tried, again. My fingers were up, Ali's pointing straight ahead. We missed, again. We each went back to our original method. We were getting nowhere. By this time Ali was laughing so hard his sides were shaking. I was shaking, too, believing I might have blown the whole thing.

Both entourages were nervous, fearing some kind of a racial incident was about to occur. However, the self-proclaimed "World's Greatest Fighter" solved the situation with a huge laugh and the statement, "Let's get this thing right and say hello to each other; we'll do it your way." We both extended our hands with our fingers pointing at each other and my hand disappeared. He had the biggest mitt I had ever seen, including Kareem Abdul-Jabbar's. Fortunately, he was a gentle man and didn't squeeze. We chatted for a minute and separated. I can't forget Ali as he was then. Even though I am not a boxing fan I admired the "Great Man" for his athletic ability, his commitment to his religious principles, his marketing ability, and his charming personality.

～✕✕✕～

When I first became a country doctor, my colleagues in city practice used to kid me about the description—straw in the hair, manure on the boots, and a case to discuss—of a country doctor. Julie London's coiffure was impeccable, her silver spiked-heel pumps were uncontaminated, and she was no country doctor but she, also, had a case.

She said, "On *Emergency* we had this case, a few weeks ago, in which a patient came into the hospital having had a heart attack and went into cardiac arrest. We did CPR but it wasn't doing any good, and the script said to stop trying to start this man's heart; but it didn't give the director any dialogue or instruction about who should make the decision. I suppose they just meant for us to have a fade-out and go to the next scene. The director wasn't happy with this and had the doctor leave the room and the fade occurring while I was disconnecting the tubing and all the electrical stuff. I didn't want to do it because it made me feel like I was killing the poor soul. The director and I got into an argument. I wanted the doctor to do it. Who was right?"

The question startled me. It was too close to an experience I'd had a few months before. Maurice Criblan complained of chest pain late one Saturday afternoon while working in his yard. Maurice, at just over sixty years old, was retired. He was overweight and hypertensive, but he loved his flower garden. When the pain started in his chest he told his wife, Flora, that it was a little indigestion. He took some bicarbonate of soda and continued to work. Abruptly, the pain worsened and he collapsed. Flora called an ambulance and then called me. I rushed to South Bay District Hospital, where I admitted most of my private patients.

I arrived at the hospital shortly after the ambulance did. Maurice was in the emergency room surrounded by the Code Blue staff (the hospital name for a cardiac arrest team). Broadcasting a Code Blue over the hospital's P.A. system automatically and quickly assembled the doctors, nurses, and technicians necessary to carry out cardiopulmonary resuscitation. The E.R. doctor was placing an airway in Maurice's throat, the I.V. team was installing an intravenous catheter, respiratory therapy was standing by with their equipment, and one of the nurses was doing external cardiac massage. I pulled off my jacket and took over for her. In seconds, the E.R. doctor had finished intubating, the airway was complete, and the respiratory people began breathing for Maurice.

I told Julie about Maurice, leaving out his name. Periodically she would nod sagely or make little agreement sounds such as, "Ah," or "Oh yeah!" I wondered why I was telling her all of this. Maybe I just wanted to get it off my chest.

I went on with my tale. "The EKG monitor showed bursts of ventricular fibrillation, a very dangerous sign, so the E.R. physician asked for the defibrillator paddles and administered the first defibrillating shock of 200 joules. A normal rhythm returned for a few minutes, but then fibrillation resumed and a second shock, set this time at 300 joules, was given.

"Once the other doctor had used the defibrillator, I was out of a job. Nominally I was in charge as the physician of record, but the team was functioning smoothly and quietly, as everyone knew their jobs. I left the room briefly to see Flora. I explained the gravity of the situation and told her we would do all we could, then returned to Maurice's room."

Julie said, "Oh, the poor woman."

I continued, "The EKG had become flat, functioning only in response to the closed chest massage that was being administered by the E.R. doctor. The automatic positive pressure breathing machine aerated the lungs. The proper drugs had been administered through the I.V. tubing. Now it was necessary to continue to do what we were doing and hope that the heart would start on its own. One of the nurses asked, 'How long do you plan to keep this up?' I responded, 'As long as there is a flicker.' The nurse replied, 'Then, I'd better get the thumper.'"

I explained to Julie and the two or three others who now were listening, that the thumper was a large pillow-like device which, when strapped to the chest of a patient and connected to an electrical outlet, compressed the chest. The number of pounds of pressure and the frequency of the compression was set by the operator to conform to the needs of the patient. The machine was not a quiet one because, in addition to the electrical motor noise, it gave off an eerie thumping sound each time it pushed down on the chest; hence its nickname.

As I continued with my tale, I noticed that most of the group at our table was listening. Peter Falk was wandering off somewhere. "There comes a time in a situation such as this when any more treatment is futile. Unfortunately, no one knows exactly when that time has arrived. There are physical signs that help. One of these is the condition of the pupils of the eyes. In death the pupils become stationary and dilated and unresponsive to light. Maurice had been this way for half an hour. He was not breathing on his own, nor was his heart beating except when the thumper caused a blip on the EKG monitor. I made the difficult decision that no one likes to make and said, 'Folks, I guess it's over; we had better pull the plug.' And, Julie, I was faced with the same dilemma that you faced in the studio when you didn't want to be the one to turn off the machines. In this real emergency room everyone immediately left, leaving me standing there alone. I had to do the job."

I didn't tell the people at our table how I had felt; it was just too personal. But I remembered, as I looked around the room that day, I had seen the sickly green-painted walls. Someone long before had decided green was more restful than white. *Maurice doesn't care what color the walls are—he is at rest except for the damned machines. Maurice has gone, probably an hour ago, but here he is—lying in this green room, having the final indecency performed on him that places him in a state of pseudo-life, because a bunch of machines are pumping the blood around his dead body and are still doing their macabre job because no one wants the responsibility of closing the case by saying, "Maurice is dead." I have to say it. I am the one responsible. I am the doctor of record.* I walked over to the thumper and turned it off, shut the valve on the oxygen machine, and removed the I.V. from the back of his hand. It was over.

Then I had to tell Flora. I hated doing that! However, Maurice would be saved the final indecency; I would sign the death certificate, giving the cause of death as cardiac arrest due to myocardial infarction. He would not have to be autopsied.

As my mind returned from its journey to Maurice's bedside, I realized that people were waiting for the conclusion of the story. I couldn't remember why I had been talking about Maurice until Julie London said, "You make my part on the show a real, living thing. I'm so glad I didn't turn off those machines but had the doctor do it. I couldn't have lived with that."

Bob Young said, "For God's sake, Julie, it was just a TV show. Remember, you're an actress…." Fortunately, at that point, a musical flourish heralded the approach onstage of the M.C. for the evening's award show, shutting off any further conversation.

Welby, Emergency, and *Columbo* were not winners that night, so it was a sour little group that parted company. The Youngs had stopped to chat with someone when, suddenly, I heard my name being called. Julie London was making her way back against the grain of the departing audience, shouting, "Doctor, Doctor, come quickly! I need you!"

She was dragging that sable coat again, but I realized that dragging it this time wasn't an affectation. She was excited, not paying any attention to her style and unthinkingly dragging her beautiful coat. Apparently that was the way the coat usually lived, half on the floor. With her other hand, Miss London waved wildly, gesturing me to come her way. At about twenty feet away she shouted, "Come quickly, there's an emergency!"

By now she had attracted a crowd. "What's the matter, Julie?"

"There's a woman passed out in the ladies' john and I think she is in diabetic coma."

That's a pretty technical diagnosis, I thought, "How do you know?" I asked.

"Her breath smells sweet."

I said, "Maybe she's been eating candy."

"No, dammit—come on! She needs you right now!"

Jeez, I thought, *Julie has her smells mixed up. If the woman was diabetic her urine would taste sweet, but doctors haven't been checking urine that way for quite a while and I was sure they didn't do it that way on* Emergency. *I was equally sure that Julie had never done it. Besides, if the woman were in diabetic coma, her breath would smell like acetone or nail polish.* I said, "Have someone call the hotel's house physician."

By this time Julie stood beside us. Bob's comment on her frantic dialogue was, "Julie, you've been on that show too long." She paid Bob no attention, grabbed me by the hand, and pulled me vigorously toward the ladies' room. I stopped resisting and went with her. We went through the swinging door into a large room where there were about twelve or sixteen stalls, all with their doors facing the double-door entrance. Because of the emergency, I had assumed the room would be cleared. Not so. All the stalls were occupied and there were ladies lined up at the mirrors and wash basins putting the last-minute touches to their faces and hair before going out to meet the public. One stall door, right in the middle, was open, and in there was the patient, crumpled on the floor.

I knelt down beside the toilet, in my tuxedo, and felt the lady's pulse. Her eyelids flickered and opened. Immediately her respirations increased. She was hyperventilating. She had overbreathed so much that she had passed out. Now, awake again, she resumed panting.

Julie's case of diabetic coma turned out to be nothing more than the young lady's anxiety reaction to telling her boyfriend that she was pregnant and what was he going to do about that. She hadn't been able to get enough courage to confront him before or during the show but now, on the way home, she was going to do it—and it scared the hell out of her.

All the while I was holding her hand and she was blurting out this story, I realized two things. First, my dinner partner for the evening and the person responsible for my being on the floor of the ladies' room had fled, leaving me with the problem; and second, here I was, a male on the floor of a women's toilet stall, totally ignored.

As I looked up, Miss Carol Burnett came through the swinging doors and entered the stall next to the one in which I was kneeling. I had always admired the talents of this fine comedienne and would have enjoyed meeting her. I glanced to the side and recognized that the very large feet that I saw, under the partition, belonged to Miss Burnett. At the moment I heard the telltale tinkle-tinkle, I knew that I could never meet Carol Burnett face-to-face. I had invaded her privacy, and even if she never found out, it would be an awkward moment. What would I say if we were ever to meet? "Charmed, I'm sure, but I already know you from the sound of your tinkle."

Later we went to a crowded and smoky party in the hotel. Bob Young wanted to stay only long enough to avoid the crowds out in front and the gauntlet of autograph seekers that was sure to be there. When the four of us emerged from the door of the hotel, the driver left to get Bob's limo. The red velvet ropes were still in place. Only one persistent couple remained with their autograph books. The man was short and round. He wore colorful shorts and a tank top. His female companion was even rounder and shorter and similarly attired. They slipped under the ropes and accosted Bob for an autograph. He refused quickly and bluntly. The man circled me and looked up into my face. When his companion was about to present her book to me for my signature, the short man grabbed her arm and said, "Don't bother. He's nobody!"

❧

Two weeks later during my last days on the job, I visited a location shoot in Westwood Village near UCLA. The scene was being shot in a fraternity house. As always, there were sound trucks, camera crews, huge electrical cables running from generators to service the lights necessary for the cameras, and a lot of people—including the necessary ones, and spectators attracted by the chance to see a star.

The commissary truck was parked at the curb, and the staff and actors took any time they could during a break in the shooting to go to the truck to eat lunch. Tables were set up on the grassy parking strip adjacent to the sidewalk.

If you believe that location shooting is fun, think again. The amount of wasted time, the inconvenience, and the quality of food—equal to that usually found only in hospitals—make it a less than enjoyable event. Nevertheless, during a quiet time, Jim Brolin and I were having a quiet conversation sitting at a table along the street, all by ourselves, when we noticed an elderly lady walking toward us on the sidewalk. She was not remarkable for anything other than her tennis shoes, which were an unusual sight on an older person at that time. She might have been the little old lady from Pasadena that the Beach Boys sang about, a character that comedians of the day joked about. She stared at all the hustle and bustle that had been created in her usually peaceful Westwood neighborhood when she spied a star. She stopped in front of Jim, smiled sweetly and said, "Dr. Kiley—ooh, I mean Mr. Brolin, may I have your autograph?" She was a very appealing person, with her sweet smile, quiet good looks and gentle manner.

Jim said, "Of course. Do you have something to write on?"

The lady looked flustered; she opened her purse, but came up with nothing. Then, holding up the paper shopping bag she was carrying on her way to the market, said, "I have this."

Jim took the bag, asked her name, wrote a little message to her about chance meetings on the street, and handed the bag back to her. The lady took a step to her left and was standing in front of me. She asked, "Sir, would you give me your autograph?"

Remembering my experience of a couple of weeks before at the Golden Globes, I replied, "I don't think you want my autograph. I'm nobody!"

This wonderful lady looked straight into my eyes. What she saw, I don't know. But I know what I saw in hers: beauty. She was a beautiful person who knew only goodness of spirit.

She said, "Oh sir, you must be somebody!" And she handed me the shopping bag.

About the Author

Thomas L. Stern, M.D., practiced family medicine in Sherwood, Oregon and in Manhattan Beach, California, for a total of twenty-two years. Dr. Stern's lifetime of service is marked by awards, honors, peer and public recognition, academic appointments and professional achievements.

A few highlights of his illustrious career are service as: Vice President for Education and Scientific Affairs of the 90,000 member American Academy of Family Physicians; Past President of the International Center for Family Medicine for the Americas, Spain and Portugal; consultant to both the United States Army and Navy in the specialty of Family Practice; Chairman of the editorial board of the magazine *Diagnosis;* Editor of the AAFP Home Study Audio Tape Program and on-tape host; Vice President for Professional and Corporate Affairs, American Academy of Family Physicians Foundation.

Among his many honors Dr. Stern was selected to be President of the California Chapter of the American Academy of Family Physicians in 1972 and was the recipient of the Willamette University Outstanding Alumnus Award in 1973. In 1981, he received an honorary Doctor of Science degree from the Medical College of Ohio at Toledo. The Thomas L. Stern, M.D., AAFP Annual Lectureship on Quality in Family Practice Education was created in 1991. From 1971 to 1975, Dr. Stern served as technical advisor to the *Marcus Welby, M.D.* television series.

Throughout his career, he has published generously and presented countless papers to both lay and professional audiences.

To order additional copies of

House Calls

Book: $17.95   Shipping/Handling: $4.50

Contact: ***BookPartners, Inc.***
P.O. Box 922
Wilsonville, OR 97070

E-mail: bpbooks@teleport.com
Fax: 503-682-8684
Phone: 503-682-9821
Order: 1-800-895-7323

Visit our Web site:
www.bookpartners.com